. . . .

The Media of Conflict: War Reporting and Representations of Ethnic Violence

edited by
Tim Allen and Jean Seaton

. . . .

Zed Books
LONDON AND NEW YORK

The Media of Conflict: War reporting and representations of ethnic violence was first published by Zed Books Ltd, 7 Cynthia Street, London N1 9JF, UK and Room 400, 175 Fifth Avenue, New York, NY 10010, USA in 1999.

Distributed exclusively in the USA by St Martin's Press, Inc., 175 Fifth Avenue, New York, NY 10010, USA.

Cover designed by Andrew Corbett
Set in Monotype Dante by Ewan Smith
Printed and bound in the United Kingdom by Biddles Ltd, Guildford and King's Lynn

A catalogue record for this book is available from the British Library

ISBN 1 85649 569 8 cased
ISBN 1 85649 570 1 limp

Contents

About the Contributors

Jocelyn Alexander teaches history at the School of African and Asian Studies, University of Sussex.

Tim Allen is a lecturer in development studies at the London School of Economics.

Philippa Atkinson is a doctoral candidate at South Bank University, working on the wars in Sierra Leone and Liberia.

Marcus Banks is a lecturer in social anthropology, University of Oxford, and Fellow of Wolfson College.

Richard Fardon is professor of social anthropology at the School of Oriental and African Studies, London.

Fred Halliday is professor of international relations at the London School of Economics.

David Keen is a lecturer in development studies at the London School of Economics.

Mark Leopold is Ioma Evans-Pritchard junior research fellow at St Anne's College, Oxford.

Peter Loizos is professor of social anthropology at the London School of Economics and a former television documentarist.

JoAnn McGregor lectures in geography at the University of Reading.

Mel McNulty is a lecturer in French at Nottingham Trent University.

Jean Seaton is reader in the Centre for Communication and Information Studies at the University of Westminster.

Spyros A. Sofos is a research fellow at the Centre for European Studies Research, University of Portsmouth.

David Styan is currently based in the Department of International Relations at the London School of Economics.

Roza Tsagarousianou is a lecturer at the Centre for Communication and Information Studies at the University of Westminster.

Monica Wolfe Murray was educated at the universities of Bucharest and Oxford, and has worked for several years with NGOs in northern Yugoslavia and elsewhere.

Croatian refugees arriving in Croatia after crossing the Sava river
(photo credit: UNHCR, R. LeMoyne).

A refugee from Bosnia arrives at Ngenda Camp, Rwanda
(photo credit: UNHCR, B. Press).

Introduction

Tim Allen and Jean Seaton

> *The death of President Tito and the end of communist domination of the former Yugoslavia raised the lid on the cauldron of ancient hatreds. This is the land where at least three religions and a half-dozen ethnic groups have vied across the centuries. It is the birthplace of World War I. It has long been a cradle of European conflict, and it remains so today. (Warren Christopher, US Secretary of State, Department of State Dispatch, 4, page 81, February 1993, quoted in Turton, 1997: 33)*

> *The most intransigent conflicts of all have arisen in regions of ancient mixed ethnicities, as in former Yugoslavia and Caucasia. In both places the withdrawal of superordinate authority has cast the populations back into a condition that, though anthropologists disagree over whether what they call primitive warfare is primordial or not, is certainly a regression from civilized order.*
>
> *The practices of territorial displacement, massacre, deliberate desecration of cultural symbols and systematic mistreatment of women, all evidently rife in recent non-state warfare in the Balkans and Transcaucasia, undeniably resemble those of the surviving Stone Age peoples of the world's remote regions – at their most savage. (*Daily Telegraph, *7 May 1998)*

> *They were driven by that atavistic fury that goes back to the times when human beings moved in packs and ate raw meat. (*Guardian, *25 April 1998)*

This book is about representations of contemporary ethnic violence and war in the media. Much of it is aimed at interrogating and countering the kinds of statement illustrated above. They have become very prevalent, and are commonly presented in news media reports as facts. The last quote, taken from the *Guardian*, is one of numerous examples cited in two studies of war reporting in Britain carried out by the Glasgow Media Group, based mainly upon close monitoring of newspapers and television news in mid-July 1994 and between October 1996 and May 1997 (Philo, 1998; Philo et al., 1998). During these periods it was found that the majority of reports of the situation in Rwanda and

Zaire made no attempt at a coherent political analysis, but concentrated on presenting shocking scenes of refugee movements and commenting on humanitarian responses (or the lack of them). Most attempts at explaining what was occurring 'reduced it to fighting between two different groups of "tribes", and some spoke directly of the "wild", "volatile" and "mad" nature of the people' (Philo, 1998: 50). Our aim here is not so much to blame the media for propagating such nonsense, but to ask why these kinds of views are expressed, and why so many of those who consume media products find them unproblematic.

The chapters have been collected together under the auspices of an organization called the Forum Against Ethnic Violence. The Forum was established by a group of mainly British anthropologists and sociologists in 1993, initially in response to the crisis in Bosnia. Its founders were concerned by the resurgence of primordialist conceptions of social difference among protagonists in former Yugoslavia, and by the accept- ance of these conceptions at face value by many journalists and political analysts. They took the view that this primordialism was both a danger- ously misleading interpretation in itself and also a way of cynically distancing events for political purposes. It enabled the governments of rich industrial states to absolve themselves of responsibility for what was happening, and helped them to adopt increasingly oppressive measures against refugees and immigrants. The members of the Forum are not foolish enough to believe that their efforts will have a significant impact on the ways in which ethnic violence occurs. The aim is more modest: to make available alternative understandings of ethnicity which may assist concerned individuals and organizations in making assessments of what is happening. Members have sought to argue their position with journalists, non-governmental organizations, students and other aca- demics through conferences, workshops, commissioned reports, and publications such as this one.

Although there are contributions dealing with the 1991 war in the Gulf and with ethnographic film and the internet, most of the following chapters deal with aspects of news media reporting in situations of wars occurring within, rather than between, recognized states. Much of what is most interesting relates to the specificities of particular situations. The authors have little time for the trite shibboleths of 'globalization theories'. Nevertheless there are some general themes, issues and arguments which are reiterated. Here are ten examples.

First, contrary to the implicit, and sometimes explicit, view of many accounts, wars are not the product of natural difference, but of social processes. To treat ethnicity as something primal and natural is to conflate the concept with discredited understandings of race.

Second, as ethnicity does not have a biological basis, it must refer to the socially constructed relationship between groups, often expressed in the form of conflicted social boundaries. All definitions of war include the idea of organized violence against an enemy group. It follows that there is no special category of ethnic war, but that all war has an ethnic aspect.

Third, it would be foolish to suggest that ethnicity does not influence behaviour. Once violence starts, ethnic identities become social facts, they are quickly ascribed to people whether or not they want to have them, and many protagonists will not hesitate in giving highly essentialist ethnic explanations for what they are doing. The power of ethnicity comes from an acceptance by enough people that particular social divisions are natural and inevitable. Analysts should be careful not to base their own interpretations on such insiders' perspectives, but should try to understand how such beliefs have become established.

Fourth, in some circumstances, national news media coverage has had the effect of exacerbating conflict as a result of conscious political strategies by political activists. It is also the case that the new technologies of the international media have helped make reporting less insightful and more sensationalist. This has often had the effect of lending credence to culturally functionalist (and inherently racist) views.

Fifth, news value depends on contingency. The public in Western countries is, or is believed to be, interested in what affects them directly. The collapse of the Cold War means that it is harder for journalists to explain the relationship of things happening to people far away from domestic audiences. In this way 'ethnic conflict' emerged in part as a kind of lazy shorthand for beastly wars of the kind that we had hoped were over.

Sixth, wars are partly what the media make them. This is so in the sense that the media can shape military strategies and the intensity of fighting. But it is also true in a more fundamental sense. To a large extent the term 'war' is ascribed to situations by journalists in such a way as to accord them a degree of status. Often use of the term implies that killing is at least partially acceptable, and sometimes a choice about referring to violent events as war has a political dimension. Many governments facing insurgencies like to avoid the word, preferring to label rebel factions as criminals. Since most contemporary armed conflicts are internal to states, it seems likely that relatively few of them would end up being called wars if official approval was required. To a large extent general recognition that a war is happening is now dependent on international news media coverage, and increasingly this means that they exist in a meaningful sense only if there are real-time pictures.

Seventh, the media are not homogeneous, as is sometimes suggested by use of the term. 'Media' is a plural form of the noun 'medium', and refers to the mechanisms by which information is transmitted. Thus, the media cannot themselves make decisions and, while they are persistently manipulated, there is no big, underlying meta-conspiracy. The media, like war, have to be de-mythologized if we are to understand them.

Eighth, the media do not exist outside the political and social world they describe, although sometimes they seem remote from what they report. On the contrary, understanding the impact of the contemporary media is a fundamental aspect of understanding wars and how they develop and, perhaps, how they might be ended. How wars are made, how participants strategize their interests, how and if 'the international community' reacts, how audiences in other, more comfortable places comprehend what is happening and how responsibility is structured and action planned are all, in the modern war, in part, a media story.

Ninth, the arbitrary and superficial qualities of much international media coverage of wars raise the issue of what kind of voice war-affected populations can hope to have. One of the most depressing aspects of the current recourse to ethnic explanations in the media, and indeed in some academic analysis, is that those caught up in wars are drawn into colluding in their own 'othering'. Most wars occur in parts of the world which, in global economic terms, do not matter much. Indeed, the wars have partly emerged because of these regions' relative or absolute levels of poverty. From the point of view of observers in affluent and politically stable countries, there may be no incentive to care about what happens in such places. Use of ethnic categories to interpret events helps reinforce such a view. Ethnicity is seen as something exotic and alien, it is something that those strange and wild people have, not 'us'.

Tenth, history is powerful, and can be used and abused. In many ways this is a book about historical understanding. It counters mytho-logized history with discussion of the role of media in history-making. Several contributions point to the way in which the present divisions have emerged from recent social processes, and to the construction of competing mythical pasts by nationalist movements, émigré groups and the external world. Modern conflicts, it is argued, are political and have real histories. Responsibilities can be determined. This book is therefore about re-politicizing war. Ethnic mythologizing by protagon-ists and by journalists is precisely a means of taking the politics and the history out of wars, and reducing them to fantastic emanations. In this context, unfashionable, accurate, balanced, old-fashioned evidence-based narratives, which explain how one event led to another, retain their value as an anchor for our investigations into what is actually going on.

The book is divided into two parts. The first five chapters deal with general themes. In Chapter 1, Tim Allen investigates meanings ascribed to the concepts of war and ethnicity, and suggests ways in which contemporary warfare might be analysed more effectively. This chapter serves as a theoretical introduction to the book as a whole. Chapters 2, 3 and 4 take up key issues that have been raised, and discuss them more thoroughly. Jean Seaton overviews the complex part that the media play in modern wars, and also comments on war reporting in the past, notably during the Second World War. Richard Fardon comments on problems associated with the notion of ethnicity, suggesting that it has become pervasive in such a way as to mean almost everything and almost nothing at the same time. David Keen critiques the assumption that contemporary warfare is essentially confusing and pointless, and argues that there is a need to address the rational functions of conflict. Chapter 5, by Peter Loizos, adds a somewhat different perspective. Like Jean Seaton, he draws attention to the capacity of the media to be remarkably insightful, when knowledgeable people are given the space and time to demonstrate their skills. He reviews three recent ethnographic films about people living in war zones, all of which demand active engagement from a viewer and provide a moving, discomforting and insightful experience. He reminds us that we must value such media products highly, and avoid dismissive generalizations.

The second part of the book comprises nine case studies. The first of these, Chapter 6 by Fred Halliday, stands out in that it is about a war directly involving the USA and its close allies. It examines media coverage of the 1990–91 Gulf War. Halliday shows that, while there was certainly distortion of events in news media coverage, notably the lack of concern about Iraqi casualties, it is misleading to suggest that there was simply collusion with Western government policies. An interesting aspect of this chapter, in the light of those that follow it, is that news reporting of the conflict did not highlight ethnic aspects, but rather focused on the strategies and technological capacities of the armies, and on the evil nature of Saddam Hussein as an individual. This perhaps reflected the fact that the Western powers had important Arab allies, but it was also surely because this was seen as a conventional kind of war. One internationally recognized state had invaded another internationally recognized state. There are long-established ways of describing such circumstances in terms of politics, using relatively restrained language, just as there are international laws, treaties, protocols, conventions and other mechanisms which can be drawn upon for intervention and mediation. The remaining chapters deal with wars that do not fit categorizations so easily.

Chapters 7, 8 and 9 provide different perspectives on the dreadful developments in former Yugoslavia. Marcus Banks and Monica Wolfe Murray discuss the prevalence of ethnic explanations in the British media, and in particular the use of the expression 'ethnic cleansing'. Spyros A. Sofos shows how the disintegration of Yugoslavia was linked to the emergence of populist ethno-nationalist discourses in the political spheres of the former Yugoslav republics, which were vigorously propagated through the local mass media. Roza Tsagarousianou analyses some of the effects these events had on neighbouring Greece. She looks at links between mass communication and nationalist discourse in the country, and explains how this has been influenced by the emergence of an independent state of Macedonia.

Chapters 10, 11, 12, 13 and 14 all concentrate on Africa. For Philippa Atkinson, international media coverage of Liberia has been both of a low quality and irresponsible. She vigorously sets about deconstructing what she sees as 'media mythologies'. Mark Leopold is similarly concerned with challenging mythologies, but his are generated by the Ugandan press, mostly print media published in the south of the country. He demonstrates that in an African country in which press freedom is quite extensive, news about the so-called 'war in the north' is just as misleading as some international reporting, often doing no more than elaborating ethnic ideologies. In Chapter 12, Jocelyn Alexander and JoAnn McGregor survey the Zimbabwean media coverage of the conflict in Matebeleland during the mid-1980s, and place the adoption of ethnic explanations in historical perspective, noting that increased government control was a crucial factor. The authors also comment on the importance of the internet in opening up debate within Zimbabwe about what happened, although it is striking that some of the internet discussions have been no more insightful than those which have appeared in government-owned newspapers.

Chapter 13, by Mel McNulty, is another very critical commentary on international news reporting, this time with respect to war and genocide in Rwanda. It is suggested that the Western media swallowed politically motivated disinformation that the conflict was ethnically driven, helped to legitimize this view, and served to exacerbate the situation, with tragic consequences. The final chapter, by David Styan, again takes up this theme of media misrepresentation. He mostly uses examples from Ethiopia to highlight aspects of media representations both in and of Africa. He emphasizes the role of northern non-governmental organizations in defining international news agendas, and comments on changes and contradictions within domestic and foreign media reporting of Ethiopia since 1991. Like Mark Leopold, he concludes that a change in government and the rapid development of privately owned newspapers does not in itself appear to facilitate a better understanding of ethnicity. In Ethiopia's case, the administration's promotion of a specific set of ethnic labels has just created a new set of biases and distortions.

The editors would like to express their thanks to all the contributors for responding so quickly to requests for revisions, to the participants in seminars at which chapters have been presented and discussed, and to various readers for their valuable comments, particularly Melissa Parker. We would also like to thank Louise Murray of Zed Books for her enthusiasm and encouragement, and Sue Redgrave at the LSE for all her efforts, which involved much more than tidying up and formating the manuscript.

References

Philo, G. (ed.) (1998) *The Zaire Rebellion and the British Media*, Background Paper to the 'Dispatches from the Disaster Zones' Conference, London, 28 May.

Philo, G., Hilsum, L., Beattie, L. and Holliman, R. (1998) 'The Media and the Rwanda Crises: Effects on Audiences and Public Policy', in J. Pieterse (ed.), *World Orders in the Making*, Basingstoke: Macmillan.

Turton, D. (ed.) (1997) *War and Ethnicity: Global Connections and Local Violence*, New York: University of Rochester Press.

Refugees from Azerbaijan at a boarding house in Armenia, May 1993
(photo credit: UNHCR, A. Hollman).

Returning to their destroyed houses in Croatia, people still cannot
comprehend the sudden disruption of their lives (photo credit: UNHCR,
A. Hollman).

. . . .

PART ONE

War, Ethnicity, Media

The 1992 conflict between Osset and Ingush caused massive population displacement, and 80% of Ingush houses in North Ossetia were destroyed. This woman has been trying to repair her bullet-riddled house. The photograph was taken in December 1996 (photo credit: UNHCR, T. Bølstad).

In April 1997, more than 80,000 refugees from Rwanda were in two makeshift camps south of Kisangani, Zaire. Thousands more were huddled in small groups, too weak to move (photo credit: UNHCR, R. Chalasani).

CHAPTER I

. . . .

Perceiving Contemporary Wars

Tim Allen

Representations of contemporary war in the news media are sometimes muddled and misleading, but it is hardly surprising. Specialists themselves have very different views of what is occurring, and even disagree about whether warfare is becoming more or less of a problem or what sort of a problem it is.

At one extreme there is John Keegan, the eminent military historian, former lecturer at Sandhurst and Defence Editor of London's *Daily Telegraph*. He began his 1998 BBC Reith Lectures on 'War and Our World' with the statement that 'the worst of war is now behind us and ... mankind, with vigilance and resolution, will henceforth be able to conduct the affairs of the world in a way that allows war a diminishing part' (*Daily Telegraph*, 9 April 1998: 24; Keegan, 1998: 1). His newspaper published the text of his talk under the heading 'Goodbye to all this', and illustrated it with a scene from the First World War. In contrast there is Lawrence Freedman, Professor of War Studies at King's College, London, who tells us in *The Economist* that 'stability is no more than a fond hope. Things will never settle down, and that is why we are unlikely to be able to stop worrying about war' (*The Economist*, 11 September 1993; Freedman, 1994: 363). There are also those who go much further in their pessimism. The US Senator and former Harvard professor Daniel Patrick Moynihan describes a world in 'pandemonium', torn apart by ethnic strife, and the influential travel writer Robert Kaplan warns us of 'The Coming Anarchy' (Moynihan, 1993; Kaplan, 1994).

To a large extent the confusion about the significance of war stems from the ambiguity of the concept itself. Although wars are sometimes discussed as if they are phenomena objectively existing in nature, in practice there have always been important differences in the application of the term. But such differences seem to have become more marked, or at least more apparent, since the early 1990s. This is partly because so many of the events now described as wars do not conform with various established ideas – including the standard dictionary definition – of what 'proper' wars should be like. In this chapter, I comment on ways in which war is studied and represented. Some of my points may seem self-evident, others rather less so. But it is striking how even the most obvious are frequently overlooked by academics, let alone by hard-pressed journalists who are required to present news about horrific events almost simultaneously with their occurrence.

My remarks are divided into four sections. I begin by examining various ways in which war is defined, and show how analyses are shaped by underlying conceptions, which are often made evident only by the ways in which the word is used. I point out that in practice, application of the term allocates status to collective violence, suggesting either that killing is in some sense acceptable, or that the level of violence in a particular place is especially disturbing. In the second section I make some observations about the current scale of the problem, weighing the value of different kinds of indicator. I show that it is difficult to locate objective data on war, but observe that the evidence suggests a rising number of internal or civil wars over the past 40 years, not a dramatic rise in the 1990s as is commonly suggested. However, I also note that there are signs that the socially traumatizing effects of wars have worsened, particularly since the early 1980s. In the third section, I discuss the assumption that the brutality of modern wars is something to do with their ethnic characteristics. Here I argue against the notion that most contemporary wars are remote from the Western world in that they are the product of uncivilized and primordial motivations. I point out that when we properly interrogate the meanings of the terms we use, then it is apparent that all war is ethnic war. In the final section I highlight certain issues which might form part of a more adequate understanding of the contemporary situation. The purpose of the chapter is to provide a general theoretical context for the book as a whole.

Conceptions of war

War is an emotive and resonant word, one which conjures up powerful images and associations, and it appears to have such distinctive substance as a social phenomenon that it can be readily perceived. In the first four of his 1998 Reith Lectures, John Keegan ranges from discussion of the two world wars, to warfare in ancient Greece, to civil war in Bosnia, to wars among what he terms 'primordial societies' in the South American rainforest and highland New Guinea. He is able to do this in the assumption that his audience will know what he is talking about, or at least that they will think that they do. Yet war is elusive of exact definition, and has become more so in recent years, such that most standard attempts to explain what it is seem inadequate.

The *Concise Oxford Dictionary*, for example, tells us that it is strife, usually between nations, conducted by force, involving open hostility and suspension of ordinary international law, while the definition provided by Quincy Wright in Lawrence Freedman's edited reader on war combines various points of view, describing war as 'a species of wider genus'. For Wright, war is one of many abnormal legal situations and numerous conflict procedures, 'an extreme case of group attitudes', and 'only a very large-scale resort to violence'. He concludes by stating that war can be seen as:

> a state of law and a form of conflict involving a high degree of legal equality, of hostility, and of violence in the relations of organized groups, or, more simply, the legal condition which equally permits two or more hostile groups to carry on a conflict by armed force. (Freedman, 1994: 70, extracted from Wright, 1966)

Both of these conceptions seem too formalized and legalistic, as they relate more to the rhetoric of international relations than what is actually happening on the ground. In many cases we seem to be dealing with something much more nebulous, and if the definitions are stretched to encompass events that are nowadays described as war in the international media, this would mean that exceptions have become the rule. Numerous wars are not conflicts between states, nor do they necessarily involve a very large-scale resort to violence, nor are they much influenced by formal legal provisions or their suspension, nor are they openly declared and resolved at certain moments and thereby clearly distinguished from situations of peace. Ostensibly recognizing the problem, Keegan makes the following observations towards the end of his fifth and final lecture:

> War is a protean activity, by which I mean that it changes form, often unpredictably. It is for this reason that I have avoided attempting to define the nature of war throughout these lectures. Like disease, it exhibits the capacity to mutate, and mutates fastest in the face of efforts to control or eliminate it. War is collective killing for some collective purpose; that is as far as I would go in attempting to describe it. (*Daily Telegraph*, 7 May 1998; Keegan, 1998: 72)

However, this is an all-encompassing formulation (notwithstanding the odd analogy with disease – a clinically observable phenomenon), which does not correspond well with his own usage. It should include kinds of criminal activity which are not usually thought to be manifestations of war, as well as various forms of human rights abuses, including genocide. Keegan himself does not refer to such things as war. Moreover, 'collective killing for some collective purpose' comes close to notions of warfare used by social and cultural anthropologists, and suggests that analysis should include violent feuding and other innumerable small-scale and locally contained conflicts. In one of his lectures, Keegan mentions in passing things like the military practices of the Yanomami tribesmen of Brazil, and the *Daily Telegraph* illustrates his comments with a picture of naked warriors holding spears (*Daily Telegraph*, 16 April 1998). But the vast majority of Keegan's examples are drawn from big wars fought between states or for the control of states, and most of them took place in Europe or North America.

He accepts that there are non-state wars, but he seems to regard them as not very important in the global scheme of things, either because they have been marginalized from the mainstream, or because they are aberrations and throw-backs to a barbaric past. He contrasts, for example, what he sees as the transformation of Western states from belligerent to benevolent entities, with the hostilities affecting some newer states, and maintains that the most intransigent conflicts of all have arisen in regions of 'ancient mixed ethnicities, as in former Yugoslavia and Caucasia' following the ending of the Cold War. He argues that:

> In both places the withdrawal of superordinate authority has cast the populations back into a condition that, though anthropologists disagree over whether what they call primitive warfare is primordial or not, is certainly a regression from civilised order. The practices of territorial displacement, massacre, deliberate desecration of cultural symbols and systematic mistreatment of women, all evidently rife in recent non-state warfare in the Balkans and Transcaucasia, undeniably resemble those of the surviving Stone Age peoples of the world's remote regions – at their most savage. (*Daily Telegraph*, 7 May 1998; Keegan, 1998: 67–8)

Leaving aside for the moment the validity of these assertions (which seem to me to be highly dubious), it is apparent that, while Keegan may have a generic understanding of war at the back of his mind, his usage of the term is in fact decidedly Eurocentric. His topic 'War and Our World' really does refer to *our* world. He wants to show that the threat of war has receded for 'us' in Britain, and his principal argument for the possible reduction of war in 'the newer states' is that we should provide them with fewer weapons. In practice he uses a kind of common-sense approach to war, one which he anticipates most readers of the *Daily Telegraph* and listeners to the Reith Lectures will share. Whatever his stated definition, the term is given meaning by the specific events to which it refers.

It is striking in this context that almost all his remarks about small-scale warfare are set in a discussion about the origins of war as a social institution. This too is a widespread practice both in popular discourse about war in Western countries, and among many scholars. While the origins of particular big wars, such as the First World War or the American Civil War, are normally studied in terms of contemporary economic and political processes, the origins of war itself are frequently explored with reference to archetypal models derived from literature on groups like the Yanomami of Brazil. The purpose is to suggest models of primordial behaviour, and to explore the possibility that human beings need to wage war either because of some sort of innate propensity, or because of the manner in which they cohere and survive as social groups.

There are various difficulties with this. To begin with, as Keegan himself admits at one point, there is no certainty at all that the people that he calls 'primitives' are primordial, 'or that their ways of war represent those of our ancestors of the main stream' (Keegan, 1998: 25). Certainly most anthropologists would reject such ideas, and would also emphasize that the conflict customs of the groups they have studied vary widely and rarely involve the kinds of atrocities witnessed in Bosnia or, for that matter, perpetrated by United States forces in Vietnam. Moreover, the search for the origins of war in the livelihood strategies of small, exotic and relatively isolated populations assumes that the events being described as war in the Amazon forests are the same sort of thing as what happened in the Gulf in 1991, but in a purer, distilled or more natural form. It suggests that the fundamental essence of war can be found among groups that fight without states being involved and without regard for formal legislation. Clearly, if war is defined as it is in the *Concise Oxford Dictionary* or in the reading from Lawrence Freedman's *War*, then this is nonsense. Keegan, as has been noted, claims not to have adopted a restrictive definition of war. Nevertheless, the majority of the wars he discusses are not non-state conflicts, and he makes little attempt to link his remarks about the origins of war with the rest of his analysis. Where he does do so, it is in reference to 'areas of high ethnic hatred', and here he resorts to the simplistic and misleading primordialism quoted above.

This misplaced search for the deep motivations for large-scale warfare in traditional ethnographic monographs is often combined with a quest for biological and psychological roots. Freedman's book has a reading on the topic, and Keegan briefly discusses both genetics and ethnology. It is an approach that informed the arguments of many Social Darwinists, as well as psychoanalytic thinkers, including Freud, and retains a grip on the popular imagination in Western countries (for a useful review of debates on the subject, see Groebel and Hinde, 1989). In recent years, sociobiologists, notably E. O. Wilson, have promoted it most strongly. For Wilson, 'war is only the most organised technique of aggression ... endemic to every form of society' (E. O. Wilson, 1978: 101, quoted in Crook, 1994: 194).

Neither Keegan nor Freedman seems altogether convinced, preferring to give more emphasis to sociological characteristics of the factions that engage in conflict, rather than dwell on individual motivations. In Keegan's view, laboratory experiments with the limbic system and controlled genetic selection are insignificant in the study of collective behaviour (Keegan, 1998: 22). It might be added that there is also a fundamental epistemological confusion involved here. However ambiguous the term 'war' may be, there seems no point in conflating it with other forms of violence. We lose capacity for specificity if aggression, force, killing and war are all perceived as interchangeable terms. It also leads to a position which is inherently ludicrous. As Creighton and Shaw put it in their 'Introduction' to The Sociology of War and Peace:

> It really is quite absurd to suppose that it follows from the fact that individual people show aggression towards each other in certain social situations, that superpower states must prepare to annihilate each other's populations with thermonuclear weapons. No such link makes any logical or scientific sense. (Creighton and Shaw, 1987: 3, quoted in Crook, 1994: 195)

Modern anthropologists would generally share this point of view. Indeed, it is a position that is implicit in their usual approach to war which, as has been mentioned, comes closer to Keegan's definition than his own usage of the concept. As Simon Harrison has explained in his entry on war in the Encyclopaedia of Social and Cultural Anthropology:

> definitions of war put forward by anthropologists usually envision war as a particular type of political relationship between groups, in which the groups use, or threaten to use, lethal force against each other in pursuit of their aims. Warfare is therefore distinct from other kinds of hostile or violent behaviour because war is made by organized collectivities rather than by individuals, and for collective ends rather than merely personal ones. To define war in this way has the very fundamental implication that the causes of war must lie in the nature of these collectivities and not in the individual. (Harrison, 1996: 561)

The dominant explanations for the occurrence of war in anthropology tend to be materialist. War tends to be viewed as a type of competition for scarce resources, particularly land, food and trade. This is important to note because it is often supposed that anthropologists study war as a manifestation of cultural difference. This is perhaps one reason why Keegan makes reference to anthropological studies. Anthropologists are supposed to know about ethnicity, and ethnicity is supposed to have become much more important. In fact, most anthropological work on ethnicity is similarly materialist and is very critical of simplistic prim-ordialist interpretations (Eriksen, 1993; Comaroff and Stern, 1995; Allen and Eade, 1997). It is also poorly integrated into the mainstream of anthropological studies of war. There is, for example, no mention of ethnicity in Harrison's encyclopaedia entry.

More generally, anthropologists have often resisted engagement with debates in political economy and international relations. Although the anthropological approach to war obviously includes large-scale conflicts, the focus of investigation is on wars that would not be registered as such in the international media or in the work of most other social scientists, except in the rather misinformed and misleading way dis-cussed above. For most anthropologists the category of 'small wars' sometimes used by political scientists refers to events that are too big to be studied. There are exceptions to this rule, and there are signs that things are changing – partly because it is becoming more common for the advice of anthropologists to be sought by journalists and aid agencies, and partly because many anthropologists have found that the groups that they have been living with have become caught up in wider conflicts, such as those in Bosnia and Sudan (e.g. Wendy James and Tone Bringa, whose collaboration with documentary film-makers is discussed in Chapter 5 in this book by Loizos). Nevertheless, it is striking that Harrison's entry in a publication which purports to offer a broad summation of the discipline's insights and achievements, makes no reference to the sorts of wars usually covered in the international media, nor to the insights of those anthropologists who are contributing to debates about them.

Harrison does, however, end with a valuable observation. He suggests that the circular arguments and confusions that affect theorizing about war: '... seem to arise from trying to understand war without having grounded it in its proper theoretical context: namely, in the deeper and more general phenomenon of violence of which it is an aspect' (Har-rison, 1996: 562). I would add that it is an aspect of violence that is accorded a particular kind of status. We are not investigating something located at some point on a continuum, at one end of which is a family argument and at the other is nuclear conflagration. Rather the term 'war' is a negotiated social categorization which draws attention to situations in which collective public killing can be expected to occur.

The killing may be on a huge scale, as it was during the Second World War and the war between Iran and Iraq, or it may be intermittent and limited, as it was in Nicaragua in the 1970s. In some instances it is restricted almost entirely to pitched battles between professional soldiers, and in others to a series of ritualized engagements in which casualties have been very low. Sometimes too, governments may dismiss a series of violent incidents as the work of bandits, and a condition of war may be recognized only by one group. In such cases, international recognition that a war is occurring may be as much to do with use of the term in the international media as any other factor, something which is closely linked to the capacity of governments to limit the activities of journalists, camera crews and human rights activists. For example, in early 1994 the lifting of reporting restrictions in South Africa, combined with international interest in the elections, led to frequent use of the expression 'low intensity war' to describe incidents in Natal which had in fact been occurring for many years. In contrast, the contemporaneous conflicts involving Ossetians in Georgia and Russia were almost entirely ignored, even though there was heavy fighting and large-scale population movements.

Thus, in practice, the term 'war' is employed as a means of conferring status. It indicates that a conflict should be taken seriously and not just treated as criminal activity or dismissed as petty squabbling. It can suggest that organized killing may be condoned, or that it is ocurring in a particularly disturbing way. The conferring of such status can be a point of controversy, especially in situations occurring within a state, and use of the label sometimes reveals as much about the user as it does about those who are fighting. Where use of the term is contested, consensus may emerge over time or be created by a new turn of events. For example, the fact that the British government is now prepared to discuss the special status of IRA and Loyalist prisoners suggests that it accepts that a war has been going on in Northern Ireland. More broadly, there seems to have been an increasing acceptance of the term 'war' at international fora and in the international media for localized conflicts which formerly would have been ignored.

This raises the question: is the violence which is commonly called war really becoming more serious or is it just that some commentators are allocating the status of war to conflicts more readily? Keegan believes that much of what appears in the British media about war is alarmist rhetoric, more to do with the need to sell a story than a reflection of reality. Taking a very different line of argument, in *The Warrior's Honor: Ethnic War and the Modern Conscience*, the intellectual journalist Michael Ignatieff suggests that it is not really that the world is becoming more chaotic or violent, it is our failure to understand and act that makes it seem so, and television makes it harder to sustain indifference or ignorance (Ignatieff, 1998: 8). What then is the current scale of the problem?

The current scale of the problem

It follows from the above that assessments of the current problem of war depend on the way in which the term is employed. If the dictionary definition is used, then it would seem that first, the total number of full-scale wars has declined since the Second World War and, second, that they have been successfully contained in particular regions. Similar, Keegan's Eurocentric perspective allows him an optimism reminiscent of the euphoric statements prevalent in Western countries when it became apparent that the Cold War was over in the late 1980s. On the other hand, if a more anthropological definition is adopted, then it is impossible to give an overall figure for the number of wars because there are limits on the number of conflicts that could possibly be studied, and there will always be disagreements about when the status of war should be allocated and where the distinctions are between one war and another. In southern Sudan, for example, it could be maintained that there is just one war going on, or the term might also be applied to the many clashes between different militia, and perhaps to the livestock raiding of pastoralists.

So does this mean that no objective assessment of the scale of war is possible? Should we abandon the question 'how many wars are there?' Strictly speaking the answer would have to be yes. We ought to ask something rather more complicated and relativistic, such as 'how many wars are perceived to be going on by a particular analyst and why?' However, provided we are clear about what we are doing, the ambiguities in the concept of war may be avoided by adopting sets of specific, recognizable characteristics as qualities of certain sorts of wars. It is then possible to make an assessment of their prevalence – at least in theory. Obviously, if we do this for openly declared wars between states, it is quite straightforward, whereas it is much more difficult to arrive at measurable criteria that can be used to assess the scale of non-state wars. Nevertheless, various methods have been promoted.

Probably the most established approach is that employed by the Stockholm International Peace Research Institute (SIPRI). This is commonly used as a source for the number of wars (e.g. Thomas, 1994;

Carnegie Commission, 1997), even though it actually avoids the term 'war' itself in its annual *Yearbook*, preferring to use the less overtly problematic expression 'major armed conflicts'. It defines these as 'prolonged combat between the military forces of two or more governments, or of one government and at least one organised armed group, involving the use of weapons and incurring at least 1,000 battle-related deaths' (quoted in Thomas, 1994: 80). According to SIPRI there were 32 such conflicts in 1990 and 35 in 1995. Others adopt a similar method, but take different casualty rates, and end up with very different results.

At one end of the spectrum is Peter Wallensteen and Margareta Sollenberg. They use a sliding scale of three categories: (1) minor conflicts, defined as those resulting in fewer than 1,000 battle-related deaths in total; (2) intermediate conflicts, defined as those which have produced more than 1,000 battle-related deaths in total; and (3) civil wars, defined as a conflict producing more than 1,000 battle-related deaths in a given year (Wallensteen and Sollenberg, 1996, 1997). According to this source, the annual number of all armed conflicts between 1990 and 1994 rose from just over 40 to just over 50, but subsequently declined to 36 in 1996. The number of civil wars ranged from 19 in 1989 and 1990, rose to 20 in 1991 and 1992, and then dropped to 14 in 1993, seven in 1994 and just six in 1995 and 1996.

At the other end of the spectrum is Dan Smith's *The State of War and Peace Atlas* (produced in collaboration with the International Peace Research Institute, Oslo) (Smith, 1997). Like SIPRI, Smith used a mix of criteria. He allocates the label 'war' if: (1) there is open armed conflict, (2) the conflict is about power or territory, (3) the conflict involves centrally organized fighters and fighting, and (4) the conflict involves continuity between clashes. There are two important differences between this source and the SIPRI classification of 'major armed conflicts'. First, the assessment of open armed conflict is linked with a low casualty rate of more than 25 war deaths in any one year. This figure is adopted on the grounds that there may be prolonged periods of relative calm between clashes, as resurgent forces withdraw from combat, regroup, rethink and recruit. Second, the criterion of centrally organized fighters and fighting does not necessarily require one of the protagonists to be the forces of a recognized government of a state. This is so that Somalia, Kurdistan and other conflict zones, in which formal armies are not directly involved, can be included. According to Smith's atlas, between 1990 and 1995 there were 70 states affected by 93 wars, in which five and a half million people were killed as a direct result of combat. The numbers of wars occurring in particular years rose from 47 in 1989 to a peak of 66 in 1992, declining to 55 in 1995.

A problem with all three of these assessments (although much less so for the third) is that it is impossible to know if combat-related casualty rates are accurate. They are often no more than a guess, and they are commonly linked to a political agenda. For example, estimates of those who have died in Bosnia-Herzegovina in 1992–95 vary by a factor of ten or even more. The most commonly quoted figure is 200,000, which seems to have emerged from the Bosnian Information Ministry in June 1993 (Smith, 1997: 100). Earlier in the same year a UN official had predicted that the total would be 400,000, but this did not gain much currency. Some reporters suggested 250,000. All of these are probably over-estimates, and the most sober analysts tend to refer to a much lower estimate published in *The World Disasters Report*. This indicates that about 20,000 died, but there seems no good reason why this should be accepted. The report is published by the International Committee of the Red Cross and Red Crescent Societies, which gives it a certain kudos, but the data presented must still be largely based on guesses.

Moreover, even if it were possible to use data on combat-related deaths with confidence, it may be a misleading indicator. In many modern wars, being a combatant can be relatively safe. According to some sources, at the beginning of the twentieth century, 90% of all war casualties were military, whereas today about 90% are civilian (UNDP, 1994: 47). This too can be no more than a good guess, and it also begs the question what is a civilian in a civil war? Nevertheless, it is the case that many insurgents and government forces seem to spend most of their time avoiding each other. In Southern Sudan, for example, there have been periods when different market days have been allocated for the local garrison in Yei town and the Sudan Peoples' Liberation Army (SPLA). The immediate military objective of warring factions may not be to defeat the other side in combat, but to extort a livelihood from or traumatize a population as a whole. In Liberia, unpaid, un-trained and young militiamen have often been based in areas that are well endowed with resources, and maintain themselves by preying on local people (see Keen, Chapter 4). Most of those who were killed in Bosnia were not directly involved in fighting. They were the victims of mortar shells landing in market-places, or they were shot by snipers while going about their daily business, or they were unarmed families who were rounded up and butchered. In Sudan, thousands of people have been deliberately separated from food sources as a military tactic. According to one source, in the summer of 1988 the death rates in some camps for the displaced 'reached the unprecedented level of 1% per day, far higher than any levels that have been recorded before or since for famines in Africa'. Perhaps 30,000 died in Western Sudan alone (de Waal, 1997: 94). Are these victims to be included in estimates of war-casualty rates?

Liberia, Bosnia and Sudan are perhaps extreme cases, and in fact would all register as wars even in the narrow categorization of Wallensteen and Sollenberg (at least for particular years). But the fact is that we do not really know how many people have been casualties of war, even in places where aid agencies and reporters have access. The data are not nearly robust enough to be used as a basis for making fine distinctions on a scale indicating the seriousness of armed conflicts. Moreover, if war casualties include all those who would have survived if the fighting had not occurred, then it would be possible to make informed assessments only after the event (and only where good demographic data become available). It is also likely that the number of conflicts that could be defined as wars would be even higher than suggested in Smith's atlas.

One response to the difficulties of using casualty rates is that adopted by the Study Group on the Causes of War at Hamburg University. This group works with a similar set of criteria as Smith, but it sets aside the issue of casualty rates as a defining characteristic, and retains the provision that regular armed forces of a government must be engaged at least on one side. The group has recently published findings for the period 1945 to 1993 (Gantzel, 1997). They are particularly interesting for the longer-term perspective they offer.

According to this source, there have been 184 wars between 1945 and 1993. The annual frequency of outbreak oscillates in an irregular way, which does not differ from earlier periods. However, since the end of the 1950s, the number of wars ongoing from year to year has increased. This means that more wars have begun than have ended, and that new wars last longer. From five wars in 1945, the trend resulted in a peak of 51 ongoing wars at the end of 1992. In 1993 the number declined to 42, but this still indicates that nearly one-quarter of all wars which have broken out since the end of the Second World War were being waged in that year. This increase is accounted for almost entirely by the increase in intra-state wars in developing countries. Of the wars counted in the study since 1945, 66% have been internal, a further 11.2% have been intra-state wars with an international involvement, and 22.8% have been waged between states; 93% have taken place in developing countries.

Clearly this method of classification presents other problems to those who depend on casualty rates. For example, in the data for 1993, Northern Ireland is included (presumably because of the involvement of

British troops), whereas other places, in which it is reasonable to assume that many more people were being killed both as a direct and indirect result of combat, are not (e.g. South Africa and Burundi – presumably because government forces were not officially involved). There also appear to be some anomalies, which are doubtless due to value judgements made by the researchers about the significance of insurgent forces, and the distinct nature of conflicts occurring in the same country. For example, two wars are registered for a few states in 1993, such as Peru and the Philippines, but only one is registered as occurring in Sudan, Afghanistan and Somalia. The latter should arguably have been excluded altogether for the reason noted by Smith (i.e. the country had no formal military forces in 1993, because it did not have an internationally recognized government), but it was obviously considered too important. On the other hand, there are several conflicts that have been omitted from the list, even though government soldiers were certainly involved (e.g. Uganda), probably because a decision was made that they were relatively insignificant.

In spite of these limitations, the study does demonstrate something very significant: that the military forces of more and more states have become involved in serious armed conflicts within the territories which they are supposed to govern. Many of the affected states were created in the decade and a half after the Second World War, and it seems that their political integrity and legitimacy has increasingly been challenged. The data also suggest that the challenge has been growing in significance fairly consistently since the late 1950s. In other words, the end of the Cold War is not in itself an adequate explanation. This is an important point, given the current tendency to view the spread of conflicts as having suddenly occurred since the late 1980s due to the lifting of bipolar constraints – as if the lid of a pressure cooker had been removed. In fact it is only necessary to glance at older surveys of wars to confirm the fallacy of such a view. For example, the *Strategic Atlas* by Chaliard and Rageau has maps indicating the location of over 100 wars between 1945 and 1983, including 37 civil wars, 16 wars of succession and 23 wars of liberation, almost all of them located in developing countries (Chaliard and Rageau, 1986: 47–50).

All these assessments of the global problem of war according to specific categories indicate that the vast majority of wars occur outside affluent Western states. This helps to explain Keegan's optimism. It also explains why those who are among the most vociferous in asserting the seriousness of the current situation are individuals and organizations representing the interests of people from developing countries. They seek access to the international media in order to make alarming statements, which they illustrate with harrowing images and personal accounts. Usually they will offer statistics too, sometimes using figures from the sources discussed above, or making their own estimates of the number of wars (often without explaining their categorizations and data sources). In addition they commonly refer to other kinds of indicator, notably the growing numbers of refugees.

The following are examples of statements about the current situation taken from recent aid agency reports. The *1994 Human Development Report*, published by the United Nations Development Programme, calls for a 'profound transition – from nuclear security to human security'. It asserts that, during 1993, there were 52 'major conflicts' in 42 countries and that another 37 countries were affected by 'political violence'. Of these 79 countries, 65 were in the developing world. The report also claims that 'about half of the World's states' had recently experienced 'interethnic strife' (UNDP, 1994: 22, 32 and 47). *The Oxfam Poverty Report*, published in 1995, claims that 50 years after the signing of the UN Charter, 'the world's citizens are in greater need of some form of collective security system than ever', and that unless something is done, there may be 100 million refugees by the year 2000 (Watkins, 1995: 42 and 43). The first chapter of a 1997 Médecins sans Frontières (MSF) report, entitled *World in Crisis*, begins with the observation that 'Civilians have always been under threat in war. But the methods of modern warfare seem sometimes to threaten more of them more of the time. In recent years wars have seemed characterised by endless streams of wretched refugees, fleeing violence or mayhem or starvation ...' (van Mierop, 1997: 1). A later chapter refers to 'a world in a state of upheaval', and notes that the 'multiplication of conflicts and violent situations has swollen the ranks of refugees and displaced populations to over 50 million people' (Jean, 1997: 42). A similar figure is given in the 1996 edition of *The Blue Helmets*, the United Nations official report on peace-keeping, which also draws attention to the fact that, of the 41 peace-keeping operations mounted between 1948 and 1996, 26 have been set up since 1989 (United Nations, 1996: 3–4). For one staff member of the office of the United Nations High Commissioner for Refugees (UNHCR): 'We are living a scenario ... that not even the most pessimistic among us could have predicted' (UNHCR, 1995: 97).

It can be argued that estimates of population displacement are a relatively good indicator. Longitudinal data are readily available on refugees in annual surveys, and an assessment of social upheaval is in many ways more valuable than simply attempting to count conflicts. However, even those organizations which compile refugee statistics accept that their data have limitations and must be treated with caution.

Reasons for this include: (1) the fact that reported refugee numbers may be exaggerated in order to secure international aid; (2) that it can be impossible to register refugees accurately when they are dispersed in a host population; and (3) that it may not be known when refugees have returned to their place of origin. Moreover, in non-state wars, most of those who flee the fighting may not actually cross an international border. This may be because the border is too far away or too dangerous to reach, or because a neighbouring country offers no advantages in terms of security, or because a border has been closed. Internally displaced people are not technically refugees, and there is no established system for effectively categorizing, surveying or protecting them. It is therefore hardly surprising that figures quoted sometimes vary widely. The World Refugee Survey, for example, claims that in 1996 there were 1,000,000 internally displaced people in Liberia alone – more than three times the corresponding UNHCR figure. Nevertheless, even the most conservative estimates of the overall numbers of internally displaced people indicate a large rise.

A recent attempt has been made to collate the best available information on refugees and internally displaced people by the Norwegian Refugee Council (Norwegian Refugee Council, 1998). Drawing on data from UNHCR and the US Committee for Refugees, this survey suggests that official refugee numbers rose from under three million in the early 1970s to over ten million in the early 1980s to around 17 million in the early 1990s. They subsequently declined to around ten million in 1996. However, this is somewhat misleading, because from 1993, UNHCR became responsible for so-called 'safe havens' – areas within war-torn countries in which people were supposedly protected, and from which they were effectively prevented from fleeing across international borders. Figures for internally displaced people from the mid-1990s include around ten million people in these safe havens, classified as 'other persons of concern to UNHCR' in *The State of the World's Refugees* (1995). Assessments of the overall number of internally displaced people suggest a rapid rise from the early 1980s, from under ten million to around 25 million in 1994, then a decline to about 18 million in 1996. The decline in both estimates of the number of refugees and internally displaced people since the early to mid-1990s seems to coincide with a small decline in the number of ongoing wars suggested in the surveys discussed above. This may be significant, or it may reflect a growing unwillingness of many governments to recognize and take responsibility for displaced populations. This has been evidenced by the concerted attempts of rich countries to restrict the arrival of asylum-seekers on their territory as well as attempts to prevent populations from moving out of war zones (something which was, for example, an explicit strategy of Western European countries in former Yugoslavia). There have also been an increasing number of violations of the principle of voluntary return, with 20 countries expelling refugees in 1996 (including Zaire and Tanzania, which between them forcibly repatriated 1.2 million Rwandans) (ODI, 1998: 2).

This section, like the previous one, has drawn attention to the difficulties of maintaining a detached and analytical view of war. In addition to the basic conceptual problems associated with the term itself, it is hard to locate a range of specific characteristics of kinds of war or armed conflict which are not themselves debatable, or for which adequate data are available. However, drawing on a combination of the approaches reviewed, a few conclusions are possible. While it is not possible to be exact about the scale of contemporary warfare, there does not seem to have been a massive increase since 1990. Rather, the prevalence of wars involving formal armed forces or their equivalent has continued to rise at about the same rate as previously, and may have declined slightly since the middle of the decade. It is also apparent that most of these wars are not being fought between states, and that they mostly occur in parts of the world which are relatively poor and which are least equipped to recover quickly. Finally, there is evidence that the adverse social effects of wars have become more extreme, including a dramatic rise in the number of forcibly displaced people between the early 1980s and mid-1990s. The usual reason given for the latter development is 'interethnic strife' (as the *1994 Human Development Report*, quoted above, puts it). This perceived quality of modern war is the subject of the next section.

War and ethnicity

Whether or not the overall scale of warfare is becoming better or worse, no one can deny that some modern wars are truly terrible. We know because we have seen dreadful images of what is happening, and we have read articles or heard interviews with journalists like Martin Bell, who insist that things are even worse than the television cameras are allowed to show. We may suspect that some reports are exaggerated to raise money from charitable donations or to make a dramatic impact in a news broadcast, but the figures for population displacement speak for themselves, and even the most dispassionate descriptions of events in Bosnia, Rwanda, Liberia, Sudan, Zaire/Congo and elsewhere are very disturbing.

John Keegan, it will be recalled, is one of those who explains such horrors with reference to ethnic divisions. He discusses intransigent conflicts in regions of 'ancient and mixed ethnicities', which are marked by 'a regression from civilised order'. Many politicians and journalists take a similar view. In a book called *Pandaemonium: Ethnicity in International Politics*, the US Senator and former Harvard professor Daniel Patrick Moynihan argues that the world entered 'a period of ethnic conflict, following the relative stability of the Cold War', and that this can be explained by the fact that, as large formal structures broke up, and ideology lost its hold, people reverted to 'more primal identities' (Moynihan, 1993: v). The journalist and travel writer Robert Kaplan takes this line of argument further, warning of 'the coming anarchy' in a series of widely quoted publications. The subtitle of one of his articles makes his position very explicit: 'How Scarcity, Crime, Overpopulation, Tribalism and Disease are Rapidly Destroying the Social Fabric of Our Planet' (Kaplan, 1994). Here Kaplan uses examples from West Africa to analyse the withering away of central governments and the growing pervasiveness of local wars. He sees a future characterized by 'nebulous and anarchic regionalism' in which people are as much at war with themselves as each other (Kaplan, 1994: 45). Elsewhere he has suggested that there is a 'formlessness' in contemporary African conflicts which recalls the age of warfare in tribal or feudal Europe (Kaplan, 1996: 41). He has also written about the Balkans, painting a picture of innate and inbred hatreds in a book called *Balkan Ghosts: A Journey Through History* (Kaplan, 1993), which is credited with dissuading the Clinton administration from its initial interventionist line in Bosnia (Duffield, 1996: 176).

For Kaplan and Moynihan, as well as for Keegan, efforts should be made to contain the risk of ethnic warfare spreading. Their analyses differ in that the latter seems optimistic that the structures for doing so are in place, at least as far as affluent Western countries are concerned, while the others are worried that they are not. For Kaplan in particular, ethnic war is less an aberration than a possible shape of things to come. However, whatever their vision of the future, all three authors take it for granted that ethnicity is an explanation for what is occurring. Just how prevalent this assumption has become is evidenced throughout this book. Numerous contemporary wars are either viewed as the result of certain ethnic groups expressing their true qualities following the lifting of external controls, or as revealing atavistic drives existing in all of us, which are manifested the moment that the rule of law is undermined. This section asks what it means to perceive contemporary warfare in these terms, and the following section discusses other factors that might help explain the apparently escalating social costs of conflict.

Although words that share similar linguistic roots have been used in some European languages for a long time, the terms 'ethnic' and 'ethnicity' are quite new concepts in English. A rare eighteenth-century usage of 'ethnic' was to mean 'heathen superstition', and it was occasionally employed in the nineteenth century with explicit racial (and biological) connotations. By the 1940s it was quite commonly used in the USA as a way referring to 'Jews, Italians, Irish and other people considered inferior to the dominant groups of largely British descent' (Eriksen, 1993: 4), and it was essentially along these lines that Glazer and Moynihan used the term in an influential book called *Beyond the Melting Pot: The Negroes, Puerto Ricans, Jews, Italians and Irish of New York City*, first published in 1963. This book explained why these kinds of identities were maintained rather than abandoned in the USA, the main thrust of the analysis being that they were instrumental to livelihood strategies, a rather different thesis from that argued by Moynihan more recently (1993). The concept was then taken up by various academics, particularly anthropologists working in Africa, who used it as a way of categorizing the new identities that had emerged in the towns, or as a euphemism for 'tribe'. It was only from the end of the 1960s that the term began to be used more generally to refer to many different kinds of collective identity, including the identities of people in industrialized countries not necessarily perceived as minorities. At the same time, the adjective began to be employed as a noun, either to refer to the qualities of a particular ethnic group or to refer to the relationship between ethnic groups. Frederik Barth's edited book, *Ethnic Groups and Boundaries* (1969), was particularly important in establishing this usage, and 'ethnicity', made its first appearance in the *Oxford English Dictionary* in 1972 (Glazer and Moynihan, 1975: 1).

Although some scholars continued to use the terms 'ethnic' and 'ethnicity' merely as ways of referring to minorities without using the problematic notion of race, or as a way of avoiding the primitive connotations of the word 'tribe', a sophisticated body of literature developed in anthropological studies (and increasingly also in historical studies) in which ethnicity was thought of as something negotiated, usually fluid and often instrumental. People were viewed as having multiple, overlapping ethnicities, and sometimes they were aware of an ethnicity only when they came into contact with social groupings which they perceived as being different (or which perceived them as being different). Thus, English people have an ethnicity *vis-à-vis* Scottish people, and Cornish people have an ethnicity *vis-à-vis* the rest of the country. Abner Cohen even went so far as to argue that London stock-brokers may be said to constitute an ethnic group in that they tend to marry into their own class and have a shared sense of identity (Cohen,

1974). From this perspective, ethnicity is socially constructed, and while analysts such as Barth and Cohen do not agree with each other in all respects, they share an antipathy to primordialist interpretations.

It is recognized that protagonists themselves may sometimes assert that their collective identities are natural, and that the power of ethnicity to influence behaviour may depend upon such beliefs. It is also accepted that once mythologies of ethnicity are sealed in bloodshed, to all intents and purposes, ethnic identities become objective social phenomena. At least for a period, it becomes impossible for people to 'unwrite what others have written'. Nevertheless, ethnicity is not in itself an explanation, but rather the product of social processes. It is not difficult to show, for example, that many African tribal identities were partially or wholly created under European rule, and that they were adapted and changed after independence. Nor is it hard to demonstrate that it is highly misleading to characterize the ethnic divisions of former Yugoslavia and the Caucasus as things that have resurfaced after 45 years. It can be shown that they are a product of more recent events, including the effects of 'nationalities' policies under communist rule, acute economic stress, local media coverage, and the machinations of politicians seeking a power base. To suggest that people kill each other in Bosnia because Muslims are Muslims, Serbs are Serbs and Croats are Croats is no more insightful than to suggest that the Iran–Iraq war was fought because the Iranians were Iranian and the Iraqis were Iraqi. The challenge is to explain why various forms of ethnicity become so significant at certain times and in certain places.

It has been commented that anthropological studies of ethnicity have not been well integrated into anthropological studies of war. A reason for this now becomes apparent: the two concepts are not distinct. If ethnicity is understood as the relationship between collective identities, often expressed with reference to conflicted boundaries, and war is a particular type of political relationship between groups, in which the groups use, or threaten to use, lethal force against each other in pursuit of their aims, then war itself is just a particularly violent form of ethnicity. Or to put it another way, all war is ethnic war, including war between nation states. People in Britain did not decide to fight in the Second World War because everyone in Britain hated Germans, but Britain was a social category that existed in juxtaposition to the social category of Germany, and once the two populations started killing each other, they tended to dislike each other intensely.

Along similar lines, it can be pointed out that just as the maintenance of boundaries between social groups facilitates the internal cohesion of each of them, so war is a mechanism for promoting social integration.

Recognizing that use of the term 'war' suggests a legitimization of slaughter does not mean that institutions that normally hold violence in check are necessarily abandoned when war is perceived as having broken out. On the contrary, political leaders are likely to maintain that armed conflict is essential to defend such institutions, and thereby to protect the fabric of social life. Indeed, it is a prerequisite of certain kinds of political entity that its members have a capacity, or potential capacity, to fight other groups as a unit. This is why it took the experience of two world wars and the fear of nuclear holocaust to make mutual belligerence less attractive for the governments of industrial states. Even now, in most industrialized states, to die for one's country is still sometimes equated with religious conceptions of sacrifice, while assertions of national pride are commonly linked with military achievements in the past and military capability in the present. Interestingly, even the effectiveness of the UN is sometimes judged in these terms. The emergence of a New World Order has been linked to the UN's facility to act as an instrument, enabling a group of powerful industrial countries to cooperate with each other and with less powerful countries, in order to fight a common enemy, most obviously Iraq in 1992.

A problem that may be raised with this approach to ethnicity is that the concept can become so broad that it encompasses too much to be analytically useful. However, a much more serious issue is that the term has escaped from anthropological debate, and is now widely used by journalists, by politicians and by some academics to mean something very different. Although the use of 'ethnic' is far from being consistent, its older connotations have been retained, such that it can indicate something 'exotic' or 'culturally different'. In Britain, 'ethnic' clothes are colourful and look African or Indian, and an 'ethnic riot' means that immigrant groups are involved. Sometimes this can be innocuous, but the last mentioned example points to a tendency for a counter-productive connection to be made between ethnicity and a Victorian conception of race.

Especially since the Second World War, biological understandings of race have been discredited in academic analysis, and in many countries they have become unacceptable in public political discourse. What is recognized to exist is racism, usually understood as the socially constructed ranking of people into hierarchies, commonly linked to unfounded assertions about natural superiority. Direct references to race can be highly sensitive, and any open explanation of behaviour that categorizes a group in terms of race and implies the existence of primordial dispositions is likely to be highly provocative. However, at the same time there has been a growth in what Mark Duffield has called 'cultural functionalism' (Duffield, 1996: 174), a view that suggests that certain distinctive groups have their own discrete qualities and characteristics. In Britain this has become the basis of official multi-cultural policies, which promote the recognition and acceptance of different world-views and customs, particularly when they are associated with people of Caribbean or Asian descent. Although such strategies may have positive effects, if pushed a step further, they can quickly become divisive. It is only a small step to a shift 'from racial discourse structured around categories of hierarchy and superiority to one in which cultural difference is argued to be the key operational factor' (Duffield, 1996: 175). As Barker has put it in *The New Racism*, 'You do not need to think of yourself as superior – you do not even need to dislike or blame those who are so different from you – in order to say that the presence of those aliens constitutes a threat to our way of life' (Barker, 1982: 18, quoted in Duffield, 1996: 176).

Usage of the term 'ethnicity' has been affected by this trend. While explicit statements about racial determinism are controversial, the suggestion that ethnicity determines behaviour is more acceptable, even if in practice this can often mean the same thing. In other words, there has been a conflation of ethnicity with the old meaning of race as social differentiation with a biological basis, and many ethnic explanations of conflict are in fact inherently racist. They suggest that natural divisions motivate action, that some social groups are inherently predisposed to violence, and that their primal barbarity can be contrasted with our humanitarianism. Echoing Barker's 'new racism', Paul Richards has described such a view as the 'new barbarism' in his critique of Robert Kaplan's article on West Africa which warns of 'the coming anarchy' (Richards, 1995).

In fact 'new barbarism' and 'new racism' have been apparent in discussions of Africa for some time. The academics who adopted the term 'ethnic' in the 1960s did so partly to avoid the primordialism associated with usage of the word 'tribe', but soon found that it was not so easily avoided. Tribe, ethnicity and often some reference to Conrad's *Heart of Darkness* are elided together in the international media's representations. In this respect, Somalia is an interesting exception, but one which proves the rule. Many journalists and some academics have maintained that this is not an ethnic conflict, but have done so on the grounds that all Somalis have the same ethnicity, a position which itself implies that ethnicity is something biological. Thus, in their chapter on Somalia in *War and the Media*, Miles Hudson and John Stanier (a former senior British military officer and a retired Tory Party *apparatchik*) state that 'the people of Somalia all come from basically the same ethnic stock'. They go on to explain that the inter-necine conflict in the country has nearly all been 'multi-tribal' (Hudson and Stanier, 1997: 245 and 247). Here is an interesting instance of the initial reason for adopting the term 'ethnic' in Africa being turned on its head. Rather than 'ethnic' referring to the new identities being forged in the towns, it is used to mean something naturally primordial. If anything, it seems to be 'tribe' that is perceived to be the socially constructed category.

In Eastern Europe the 'biologizing' of ethnicity has occurred some-what differently. Although there have long been derogatory views about a 'Balkan mentality', the early international media reports of the fighting in Bosnia were careful to place the term 'ethnic cleansing' in quotation marks, indicating that this was a local interpretation of events and not one that the journalists necessarily accepted. However, within a year the inverted commas were removed, and many foreign analysts had increasingly come to accept such a local perspective at face value. While it never became acceptable to explain events with reference to the Serb, Muslim or Croat races, references to ethnic groups, or often just to 'peoples', carried the same meaning.

This drift towards biological determinism was actively encouraged by several local politicians and local academics, because it conformed with their own ethno-nationalist agendas. It was also a logical extension of well-established local understandings of how social groups are formed. Approaches to the historical emergence of identity in Eastern European folklore studies are highly primordialist, and so were Soviet and Yugoslav nationalities policies, and the influential 'ethnos' theories which had been developed at the Academy of Science in Moscow by Yulian Bromley and his colleagues from the late 1960s (Bromley, 1974). By the second half of 1992, the conflation of popular understandings of race and ethnicity had become so entrenched that even some critiques served to reinforce it. Banks and Wolfe Murray provide the example of an article in the British *Guardian* newspaper which adopted a similar line on Yugoslavia to that taken by Hudson and Stanier on Somalia. It asserted that 'there are no ethnic divisions among the Slavs of Yugo-slavia', and claimed that the divisions were 'religious and cultural', thereby implying that other things are relatively ephemeral, but ethnicity is underlying and fundamental (Banks and Wolfe Murray, Chapter 7).

Awareness of the dangers of using ethnicity as a straightforward explanation for war, and in particular of the racist connotations of biologizing the concept, leads to a sceptical view of many accounts. *The Century of Warfare*, a book published to go with a recent BBC television series, finds nothing problematic in asserting that 'African tribalism caused a bloody civil war in Liberia in 1989 and another in Rwanda in April 1994'. It also tells us that 'Outside of Africa tribalism is known as ethnicity', and that this has 'provided a trigger for conflict in the aftermath of the break-up of the Soviet empire' (Messenger, 1995: 394 and 390). Numerous other examples of such statements are given in the chapters that follow. There is a need to interrogate them and to view them as, at best, misinformed and misleading.

However, it is not helpful to swing to the other extreme, and dismiss all statements by protagonists about ethnicity as mere 'false consciousness'. Arguing that ethnicity is socially constructed is no consolation to a woman who has watched her family being beaten to death, or even been forced to participate in the killing of loved ones. There is a need to find answers to the question of why so many people caught up in modern wars find highly ethnicized, and often highly apolitical, explanations for what has happened to them (and what they do to others) so convincing. At one level, all wars may be ethnic wars, but it is clear that protagonists in several modern conflicts embrace extreme forms of ethnic essentialism. This has happened in the past, for example in India at the time of partition, but what makes it so prevalent today? It also still needs to be asked why the socially traumatizing effects of wars appear to have been escalating, particularly as measured in terms of mass population displacements since the 1970s. Full answers to these questions require an analysis which cannot be attempted here. But the following seem to be important points to bear in mind.

Towards an understanding of contemporary wars

The weakening of state institutions It is clear that the governments of a large number of states are using their formal armed forces in wars against groups of their own people. This indicates that the integrity of many internationally recognized political units is being threatened. In the 1990s the term 'complex emergency' has gained a currency to describe some of the worst of these situations, usually where state institutions seem to have all but collapsed. It is, however, inaccurate to view this as a post-Cold War development. It is certainly the case that the end of the Cold War removed external alliances that helped keep some regimes in power, notably in Ethiopia and parts of Europe, but there was an incremental rise in the number of internal/civil wars in the 1990s, not a sudden proliferation. As mentioned above in the section on the current scale of the problem, the number of ongoing wars has been increasing since the end of the 1950s. It has been a consequence of many factors, including the rapid process of de-colonization, the setting up of unsustainable state structures, economic poverty and various forms of external involvement. In Africa in particular, the oil-price rises of the 1970s and the structural adjustment programmes of the 1980s had the effect of slowing or reversing the small developmental gains of previous decades, and led to a crisis of governance. Many states lost the capacity to assert a monopoly on the use of force, and could offer little in terms of services. It is small wonder that resistance movements emerged, and even the World Bank now recognizes that there is an urgent need to 're-invigorate' state institutions (World Bank, 1997).

War within social groups I have argued that war may be viewed as a form of ethnicity in that it promotes social cohesion in relation to groups perceived as outsiders and as enemies. It follows that the 'ethnic' aspects of many internal wars do not reveal the existence of a clearly differentiated category of 'ethnic war'. Rather, these are conflicts in which the link between violence and the expression of collective identity are especially apparent. One reason why this link is so clear is that the mechanisms which have been developed to mediate, diffuse and disguise such a tendency in inter-state conflicts cannot readily be applied to armed strife occurring inside states. It is also to do with characteristics of wars occurring within any social group. Whereas inter-state wars have normally helped to reinforce an existing political entity, such as 'France' or 'Argentina', even in defeat, in an internal war the promotion of social integration will often directly challenge former notions of where the boundaries of collective identity should be located. As a result, established institutions regulating cultural specificity and social order are likely to be threatened. In other words, many internal wars are waged over competing ideas about the way social integration should occur.

Here is certainly one reason why internal/civil wars can have such traumatic qualities. If they are prolonged or intense, they are likely fundamentally to transform affected populations, because it is the populations as a whole that are the object of the fighting and who bear most of the consequences (in some instances they also do most of the slaughtering). The material resources and social networks which have made former activities of daily life possible are deliberately destroyed. People have no option other than to find alternative modes of liveli-hood, often necessitating an antagonistic relationship with old friends who are now defined as outsiders. Customs of trust, moral probity and duty no longer suffice to ensure social accountability, except perhaps within a 'purified' locality or an extended family, which are defined in relation to the violent exclusion of others. This characteristic of internal war also has a discomforting corollary. The relative success in the development of mechanisms for limiting the occurrence of wars between states since the Second World War has restricted opportunities for governments to promote (or create) 'national' cohesion, and has perhaps made internal wars more likely.

Arms supplies and the decentralization of conflict During the Cold War, most wars involving guerrilla armies conformed to a certain pattern. Usually resistance was supported, directly or indirectly, by one of the superpower blocs, and anti-insurgency was supported by the other. This meant that lines of command tended to follow centrally organized supply routes. For the government this was likely to be from the capital city or ports. For the guerrillas it was likely to be base camps, often located in a neighbouring country. Atrocities were common, but there were ways in which some constraints could be imposed. The International Committee for the Red Cross and other organizations could apply pressure behind the scenes, usually in Washington or Moscow, and warring factions could sometimes be forced to limit human rights abuses. It was also the case that, whatever the other motivations for fighting, the publicly expressed reasons for conflict normally had to be political, because it was usually not possible to maintain the supply of arms and other resources with an ideology premised on ethnic essentialism. In some parts of the world huge quantities of weapons were channelled into war zones in this way.

However, with the unwillingness of the USA to become too closely involved in wars, following the defeat in Vietnam, and with the over-commitment of the Soviet Union, external regulation of these supply routes tended to become more remote. US support for the guerrillas in Afghanistan, for example, which at its height in the 1980s exceeded $600 million per year, was provided by the CIA through Pakistan with the cooperation of the Pakistan Inter-services Intelligence. It was accepted that there would be considerable leakage, and large quantities of military equipment ended up in local markets, contributing to a splintering of *mujaheddin* resistance. A comparable situation developed in north-east Africa, where arms supplied to the region's militarized regimes and guerrilla armies quickly found their way into new war zones in which there might be no superpower involvement. Small arms in particular became widely available, and automatic assault rifles became a weapon of choice, even in some small-scale conflicts, such as those between pastoralists over grazing land. In 1987, for example, Nyangatom warriors attacked their neighbours in south-east Ethiopia.

Raiding had occurred between the two groups in the past, but on this occasion the Nyangatom had obtained automatic rifles, and they killed between 500 and 1,000 people, between 10 and 20% of the entire Mursi population (Turton, 1989).

The ending of Cold War alliances (which occurred in most of the world well before it happened in Europe) exacerbated these processes. One way or another, the weapons of demobilized armies were distributed into populations. Initially this was mostly in the vicinity of long-standing Cold War conflicts, but from the 1980s, the vast Cold War arms stocks began feeding into the growing world-wide informal arms trade. According to one unpublished Polish military audit in 1992, about 30% of total military stock had disappeared, and as long ago as 1985 the US Department of Defense admitted that at least $1 billion-worth of equipment was being lost or stolen from stocks each year (Louise, 1994). The relative ease of access to cheap weapons, especially land mines, mortars and small arms, has inevitably encouraged increasing levels of violence. This in turn has created a growing demand, and several smaller arms-exporting countries, such as South Africa, now compete with criminal organizations to supply arms wherever there is the cash or resources to pay.

The process has also had the effect of changing the character of military strategies. Concentrated supply routes and lines of command have become increasingly redundant, and war lords are often able to provide for their clients without recourse to international political ideologies. States too have tended to decentralize anti-insurgency operations, sometimes engaging a particular group as local militia to attack neighbouring areas in which rebel factions are active. All of this has facilitated a localization of conflict. Clearly there are international interests at stake in many war zones, but many aspects of the war economies which sustain the fighting relate to the particular areas in which it occurs (such as the availability of exportable minerals), and the motivations for ongoing violence may have little to do with conventional national, let alone international, power politics.

The media Finally, there are the media, the subject of this book as a whole. Debate about their role is another example in which differences in views partly relate to usage of the concept itself. An unsatisfactory quality of 'the media' as a term is that 'media' is a plural noun, which in this connotation cannot be used in the singular. To refer to a journalist as being a representative of a medium would suggest metaphysical proclivities, and certainly not empirical investigation and reporting. Sometimes there are references to 'medias', but this is an abuse of the

English language, whatever the apparent gains in analytical clarity. One consequence of the problem is that 'the media' can be used to refer to something quite specific, such as partisan radio broadcasts in Rwanda, and also to a wide range of things from CNN, to novels, to church sermons. It is hard to avoid the trap of conflating the term's diverse applications, and for analysts to end up suggesting implications for the media generally from discussion of some forms of the media in a particular place at a particular time. Moreover, the linking with the definite article encourages a tendency to treat the media as a conscious as well as a homogeneous entity. In *War and the Media* (1997) by Hudson and Stanier, for example, we are told that 'the media' did all they could to raise anxieties about the length and cost of the war in the Gulf in 1991, led the intervention in Somalia in 1992, supported Milosevic in former Yugoslavia, and that they often find common cause with aid agencies, because both benefit from sensationalizing horrific situations (Hudson and Stanier, 1997: 242, 260, 267, 318).

In fact Hudson and Stanier's book, like most of the following chapters, focus on a specific kind of media, the news reporting of events in war zones. In this context it is all the more important to be clear that we are dealing with a means of transmitting information and views, and that when decisions are made about what to transmit, they are not made by the media, but by those who use them. It is therefore highly misleading to equate Serbian propaganda with the BBC World Service. However, it is also the case that the news media technology now available to many journalists, politicians and aid agencies has dramatically changed since the 1980s, with a consequence that scope for subtlety and insight have become more limited, and that a certain kind of international reporting has become an established norm.

Equipment has been developed which allows film to be very rapidly transmitted from one part of the world to another. This has created a demand in affluent countries for real-time news coverage, and an event, including the existence of a war, nowadays does not exist unless there are pictures available to illustrate it. There is intense competition for dramatic images, linked to simple stories which may be presented in the form of stereotypes, and even the most courageous and motivated of journalists often find that no time is available for reflection and thorough assessment. Martin Bell of the BBC has described the 'glamorising and prettifying' of war at the hands of British broadcasters. Soldiers are shown blazing away in the ruins, but audiences do not see what happens at the other end (quoted in Owen, 1996: 177). They never find out what is really going on.

In Africa, wars are certainly not glamorized in the same way, but journalists find themselves no less constrained. Writing in the *Guardian*, John Ryle has described a conference which he had himself been involved in organizing called 'The Fate of Information in the Disaster Zone'. He noted:

> There was plenty of criticism of media coverage of African disasters – often from journalists themselves. The media were to blame, it was argued, for lazy explanations of political crises, for the invocation of ancient tribal hatreds, for example, as an explanation for the genocide in Rwanda, when deliberate manipulation of communal conflict by a ruthless government was the immediate cause. When reporters in a conflict situation cannot make out what is happening, a noted journalist explained, they call it anarchy. Since they have usually arrived in town only a day or two before, this is quite often. (*Guardian*, 29 September 1995, quoted in Philo, 1998: 4)

It also seems to be the case that warring factions are becoming increasingly sophisticated at manipulating the international media. The very short amount of time available to obtain a story and the requirement that real-time images are available, means that it can be relatively easy both to prevent some information from being reported and to feed journalists a certain line of interpretation. Nik Gowing has recently suggested that such strategies were effectively used by Laurent Kabila's forces and the Rwandan government to deflect attention from the mass-killing of thousands of refugees in eastern Zaire (Gowing, 1998).

Such difficulties confronting serious-minded journalists are compounded by the fact that some of the most influential news organizations now make a virtue out of a minimal approach to analysis, and avoiding criticism of powerful government and other entrenched interests which jeopardize their global access. The extraordinary success of both CNN and News Corporation have been linked to this strategy, and have set the agenda for their competitors. In the West, the era of investigative TV journalism seems to be coming to an end, particularly when it relates to parts of the world thought to be far away. Rapid-fire, bullet-point summaries of events, combined with images that are heart-rending but sanitized, 'real-time' but manipulated, have become the dominant model. The entire script contents of the CBS nightly half-hour news would fit on three-quarters of the front page of the *New York Times* (Ignatieff, 1998: 26). Usually, no attempt is made to explain events in more than the shallowest of terms. The objective is often to elicit sympathy for the apparently innocent and helpless, or sometimes to rail against the manifest horrors of the world. But it is rarely to attempt a deeper understanding.

There is some disagreement about the impact of this kind of TV news. For John Keegan, its superficiality and sensationalism make it untrustworthy. He was one of the few public commentators who took issue with the coverage of the 1991 Gulf War at the time, castigating 'television opinion-makers' as 'contemptible' in their exaggerations (*Daily Telegraph*, 1 March 1991, quoted in Hudson and Stanier, 1997: 240). To some extent his line of argument in his 1998 Reith Lectures can be interpreted as an attempt to reverse what he views as doom-mongering misconceptions about 'war and our world' propagated through the British media. Like Hudson and Stanier, he is perhaps concerned that such media accounts may end up dictating policy, and certainly there are some instances where this seems to have occurred. For example, when Bosnian Serbs fired a single mortar shell into a Sarajevo bread queue, in local terms it was not an especially shocking atrocity. It was the fact that it was captured on film that made the difference, and prompted a threat of military action by NATO. Others, such as Warren Strobel, argue that these kinds of pressures tend to be quite short-term and can be weathered with relative ease if a government has a clear policy agenda and sticks to it. Based on evidence from the USA, he maintains that CNN-style news reporting may have made governance more difficult, but it has not resulted in the loss of policy control that is sometimes asserted (Strobel, 1996).

There is, however, another aspect to the influence of real-time TV media coverage, which in this context is even more significant than its possible effects on the policies adopted by the governments of the major powers. It seems likely it has an important influence on the fighting itself. This is particularly so where coverage makes no effort to look beyond the public ideologies of combatants or highlights what appear to be exotic aspects of a conflict. As Spyros Sofos points out in Chapter 8 of this book, in former Yugoslavia, the national media played a part in encouraging the emergence of populist nationalisms, and in the creation of mass panics that reinforced closed definitions of community, and little was done to reverse this trend in international coverage as warfare spread. The ethnicity of 'Serbs', 'Croats' and 'Muslims' was reported as if these were perduring, obvious and a natural focus for group division – the product of biology. Although some newspapers and reporters tried to dig deeper into events, the main thrust of international coverage was not to provide an alternative, more objective commentary on the fighting, but to confirm as 'facts' the constructed populist nationalisms of local politicians and war leaders. This both lent credibility to such views within former Yugoslavia, and probably helped encouraged participation in the conflict by many migrants and others with no direct experience of the fighting. As Philippa Atkinson and Mel McNulty show in their Chapters 10 and 13 of this book, similar observations can be made about international reporting of wars in Africa. Here the impact can be even more important, because the capacities of local news organizations may be very limited. International TV coverage percolates back into a conflict through world radio broadcasts, satellite TV transmissions, and the use of international news services by the national media, and may serve to reify divisions by concentrating on apparently mindless atrocities motivated by primal urges. If the power of ethnicity to propel people towards war rests in the subjective acceptance, by at least some protagonists, that social divisions are natural, then the fact that international news coverage promotes such views is grounds for serious concern.

Note

I would like to thank Chris Dolan, David Keen and Melissa Parker for their comments on drafts of this chapter.

References

Allen, T. and Eade, J. (1997) 'Anthropological Approaches to Ethnicity and Conflict in Europe and Beyond', *International Journal of Minority and Group Rights*, Vol. 4, Nos 3/4, pp. 217–46.

Barker, M. (1982) *The New Racism*, London: Junction Books.

Barth, F. (1969) 'Introduction', in F. Barth (ed.), *Ethnic Groups and Boundaries*, London: George Allen & Unwin.

Bromley, Y. (1974) 'The Term Ethnos and its Definition', in Y. Bromley (ed.), *Soviet Ethnology and Anthropology Today*, The Hague: Mouton.

Carnegie Commission on Preventing Deadly Conflict (1997) *Final Report*, Washington, DC: Carnegie Corporation of New York.

Chaliard, G. and Rageau, J. (1986) *Strategic Atlas*, Harmondsworth: Penguin Books.

Cohen, A. (1974) *Two-Dimensional Man*, London: Tavistock Publications.

Comaroff, J. and Stern, P. (eds) (1995) *Perspectives on Nationalism and War*, Luxembourg: Gordon and Breach Publishers.

Creighton, C. and Shaw, M. (eds) (1987) *The Sociology of War and Peace*, London: Macmillan.

Crook, P. (1994) *Darwinism, War and History*, Cambridge: Cambridge University Press.

de Waal, A. (1997) *Famine Crimes: Politics and the Disaster Relief Industry in Africa*, Oxford: James Currey.

Duffield, M. (1996) 'The Symphony of the Damned: Racial Discourse, Complex Emergencies and Humanitarian Aid', *Disasters*, Vol. 20, No. 3, September, pp. 173–93.

Eriksen, T. (1993) *Ethnicity and Nationalism*, London: Pluto Press.

Freedman, L. (ed.) (1994) *War*, Oxford: Oxford University Press.

Gantzel, K. (1997) 'War in the Post-World War II World: Some Empirical Trends and a Theoretical Approach', in D. Turton (ed.), *War and Ethnicity: Global Connections and Local Violence*, New York: University of Rochester Press.

Glazer, N. and Moynihan, D. (1963) *Beyond the Melting Pot: The Negroes, Puerto Ricans, Jews, Italians and Irish of New York City*, Cambridge, MA: MIT Press.

— (1975) 'Introduction', in N. Glazer and D. Moynihan (eds), *Ethnicity: Theory and Experience*, Cambridge, MA: Harvard University Press.

Gowing, N. (1998) *New Challenges and Problems for Information Management in Complex Emergencies*, Background Paper to the 'Dispatches from Disaster Zones' Conference, London, 28 May.

Groebel, J. and Hinde, R. (eds) (1989) *Aggression and War: Their Biological and Social Bases*, Cambridge: Cambridge University Press.

Harrison, S. (1996) 'War, Warfare', in A. Barnard and J. Spencer (eds), *Encyclopaedia of Social and Cultural Anthropology*, London: Routledge.

Hudson, M. and Stanier, M. (1997) *War and the Media*, Thrupp: Sutton Publishing.

Ignatieff, M. (1998) *The Warrior's Honor: Ethnic War and the Modern Conscience*, London: Chatto & Windus.

Jean, F. (1997) 'The Plight of the World's Refugees: At the Crossroads of Protection' in Médecins sans Frontières, *World in Crisis: The Politics of Survival at the End of the 20th Century*, London: Routledge.

Kaplan, R. (1993) *Balkan Ghosts: A Journey Through History*, London: Papermac.

— (1994) 'The Coming Anarchy: How Scarcity, Crime, Overpopulation, Tribalism and Disease are Rapidly Destroying the Social Fabric of Our Planet', *Atlantic Monthly*, February, pp. 44–76.

— (1996) *The Ends of the Earth: A Journey at the Dawn of the Twenty-first Century*, New York: Random House.

Keegan, J. (1998) *War and Our World*, London: Hutchinson.

Louise, C. (1994) *Societal Impacts of Small Arms Availability and Proliferation*, mimeo, International Alert, June.

Messenger, C. (1995) *The Century of Warfare*, London: HarperCollins.

Moynihan, D. (1993) *Pandaemonium: Ethnicity in International Politics*, Oxford: Oxford University Press.

Norwegian Refugee Council (1998) *Internally Displaced People: A Global Survey*, London: Earthscan.

ODI (1998) 'The State of the International Humanitarian System', *Overseas Development Institute Briefing Paper*, No. 1, March, London: ODI.

Owen, J. (1996) '"No Body, No Story": Representations of War and Disaster', in T. Allen, K. Hudson and J. Seaton (eds), *War, Ethnicity and the Media*, London: South Bank University.

Philo, G. (1998) (ed.) *The Zaire Rebellion and the British Media*, Background Paper to the 'Dispatches from Disaster Zones' Conference, London, 28 May.

Richards, P. (1995) *Fighting for the Rain Forest: Youth, Insurgency and Environment in Sierra Leone*, Oxford: James Currey.

Smith, D. (1997) *The State of War and Peace Atlas*, London: Penguin Books.

Strobel, W. (1996) 'The Media and U.S. Policies Toward Intervention: A Closer Look at the "CNN Effect"', in C. Crocker and F. Hampson (eds), *Managing Global Chaos*, Washington, DC: United States Institute of Peace Press.

Thomas, A. (1994) *Third World Atlas* (2nd edn), Buckingham: Open University Press.

Turton, D. (1989) 'Warfare, Vulnerability and Survival: A Case from South-western Ethiopia', *Cambridge Anthropology*, Vol. 13, No. 2, pp. 67–85.

UNDP (1994) *Human Development Report 1994*, New York: Oxford University Press.

UNHCR (1993) *The State of the World's Refugees*, New York: Penguin Books.

— (1995) *The State of the World's Refugees*, Oxford: Oxford University Press.

United Nations (1996) *The Blue Helmets: A Review of United Nations Peace-Keeping*, New York: United Nations.

van Mierop, E. (1997) 'Protection of Civilians in Conflict', in Médecins sans Frontières, *World in Crisis: The Politics of Survival at the End of the 20th Century*, London: Routledge.

Wallensteen, P. and Sollenberg, M. (1996) 'The End of International War? Armed Conflict 1989–95', *Journal of Peace Research*, Vol. 33, No. 2, pp. 353–70.

— (1997) 'Armed Conflicts, Conflict Termination and Peace Agreements, 1989–96', *Journal of Peace Research*, Vol. 34, No. 3, pp. 339–58.

Watkins, K. (1995) *The Oxfam Poverty Report*, Oxford: Oxfam.

Wilson, E. O. (1978) *On Human Nature*, Cambridge, MA: Harvard University Press.

World Bank (1997) *World Development Report 1997*, Oxford: Oxford University Press.

Wright, Q. (1966) *A Study of War*, Chicago: University of Chicago Press.

CHAPTER 2

. . . .

The New 'Ethnic' Wars and the Media

Jean Seaton

Oh those unspeakable Serbs! And then there are the envious Hutsis and the arrogant Tutsis, not to mention the aggressive Dinka. Consider how many groups of people and cultures about whom – until they were recently engaged in bloody civil wars – you knew little, but of whom you now have a clear, despairing, view. It seems that we have come to see whole continents like Africa and regions like the Middle East or the Balkans as subject to barbaric conflicts which are caused by the character of the peoples involved. Contemporary butchery is increasingly explained as a perverse blossoming of how people 'really' are, their inner ethnic core.

The use of ideas of ethnic enmity to explain conflict is not new. Such wars have usually been analysed as products of nineteenth- and twentieth-century nationalism and colonialism, which attempted to put boundaries around untidy social groups. These boundaries were convenient for the powers that imposed them, but often not coherent, and they have led to recurrent disputes about minority populations. There have been bitter quarrels about definitions of national identity, struggles about the location of borders and competition between ethnic groups for the control of state power. The losers in these conflicts have often been persecuted. Thus from the Russian and Polish pogroms of the nineteenth century, through the massacres of the Armenians, to many present-day conflicts, a repeated theme in contemporary history has been the eruption of peculiarly brutal, sub-national, ethnic warfare.

However, the ubiquitous re-emergence of ethnicity as a way of explaining the origins of wars all over the world is new. The problem is that reducing the social and economic realities, and the complex historical causes, that underlie and prolong these conflicts to 'ethnicity' de-politicizes them. Such explanations collude with protagonists' nationalistic, mythologized interpretations of history that form part of the ideological battle that accompanies persecution. But these media-based interpretations also, perhaps comfortingly for the outside world, obliterate the origins of conflicts in the politics of the Cold War and the colonial past and serve to conceal the impact of recent political decisions. Nowadays, 'ethnic' wars are described, all too often, as more or less inevitable and more or less intractable, because they are perceived to be the consequence of qualities inherent in the character of the communities involved.

The media play a complex part in the conduct of these new emergencies. They often provide the first, influential, definition of the social groups taking part in the conflicts. Individuals within the groups may be portrayed as alternatively culpable or innocent of war-mongery, or even its hapless victims, but it is nevertheless as if all of them bear the marks of their history and identity. We have almost come to see their fate as hereditary and predestined. Then the media act in their traditional role as messengers, although now ones with instant impact, so that White House officials make decisions with one eye on the CNN report on the screens beside the telephones on their desks (Sabato, 1996). But the media also act as agents of war and the press and broadcasting increasingly have become the institutions that accord wars legitimacy, and judge their outcome. Moreover, the media have become one of the primary means of assessing the effectiveness of intervention by outside forces, whether humanitarian or military. Our dazzling, new communications technologies bring us pictures of wars from all over the world, many of which we would previously hardly have known about. That we require new ways to come to terms with how vividly we now see these wars and what our relation to them ought to be, is hardly surprising.

Yet 'ethnic' conflicts, as David Turton (1997: 1) points out, are often perceived as having been 'deep-frozen' for the period between some historical moment when they first erupted, until their contemporary reappearance. So that the time when combatants were not fighting is explained by the restraining force of external factors, for example the power of the Communist Party in the former Yugoslavia, or the discipline – however unpalatable – of the colonial rule in the former empires of Europe, or even the draconian centralizing influence of the former Soviet Union over its satellites. But once these powers fade, the conflict that emerges is seen as the 'same old' hostility, inexorably bubbling up, even though it last erupted 60 or 100 years ago, even though it never previously took its current form, even though the form it takes is inevitably the result of the recent history of outside domination.

Why has ethnicity – quite recently having become the name we gave to benign marks of cultural distinction (which we usually wished to preserve) and now revealed as a close cousin of racial difference (which we wished to eradicate and indeed to demonstrate to be an illusion) – emerged as such a dangerous motor of brutality? Indeed, is it the wars themselves – or the explanations we attach to them – that are 'ethnic'? The role of the press, broadcasting and journalism in establishing how and why conflicts occur, and how the outside world understands them, is complicated. This is partly because the media are so implicated in how conflicts develop domestically, as well as internationally, and these two spheres may (or may not be) related.

However, a far more important influence on the ways in which the media handle these events is the economic and commercial situation of the media. The press and broadcasting have another life – as businesses. Contemporary news is processed in what are really multinational news factories, and is as subject to the rationalizations of the market as any other commodity. The institutions that produce news are themselves in turn only minor parts of vast entertainment industries, although news, because of its democratic role, is still accorded some legal and indeed economic privileges not enjoyed by other goods. Nevertheless how news of wars is constructed and sold is, more than ever, subject to the constraints of a ferociously competitive market. Stories of wars in far-away places have to attract audiences to sell to advertisers in competition with soap operas and game shows. Indeed, it is quite beside the point, as many critics of the role of the media in contemporary wars have done, simply to blame the media for inadequate or misleading reporting. The pressures on the media industries also have to be explained.

Media characterizations of conflict as ethnic in any case involve the interrelation between several partly distinct, partly dependent, media systems, each with its own structure, pressures, economies, and even styles. The first is how a group tells itself the ways in which it and its enemies are different. Then, in a world of diasporas, how the scattered members continue to remind themselves of their origins and differences, and finally, how the outside world, when conflict has broken out, comes to understand the violence as a consequence of ethnic hostility.

Internal media and ethnicity

The process of elaborating and allocating characteristics to groups of people defined as the enemy, and disseminating a view of them, is critical in the internal mobilization of opinion that is required to move populations towards war with each other. Rhetorics of national and cultural identity are revived and invented, in order to stimulate feelings of homogeneity within groups, and identify the enemies as excluded. Much of the work on this aspect of the role of the media has emphasized the content and imagery of the press and broadcasting. Indeed, the part played by 'regional' television, literature, intellectuals, and the continuous politicizing of history in the media in these conflicts is well documented. As Ed Vulliamy, in his book on Bosnia, commented, 'the answer to a question to a Serb about a Serbian artillery attack yesterday will begin in the year 925 and is invariably illustrated with maps' (Vulliamy, 1994: 5). He goes on to discuss how common interpretations of the past are elaborated by the media in these situations.

Depicting your enemy as a mad, ravaging tyrant has been part of the stock-in-trade of propagandists since wars began, and the role of the media in inciting these feelings is part of twentieth-century warfare. 'Day after day the Bulgarians were represented in the Greek press as a race of monsters,' reported the Carnegie Endowment for International Peace, 'and public feeling was roused to a pitch of chauvinism which made it inevitable that war, when it should come, should be ruthless ... Deny that your enemies are men and you will treat them as vermin.' This report was submitted in 1914 (Judah, 1997: 73). What is important in this process is the success of the media in helping to make a monster out of the man you know personally, who has lived next door. Yet this too is a process, not a natural phenomenon. It is also one that depends on media structures, the existence of regional monopolies, the regulatory tradition or lack of it, the ownership of the media and how they are financed, quite as much as more familiar issues of biased content. Beyond the direct influence of the media it also depends on the emergence of a willing-to-be-persuaded audience.

However, as Robert Fisk, the distinguished reporter who has filed from many of the world's most brutal wars, points out: 'The old barbarities are revived by new atrocities. Once the process gets going the murderous circle is closed. That is what "ethnic cleansing" is about' (Fisk, *Independent*, 3 July 1992). He goes on to argue that the local media play a vital role in reiterating old grievances. Vulliamy quotes a Bosnian describing how this process felt: 'I never saw any difference between a Serb or a Muslim or anyone. But how could I never look at them or greet them or live with them again? We liked each other for 45 years and in the 46th we hate each other' (Vulliamy, 1994: 208).

Of course, the image of the sudden breaking of the seemingly secure bond of neighbourliness may be peculiarly threatening to the external, watching world beyond. It seems to suggest a threat lurking in all multi-ethnic, urban populations. Yet even this picture of what happens in ethnic wars is misleading. As Strobel points out, the realities of which communities fall into conflict is far more complex than the media's picture of sudden fracture implies. Thus, in fact, research in communities under intense pressure has shown that urban mixed neighbourhoods often remain remarkably intact. In the city of Sarajevo, Serbians, Bosnians and Croats continued to live together under Serbian fire. Neighbourliness, knowing the man from the opposed community, remained a remarkably strong link, and people were not easily turned against each other on ethnic lines. It was in other rural areas that communities – even long-established and mixed ones – split rapidly and brutally (Strobel, 1997).

The external republics

A new factor in modern conflicts, however, is the existence of 'external republics': the groups of immigrants who remain fiercely committed to the communities they have come from, and the ways of life they have left behind. Nationalism – at a distance – is a contemporary phenomenon, and one especially dependent on the media. It is often more virulent than the home-grown variety and it has become a powerfully destabilizing force in some of the conflicts seen as 'ethnic' in origin.

In the case of the former Yugoslavia, the 'openness' of the borders had made it seem like the *least* Soviet of Eastern Bloc nations and as one of the most modern, most secular, and most economically developed of these countries. Thus by 1970, one-fifth of the entire workforce worked abroad. It was seen as a nation close to Western European patterns of politics and development, and as one likely to make the transition to democracy in the post-Cold War period most easily. Nevertheless, as the proportion of the population who worked abroad grew, and as the *émigrés* stayed away longer, the theory that these migrants would merely assimilate into their adopted societies and become first and foremost citizens of their new homes became increasingly inaccurate. Migrants became members of their new communities, but this did not diminish their attachment to the regions from where they had come, although it did change the nature of that attachment. As Walter Zimmerman wrote in a prescient book published in 1982:

> One cannot write the history of the internal evolution of post-war Yugoslavia without describing the role of actors outside it. Their role is likely to intensify in the near future ... and because of developments in modern

communications they are increasingly influenced by the local media, however narrow, however unbalanced, 'back home'. (Zimmerman, 1982: 219)

By 1990, every republic in Yugoslavia had its own satellite service to
the world, often transmitting an increasingly rabid local nationalism
which was avidly consumed by *émigrés* abroad.

The problem of how to 'govern' these distant, but related citizens,
was taken very seriously in the former Yugoslavia. Yet as Zimmerman
goes on, 'For a sizeable number of Yugoslavian citizens abroad, a major
consideration has not been preserving the independence or sovereignty
of Yugoslavia, but rather securing the independence of a component
part of the country from Yugoslavia' (Zimmerman, 1982: 4). Thus,
modern communication encouraged citizens of the 'external republics'
to become part of the jingoistic separatisms dominant 'at home', which
they financed and encouraged.

Zimmerman's book demonstrates that the emergence of this extreme, international nationalism is not a recent, or indeed a sudden,
development, but part of a protracted process. It has a history and
politics of its own. Paradoxically, the book also demonstrates how global
communication facilitates the dissemination of narrow, particularistic
'ethnic' points of view in the citizens of the 'external republics'.

The outside world

Then there is the problem of how the outside world comes to
understand some conflicts as being 'ethnic' in origin. The role of the
media in this is important because it affects what the outside world
does about these wars. However, the interaction between the media
and foreign policy also has to be understood in an historical context.
There may always have been wars, famines and at times the systematic
attempt to exterminate populations, but whether we knew, understood,
cared or thought that something ought to be done about them has
changed over the twentieth century. So, too, has the relationship of
these events to the press and broadcasting. Indeed, the impact of mass-
produced, widely available images of various kinds of conflict through
drawings, photographs, film and television has also altered. The idea of
'atrocity-mongering', the pejorative description of the use of pictures
and stories of cruel and savage acts to mobilize foreign opinion, only
emerged in the 1890s, and was itself a response to a new journalism.
Private, public, national and international reactions to foreign wars and
suffering may even have a history which is somewhat independent from
the events themselves. Our response to tragedy has a past.

Within this history the role of the media has been critical. On the one hand, journalism is seen to be a 'watchdog', alerting, alarming and mobilizing response. On the other, it is seen as ignoring or mis-representing the seriousness or relevance of events. While it may often have been prudent or expedient – or indeed even right – not to respond to some particular event, nevertheless the explanations advanced for action or inaction have also developed independently. We are always developing rhetorics of intervention or abstention from action. The media do not merely incite or dampen down calls for action, nor do they act like magic wands, imposing a point of view on other policy-makers; the press and broadcasting also articulate and rationalize the legitimacy of whatever position is adopted. Whether they are critically clamouring against government policy, acting in concert with it, or unreflectively smoothing its path, the media are an intrinsic part of the political processes of official and public response.

It is worth emphasizing how much our response to international crises has varied, because it helps situate what looks like a new mood of fatalism among many contemporary political leaders. This in turn has been justified by the related notion that conflicts are caused by primitive ethnic identification, rather than by determinate historical events. Thus when Warren Christopher, the American Secretary of State for Foreign Affairs, searched for words to describe the situation in Bosnia as it evolved in the 1990s, he argued colourfully that it was 'a problem from hell', 'like one of those beasts down there', 'one of those great messes' (*Newsweek*, 2 December 1992). Douglas Hurd, the British Foreign Secretary, claimed in another speech that 'there is nothing new in mass rape, in the shooting of civilians, in war crimes, in ethnic cleansing, in the burning of towns and villages. It has always happened. What is new is that a selection of these tragedies is now visible, within hours, to people around the world' (Douglas Hurd, *The Times*, 18 August 1994). In a similar vein Foreign Office officials argued that it 'could not be the object of foreign policy to wipe a tear from every suffering eye, however much the cameras would like to see us doing so' (Glenny, 1994: 123). Of course, there is nothing new (nor is it necessarily wrong) for govern-ments to say they cannot, or will not act in a particular crisis. The problem may well be what to 'do' for the best. But what is noticeable in recent arguments is how prominently the media and their impact figure in a debate that is ostensibly about foreign policy.

Recently, politicians have taken to giving the public earnest lectures on decoding images, attempting to inculcate caution. In America, in the aftermath of the Gulf War, there was a vigorous public debate about the extent to which 'real-time' television had come to determine policy by making politicians hopelessly vulnerable to domestic, media-stirred, public opinion. The debate has focused on the problem of whether foreign policy may not be permitted to 'do' what it needs to, because the consequences (dead American soldiers) are unacceptable when directly seen by the public. A related concern is that foreign policy may be inappropriately driven to action by public outrage at what is seen on the screens. The new, and in many ways inadequately thought-out, policy of supplying 'humanitarian aid' to the suffering innocent, while doing nothing militarily to stop the aggressors, has developed in response to these powerful, media-driven cross-pressures.

In reality, it is often difficult to separate humanitarian aid so neatly from political intervention. The acceptable plea for help for the suffering, all too often, becomes a disguised form of political intervention. The media and public opinion are the territory in which the battle for intervention is fought. Is part of the explanation for the rise in 'ethnic' wars that the media need to be able to explain conflicts in ways that do not involve complicated political calculations?

The rise and fall of ethnicity

However, even the use of 'ethnicity' has a history. Until the Second World War, notions of essential national characteristics were widely accepted, repeated and used to explain political action, personal behaviour and social patterns in the press. Such ideas were given credibility through myriad sources of authority from academic study and public policy as well as the media. They were unthinkingly shared by officials, intellectuals, journalists and the person on the Clapham omnibus. That individuals exhibited the stereotyped characteristics of their native country, and national populations exhibited sharply differing propensities and habits, was simply axiomatic. It was how people saw the world.

However, the Second World War changed the conventions. What is interesting about this is not that in some sense a superior, more desirable attitude prevailed, but that it shows how swiftly views can alter, and also how instrumental such shifts are. The decisive factor for the Allies was, of course, how to handle the racialism of the enemy. The fear was that the German claim that the war was really 'a war over Jews' would convince the hardly pro-Semitic domestic population that this was indeed the real cause of the war and undermine the public will to go on fighting. Robert Bruce-Lockhart, a journalist and diplomat, wrote in 1942, 'Max Aitken got going on the Jewish problem, after we listened to young Amory, who did a pro-Nazi broadcast from Berlin, the theme being we were being deceived "by the Jews". Max thinks that the anti-Semites will be a big problem here' (Robert Bruce-Lock-hart, in K. Young, 1980: 231). Government policy was influenced by the considerable anxiety about stimulating anti-Semitism, either by talking about the problem at all, let alone by using positive propaganda to change the views of the public (see Seaton, 1987).

It was also suggested that the attempt to correct anti-Semitism in the domestic population would in itself fall into the fascist trap: 'We do not recognise the German theory of a Jewish race and we maintain that Jews are citizens of the country to which they belong,' went one representative memo of the period (BBC Written Archives, 15 August 1941). The official attitude was that the war was being fought against a society that depended on theories of race discrimination, which conse-quently must be undermined. This 'anti-ethnicity' policy even extended to official attitudes towards the Germans themselves: 'Many people now adopt a sort of racialist theory that Germans are wicked by nature,' wrote one official. 'This must be opposed as a priority' (BBC Written Archives, 7 July 1944). On the face of it, this was a somewhat unexpected priority in the middle of a war. But it was argued that racialist anti-German views were not only proto-fascist in their implications, but that in any case, they were inefficient. If the Germans were portrayed as congenitally evil, it was argued, they could hardly be held responsible for what they did. Thus, one of the problems in dealing with the way in which Jews were being treated in Germany (on the basis of their ethnic identity) was that racialism as an ideology was seen as an irrational mistake. So that from the government, down to the BBC and the press, attempts to explore or explain German racialism to the public were actively discouraged.

However, the British public did not share this point of view. The public were often enthusiastic about programmes and articles that explained the war in terms of the ethnic origins of their enemies. However, even anti-German propaganda caricature often involved the notion that the enemy was irrationally racialist, and contrasted this ethnic view of the world with the democratic and principled attitudes of the Allies who made no distinctions between citizens. Yet it was only when the full horror of the consequences of Nazi racialism in the Holocaust was recognized at the end of the war that 'ethnic' explana-tions and references were made finally unacceptable. The experience of the Second World War and the media policies that were pursued made a previously acceptable dialogue about ethnic characteristics – for a time at least – taboo. This shift in public mores was profound, and was above all concerned with what was acceptable in public discussion. It makes it very difficult not to be anachronistic in dealing with pre-war expression. Thus Hugh Dalton, an eccentric old-Etonian Labour Party politician, and eventually a radical Chancellor of the Exchequer in the 1945 Attlee government, spoke at all of the public rallies about the fate of European Jewry during the war, was a prominent advocate of Israel, had Jewish refugees living in his own home ... and routinely made anti-Semitic jokes in speeches and in his immensely important diaries. The war made this appear an almost impossible contradiction. What was clear, was that by the end of the Second World War ethnicity had become seen as an unacceptable reference for explaining social and historical developments in public discourse. Wars certainly could not be explained by reference to anything as nebulous, or by then as suspect, as ethnicity.

The rapid post-war emergence of the Cold War confirmed the exclusion of 'ethnicity' from the lexicon of the explanation of wars. The Cold War provided a stable background framework for situating conflicts, which was quite separate from any 'ethnic', or indeed historical, explanations. From the 1950s through to the 1980s, all wars, throughout the world, could be interpreted as part of the grand supranational chess game of the Cold War. Henry Kissinger, the American Foreign Affairs Adviser to successive American presidents, put it clearly:

> In the relatively simple bi-polar world of the Cold War, although in an important sense we had only begun to scratch the surface of the long-term problem of our relationship with the Soviet Union, conflicts in the periphery were easy to categorise – if not to handle. Containment and diplomacy followed understanding. We would ask which side in this war is ours? And which side is really acting as a stooge for the Soviets? ... Journalists and governments had a relatively clear job in working this out and explaining it to the public. (Kissinger, 1979: 47)

Wars were 'explained' by the action of the – occasionally disguised – political interests of the great powers.

However, with the collapse of the Cold War in 1989, this convenient explanatory framework also disappeared. Perhaps even more significantly, the Cold War had also provided a flexible rationale for intervention in conflicts. 'Why were we worried about this war? Because of what it meant for the domino theory. Of course, if it was really the Russians at work, then we had to do something. That was the theory we worked on,' observed one seasoned journalist (Cameron, 1985: 172). Many contemporary conflicts are a legacy of these Cold War machinations, yet this history is conveniently buried in the myth of ethnic warfare.

What interests were to move the outside, watching world, in the post-Cold War era? There was a dramatic collapse of the simple calculus that had linked foreign wars to Western domestic self-interest. The problem was made worse by a change in the kinds of war journalists were observing. Increasingly in the post-Cold War, conflicts were sub-national: between competing groups, within and sometimes across national boundaries. In the former Yugoslavia, maps became immensely political as groups competed to establish the legitimacy of their claims to territory. Post-Cold War conflicts crossed boundaries of all kinds. Yet journalists still had to try to translate the bewildering conflicts they observed into stories that would engage the attention of their audiences (in competition with all the other sources of entertainment at their disposal). In addition, journalists had to develop some new way of explaining why wars in distant places still affected the interests of their audiences. It was an increasingly difficult job on both counts.

If 'ethnicity' seeped back into how journalists explained why conflicts developed, another rationale was needed in order to explain why distant audiences and governments should consider it their responsibility to 'do' anything about the carnage. An old comrade of war, all too real, but used for new purposes, was set to the task. If 'ethnicity' was commandeered to explain why conflicts occurred, misery and human suffering were used to argue that something ought to be done.

Misery and action

Famine, civil war, atrocities and natural disasters are quite different events, yet they have become increasingly conflated in international media accounts, and perhaps in political calculation as well. The problem is that, historically, the victims of nature were seen as deserving innocents, while the victims of culture, wars and religious conflicts might be undeserving. Now the separation is less clear. In part, this merging of the categories of disaster has come about because they are, in fact, very closely related phenomena. Amartya Sen, in his famous book on the 1947 Bengal famine, argued that the catastrophe was the consequence of the loss of people's entitlement to food, not the absolute shortage of food in an area. He commented that 'wars, conflicts, the collapse of civil order, an over-ideological political system, are all associated with, and are pre-conditions for famine' (Sen, 1983: 162). However, there are clear advantages in the previous view of politically neutral disasters for agencies who have to try to move the sympathy of donors; they find it easier to argue for the relief of innocent victims of circumstance. The complex interconnections of problems that lead to catastrophes is getting more difficult to communicate when there is so much emphasis on 'hot' news. While the argument for the kind of long-term commitment to development that might avert disasters before they occur is peculiarly difficult to place in the frantic market-place of modern news-making. These pressures have led to damaging media generalizations about chaos and disorder in needy nations.

One important theme in Sen's work is the powerful prophylactic role he argues for adversarial politics and journalism as defences against famine. An active press and opposition alert governments to impending disaster and 'operate even if there is no other more sophisticated monitoring, as an early warning system' (Drèze and Sen, 1989: 147). Although the authors point out that the media provide far less protection against endemic under-nutrition than they do against a more dramatic famine, nevertheless the media are given a significant role in the battle against hunger. But there is a confusion in all of these discussions between the internal national role of the press and the international impact. Sen suggests that the media not only 'carry information that the authorities may use, but also elements of pressure that may make them respond and make them do something urgently' (Sen, 1983: 113). However, while the international media share some of the characteristics of a local free press – they alert, they may mobilize – they are also far more potentially distorting. Above all there is the problem of counting the consequences of wars internationally.

Recently, there has been a vigorous debate about the political meaning of the messages sent by imagery of the Third World used to move pity – and charity – elsewhere. Some have argued that by perpetuating images of suffering the real possibilities of development are ignored. Thus Jonathan Benthall has pointed out how severe the pressures are to commoditize misery, yet how the agencies that are more self-critical in their use of imagery may be less effective in their fund-raising (Benthall, 1994: 14). Earlier, Peter Gill, in his book on the famine in Ethiopia, explored the perturbing distortions imposed on campaigns by the need to fit Western news agendas, as well as Western charitable calendars: people are more philanthropically inclined before Christmas (Gill, 1986: Chapter 3). However, there has been far less interest in the way in which media accounts of disasters interact with domestic political processes.

Thus the argument that democratic media protect societies against famine needs modification if it is considered in a wider context. Drèze and Sen suggested that one of the 'roles of the press is to make it too expensive in political terms for governments to be callous and lethargic ... Indeed it appears that no country with a free press and scope for opposition politics has ever experienced a major famine' (Drèze and

Sen, 1989: 237). However, the possession of democratic liberties does not necessarily make one nation sympathetic to the plight of another. Indeed, the 'expense' of another, distant, nation's disaster may be calculated quite differently. Sen's argument that catastrophes are a consequence of a lack of political rights may be accurate, both nationally and internationally. However, the 'cost' of not doing something, internationally, is often difficult to calculate. Moreover, misery which is distant (or in the case, for example, of Bosnia, or Kosova, misery which is made to seem more distant than it is – precisely because of the shared characteristics of misery wherever it occurs) is more frequently explained in the international media as a consequence not of processes, like the political rights Sen is describing, but in terms of inevitabilities, like ethnicity.

How should journalists report what they see when public pressure to act is generated by television images of human suffering, but when there is no clear – or vital – national interest at stake? In this increasingly common situation, it is, however, evident that the media do have an impact on policy-making. Ironically, this is most powerful on either end of the process of intervention, the decision to go in, the decision to pull out, when policies themselves are uncertain, or weakly held. Politicians should perhaps complain less about what the media make them do, and devote more energy to how they make policy in the new uncertainties of the post-Cold War world.

In addition, in old-fashioned, national wars, the military have always sought to control, manipulate and minimize the action and role of reporters. Yet, in the changed conditions of contemporary military operations, 'peace-keepers' actually depend on the media in a quite novel way. At least in a conventional war the goal was relatively clear; in today's untidy conflicts, peace-keepers from outside need the media to demonstrate their success: the media become the agents (not reporters) of achieving goals. Douglas Hallin, in a classic account of the role of the media in Vietnam, argued that the impact of the news media on policy was proportional to the level of consensus in society about the aims of the war (Hallin, 1982). In a world without the consensual 'glue' of the Cold War's agreed framework, the scope for media influence is thus increased. As Strobel argued in his analysis of the media–policy nexus in the Gulf War, the Balkans and Korea, 'I found no evidence that the news media, by themselves, force US government officials to change their policies. But, under the right conditions, the news media nevertheless can have a powerful effect on the process. These conditions are set by foreign policy-makers themselves' (Strobel, 1997: 5).

Gangsters and winners

Journalists' explanation of the origins of modern wars in 'ethnic conflict', and their appeal for intervention on the basis of (all too real) suffering, have tended to exclude other inconvenient aspects of these brutal affairs: for example, that some groups have done very well out of them.

The emergence of 'gangster' politics may not be a new political form, but it has become as prevalent in the more developed as in the less developed world when rabid conflicts between communities have emerged. However, it is a difficult phenomenon for journalists to report or even perhaps describe and think about – let alone for other governments to deal with. Journalists from liberal democracies, reporting to news organizations with rigid hierarchies of news values, are used to working within tight frameworks of predictable political structures. They report on the activities of parties, leaders, assemblies, political pressure groups, governments and officials, all of whom may have a relationship – but a tangential one – to the sources of economic and physical power in the new areas of conflict.

Thus 'winners' in these conflicts remain obscure and unspoken of despite their very real interest in the continuation of the war. Tim Judah writes in his book on Serbia of the 'flashy cars, designer clothes, and opulent lifestyle of the gun runners and gangsters who were the real authority in the war' (Judah, 1997: 309). Shattered Vukovar, he argues, was full of gangsters' cars, and the imposition of Western economic sanctions against the Serbs ironically simply effected the final transference of the economy into their hands, by destroying the remaining legitimate businesses. But this paradoxical wealth was never seen on Western screens. In contemporary wars, fortunes are made out of gun-running, extortion, and the buying and selling of humanitarian aid. Similar developments, which have made the work of aid agencies peculiarly complex, have been common in Somalia and Rwanda. John Lloyd, in his authoritative account of the reshaping of Russian society, points out that Western journalists have too frequently reported what they expected to find, not on the reality of an economy where violence has become endemic, but which is nevertheless fast developing (Lloyd, 1998).

Of course reporting – not on anarchy, though that is what it may look like – but on the very unstable, violent, illegal order that may characterize modern wars is also hard to do because it is dangerous. More journalists have been killed in recent conflicts than ever before, and there is evidence that they are more frequently deliberately murdered than in the past (Freedom Forum, 1998). Reporting is also difficult because profiteers have nothing to gain from publicity and are secretive. Nevertheless, a discussion of the instrumental rationality of some groups who further and prosper from the savage civil conflicts is so at odds with how the wars have been described that it has frequently been ignored. Consequently the conflicts appear all the more strange, and irrational – in other words, ethnic.

The news industries and the new world order

Journalists can report only the news their organizations will publish or broadcast. News is a commodity, and the expensive reporting of news from far-away places, where they are doing horrible things to each other, is not always easy to place. The situation of journalists in extreme predicaments, wars, famines, natural disasters, is unusual. However much journalists ritualize their response to it – the jokes, the drink, the media-bared routines in the face of death, the deadlines – there is always an appalling gap between journalists' own front-line experiences and the places in which their reporting is received: in comfortable, remote homes. Martin Bell and Fergal Keane reticently describe the nightmares that attend their work. The massacre in Rwanda, wrote Keane, was 'unlike any other event I have reported on … it changed everything. The survivors most of all, but also the doctors, the aid workers, the priests and the journalists. We had learned something about the soul of man that would leave us shamed long into the future' (Keane, 1995: 45). Journalists in these conditions occupy a strange territory, one with burdens, and privileges. Yet the assessment of the role of journalism in wars has, in general, been highly critical. The parasitical nature of journalism is more evident in these conditions. From Phillip Knightley's classic book, *The First Casualty* (1981), through Bruce Cummings's more complex work on television and the Korean War, to Mark Pedalty's account of the media in Nicaragua, observers have delineated the bureaucratic and narrow focus of much war report-ing, and have compared it unfavourably with the hyperbole of the journalists' own myths. 'Journalists often lie,' argues Knightley, 'pictures very often lie. In war, truth is the first casualty' (Knightley, 1981: 186).

However, contemporary journalists, reporting on the making of the New World Order and its savage wars, seem to be identifying changes in the habits of the news organizations for which they work. The first new feature they identify is the increasing pace in the industrialization of news. Pressures on news have greatly intensified. There is the growth and consolidation of the vast media empires. Unlike the previous generation of press barons, the new masters of the universe do not invest in news: on the contrary, they ruthlessly cut costs by asset-stripping news rooms. Fewer journalists, fewer experts, but more news programmes. There is more news in the world, but it is produced by less specialized, more general reporters. They know less, they cost less, but they produce news that is disseminated more powerfully than ever before (Seaton, 1998).

In addition, new technology, the proliferation of stations, channels and programmes, and the idea of the rolling news day with its almost continuous flow of news, literally means that deadlines occur so frequently that journalists have less and less time to collect news themselves. Not only has news become increasingly metropolitan, but under pressure journalists take it from easily accessible sources. 'More means worse,' writes Bell, 'the multiplicity of deadlines takes us away from the real world and drives us back into our offices and edit suites. It is safer there and we may find reason to stay' (Bell, 1995: 271).

Another important factor is speed. 'News dies faster now than ever before' comments Nik Gowing (1995: 12). News can often now be live, but unless it is ingeniously managed this has come to mean that news is what is happening now, however trivial. Important things, the news that journalists like Bell, Gowing, Keane and Lloyd think matters, dies just as fast as the silly, absurd and unimportant. The pantheon of significance that is at the centre of good journalism may be being undermined. Thus a greater volume of news should not be confused with a greater variety of news. 'More' news does not mean more generous news values, more different, more in-depth stories. Editors making choices in domestic news rooms far from conflicts are all too often what Bell calls 'departments of preconceived notions', and stories which challenge the narratives that they believe to be developing will be discounted and not shown. In a war in which the Serbs had been the aggressors, stories of the murder of hapless Serbs were too 'emotionally confusing', one editor explained to Bell, 'to be good for the public'.

In the past, war reporting was highly developed to fit simple narratives of moral 'neighbourliness'. There were, from whatever your national point of view, goodies and baddies. A great deal of creative energy was devoted to making these conventions clear, and the visual codes of war reporting have always been fiercely tamed to these codes. Thus, in the great path-breaking documentary histories of twentieth-century war, 'The Great War' (1969) and 'The World at War' (1972), programmes that were subtle, powerful, informed and immensely influential in discussions of the origins and consequences of the conflicts they described, the Allies were nevertheless always to be seen shooting from the right, and the enemy from the left. In Ted Turner's epic series on 'The Cold War' (1998) decades later it was the same. This helps illuminate the problems reporters have had with contemporary 'ethnic' conflicts. Think about pictures of snipers, a lethal feature of wars in Bosnia, and before that in the Lebanon, a feature of wars played out in mixed communities and particularly in cities. 'Sniper view' shots on television are technically quite possible, but at least so far unacceptable. It is perhaps significant that in the film *Schindler's List* (1992) such a random, but intentional, shot was the moral pivot of the story, yet most Jews in most camps were not killed by sniper shots. In the film, the picture demonstrated the depravity of the sniper, but news cameras cannot share such pictures without being complicit with them.

Furthermore, the politics of reporting peace-keeping missions, the most common form of intervention that has developed in response to the 'ethnic' wars, is as undeveloped as the interventions themselves seem to be. The vulnerability of the media in these situations may reflect the ambiguities of the peace-keepers' own, inadequate, mandates. Warring groups all over the world now seem to understand perfectly well how cynically to exploit their own civilian suffering and the frailty of the position of the peace-keeping forces in order to manipulate the media. Journalists thus play an important part in defining the meaning of conflicts but are not always clear as to how they should use this role. They are now attending civil wars in which civilian suffering, and sometimes manipulation of the images of it, are ruthlessly played pawns in nationalist conflicts.

What language do journalists use to describe these conflicts? Journalism is the art of the cliché. Great journalism may inflect or bend the language for new purposes, but it is still dependent on the language and ideas that audiences recognize. Under pressure from deadlines, narrow news values, in highly involved situations which they have little time to understand, and constrained by audiences with very short attention spans, some journalists and news editors have used 'ethnicity', 'tribalism' or 'history' to explain contemporary conflicts. Many of the most committed have attempted to escape from the cliché. However, commitment is not merely a moral category distinguishing the good journalist from the bad, although the quality of journalism is a critical consideration. Commitment is also an organizational category, it denotes those journalists with the time, the resources, the backing from their news organizations and the editors in their news rooms. Misha Glenny, Fergal Keane, Robert Fisk, Martin Bell, Ed Vulliamy, John Lloyd and so on know that the conflicts they see are complex affairs with real histories. They know, all too well, that it is not the differences between the groups that have caused the wars, but on the contrary, the purposes that these differences are used for.

Media watchdogs dying?

In the post-Cold War, de-aligned New World Order, the media watchdogs seem to be complaining that they are no longer wanted. The capacity of journalism to move, alarm, shame and stir the public and the politicians has, many good journalists say, been diminished. They say that they find it increasingly difficult to influence policy and politics. Recently, a number of distinguished reporters, writing about plagues and famines, catastrophes and wars, are claiming that news, and their own stories, are being treated differently from the way they had expected. What is odd is that journalists are saying that what they do has less effect, at the same time that politicians are saying that the news is having greater effect. Are the politicians merely using a ploy to diminish the power of reporting? Or are they both right?

While journalists have complained of a bland political indifference to the terrible events they have reported, they are also clear about the conditions when what they say does have an effect – and are often as suspicious of these as the politicians. When there is a policy vacuum, and when pictures have a sudden, jolting, impact on the public, then suddenly and radically policy can change. Thus the fate of an individual child will catch attention, and as a consequence recourses will be found, logistics worked out, and for a time sick children will be air-lifted to medical attention. Bell, Gowing, Keane and others worry about this. They compare what may suddenly move opinion to the terrible destruction that they have witnessed and find the reaction not merely inadequate, but bizarre. All too often it seems contemporary political responses to conflict do nothing to address the causes of the violence, and may indeed even only appear palliative. 'It is', writes Bell, 'the story of the containment of politics by humanitarian assistance' (Bell, 1995: 134).

To those beyond the media they look like magically powerful institutions, capriciously determining the fate of peoples and nations. Bernard Kouchner, the founder of Médecins sans Frontières, summed up what many feel to be the situation: 'Men are dying at this moment in Burma, and Tibet and Sri Lanka and no one cares because they are not known, and they are not seen to die' (Kouchner, quoted in Benthall, 1994: 170). To those trying to command world attention – or needing to be attended to – the media gaze looks like that of an over-indulged tyrant, irrational, self-regarding and all-powerful. An inverted Medusa whose eye delivers life, and whose inattention condemns to death. Of course, for many journalists themselves the problem is how to mobilize the public into action about the terrible suffering they witness. They have argued that if politicians and the public could see the unedited brutality of what they have seen, they could not fail to be moved to responsibility. Bell fiercely condemns the BBC guidelines which mean that all the torture and the consequences of violence are 'good tasted' away. We are, he argues, in danger not only of sanitizing war but even of prettifying it.

Moreover, another problem is that wars, famines and natural disasters seem to have exchanged explanatory frameworks in contemporary media accounts. They have become like the ideas in Samuel Butler's great nineteenth-century satirical novel, *Erewhon*, in which everyone who is ill is treated as bad and everyone who is bad is treated as ill. We have come to recognize that famines and natural disasters have causes. They are not inevitable. In contrast, we have come to regard civil wars as 'ethnic' conflicts: unavoidable and irresolvable.

Interestingly, the journalism that seems to deal with these complex new emergencies with greatest clarity often depends on an old-fashioned narrative technique. By placing events in sequences, as Brian Lapping and Norma Percy did in the series 'The Death of Yugoslavia' (1996), or more recently in 'The Arabs and the Jews' (1998), journalism can at least bring order to the consideration of consequences. Narrative history also powerfully repoliticizes events. The aim of 'The Death of Yugoslavia', claim its makers in an accompanying book, was to 'shed light on the decisions which led to the horror of destruction. And to identify dispassionately and clinically the crucial events that led up to the war' (Silber and Little, 1995: 3). Authoritative narratives emphasize the contingency of events, and display them as parts of an historic, never inevitable, and consequently reversible process. This is far removed from the blind working out of a fatalistically conceived notion of 'ethnic' identity. Eric Hobsbawm writes in his latest book of the way in which the manipulation of history has become the raw material for nationalist, or ethnic, or fundamentalist ideologies: 'I used to think that the profession of Historian, unlike that of, say, Nuclear Physicist, could at least do no harm. Now I know that it can' (Hobsbawm, 1997: 15). He also goes on to point out that history is never the product of ancestral memory; it is what educated people make it. Nevertheless, he argues that the only corrective to myths is evidence. Yet, it is the considered, well-informed, disciplined journalism that produces such corrective and well-founded accounts which is most under threat in the highly competitive markets of contemporary broadcasting.

However, the politicians of the policing world need to sort out what they want to do more clearly as well. Humanitarian aid, thrown at needy emergencies to ward off domestic public outcry, may not merely be inadequate, it may even protract and intensify awful conflicts. If policy-makers are clearer about the politics and the goals of intervention, then in turn, all the evidence suggests the media will support them.

Brutal, complex wars involving appalling consequences for civilian populations are becoming more, not less, frequent. Both the media and the policy-makers have to find ways of addressing the political realities of these affairs – and explaining them to their audiences and electorates. They cannot hide behind naïve inevitabilities of 'ethnic' explanation and the mask of neutral peace-keeping, because they do not work. Neither politicians nor journalists can go on avoiding the political realities that cause and prolong these conflicts. As Thomas Hobbes observed in Part One Chapter 13 of *Leviathan*, describing the bloody civil war he lived through, the costs of not dealing in political realities are 'fear and danger of violent death; and the life of man, solitary, poor, nasty, brutish, and short'.

References

BBC Written Archives, R341/952, 15 August 1941.

BBC Written Archives, R341/36, 7 July 1944.

Bell, M. (1995) *In Harm's Way: Memories of a War Zone Thug*, London: Hamish Hamilton.

Benthall, J. (1994) *Disasters, Relief and the Media*, London: I.B.Tauris.

Cameron, J. (1985) *Reporting Yesterday*, London: Weidenfeld and Nicolson.

Christopher, W. (1992) 'New Conflict in Bosnia', *Newsweek*, 2 December, p. 117.

Drèze, J. and Sen, A. (1989) *Hunger and Public Action*, Oxford: Oxford University Press.

Fisk, R. (1992) 'What Ethnic Cleansing Means', *Independent*, 3 July.

Freedom Forum (1998) *Journalists under Fire* (Report), London and Washington: Freedom Forum.

Gill, P. (1986) *A Year in the Death of Africa: Politics, Bureaucracy and Famine*, London: Paladin.

Glenny, M. (1994) *The Fall of Yugoslavia*, Harmondsworth: Penguin.

Gowing, N. (1995) *Real Time Television and American Foreign Policy*, Cambridge, MA: Joan Shorenstein-Barone Centre for Politics and the Media, Paper No. 29.

Hallin, D. (1982) *The Uncensored War: The Media and Vietnam*, Oxford: Oxford University Press.

Hobsbawm, E. (1997) *On History*, London: Weidenfeld and Nicolson.

Hurd, D. (1994a) 'Foreign Secretary Warns of Media's Role', speech to the Travellers Club, reported in *The Times*, 17 August.

— (1994b) *The Times*, 18 August.

Judah, T. (1997) *The Serbs: History, Myth and the Destruction of Yugoslavia*, New Haven, CT: Yale University Press.

Keane, F. (1995) *Season of Blood: A Rwandan Journey*, Harmondsworth: Penguin.

— (1996) *A Letter to Daniel: Dispatches from the Heart*, Harmondsworth: Penguin.

Kissinger, H. (1979) *The White House Years*, London: Weidenfeld and Nicolson.

Knightley, P. (1981) *The First Casualty*, Harmondsworth: Penguin.

Lloyd, J. (1998) *Russia: Rebirth of a Nation*, London: Weidenfeld and Nicolson.

Pedalty, M. (1995) *War Stories: The Culture of Foreign Correspondents*, London/New York: Routledge.

Sabato, L. (1996) *Feeding Frenzy and the Media*, New York: The Free Press.

Seaton, J. (1987) 'Atrocities and the Media', in Jean Seaton and Ben Pimlott, (eds), *The Media in British Politics*, Aldershot: Avebury.

— (ed.) (1998) *Politics and the Media*, Oxford: Blackwell.

Sen, A. (1983) *The Famine in Bengal*, Oxford: Oxford University Press.

Silber, L. and Little, A. (1995) *The Death of Yugoslavia*, London: BBC and Penguin Books.

Strobel, W. P. (1997) *Late Breaking Foreign Policy: The News Media's Influence on Peace Operations*, Washington, DC: US Institute of Peace.

Turton, D. (1997) 'Introduction' in David Turton (ed.), *War and Ethnicity: Global Connections and Local Violence*, New York: University of Rochester Press.

Vulliamy, E. (1994) *Seasons in Hell: Understanding Bosnia's War*, London: Simon and Schuster.

Young, K. (ed.) (1980) *The Diaries of Bruce-Lockhart*, Basingstoke: Macmillan.

Zimmerman, W. (1982) *Open Borders, Non-Alignment and the Political Evolution of Yugoslavia*, Princeton, NJ: Princeton University Press.

CHAPTER 3

Ethnic Pervasion

Richard Fardon

Covering ethnicity? Or, ethnicity as coverage?[1]

To give credit its due: as an academic anthropologist and specialist on West Africa, most of my working life is spent in the Bloomsbury area of central London immersed in teaching and administration. To follow day-to-day events in the West African countries I have known best (and others I have never visited) I rely upon African visitors and coverage provided by the media – especially print media: specialist journals, like *Africa Confidential* or *West Africa*, and the diminishing flow of African news to be found in the 'quality' daily newspapers. When organizing business or diplomatic briefings through the Centre of African Studies, I am as much reliant on journalists and consultants as academics for up-to-date reports. So I have more admiration than criticism for the efforts of journalists and more daily reasons to be grateful to them than most.[2]

It is all too easy to generalize about the media or those who work in it but, if journalists spoke for themselves, I hope they would insist on differentiating between types of report: contrasting those of the on-the-spot specialist – whether local stringer or regional specialist with long-term knowledge – with those of visiting 'crisis' reporters; and explaining the negotiation which has to take place over the report that reaches its final consumer (whether in print, sound or image). What might be construed as criticisms of journalists are meant as observations on the state of our times, and apply to anthropologists as much as they do to journalists.

Over the course of the twentieth century, but most startlingly since the end of Eric Hobsbawm's 'short twentieth century' (Hobsbawm, 1994), it has become difficult to envisage acts of collective violence that may not, from some or other perspective, be deemed ethnic. Some violence is still described in class terms; gender and generation are more generally seen as axes of violence that have collective aspects.

But the overwhelming tendency is for an ethnic account to be available for collective acts of violence. To be against ethnic violence goes a long way towards being against collective violence in short; often the adjective 'ethnic' adds little further specification to the adjective 'collective'. What kind of understanding do we really gain from ethnicity?

Ethnicity seems to be in the air we breathe so that it becomes increasingly difficult to decide whether news reports cover the global phenomenon of ethnicity or whether ethnicity is the covering in which events are globally wrapped. Do reports document ethnicity or produce it? Is ethnicity part of the medium in which information is communicated, or is it the message? Can we even make this distinction? I believe these undecidabilities are principled; from which it follows that what we need to begin to understand is a world in which such unresolvable questions arise constantly in the mind of every intelligent commentator but cannot in essence ever be resolved.

One of these undecidabilities is not particular to ethnicity but may be particularly perplexing in that case. Is ethnicity a term of translation or of explanation? When we are told that 'such and such' is an ethnic term, are we simply being told, 'You may understand this best by thinking of it as, in some respects, like something you already know about', or, are we being told, 'You've seen this before and so you know what follows'? In practice, the line between translation and explanation is always difficult, sometimes impossible, to draw, but with terms like ethnicity there is the additional problem that it is not only reporters who may want to make local identities globally comprehensible but local proponents may also see, or want to see, their own situation as a variant of a global condition from which certain things are generally conceded to follow. Most obviously, there is an argument which can be made to run directly from concession of a local collective identity to ceding that identity the right to equality with other such identities, which equality entails representation among other like collectivities and the right to complete or partial self-determination. While all translations are purposeful, translation of a local identity is motivated in particularly urgent fashions because so much can seem to be entailed by it. For instance, immediate translation of bloodshed in Rwanda as an ethnic conflict between Tutsi and Hutu subsequently transpired to have been a gross oversimplification of a complex set of circumstances. Subsequent reportage had to concentrate on redescribing the hasty short-circuit by virtue of which the international community seemed to know already what followed from 'Hutu' and 'Tutsi' being ethnic terms (*Article 19*, 1996). There is a constant danger that too much becomes self-evident once an identity is construed as ethnic.

The self-evidence of ethnic terms

I ask the reader's forgiveness for an autobiographical aside which helps me explain how this argument might develop: about a decade ago, when in the throes of writing an ethnography of a people of Nigeria and Cameroon who – regardless of great differences in language and dialect, political organization, history, and much else – claimed a single ethnic identity for themselves in certain contexts, I was asked to reflect for a symposium upon the relation between ethnicity and comparative anthropology (Fardon, 1987). The problem then looked to me like this: comparative anthropology usually sought to compare some facets of the systematic relations between a situation among the X with facets of the same situation among the Y. So, for instance, comparative anthropologists might ask whether there was some consistent relation between, on the one hand, rules of residence and descent and, on the other, the frequency of divorce in different societies. The grandest examples of such a thought style relied upon coded, and now computerized, banks of such apparently comparable information.[3] No exercise of this kind would be writable, or presumably even thinkable, without some short-hand way of establishing who were the X and Y. Moreover, the X and Y would need to be unproblematic, since the thrust of the argument was elsewhere (in the comparison of other systematic features). Where did these X and Y terms come from and how were they able to do their job?

The answer to the question, 'Where do ethnic terms come from?' was practically simple but historically and epistemologically complex. Practically, the names were – more often than not – simply those used by ethnographers to title the descriptions from which the comparative anthropologist's information came. However, an answer to the question where the ethnographers got the name from was far from singular. Each ethnonym (ethnic name) had its own contexts of local use, local history, relations with other local terms (some of smaller scale which it encompassed, some larger which englobed it, some of which constituted its 'others' in different respects), and the ethnographer had decided – under conditions, as they say, not entirely of his or her choosing – what term to adopt and what to mean by it. Comparative anthropology was necessarily naïve about the uses of ethnic terms reported in the very ethnographies it drew upon. Over a long period ethnographers had been developing a 'hermeneutics of suspicion' towards ethnic terms: people's use of them was highly situational, some African ethnic identities were demonstrably colonial or post-colonial inventions and so forth. In short, it became difficult to define briefly what all the X, Y, Zs of comparative anthropology had in common other than that they were unit markers that could be used to play the game of comparison. Here, I use 'game' not as an easy insult but to describe an intellectual exercise with its own starting conventions and ways of going on.

Adding together all these ethnic unit markers, the analyst could not help but be struck by how much they differed from one another. From a viewpoint of Olympian detachment, the analyst might then ask what sort of synthesizing definition of 'ethnicity' – the general phenomenon – might allow all these identities, translated as 'ethnicities' – in the plural – to be considered its instances. No simple definition would capture them all. Ethnicity would have to be described as both a polythetic and a residual category. By borrowing the term polythetic,[4] I meant only that ethnic terms did not share a single essential trait; instead, a term was recognized as an 'ethnic term' by virtue of having some, but not necessarily all, of the characteristics of that class. As a theoretically limiting but unlikely case, if we decided ethnic terms had ten defining features, it could happen that ethnic term X had characteristics one to five while ethnic term Y had characteristics six to ten. In other words, both could be construed as ethnic terms without sharing any of the defining features. To complicate matters further, any polythetic class capable of capturing all the instances of differences that might be considered ethnic was likely to cast a large net so widely as to catch examples of difference that had to be taken out and put into another category where they seemed more at home (under race, nation or class, for instance). So the design of our definitional net devised to capture ethnic differences, but only ethnic differences, would need to be both polythetic and residual. Put another way, ethnicities are only partially connected to one another: their resemblances are complex rather than simple.

From the point of view of the ethnography of a very varied people I was trying to write up, this meant that the game of comparative anthropology worked only at the cost of impoverishing the differences between local ethnicities that my ethnography demonstrated. My point, to reiterate, was not to demean comparative anthropology but to point out the necessary cost of playing that game (a cost one had to bear if taking part in the project warranted it). The cost, in short, was that highly divergent local phenomena had to be objectivized and treated as if they were analogous with one another. We shouldn't allow ourselves to forget, just because we could play the comparative game, that the objectification of ethnicities was a convention of the game; our usage was not so much wrong as limited to the purpose of the game. The danger was that in forgetting the conventional grounds of our objectivization, we reified the identities and believed their existence to be independent both of the conventions that had made them comparable and of our reasons for having played the game.

Before this comes to seem hopelessly digressive and indulgent: isn't it the case that we are all comparative anthropologists? We all make contrastive comments about different collectivities. And, if so, we share the problem of needing the 'human kinds' (to borrow Ian Hacking's fertile phrase) we compare to exist self-evidently and to be self-evidently comparable.[5]

Recently, I rediscovered a more elegant and general formulation of this problem that I had forgotten since student days. In opening a clever little book called *Taboo* (1956) – based on lectures given at the Oxford Institute of Anthropology and edited after his death – the Czech anthropologist Franz Steiner noted how ethnography and comparative anthropology had tended to grow apart. Ethnographers sought increasing specificity in translation. Thus 'taboo', the term in European languages, had expanded its sense since first being reported by observers of Polynesia – it had been taken up widely (not least by Freud) and its relation to ta*bu*, its Polynesian original, had become so remote that it became possible to discover that *tabu* was hardly an example of 'taboo' at all. Anthropologists, Steiner said, like other bilinguals, found themselves speaking two different languages (those of comparative anthropology and ethnography) between which they had difficulty translating. What could one do? What one couldn't do was to redefine 'taboo' by reference to *tabu*: they operated in different discourses. But one could document the historical relation between the terms in order to understand better how the situation had transpired, and one could replace 'taboo' with the more general idea that human societies imbued boundaries with dangers in order to evaluate morally and control behaviour.

Steiner helps us understand the very general nature of the problem we face in our use of terms which have pretensions to global relevance. The analogy with *tabu*/taboo is also helpful to the degree that it concerns the relation between particular and general, or local and global, usages. More generally, taboo – like ethnicity – exists as a set of practices. But there are important differences: the work of translating from *tabu* to taboo, as Steiner described it, had been largely European; but the work of translating between ethnicity as global and local condition has taken place from many sides. Moreover, ethnicities as 'human kinds' are eminently what Ian Hacking further describes as 'interactive kinds' – people are changed by their relation to such types.[6] For instance, a citizen of the USA who serially identifies as a 'coloured person', Negro, Black and African-American is changed by interaction with these categories of 'human kind' as is the character of the broader society (sensitively documented in autobiography by Gates, 1995).

The argument that ethnicity is a polythetic and residual category has, as noted, a somewhat Olympian logical standing; the general consideration of 'interactive kinds' makes the same terrain problematic from a different angle. Let me revert to Steiner for a second. There might be philosophical argument whether translation is problematic because there is no corresponding usage in the target language or because there are many usages and the choice between them is underdetermined. In practice, Steiner generalizes, the world accepts an extension in sense more readily than a loss. This is not least so because we translate when we have a reason for doing so; therefore, we have an interest in translation being possible. Thus, words usually extend their sense in translation. Changing philosophers in mid-stream, it could be said that, pragmatically, translation does not require us to be able to match senses or classes but only to have conventions that allow us to identify similarities between exemplars (Goodman, 1992). It is not that Nigerians, having worked out general criteria for membership of the category 'tribe', 'people', 'ethnic group', or 'nation', then decided that Yoruba, Tiv, Nigerians or whoever were legitimate category members. Instead, what happened was that similarities could be noticed between some exemplar of what counted as a 'tribe' and 'one's own' such that 'one's own' also became an exemplar of a 'tribe'. And if 'tribe' became pejorative in some circles and for some purposes, then any 'tribe' that became an 'ethnic group' would itself become the exemplar for others to follow that route. Ethnicity and ethnicities are thus engaged in a cumulative interaction of polythetic definition, seen globally, and exemplification, seen locally. As ethnicities, as it were, join up to the general category so the polythetic definition of that category, ethnicity, has to be widened, if only implicitly, to keep pace. And, as it widens, so there are further exemplars which provide the grounds on which new human kinds can be recognized locally. Eventually, one supposes, the category must collapse under the burden of its extraordinary success. In the meantime, the dynamic by which ethnicities are created-as-already-subsumed under the label of ethnicity gives institutional grounds for our recognition of the increasing homogenization of the terms of people's identities. We find a global homogenization not of differences (although that might follow) but of the grounds for recognizing differences as similar.

To reiterate, this is not simply analytic but intensely practical. Ethnicity thrives because ethnicities thrive: they are the grounds to discover and pursue political and economic interest, seek or offer patronage, revise collective world-making and so forth. Certain questions about ethnicities become entirely normal features of our ethnic way of world-making. Of course such questions as 'Are they really an ethnic group?', 'Do they have a history?', 'Have they constructed their identity?' must flourish: they are the arguments inherent in this articulation of more and less general considerations. To attempt to explain Africa's ills as the results of ethnicity is to treat a translation as if it were a sufficient explanation.

Admitting that all ethnic and national identities – in fact all identities – have to be constructed, imagined and narrated in particular ways, their differences become just as interesting as their similarities.[7] After three and a half decades of independence, and a century of encapsulation within – more or less – what were to be the twentieth-century nation states of Africa, can one begin to detect differences in the style of making human kinds ethnically between neighbouring countries such as Cameroon and Nigeria? I think one can. What are the differences between, say, western and southern Africa with their divergent histories? The answers to these questions may begin to disturb any easy sense that much is explained when we are able to apply the label ethnicity.

A many-sided project

Assumption, in the senses both of the taking-on and the taking-for-granted, of an ethnic identity is a work of discovery which has implications for many constituencies that become apparent only as the work goes on. Translation into ethnicity is an act of transvaluation of difference.[8] Differences that become 'ethnic' are radicalized in their salience, singularity and consequentiality. Anthropologists, journalists and ethnic subjects translate differences into an idiom of ethnicity in order to achieve comprehensibility (to themselves as silent audience as much as to their eventual audience one supposes). Ethnic terms designate collective agencies that are brief and (presumably) correspond to (at least some) local versions. Ethnic subjects have attributes in terms of which stakes may be claimed. No wonder, if translation into ethnicity proceeds from all sides in a globalizing world.

Ethnic terms are proper names: not only are they highly convenient for meeting word limits, predicating subjects and objects and so forth, but proper names also suggest analogy between ethnography and biography. On this occasion, I mean by ethnography *not* the sense normal to my discipline (extended, usually written, accounts of anthropologists' local research) but a form of writing in which what the French call *ethnies* are made the agents of action.[9] (In my abuse of the term then, contemporary anthropologists would need to write anti-ethnographic-ally in order to avoid reification in what is conventionally called their ethnography. This would be analogous to biography without the unitary subject whose lifetime's development gives biographers their narrative thread, and it would be just as difficult to sustain comprehensibly.)

One of the advantages of translation into ethnographic – by analogy with biographic – conventions of reportage is that irrational behaviour is made, not understandable, but predictable. Put differently, the rational incomprehensibility of some of its actions is what gives an acting subject depth and complexity. Otherwise we are simply dealing with a calculating cipher. Just as human individuals have been conceived as motivated by their interests and by their passions, so too for ethno-graphic subjects. Thus, for instance, 'belonging' for ethnographic subjects might be analogous to what 'family' is to biographic subjects; overreaction is intrinsic to an intensity of attachment and thus always a likelihood for both types of agent. More generally, the description of ethnographic subjects by adjectives denoting personality that are used of biographic subjects is far from accidental since it evokes their in-dividuality (the proud X, wily Y, and loyal Z).

Such ethnographic accounts provoke a highly typical range of suspi-cions and distrusts; so typical, indeed, that these doubts also should be envisaged as part of the 'ethnic' (by now I have argued 'ethnographic') air we breathe – and therefore as normalizing features of current discourse.

Ethnic relations, it can be suggested, are *really* the ideological fancy dress of perfectly comprehensible self-interest. Ethnicity is a folkloristic garment claiming rustic authenticity but *actually* available locally in your branch of that global player Ethnic Identities plc. *In truth*, ethnic identities are made up, and their fast-and-loose attitude to history is not difficult to demonstrate.

Academic commentators have produced illuminating critiques of ethnicity as a symbolic disguise for other interests (economic, political or whatever), but these critiques have their own problems. If ethnicity really is disguised self-interest, then there must be a deal of bad faith abroad: either at work between manipulators and manipulated or in some psychic process of collective self-delusion. Ethnic identities may be something we can find globally, but is this because they are universal, because they are becoming globalized, or because our way of world-making characteristically organizes the reality of other people into ethnic classifications? Moreover, ethnic identities may be made up in some respects but – in an age bent on telling us that everything is more or less fictional or made up – is this particularly damaging? And if ethnicities are invented, and if there is any sense in recognizing cultural difference, can we argue that invention is an acultural feature of all culture? It doesn't sound a very consistent argument. This process of arguing about ethnicity does not have the effect of dispersing the phenomenon; on the contrary, the range of possible argument is itself the mechanism through which ethnicity is entrenched. For instance, in the history of Northern Cameroon and Nigeria which I studied, it was possible to witness the ethnic identities of minority peoples crystallizing as counters, contrapuntally related, to the arguments by which dominant ethnic groups sought to entrench their position *vis-à-vis* the colonial powers. And one could witness colonial officers in their reports lining up behind either the intrinsic capacity of the dominant people's quasiracial capacity to rule, or else the minority people's legitimate right to be allowed spheres of self-determination. It didn't have to be Africa for the choice of sides to be seen like this.

Such development occurred within institutional and personal contexts highly conducive to a conception of all collective issues in terms of identity. In an international context, only players credentialized as 'nation states' (however improbably) got to gamble at the top tables; in interpersonal terms, various rights to personal identity vested in understandings of history, representations of what language is, relations to place and locality and so forth became derivative of the inalienable personal right to ethnic identity. To lack ethnic identity is thus to be devoid of some degree of normal (late twentieth-century) humanity; and to deny the centrality of ethnic identity is symptomatic of an indefensibly low level of self-knowledge. Both personally and collectively, identity has become a master-trope. But what is identity, and how is it demonstrated? Presumably, a person or group has to be identical *to* something. But to what? By definition not to something other than itself, for that would undercut the sense of identity as particular. In short, I would think, identical to itself: itself elsewhere, or itself at an earlier time.[10]

Attempts to challenge unitary conceptions of personal and collective identity have employed a vocabulary of terms such as hybridity, creolization, mongrelism and so forth. But these words describe a condition that can exist only subsequent to speciation; as such they share the presupposition that unitary and exclusive identities have a prior or pristine existence. Because their reaction occurs on the epistemological terrain of essentialized identities, for most readers terms denoting 'mixture' actually reinforce the normative status of the presuppositions they are designed to challenge and reveal how thoroughly assumptions of human speciation in terms of ethnicity have colonized notions of difference.[11] To this degree, ethnicity has become additionally coercive.

Superficially, normalization of the expectation that people have ethnicity and identity, and that the two should be related, has had an effect similar to inviting everyone to express themselves individually: everyone has 'done their own thing' – but rather similarly. At least this is the cynical impression produced by using general (or globally relevant) notions of identity and ethnicity to make other people's events readily comprehensible. These events become directly comparable to those elsewhere and simultaneous with some of them. In short, co-evalness in time and space is suggested.

Here we encounter another indication of the epistemological air we breathe, and again it comes in the form of a characteristic dilemma. Not to suggest that people(s) living in the same age are co-evals can be a device to project the 'other' into a time different from oneself.[12] However, to suggest too easily that peoples are entirely co-eval is to risk imposing a hegemonic and homogenizing account of time and space quite contrary to an argument that the parameters of local life are – at least in some degree – locally produced. Thus, we find mutually impugning arguments.

The types of questions that arise, to reiterate, strike me as being entirely normative: they are questions intrinsic to ethnic coverage and circulate quite happily within the parameters of an ethnographic worldview to produce a comforting sense that serious thought is being given to pressing questions. Ethnicity is powerfully reinforced by its position as a middle term between the nation and the individual, drawing upon the institutional entrenchment and self-evidence of both.

Any suggestion that there are simple, quick fixes to our situation would be wrong. Commentators, whether academics or journalists, have no place into which to step wholly outside the terms of these argument nor can they navigate around and thus ignore them. We need ways to live constructively with a current thought style shared, in many respects, by observer and observed.

In and out of the whale

This brings me back to the potential role of an academic anthropologist – typically stuck in his or her university office. I realize there are anthropologists outside the academy (probably as many as within), and there are anthropologists close to the epicentre of ethnic violence. I do not wish to appear to speak for anthropology or, indeed, for anthropologists, but only on behalf of whatever generalizable aspects there might be in my own situation.

Most illuminating in the long run, I suggest, will be attempts complementary to those of on-the-spot reporters which seek to contextualize both ethnicity (the role of the somewhat ill-defined but ambitious master idea in the world) and the relation to it of particular ethnicities (local identities) and ethnically based organizations in the world. And such accounts will need to analyse the complex relations between multifaceted projects of ethnicity, nationalism and individualism.

This project lays claim to a different sort of co-evalness: through recognition of the senses of local time and local space simultaneously abroad in the world, and in the attempt to understand how these articulate contrapuntally with one another in the globalizing system of historical and spatial claims that are made in the name of collective actors.

This is not an immediately newsworthy proposition, but a sense of, if not this, then something such must be why anthropologists occasionally allow themselves the sense of reading through the surface of the news reports of some journalists. (And why more specialist journalists know how the depth – or depthlessness – of their own reportage is tailored to a particular communication slot.)

The challenge is not just to see *through* the shibboleths of the age: to argue that ethnicity is not universal, or to challenge specific ethnicities by showing them as self-interested or historically contrived. Such challenges, I have argued, actually have a normalizing effect; perversely, as a phenomenon anchored to accounts of the past, ethnicity thrives on a history of such challenges. The greater challenge is to explain how the shibboleths of the age are produced, why they convince (ethnic and outside commentators alike) and how the dynamic of increasing ethnic speciation is accelerated. The problem, precisely, is to understand the superficial: the style of thought, of which ethnicity is a characteristic 'groove' through which the currents of explanation are readily channelled.[13]

The achievement of a previous generation of Africanists was to demonstrate that African ethnic identities were not primordial, that they had histories of invention or construction that belonged, just as much as their counterparts elsewhere, to the conditions under which the contemporary world came to be what it is (Ranger, 1993). Where this is not understood, it needs repeating, for only once this is conceded is it possible to address more nuanced problems. Apart from the design of ethnic argument, these are twofold: the realization of the diversity of ethnic situations across Africa and, related to this, the diversity of grounds, other than ethnic, for identities differing.

The study of ethnicity is part of the study of how and why people objectify, reify and fetishize human collectivities on the basis of their perceived differences, and of the conditions for and consequences of their doing so.[14] Objectification, reification and fetishization are no more than arbitrary points along a continuum stretching from – something like – the capacity to recognize an ethnic group as figure against a wider ground, through treating it as thing-like (and forgetting the objectification process), to attributing to it various characteristics in which we decide not to collude. I use this loaded continuum and relate it to a 'we', because I cannot conceive how a commentary on ethnicity could be written without the commentator – whether or not by intention – also being situated in terms of an evaluation of particular ethnic differences. An outside commentator's judgement is often swayed by a broader end (perhaps liberation from domination in whatever guise) towards which an ethnicity can be envisaged as purposed. But whether or not explicitly, the question of evaluating ethnicity cannot finally be bucked.

Several recent developments strike me as helpful. One is the move from intensive study of single ethnicities – typical of ethnographers' early fieldwork – to the study of contrapuntally related local ethnicities – which can be studied intensively only on the basis of longer-term, multi-site ethnographic research. Philip Burnham's long-term study of Northern Cameroon, including collaborative study with ethnographers of neighbouring peoples, is a signal achievement in this context (Burnham and Last, 1994; Burnham, 1996). Such studies reveal the differences between local circumstances that are obscured by too ready acceptance of the global homogenization of the grounds of ethnic difference.

Building from this basis, one would also welcome more intensive studies of the grounds of African national identities and public cultures. How variable are the local idioms of difference in African languages, pidgins and in languages of European origin spoken in Africa? How varied are the 'solutions' proposed in African countries to the management of these perceived internal differences? The differences between official language policies in African countries tell us a great deal about the political imaginary of these nations that differ widely in size and in their perception of, and attitude towards, the differences among the people that make them up (Fardon and Furniss, 1994). These attitudes are susceptible of further study in, for instance, policy towards the ongoing liberalization, or simply privatization, of the air waves. How many languages are chosen for broadcast? How is air-time apportioned? How is access arranged? (Panos Institute, 1993; *Article 19* and *Index on Censorship*, 1995).

A second recent trend challenges the extent to which African identities are rooted in ethnicity. Paul Richards's study of war in Sierra Leone has highlighted the importance of youth as a category of identification (Richards, 1996). Louis Brenner has devoted a volume of essays to Muslim identity in sub-Saharan Africa (Brenner, 1993). Richard Werbner has drawn more general attention to the plurality of African post-colonial identities (Werbner, 1996). Study of identities that are not, primarily, ethnically intended may help to allay any sense that sub-Saharan Africa, as a sub-continent, is more easily and thoroughly explicable in terms of ethnicity than elsewhere.

A third more general consideration refers to the re-embedding of African ethnicity in the recent political and economic context of the countries of the continent. It is now clearer than it was at the outset, how far the Rwandan experience resulted from the failed imposition of a programme of transition to democracy (Prunier, 1995). Generalizing, the environment of scarcity resulting from structural adjustment, which has been the context for coerced 'democratization', has inevitably incited resort to identity politics as a means of rationing and distributing resources.

Ethnicity can all too easily become a way of laying not just entire blame, but responsibility for the entire circumstances at the door of the natives. If little can be done about other people's atavistic fantasies, it might be suggested, better to stand aside. But it is one thing to say that the people most immediately concerned must have final ownership of any solutions essayed to their dilemmas, and another to suggest that the circumstances of their choice cannot be ameliorated. To say we need to understand better is banal but true; to say that part of this understanding might require nothing more immediately costly than a robust resilience to ethnicity as coverage is something a little more. I have tried to suggest, in brief compass, why ethnic coverage can seem convincing and why it is often wrong to be convinced. But I am not suggesting ethnicity be ignored or wished away. The simplest reaction to arguments about ethnicity in Africa is to say, 'Ah, so it wasn't *really* ethnicity, it was *really* politics, economics, religion ...'. The simple reaction is to believe if ethnicity is not explanatory, it is entirely derivative of whatever is explanatory. Rather, my point is that reportage has to recognize the complexity of ethnicity as a project in Africa – and elsewhere. It is not *that* ethnicity explains (or indeed doesn't explain) but *how, when, why and in what form* ethnicity helps us to explain.

Picking up a phrase of Henry Miller's, George Orwell regretted the decision of those who, like Jonah, preferred the womb-like security of the whale's stomach to the raw experience of life outside.[15] The Biblical whale, as he reminds us, was really a fish, so we might add that the resident of one fish, emerging in anticipation of being dazzled by the light, might enter only the dark stomach of the larger fish that had eaten it. Is there any illuminated place outside the whale of ethnic discourse? Not in a simple sense. Yet, it seems to me that trying to discover what it feels like inside and outside this whale is as close to a method as the beast permits.

Notes

1. That this chapter retains the feel of its original, a personal, off-the-cuff, reflection on anthropologists' definitions of ethnicity offered as a discussant at the Forum Against Ethnic Violence meeting and written up briefly for the workshop proceedings (Fardon, 1996a), goes some way, I hope, to excuse its remaining self-referential quality (drawing on Fardon, 1996b, 1996c).

2. At the time of the FAEV meeting, I was in mid-term as Chairman of the Centre of African Studies of the University of London, and especially grateful for the generous support of Centre activities by a number of London-based journalists whose long knowledge of, and commitment to, Africa I found, and still find, inspirational.

3. The phrase 'thought style', to mean 'a communicative genre for a social unit speaking to itself about itself, and so constituting itself' is borrowed from Mary Douglas (1996: xii). A more faithful borrowing would go on to distinguish a variety of such styles, but I am predominantly interested here in tracing how far a single style has been adopted widely. But this does not preclude later attention to the differentiation of thought styles about ethnic difference.

4. From its anthropological popularization in Rodney Needham's important essay (1975).

5. See Hacking's incisive article (1992) and his account of the statistical normalization of human categories (1990).

6. In an article that combines brevity and serviceability, Hacking (1997) has summarized his own ideas and also registered disquiet with some of the purposes for which they have been borrowed. I hope he would agree to loan his argument in the case of ethnic identities, since these strike me as clear examples of his interactive kinds.

7. Terence Ranger has construed this as a generational emphasis: the very success of those who demonstrated the non-primordial and non-essential character of ethnic difference has led to their successor generation taking for granted their achievement and perhaps underestimating the lag in uptake among a wider public (discussion at a conference in the Institute of Historical Research 1997). The anti-primordialist and anti-essentialist arguments still require restatement until such time as they are wholly normalized. Accepting this caution, it may be that the exploration of the implications of the argument might in the longer term be the best way to normalize the suppositions on which it rests.

8. Franz Steiner, who was particularly sensitive to issues of translation,

pointedly chose to use the term, in an analysis of the circulation of economic values, for circumstances when items exchanged have values which are not fully commensurable (Steiner, 1956).

9. *Ethnies* are usually translated as ethnic categories (having identity but little organization) or ethnic groups (having both identity and organizational capacity). English lacks a single term that reifies a range of disparate entities in quite the same way as *ethnie*, but I would argue that *ethnie* does exist as a covert category in English with implications virtually identical to its French counterpart.

10. I have argued elsewhere – by reference to West African ethnographies – that some alternative African notions of personal identity might be construed, at least in narrow contrast with identity to the self, as dispersed. That is to say that the person is a point of confluence in numerous webs of resemblance to others related in various ways (through one's mother's and father's marriages, through affinal relations, etc.) (Fardon, 1996c).

11. Kwame Anthony Appiah's is a remarkable attempt in this direction (1992). However, this tendency is presently less typical of accounts of African identities in Africa than it is of, for instance, post-colonial South Asian accounts of identity.

12. With results explored in a celebrated anthropological critique by Johannes Fabian (1983).

13. The image – of thought styles having grooves, worn by persistent use and institutionally entrenched, which offer the line of least resistance to thinking as usual – is Mary Douglas's.

14. As noted earlier, Steiner's (1956) account of 'taboo' moved to subsume the 'problem' of taboo under a broader rubric. I am attempting to follow the example of his argument.

15. 'Inside the whale', originally published in 1940, in *The Collected Essays, Journalism and Letters of George Orwell, Vol. 1: An Age Like This 1920–1940*, edited by Sonia Orwell and Ian Angus (1970), Harmondsworth: Penguin.

References

Appiah, Kwame Anthony (1992) *In My Father's House. Africa in the Philosophy of Culture*, London: Methuen.

Article 19 (1996) *Broadcasting Genocide: Censorship, Propaganda and State-Sponsored Violence in Rwanda 1990–94*, London: International Centre against Censorship.

Article 19 and Index on Censorship (1995) *Who Rules the Airwaves: Broadcasting in Africa*, London: International Centre against Censorship.

Brenner, Louis (ed.) (1993) *Muslim Identity and Social Change in Sub-Saharan Africa*, London: Hurst and Company.

Burnham, Philip (1996) *The Politics of Cultural Difference in Northern Cameroon*, Edinburgh: Edinburgh University Press for the International African Institute.

Burnham, Philip and Last, Murray (1994) 'From Pastoralist to Politician: The

Problem of a Fulbe "Aristocracy"', *Cahiers d'études africaines*, 133–5, XXXIV (1–3), pp. 313–57.

Douglas, Mary (1996) *Thought Styles*, London: Sage.

Fabian, Johannes (1983) *Time and the Other: How Anthropology Makes its Object*, New York: Columbia University Press.

Fardon, Richard (1987) '"African Ethnogenesis": Limits to the Comparability of Ethnic Phenomena', in Holy Ladislav (ed.), *Comparative Anthropology*, Oxford: Blackwell, pp. 168–88.

— (1996a) 'Covering Ethnicity? Or, Ethnicity as Coverage?', *Contemporary Politics*, Vol. 2, No. 1, pp. 153–8.

— (1996b) '"Crossed Destinies": The Entangled Histories of West African Ethnic and National Identities', in Louise de la Gorgendière, Kenneth King and Sarah Vaughan (eds), *Ethnicity in Africa: Roots, Meanings and Implications* (Proceedings of the 1995 Conference of the Centre of African Studies), Edinburgh: University of Edinburgh, 1996, pp. 117–46.

— (1996c) 'The Person, Ethnicity and the Problem of "Identity" in West Africa', in Ian Fowler and David Zeitlyn (eds), *African Crossroads: Intersections between History and Anthropology in Cameroon* (Cameroon Studies Vol. 2), Oxford: Berghahn, pp. 17–44.

Fardon, Richard and Furniss, Graham (eds) (1994) *African Languages, Development and the State*, London: Routledge.

Gates, Henry Louis (1995) *Colored People. A Memoir of a West Virginia Boyhood*, Harmondsworth: Viking/Penguin.

Goodman, Nelson (1992) 'Seven Strictures on Similarity', reprinted in Mary Douglas and David Hull (eds), *How Classification Works: Nelson Goodman among the Social Sciences*, Edinburgh: Edinburgh University Press, pp. 13–24.

Hacking, Ian (1990) *The Taming of Chance*, Cambridge: Cambridge University Press.

— (1992) 'World-making by Kind-making: Child Abuse for Example', in Mary Douglas and David Hull (eds), *How Classification Works: Nelson Goodman among the Social Sciences*, Edinburgh: Edinburgh University Press, pp. 180–238.

— (1997) 'Taking Bad Arguments Seriously', *London Review of Books*, 21 August, Vol. 19, No. 16, pp. 14–16.

Hobsbawm, Eric (1994) *The Age of Extremes: The Short Twentieth Century 1914–1991*, London: Michael Joseph.

Needham, Rodney (1975) 'Polythetic Classification: Convergence and Consequences', *Man*, n.s., Vol. 10, pp. 347–69.

Orwell, George (originally 1940, 1970) 'Inside the Whale', in Sonia Orwell and Ian Angus (eds), *The Collected Essays, Journalism and Letters of George Orwell, Vol. 1: An Age Like This*, Harmondsworth: Penguin, pp. 540–77.

Panos Institute (1993) *Radio Pluralism in West Africa: A Survey Conducted by the Panos Institute and l'Union de Journalistes d'Afrique de l'Ouest*, Paris: Institut Panos and L'Harmattan.

Prunier, Gérard (1995) *The Rwanda Crisis 1959–1994. History of a Genocide*, London: Hurst and Company.

Ranger, Terence (1993) 'The Invention of Tradition Revisited: The Case of Colonial Africa', in Terence Ranger and Olufemi Vaughan (eds), *Legitimacy and the State in Twentieth-Century Africa*, Basingstoke: Macmillan (in association with St Antony's College, Oxford), pp. 62–111.

Richards, Paul (1996) *Fighting for the Rainforest. War, Youth and Resources in Sierra Leone*, Oxford and Portsmouth, NH: The International African Institute (in association with James Currey and Heinemann).

Steiner, Franz Baerman (1956) 'Notes on Comparative Economics', *British Journal of Sociology*, Vol. 5, No. 2: pp. 118–29.

— (1956) *Taboo*, Harmondsworth: Pelican/Penguin.

Werbner, Richard (1996) 'Multiple Identities, Plural Arenas', in Richard Werbner and Terence Ranger (eds), *Postcolonial Identities in Africa*, London: Postcolonial Encounters, Zed Books, pp. 1–25.

CHAPTER 4

'Who's it Between?' 'Ethnic War' and Rational Violence

David Keen

Warfare and rationality

War as 'pointless' To judge from the accounts of the majority of journalists, aid staff and even some academics, war is essentially confusing and pointless. A very common framework of analysis portrays war (whether international or civil) as a contest between two or more sides. Those operating within this framework, when they are confronted by a war, are like an outsider arriving at a sporting event whose first question is: 'Who's it between?' Such analysts may be quickly reassured with a set of competing initials (for example, UNITA versus the MPLA) or, better, a set of competing ethnic groups (the Serbs versus the Muslims or the Hutus versus the Tutsis). It is not always clear, however, that the roots of conflict have been illuminated in such a dialogue. A related model – also frequently dovetailing into a model of 'ethnic war' – tends to portray war as an eruption of mindless violence, often stemming from 'ancient tribal hatreds'. This model has been associated with the work of Robert Kaplan (1994), among others. In a widely quoted article called 'The Coming Anarchy: How Scarcity, Crime, Overpopulation, Tribalism and Disease are Rapidly Destroying the Social Fabric of Our Planet', Kaplan uses examples from West Africa to analyse the withering away of central governments and the growing pervasiveness of local wars. He portrays the war in Sierra Leone as savage and anarchic. His work is a prominent example of what have been called theories of 'the new barbarism' – a perspective influenced by Malthusian, Hobbesian and even Hegelian ideas, which suggest that parts of the world are populated by irrationally violent and uncivilized peoples.

This portrayal of war as confusing and pointless can be a disabling force, part of a culture of disempowerment that seems to produce a peculiar combination of outrage, indifference and inaction in wealthy countries confronted by conflicts elsewhere.

In so far as the causes of wars (and notably civil wars) remain poorly understood, it may be relatively easy for some analysts – particularly in military circles – to insist that a proper response is an isolationist one. It is becoming commonplace to hear that 'we in the West' should simply withdraw from far-away countries of which we know little and understand less. Would it not be better to 'let them fight it out until they are exhausted'? Kaplan has advocated a form of 'triage' in which interventions are concentrated on what he sees as a relatively small number of countries where effective assistance can still be administered. Former British Foreign Secretary Douglas Hurd has noted: 'It is perfectly defensible ... after examining the difficulties, to say that the international community can do nothing effective and must stay out of the way until those concerned have come to their senses' (Hurd, 1997: 253). Anyone moving from 'development' circles into strategic studies, as I did, might be surprised how common such attitudes have become.

Warfare and rational economic behaviour The models of war as an orderly contest between 'sides' or as a manifestation of ethnic hatreds do not throw much light on the political and economic processes that generate civil conflict. In particular, they do not address the complex relationship between violence and the distribution of economic resources. Although non-economic factors such as religion and simple revenge are often important in generating and sustaining civil conflict, it is suggested here that warfare frequently revolves around the rational pursuit of economic goals. Indeed war – to rephrase Clausewitz's famous dictum – may be a continuation of economics by other means. While it would be unwise to dismiss the importance of ethnicity in contemporary conflicts, what is urgently needed is a better understanding of the relationship between various forms of collective identity, on the one hand, and political and economic struggles on the other.

One set of goals relates to the state, and to the system of laws and favours which governs the distribution of economic rewards within the state. Civil conflicts can to some extent be explained as a struggle to overthrow – or maintain – a particular system for the distribution of economic resources. This struggle can reasonably be labelled as 'political'. It often has an important ethnic dimension, but is rarely illuminated by the label of 'ethnic war'. Very often, the privileged access to economic resources enjoyed by elites (often disproportionately from one geographical area or 'ethnic group') was propped up by external powers and/or international aid during the Cold War, and these elites subsequently found themselves under threat (perhaps through rebellion or processes of democratization, or both) and resorted to violence to counter this threat. Dominant groups may also define their ethnicity – for example 'Muslim' in Sudan – in ways that legitimize the political exclusion of others while simultaneously encouraging the organization of opposition along ethnic lines. Particularly where states – or rebel movements – have lacked the resources that might allow a disciplined military force, mobilizing ethnic militias has represented a practical and cheap means of mobilizing (revolutionary or reactionary) violence. It has also proved a good way to confuse and immobilize the international community, foreign governments, aid agencies and the UN Security Council, not least because many seem so ready to believe in the myth of ethnic war.

Mythologies of ethnicity have also been institutionalized into state systems. In the Soviet Union and its satellite states, for example, ethnicity was institutionalized into processes of political domination, through nationalities policies. Manipulating cultural differences was a mechanism for facilitating centralized state control. Similarly, in colonial Africa the European administrations often relied disproportionately on collaboration with people from particular geographical areas or ethnic groups, and institutionalized 'tribal' divisions within systems of indirect rule. This contributed to a 'dialectic' of ethnic conflict, most notably in the post-independence era, as other groups sprang up to challenge the hegemony of apparently favoured identities, and ethnicity was subsequently further manipulated by political elites to preserve their privileges.

In Sudan, as some ethnic groups fell behind in the allocation of education, jobs and other resources, they organized politically and/or militarily to try to catch up. The development of southern Sudan was particularly neglected, and the resulting resentment played a key role in generating civil wars from 1955 to 1972 and from 1983 to the present. However, it was not just the south that was discriminated against in a political economy that favoured a narrow riverain elite from central-northern areas. Inciting the marginalized Baggara of western Sudan into violence against southern Sudanese and Nuba has proved a largely effective way of preventing these groups from combining in some kind of 'class' alliance. And while westerners have been divided against southerners, the opposition in the south has also been divided, often along ethnic lines, notably by promoting scarcity in the area. The clearest manifestation of this was when the SPLA split in 1987.

In Rwanda, ethnic conflict was again invoked to break up threatening political alliances. In August 1993, the Arusha Accords – achieved with a high level of foreign diplomatic and head-of-state involvement – spelled the end of 20 years of autocratic, single-party rule in Rwanda and stipulated a shift to parliamentary government and the incorporation of the rebel Rwandan Patriotic Front (RPF) into the army. Since a military coup in 1973, the government of Habyarimana had been dominated by a small Hutu elite from north-western Rwanda. The Arusha Accords were a major success for the RPF (which drew most of its support from Tutsi refugees in Uganda) and for the internal opposition. There was a clear prospect that the RPF would be able to combine with internal Hutu opposition (notably from the south of the country) to upset the domination of the north-western Hutu elite.

For hard-line north-western Hutus in the government, fomenting ethnic violence against the Tutsis, first in a series of massacres and then in a carefully planned genocide in April 1994, offered the prospect of derailing the peace process, sabotaging democracy and preventing a coming-together of the RPF and the Hutu opposition. As Lemarchand observes, the wanton killing of Tutsi civilians was designed to make it unthinkable for the Tutsis and Hutus to agree on anything. Stressing that the genocide was carefully planned and was much more than an outbreak of tribal hostilities, African Rights (1994) noted that it targeted not only the Tutsi but also leading members of the Hutu opposition.

Of course, the use of 'ethnicity' as a distraction from 'class' alliances is not confined to poor countries or to contemporary warfare. In the West, the Great Depression and the perceived threat of communism in the 1930s encouraged support and tolerance for the Nazis among powerful groups both inside and outside Germany. Within Germany, the Nazis won considerable business and establishment support through offering to suppress communism, reorient politics along ethnic or racialist lines, and physically absorb many of the unemployed youths attracted to communism.

If manipulating ethnicity is a powerful technique for deflecting class alliances and for inexpensive military mobilization, it may also be a useful route to political mobilization. In his discussion of the disintegration of former Yugoslavia, Ignatieff (1993) stresses that manipulating ethnicity may be the easiest way of getting a political constituency where a plural political culture has not been nurtured (see also Keen, 1994a). But, significantly, the intensity of ethnic conflict is not written in stone. 'Ethnic warfare' may flare up among groups that had previously lived together peacefully, though there is often some history of conflict that can be invoked by those who might wish to reignite it. Even in the course of a particular civil war, the importance of ethnic divisions may increase or diminish over time. In Liberia, for example, 'ethnic war' was partially superseded by a more purely economic war, with the emergence of ethnically mixed militias. Factions came to cut across ethnic lines and even formerly hostile ethnic groups joined forces (Outram, 1997).

In Sudan, a persistent difficulty for southern rebels has been securing unity among southern ethnic groups. The importance of ethnic divisions within the south was diminished in 1987 when most of the 'Anyanya 2' (primarily Nuer) rebels threw in their lot with the SPLA (in which the Dinka were very strongly represented). However, the proliferation of militias in the south created major potential for ethnic conflict. In Ethiopia, the collapse of the Mengistu regime in 1991 paved the way for a re-emergence of open ethnic conflict within the south: deprived of the support previously emanating from Mengistu and from the refugee camps in Ethiopia, the SPLA leader John Garang was unable to maintain obedience among the diverse factions making up the 'southern rebellion' (see, for example, African Rights, 1997).

Changing relationships between the Baggara and Dinka, meanwhile, underlined how ethnicity may be taken up or discarded in a pragmatic manner. By 1989, given the growing strength of the SPLA and the diminishing returns from raiding the impoverished southern Sudanese, some elements of the Baggara were reconciled with the Dinka, and some turned to raiding northern Sudanese, including fellow Muslims. The Sudan government was dismayed at signs of accommodation between Baggara and Dinka, and the military government of Lieutenant Omer el-Bashir has sought to destabilize this threatening alliance and halt local attempts at ethnic reconciliation – notably by sponsoring raids on the Dinka by militias of the Popular Defence Forces. The case of Sudan also demonstrates the potential for using 'ethnicity' to exploit your own ethnic group. The Fur (mostly Muslim) and the Nuba (perhaps 50% Muslim) have both been attacked and exploited by Arab militias under the cover of 'holy war'.

Overlaid on an essentially 'political' struggle over the state, a second type of conflict may emerge. As a conflict progresses, we may see the development of a new political economy of war, with various groups, including government officials, traders and soldiers, taking advantage of conflict and conflict-related scarcities. Fighters, though presenting themselves as representatives of particular positions, may acquire their own vested interests in the course of a conflict. To some extent, both rebel groups and groups allied with the government may expropriate food, 'taxes' and labour for the purpose of making war (Duffield, 1990). In other words, they may exploit civilians *in order* to fight a war. But they may also fight a war in order to exploit civilians: a situation of 'war' may provide, in effect, a licence to take advantage of particular groups of civilians. We may also see the emergence of groups with a vested interest in polarizing civilians. The aim of those carrying out violence may not be simply to win, but to prolong and deepen the conflict (perhaps to reinforce their status within a government or rebel movement, or simply to make money). In other words, there may be wars you *don't* want to win.

In addition, there may be a degree of collusion between 'warring parties' against civilians, as has been evident in Sierra Leone and Cambodia (Keen, 1998). There may be economically lucrative but militarily counter-productive raiding of groups with previously minimal rebel affiliations, as in Sudan (Keen, 1994a, 1998). Such raids create their own justification. They typically encourage civilian support for rebel forces, as the government comes to be seen as neglecting or attacking its own citizens. There may be attempts by ordinary people to organize themselves to secure their own protection, and these can draw on cultural resources associated with particular ethnic groups, as when the traditional hunting societies of the Mende of southern and eastern Sierra Leone formed the basis for a powerful civil defence movement. As conflict creates scarcity, this may create further conflict, with newly impoverished groups turning to violence as a remedy for their pressing economic problems.

In so far as short-term economic goals become prevalent, the aim may be not so much to change the existing system of laws as to ignore it. Correspondingly, the boundaries between war and crime may become quite indistinct. Some of these processes could be seen quite clearly in the Liberian civil war, as Stephen Ellis (1995) has shown. Here, young militiamen – few of whom were paid or trained – tended to base themselves in areas relatively rich in resources. These were areas where diamonds were plentiful, or where villagers were still producing crops, or where humanitarian convoys could be looted. Looting of civilians and commandeering of slave labour was commonplace. Significantly, as Ellis notes: 'Only rarely did the militias attack each other head on. For the most part, they preyed on civilians' (1995: 186). Meanwhile, senior commanders (adults) exploited and neglected the boy militiamen, making sure that the boys yielded looted goods to them. This process mirrored the generally unhappy experience of boy soldiers in Sierra Leone.

Just as poorly trained and poorly paid soldiers may be unwilling or unable to confront rebels involved in a lucrative illegal economy, so also poorly trained and poorly paid policemen may – even in more developed economies – be unwilling or unable to confront criminals who are similarly involved in illegal economic activities (Keen, 1996). And if there are few hard-and-fast boundaries between war and crime, there may also be dangers in rigidly separating war and peace. In a country like Sierra Leone, government officials have long-standing links with illegal economic activities: wartime involvement in an illegal economy may simply reflect a modification – and perhaps a deepening – of relationships developed during what, in diamond-rich areas of the south-east, has always been an unsteady peace.

Closely associated with the common idea of a 'reversion' to 'tribalism' is the notion of a 'reversion' to 'medieval' patterns of warfare. Martin van Creveld (1991) has suggested that many contemporary conflicts represent a return to medieval patterns of warfare, with pillage once again an important motive for fighting. The argument has some merit. However, while van Creveld usefully highlights a weakening of the state's monopoly on violence, he provides little analysis of why this is occurring. It is not enough to point, as he does, to Vietnam and the apparent obsolescence of high-tech and nuclear weapons. Nor is it enough to advise, as van Creveld does, that 'to understand the future, study the past'. The causes of this apparent regression need more attention. In any case, changing patterns of warfare are not simply a return to medieval patterns of warfare. Indeed, if we look closely, we see that the very factors that have precipitated these changes have helped create a radically different political economy from that which existed in medieval Europe.

First, on top of the old 'medieval' patterns of looting, the forces of international capitalism have provided sophisticated weaponry as well as the incentive (and often the funding) to pursue wars over products (like oil and diamonds) whose value reflects the international demand for them. Second, contemporary conflicts are the focus of an elaborate system of international aid, which can shape the pattern of violence in various ways (for example, when armed men seek to gain access to aid or even to create the concentrations of displaced people which give rise to the aid in the first place). Third, contemporary conflicts have often accompanied the active dismantling of state institutions (for example, by IMF/World Bank-sponsored privatization schemes), and indeed the state has frequently played a role in dismantling itself (notably by devolving the right to inflict violence to particular ethnic groups in order to wage war on the cheap). For all these reasons, modern civil warfare is not simply a return to medieval patterns of warfare but the emergence of something new, albeit with economic goals often re-emerging as a central driving force.

The fact that states may play a role in dismantling themselves highlights the possible links between the two levels of economically oriented conflict that have been discussed. Specifically, short-term economic goals may be harnessed and manipulated by those with a broader brief for changing (or preserving) the political economy at the national level. Just as the state may take advantage of local rivalries and exploitation to wage war on the cheap, so too a rebel group may also manipulate local rivalries to compensate for an inability to fund a disciplined rebel army. In addition, economic grievances that have threatened a particular political economy have often been deflected by using a restive group as militias against a rebellious third party. In the Ottoman empire during the late nineteenth century, the Ottoman government armed Kurdish militias and gave them a 'licence to raid'. This appears to have served to appease the Kurds, while at the same time offering a way of suppressing dissent (among the Armenians) (van Bruinessen, 1992). In modern-day Sudan, the deflection of potential class tensions into ethnic conflict has been noted: warfare has been used as a means of manipulating the resentment of the potentially rebellious (and economically marginalized) Baggara group by turning them against politically marginalized southern Sudanese who were blocking Khartoum's access to oil in the south (Keen, 1994a).

The principal focus here is on the economic rationality of violence (including 'ethnic violence'). However, such violence may also be conducted with a view to enhancing security, particularly where a specific ethnic group is portrayed as a mortal threat. As Ignatieff argues: 'Ethnic hatred is the result of the terror which arises when legitimate authority disintegrates ... Rid yourself of your neighbours, the warlord says, and you no longer have to fear them (Ignatieff, 1993: 30). Such behaviour, abhorrent and risky as it may be, may also be construed as in some sense rational, particularly if we consider that people are often operating on the basis of very limited information. Where the state fails to ensure economic or physical security, people may turn to violence in pursuit of these elusive goals. And very often this violence takes the appearance of 'ethnic conflict'.

'Civilians' and 'fighters' In addition to looking at the functions of violence, we need to rethink the relationship between civilians and fighters. When war is depicted as a contest between two or more sides, the categories of civilian and fighter are often either unrealistically amalgamated or too rigidly separated. In some accounts, civilians may be lumped in with the warring factions, as when journalists talk about fighting between 'the Serbs', 'the Muslims' and 'the Croats' in the former Yugoslavia. On the other hand, civilians may be seen as occupy-

ing a space on the edge of the conflict: they may be portrayed as 'caught in the crossfire', the 'innocent victims' to be targeted with humanitarian aid, perhaps after negotiations to secure the 'neutrality' of relief and access to 'both sides' of a conflict.

What is most conspicuously missing, very often, is any detailed analysis of the relationship between the people who are not engaged in fighting and those carrying out or orchestrating acts of violence. Often ignored is the fact that violence against civilians may not be simply an accidental by-product of warfare between rival factions; rather, it may be one of the main tactics of warfare (e.g. to weaken civilian groups associated with a rebel faction, as in Sudan, or to polarize the civilian community to the benefit of extremist groups, as in Northern Ireland and south-eastern Turkey). Similarly, the forced migration of civilians may not be an accidental by-product of warfare so much as something that is specifically intended, perhaps as part of a policy of 'ethnic cleansing' (as in the former Yugoslavia) or as part of a policy of de-populating resource-rich areas in order to exploit them (as in Somalia, Sierra Leone and Sudan). In Sudan, oil, water and grazing land were critical scarce resources, and economically marginalized herders in the north were encouraged to use violence to secure access to the resources of the south as a remedy for their own scarcities. Even the most appalling acts of terror – though grist to the mill of those who present warfare as mindless anarchy or tribalism – may be part of an attempt to evacuate the maximum number of civilians with a minimum of military resources.

Where forced migration is specifically intended, a variety of local actors are likely to have a powerful interest in manipulating humanit-arian aid in order to influence the behaviour and movement of civilians. Famine itself may be actively intended by those seeking to secure access to one set of scarce resources (minerals, land, etc.) by creating an artificial scarcity of another resource (notably, food). Those designing aid programmes will need to take these interests and tactics into account if aid is not to be sabotaged by political opposition.

Civilians, so far from standing completely outside the conflict, will often join one or other fighting group for a variety of reasons. Indeed, particularly in the context of a 'weak state' where resources are too scarce to allow for a large, salaried army (Sudan, Sierra Leone), under-standing how civil wars deepen and proliferate will depend on understanding the circumstances – very often some combination of greed, hunger and fear – that prompt civilians to become fighters, perhaps by joining 'militias'. International aid has at least the potential for retarding the process by which civilians turn to violence as well as serving as an incentive for demobilization. However, it is unlikely that aid can serve these purposes unless the complicated reasons (including economic reasons) why people turn to violence are properly understood.

What all this implies is that we need an analysis that locates the origins of violence within particular societies, an analysis that addresses the varied and complicated functions of violence, rather than one that seeks to portray violence either as wholly 'political' (in a narrow sense, divorced from economic interests) or as wholly 'irrational' or 'ethnic'. This means avoiding the temptation to 'split off' the violence from the economic and political processes which govern the distribution of scarce resources in peacetime.

In an important article, Turton (1997) has emphasized that ethnicity may be generated by conflict, rather than simply giving rise to conflict. Yet too often newspaper accounts of conflict – even in the *New York Times* – contain a routine two or three paragraphs on the 'historical causes' of conflict, causes that are frequently divorced in the analysis from the nature of conflict or the way it evolves over time. History, particularly if it is violent, seduces us into accepting ethnic divisions as fixed and inevitable. In discussions of the Nazi holocaust, even liberal and Jewish accounts typically make a distinction (and it is not hard to imagine why this might be so) between the Germans on the one hand and the Jews on the other. And yet most of the Jews in Germany were German too, until they were stripped of their rights and separated – first legally and then physically – from the rest of society.

Conflict response

The current system of international responses to conflict seems only minimally informed by understandings of the rationality of violence. The present system of international responses to civil conflicts has two main pillars. First, it seeks to address the economic consequences of conflict, and second, the political causes, all the while operating within a rather narrow definition of the term 'political' that largely excludes consideration of the economic interests at stake.

Economic consequences For the most part, addressing the economic consequences of civil conflict takes the form of: (1) humanitarian aid; and (2) post-conflict reconstruction, rehabilitation, resettlement, repatriation – what we may call 'the system of "res"' that attempts to turn the clock back to the beginning of the conflict and reverse the damage arising from conflict. These tasks are often conducted in the absence of any detailed analysis of their likely political consequences or of the political obstacles that might stand in the way of successful implementation (Keen, 1994a). Such interventions may be seen as a classic case of 'splitting off' the violence from economic and political processes: the violence is a 'given'; the point is to 'mop up' after it. And if violence subsequently sabotages the aid intervention, it can once again be marginalized and dismissed as 'a problem of implementation' or 'a lack of political will' (see Clay and Schaffer, 1984).

Humanitarian aid is habitually based on needs-assessments and early-warning systems that are themselves based on systems of counting – on measurements of thinness, rainfall, production, numbers of displaced people, and so on. Such number-based systems may miss the more important things that are going on in a particular society, notably the causes, rather than the consequences of, violence. The danger is that they will provide an apparently unobjectionable, technological screen behind which ethnic manipulation and economic exploitation can proceed unhindered. Frequently, humanitarian aid may serve as a distraction, an excuse of inaction (e.g. diplomatic inaction) on other fronts. The need for good information on political processes is underlined by the fact that interest groups who are manipulating crises may also be manipulating the information surrounding these crises, for example through depicting inter-ethnic violence as outside government control. Clearly, the 'chaos' model of warfare makes it easier for governments to confuse the international community by manipulating ethnic tensions and by playing up to Western stereotypes of 'ancient tribal violence'.

The political consequences of the current 'system of "res"' may be damaging. Let us suppose that it was possible to achieve repatriation, reintegration, rehabilitation, reconstruction and all the other 'res' to which United Nations documents habitually pay homage. At this point, one would be able to declare the 'madness' of war was truly behind us. And yet, assuming external factors remained constant, the war would simply begin again – for precisely the same reasons that it began in the first place. Those ethnic groups entrenched by the pre-war political economy would resume their dominance, perpetuating the pattern of resentment and official backlash that perhaps characterized the descent to outright conflict. A technocratic approach to 'rebuilding' economies ignores the role of pre-war political economies in generating ethnic conflict.

An alternative model of post-war reconstruction would seek to take into account the economic goals that fuelled the conflict and would be likely to encourage a pattern of economic development that did not discriminate against particular ethnic groups or geographical areas to the same extent as the pre-conflict pattern. This model is likely to be sustained only under accountable forms of government.

As things stand, it must be doubted whether the present system of aid to conflict zones actually addresses the causes of conflict. More often, it seems simply to be 'laid over the top' of these causes – a short-term palliative, a distraction, or, worse still, something that actually fuels the conflict. Yet these shortcomings are often only dimly discerned: for although attempts to address the economic consequences of conflict are often high-profile operations, they cannot properly be said to be in the public domain. They are not subject to public scrutiny, and those taking part are only minimally subject to sanctions for poor perform-ance. This has helped to preserve systems that are failing the victims of conflict.

Political causes In addition to the existing mechanisms for addressing the economic consequences of conflict, a number of groups have sought to address the 'political' causes of violence. However, these efforts again appear to be hampered by important weaknesses. Some of these weaknesses are specific to the group concerned. Among the weaknesses that afflict them all are, first, a tendency to adopt a narrow definition of 'political' that largely excludes consideration of economic causes, and second, what Mark Duffield, in his discussion of aid agencies, has referred to as a lack of willingness on the part of those possessing power to discuss their own role in the wielding of power (Duffield, 1996). This weakness is intimately related to a lack of account-ability within the institutions involved in conflict response (see, for example, de Waal, 1997).

Diplomacy Judicious diplomatic pressure on the relevant parties may well be the most effective tool for conflict resolution and conflict pre-vention. It is not proposed to discuss this in any detail here. However, four problems with this tool must be emphasized.

First, we need to recognize the role of diplomatic (and economic) tools in generating conflict as well as their potential role in reducing it. For example, foreign aid was critical in propping up the undemocratic regimes of Habyarimana in Rwanda, Barre in Somalia and Doe in Liberia. This largely unconditional support effectively entrenched ethnic or class rivalries, storing up resentments that fuelled outright rebellion and official backlash.

Second, much of current diplomatic activity appears to be con-structed within an old-fashioned, bureaucratic model of warfare that is increasingly inappropriate. An old-fashioned paradigm where war is first declared (when the leaders of the warring parties decide to go to war) and then declared over (when they opt for peace) may be of little use in a war where short-term economic gains are paramount and violence is highly decentralized. Merely securing an agreement among 'leaders' is unlikely to secure lasting peace among those who are (conveniently) assumed to be their 'followers'. Divisions among the Palestinians over Arafat's peace agreement have provided a graphic and tragic illustration of the need to secure broad popular support for any peace agreement and to tackle the social and economic grievances that may be underpinning radical protest. In some contexts, dealing with large-scale violence as if it were a conventional civil war may be extremely dangerous. For example, during the 1994 genocide in Rwanda, the UN was insisting that the belligerents must reach a ceasefire to 'stop the massacres'. However, since it was victory by the rebel Rwandan Patriotic Front that eventually brought the massacres to an end, it appears that any ceasefire would only have prolonged the genocide (African Rights, 1994; Prunier, 1995).

Third, a willingness to use diplomacy to exert pressure for peace may depend on whether a major power perceives important strategic, political or economic interests to be at stake. It is at least arguable that much of Africa is now regarded as of marginal interest by the major powers. Even where such powers regard an African government as an important strategic ally, this may militate against diplomatic pressure for peace – as during the 1980s in Sudan, when the US and European governments were prepared to turn a blind eye to government-sponsored human rights abuses so as not to embarrass a 'friendly' regime.

Fourth, diplomatic activity – like most of the activities designed to address the political causes of conflicts – is shrouded in secrecy. This tends to insulate it from critiques that put humanitarian considerations above strategic ones, or that analyse conflict in a non-traditional way.

Criticisms of famine early-warning systems have sometimes pointed to a tendency to concentrate on variables like rainfall and production – the 'natural disaster' model (Duffield, 1994) – at the expense of political variables which might provide a better warning of conflict-related famines. Among the political variables that might usefully be monitored are media propaganda and attempts to replace government officials from one ethnic group with officials from another group. However, if early-warning systems were to become more politically sophisticated, then the topics they investigated would increasingly come to resemble the topics currently investigated by intelligence services. Although the inadequacies of early-warning systems (for conflicts as well as conflict-related famines) have sometimes been attributed to shortages of appropriate information, the real problem may not be lack of information so much as the fact that relevant political information is not circulating beyond the narrow confines of intelligence organizations and senior government officials in the industrialized world. For example, France has for some years been in a position to track the behaviour of Hutu extremists inside and outside Rwanda, but much of this information went no further than the French intelligence services (see, for example, Prunier, 1995).

Just as Sen (1981) argued that famine was caused not by an overall shortage of food but by a failure of distribution, a major reason why conflicts and conflict-related famines are allowed to evolve and persist without effective international intervention may be not so much an overall shortage of appropriate information but a failure to distribute this information to those who are ready to take appropriate action. And just as Sen's analysis brings us to the question of who can and cannot command access to existing food (e.g. by buying it, or through democratic mechanisms), so an analysis of the information flows that surround disasters brings us to the question of who can and cannot command access to existing information (again, perhaps by buying it, or through democratic mechanisms). Although Sen's analysis ultimately links famine with the absence of democratic mechanisms and free speech in afflicted countries, an analysis of information flows suggests that deficiencies in democratic mechanisms and impediments to free speech in industrialized countries may be equally significant in creating vulnerability to violence and famine. In so far as the population of an industrialized country is deprived of access to information about unfolding political crises abroad, the opportunities for international solidarity will be greatly reduced and the field will be left relatively clear for politicians to follow strategic objectives. The impediments to free speech by Western aid agencies – reflecting financial constraints on these agencies, and, ultimately, who is able to buy what kinds of information and what kinds of silence – are also part of this problem of lack of democracy and free speech 'at home'. They will be discussed further in the section on aid agencies below.

Aid agencies While many UN agencies and non-governmental organizations (NGOs) content themselves with addressing the economic and social consequences of conflict, some also claim to be addressing the 'root causes'. However, this claim is very difficult to substantiate. It may be true that poverty is, in some sense, contributing to conflict, and that alleviating poverty makes conflict less likely. But this glosses over a number of leaps in logic, and it tends to ignore the critical role of elite groups in sponsoring conflict. Many agencies have claimed to be contributing to stability by boosting 'civil society' at the expense of 'the state'. However, this stance contains a large element of rhetoric. Nor is it clear that civil society is particularly civil. (What about ethnic militias, for example?) Nor, for that matter, is it clear that further undermining the institutions of the state will benefit ordinary people in a context where the state – already under attack from internationally sponsored privatization – may still constitute the best hope of physical security (as opposed to violence) and social security (as opposed to charity) (Tvedt and Harir, 1994; Duffield, 1996). A further problem is that aid agencies' initiatives in conflict resolution are often aimed at tackling the 'trauma' of victims of violence on the assumption – unproven and very often implausible – that this will impact on the behaviour of the perpetrators of violence (Voutira and Brown, 1995). This logical leap is often obscured by referring to the so-called 'cycle of violence' under which victims later become perpetrators.

Any claim on the part of aid agencies to be addressing the political causes of conflict will be particularly difficult to assess in view of the habitual failure of such agencies to produce adequate evaluations of their own impact (Keen, 1994b). Agencies may have a powerful financial interest in exaggerating their efficacy (to get funding from donors) and thus NGOs' own economic interests in relation to conflict are an important, and neglected, area for investigation.

Human rights organizations Frequently, human rights organizations claim to be addressing the political roots of conflicts and conflict-related famines, distinguishing this response from humanitarian aid that focuses primarily on the consequences of conflict. Certainly, attention to human rights issues is vital. Human rights organizations can give a voice to oppressed people who may find no other outlet. At the same time, it is important to look at what human rights organizations don't say as well as what they do.

First, like aid NGOs, they say very little about the efficacy of their own activities. What kinds of lobbying have had what kinds of effects? It is a fair question, but not one which human rights organizations have answered in any detail.

Second, human rights organizations tend to employ the language of condemnation, rather than the language of explanation. Amnesty International is a notable example. While documenting and condemning human rights is useful, this activity does not in itself point the way towards the creation of a different system where violence will be less likely. For example, an emphasis on condemnation and punishment does not address the essentially pragmatic problem of how to convince warring parties, who are likely to have taken part in human rights abuses, to lay down their arms. In some circumstances, the need to 'wean' particular groups from violence may mean, in effect, 'rewarding' individuals who have carried out human rights abuses, rather than punishing them. This is not an idea that human rights discourse can cope with easily. If the violence in a war is an accumulation of crimes, then any human rights report that condemns but does not explain this violence will have important points of similarity with right-wing discourses that condemn – but do not explain – crime 'at home', or with those who emphasize the mindlessness, the inhumanity and the 'otherness' of human violence.

Third, human rights discourse may be taken up – and abused – by those whose agendas have little or nothing to do with human rights. Amnesty International habitually refers to 'a catalogue of human rights abuses' in this or that country. To some extent, right-wing elements in the developed world, who may seek to cut aid and to portray poor countries as a seething mass of mindless violence, can simply browse through this 'catalogue' and pick some particularly horrendous examples in support of isolationist policies and perspectives; yet these may in turn serve to exacerbate the human rights abuses. Amnesty International's investigation of human rights abuses among the Iraqi Kurds was used by those seeking to cut aid to Iraqi Kurdistan, despite the fact that competition over scarce resources in northern Iraq had helped produce these abuses in the first place.

Such unforeseen consequences are to some extent unavoidable. But they underline a need to provide context, explanation and understanding. Human rights organizations can contribute to this discourse. Some Amnesty International reports are very enlightening – not just on the question of how bad a particular situation has become, but on why it has become so. The London-based human rights organization, African Rights, has set an impressive standard in this field of explanation.

Writers Journalists' attempts to analyse the root causes of conflicts may be inhibited by a number of factors. One is the desire to 'get close to the action', something that may be particularly important for the credibility of TV journalists. On occasions, journalists have got so close to the action that they are unable to find out anything except that the situation is very dangerous. Detailed interviews with those displaced by fighting are often more revealing, if less visually stimulating. Journalists may also depend on aid agencies for access and information, something that may make it difficult to develop a perspective that is radically different from that of the agency. The dangers of journalists reifying ethnic groups as fixed categories have already been touched on. In general, of course, a mission to entertain (and simplify) may undermine any mission to explain.

Academics may see themselves as better able to provide explanations of the underlying causes of conflicts, but they too are hindered by a number of factors. First, it may take an academic so long to say anything, that the crisis has already come and gone. Second, academics are constrained by what they like to call their 'disciplines', a term that would appear more appropriate for a military institution than for an institution promoting free thinking. A 'discipline' prescribes a set of questions that one is supposed to ask; at the same time (though this is less often noted) it implicitly prescribes a set of questions that one is not supposed to ask. A particular gap is the failure to knit together political economy and anthropology,[1] or to describe the evolving relationship between economic factors and ethnicity.

In the case of conflict studies, this can be very damaging. Economists have had a major blind spot when it comes to violence, which standard texts barely discuss. Few economists have asked how economies work during civil war, or how violence shapes economic life even in peacetime. Even though Sen's famous book on the economics of famine includes a case study on the Bengal famine during the Second World War, the book does not really get to grips with the direct links between famine and violence: in the case of Bengal, Sen (1981) emphasizes the role of the war in generating inflation which in turn generated famine, but there is no sense of how some groups may violently appropriate resources from others. We hear a lot from economists about 'economically rational behaviour'. But what are the circumstances in which it is economically rational to carry out acts of violence? Too often, as Frances Stewart (1993) points out, warfare is treated by large international organizations as an exogenous variable, something that can be assumed away when making economic plans. Nor will one find much discussion of economics in a lot of 'political science'.

Many disciplines have focused on a restricted area which is to some extent ordered and predictable, and many have assumed the existence of a functioning state. Dialogue between disciplines has been weak. Traditional economics has been rooted in neo-classical market theory, and has largely set aside the problem of violence. Political science has often focused on elections and voting, the tactical battles over control of 'the state'. Military history has focused on wars between states and on wars over the state, on the tactics of international and civil warfare.

These discourses are generally too rigid and too narrowly defined to embrace adequately the complexities of internal conflict and the partial collapse of the state. When 'messy' phenomena like contemporary civil wars have not fallen easily within the orbit of these 'disciplines', the temptation to wheel out the labels of 'chaos', 'breakdown' and 'collapse' has sometimes been irresistible.

Anthropologists, for their part, have often focused on warfare at the micro level and traditionally have concentrated on small and relatively isolated social groups, such as those in the New Guinea Highlands. This literature is largely self-referential, and makes little attempt to engage in wider debates within a political economy framework. For a critique, see, for example, Wilcken (1995). Some anthropologists, such as Turton, Allen, Duffield, de Waal and Kriger have brought out the connections between local and national conflicts; Duffield and de Waal have perhaps gone furthest in the journey from anthropology to political economy. It is worth noting, however, that none of them is based in a traditional anthropology department. Psychology is another discipline within which considerable research has been done – on the conditions in which people are prepared to carry out violence, for example. Unfortunately, relatively little of this finds its way into discussions of specific contemporary conflicts.

In addition to barriers between disciplines, there have been significant intellectual barriers between nations. How many British academics, for example, are familiar with the latest thinking on conflict and conflict resolution from Germany and France? Intellectual 'bubbles' of academics exist side by side, with the members of each bubble frequently citing each other in cosy, self-referential circles.

Concluding remarks

This chapter has stressed the need to address the economic functions of civil conflict, rather than simply the economic consequences and the (narrowly defined) 'political' causes. It has also emphasized a pressing need for more openness and accountability among institutions that claim to be addressing the consequences and causes of conflict. A complex system for controlling the flow of information (a system of control that confers significant economic and political advantages) is helping to preserve the existing system of conflict response, which leaves largely unaddressed the reasons why people turn to violence or incite violence in others.

One particularly urgent task is to look at the conditions that create impunity for 'ethnic' or other violence. Very often, two parallel processes have been at work: national leaders have granted immunity from prosecution to those (often militias) carrying out ethnic violence; meanwhile, the international community has frequently granted effective impunity to national leaders. We need to be particularly aware of the possible manipulation of militias and ethnic 'hate propaganda' behind the scenes, and to avoid the error of focusing only on the army and the formal state administration. Labels like 'tribal violence' and 'ethnic war' typically impede such awareness. And manipulative governments in conflict-affected states are all too well aware of the potential leeway provided by such confusion.

To understand these issues better, more work within a political economy framework is urgently required. Political economy appears to be a more threatening – and more useful – 'discipline' than either political science or economics when it comes to the study of conflict, since it examines who does what to whom and for what purpose. A proper political economy of war will answer many of the same questions that would be addressed in a political economy of peace – notably, how is power (office, violence) used to make money, and how is money used to acquire and keep power. Unfortunately, political economy is not a conventional academic discipline, and most universities do not have departments of political economy. The discipline has been dominated, at various points, by ideological agendas that have limited its potential in conflict analysis. In the nineteenth century, most 'political economists' had a strong ideological agenda that emphasized the moral and economic damage done by state interference. More recently, the discipline came to be dominated by Marxists who emphasized the inequities in the international system. Abusive politicians and military leaders have become increasingly skilled at manipulating civil society and the language of ethnicity. Analysts, whether journalists or academics, need to be flexible and quick-witted enough to illuminate this manipulation, and this implies a conscious effort to move beyond media stereotypes and the rigidities of academic disciplines.

Note

This chapter is an expanded version of 'War: What is it Good for?' *Contemporary Politics*, Vol. 2, No. 1, pp. 23–36.

1. I am grateful to Tim Allen for discussions on this and a number of other issues.

References

African Rights (1994) *Rwanda: Death, Despair and Defiance*, London.
— (1997) *Food and Power in Sudan: A Critique of Humanitarianism*, London.
Berdal, M. and Keen, D. (1977) 'Violence and Economic Agendas in Civil Wars: Some Policy Implications', *Millennium: Journal of International Studies*, Vol. 26, No. 3, pp. 795–818.
Clay, E. and Schaffer, B. (1984) *Room for Manoeuvre: An Exploration of Public Policy in Agriculture and Rural Development*, London: Heinemann Educational Books.
de Waal, A. (1997) *Famine Crimes: Politics and the Disaster Relief Industry in Africa*, Bloomington, IN: Indiana University Press and Oxford: James Currey.
Duffield, M. (1990) 'Sudan at the Crossroads: From Emergency Preparedness to Social Security', Discussion Paper 275, Institute of Development Studies at Sussex University.
— (1994) *Complex Political Emergencies: With Reference to Angola and Bosnia – An Exploratory Report for UNICEF*, Birmingham: University of Birmingham Press.
— (1996) 'The Symphony of the Damned: Racial Discourse, Complex Emergencies and Humanitarian Aid', *Disasters*, Vol. 20, No. 3, September, pp. 173–93.
Ellis, S. (1995) 'Liberia 1989–1994: A Study of Ethnic and Spiritual Violence', *African Affairs*, Vol. 94, No. 375, April, pp. 165–97.
Hurd, D. (1997) *The Search for Peace*, London: Little, Brown & Company.
Ignatieff, M. (1993) *Blood and Belonging: Journeys into the New Nationalism*, London: BBC Books/Chatto & Windus.
Kaplan, R. (1994) 'The Coming Anarchy: How Scarcity, Crime, Overpopulation, Tribalism and Disease are Rapidly Destroying the Social Fabric of Our Planet', *Atlantic Monthly*, February, pp. 44–76.
Keen, D. P. (1994a) *The Benefits of Famine: A Political Economy of Famine and Relief in Southwestern Sudan, 1983–89*, Princeton, NJ: Princeton University Press.
— (1994b) *Image or Impact: NGOs and Evaluation*, Bergen: University of Bergen.
— (1995) 'When War Itself is Privatized: The Twisted Logic that Makes Violence Worth While in Sierra Leone', *Times Literary Supplement*, 29 December, pp. 13–14.
— (1996) 'Organised Chaos: Not the New World We Ordered', *The World Today*, January.
— (1998) *The Economic Functions of Violence in Civil Wars*, Adelphi Paper, International Institute for Strategic Studies, London and Oxford University Press.
Outram, Q. (1997) '"It's Terminal Either Way": An Analysis of Armed Conflict in Liberia, 1989–1996', *Review of African Political Economy*, Vol. 24, No. 73.
Prunier, G. (1995) *The Rwanda Crisis, 1959–1994: History of a Genocide*, London: Hurst and Company.
Sen, A. K. (1981) *Poverty and Famines: An Essay on Entitlement and Deprivation*, Oxford: Clarendon Press.
Stewart, F. (1993) 'War and Underdevelopment: Can Economic Analysis Help

Reduce the Costs?', *Journal of International Development*, Vol. 5, No. 4, pp. 357–80.

Turton, D. (1997) 'Introduction', *War and Ethnicity: Global Connections and Local Violence*, New York: University of Rochester Press.

Tvedt, T. and Harir, S. (eds) (1994), *Short-cut to Decay*, Uppsala: Nordiska Africa-institutet.

van Bruinessen, M. (1992) *Aghaa, Shaikh and State: The Social and Political Structures of Kurdistan*, London: Zed Books.

van Creveld, M. (1991) *The Transformation of War*, New York: The Free Press.

Voutira, E. and Brown, S. A. W. (1995) 'Conflict Resolution: A Cautionary Tale – A Review of Some Non-Governmental Practices', Refugee Studies Programme, Oxford, and Overseas Development Administration, London, April.

Wilcken, P. (1995) 'The Intellectuals, the Media and the Gulf War', *Critique of Anthropology*, Vol. 15, No. 1, pp. 37–69.

. . . .

CHAPTER 5

A Duty of Care? Three Granada Television Films Concerned with War

Peter Loizos

This chapter is about representations of war in anthropological films. But although there have been at least a dozen such films touching upon wars,[1] it is limited to three recent productions by Granada Television, a British commercial television company with a long record of making films using anthropologists as consultants. Granada supports a centre in Manchester University for teaching ethnographic film production. There is currently more interest than usual in Britain about such issues – a group of scholars have formed themselves into an active association called Anthropologists Against Ethnic Violence, and their deliberations have filled a recent issue of the journal called *Contemporary Politics* (Allen et al. 1996). Another recent workshop concerned with the Horn of Africa, a region which has suffered wars of various kinds continuously since the 1950s, called its working title 'The Fate of Information in the Disaster Zone'.[2] There is an increasing concern among academics with the influence of the media, particularly television, in contemporary political and aid-related issues (e.g. Benthall, 1993).

War, first: Hobsbawm began his history of the 'short' twentieth century with quotations suggesting it has been the most murderous of all time. Two immensely destructive world wars were followed by attempts to control conflict – the League of Nations and the United Nations were partly fuelled by American idealism, to find ways of reducing the frequency of war in the international system. Northern Europe enjoyed an unusually 'long peace' from 1945 to 1989, but one in which the memories of many people were full of war images. There were disruptions of various kinds – the overseas wars of colonial disengagement conducted by Britain and France in Africa, Asia and the Middle East, the Basque, and Ulster conflicts, and the Cold War nuclear tensions in the divided Germany and Central Europe which at times seemed to threaten massive destruction.

War, media and photography? The American Civil War, we are told, made photography popular with the American public (Huppauf, 1995: 97). Hollywood has thrived on the Second World War in particular, and current affairs television demonstrated its capacity to disturb through its coverage of the Vietnam War. By the time we get to the cold missile-eye weirdness, and casual horror of the Gulf War, we can say that television has become a taken-for-granted window of a highly selective character on to a world, some parts of which are at war at any one time. There is then a more or less permanent 'slot' for news, current affairs and documentary material on war, the atrocities that accompany it, the famines and epidemics that follow it. The Four Horsemen of the Apocalypse nightly come into our homes, half intruding, half invited. Why do we have them in? The war correspondent is a new breed of cinematic hero/ine and there is now an interesting level of public debate in Britain by experienced war correspondents such as Martin Bell, on whether or not television has been reporting the Yugoslav, Somali, Rwanda, Afghan and Gulf wars responsibly.

Susan Moeller on American war photographs

Susan Moeller wrote an interesting historical study of American war photographers and their impact during this century (Moeller, 1989). Having noted the way in which particular photographs become images which sum up and so miniaturize entire wars, she discusses the impact of three well-known pictures from the Vietnam War: a monk who has set fire to himself in protest against the war; the execution of a prisoner; and naked children who are being burned by napalm running towards the camera. She argues the humanitarian case that 'with photographs, people discover that human beings, not just faceless "casualties", are dying. The transformation of mass calamity into individual people and incidents arrests the viewer. Through photography, war becomes personal and comprehensible – more than just grand patriotic schemes and unintelligible statistics' (1989: 19).

Moeller is no naïve realist about photography. She insists, for example, that photographs can offer a visual evocation of war, but cannot do justice to the complex sensory experience of combat, which has tastes, smells, sounds, vibrations and wounds. She emphasizes that the viewer brings a capacity for the active appropriation of an image – there is no simple line from image to effect. She suggests that images and photo essays can lie, and indeed gives one revealing example in a footnote. An American photographer called David Duncan took some powerful photographs of American soldiers in retreat, during the Korean War. They were printed in *Life* (the famous photo reportage magazine). In one notable photograph there are heaps of American dead to be seen. Readers wrote in and praised the photographs. Some 40 years later the US government issued a 23-cent stamp with the words 'Veteran Korea' on it. It reused Duncan's photograph of the Marine retreat, but had removed the piles of bodies (Moeller, 1989: 448, note 30). But in spite of such attempts by the state's agents to distort and appropriate significant images, Moeller's general view is that some photo-journalists have moved from being patriotic enthusiasts for America's wars to disenchanted witnesses and critics of brutality, squalor, and worse. They have offered the concerned citizen resources with which to help bring elected governments to account. There is, then, some political leverage, and some small hope in the best war photography. But this view is not the only one.

Huppauf's challenge

Bernd Huppauf (1995) has raised some difficult questions about modern war and the photographic image. His argument is subtle, and compression will not do it full justice. One theme is that there is a complete mismatch in anti-war photography and films between images of suffering humans at the trench and platoon level, and the vast, mass, technological, abstract, fragmenting and industrial character of modern war. His essay starts with the American Civil War, a war supplied, as it were, by an 'invisible' munitions industry, and driven by equally 'invisible' economic issues. It gets much, much worse in the First World War: Huppauf spends some time on a war photographer called Hurley, who knew there was something wrong with his pictures because at first they could never capture the scale of destruction. Later, he used studio-manipulated images to convey complex effects, combining as many as a dozen negatives in a single composite print, to put together the images he could never capture in a single shot. He never resolved the paradox of the isolated image which could not show the complexity of interrelationships, or the scale of activity. Huppauf's judgement is that in spite of his awareness of the issues 'the pacifist intentions of his war photography are lost in the beautiful appearance of his images' (1995: 104). The same could be said of the Australian film *Gallipoli* (1981).

This problem gets worse, Huppauf insists, in films like Joris Ivens's *Spanish Earth* (1937), which has good proletarian lads stacked up against fascist machines, as if only one side had or used machines, or had fresh-faced peasant lads in it. He suggests that there was a clash over the representation of war between realists and modernists. Picasso's 'Guernica' is one focal point. The painting is rightly famous because there is no centre, no heroic or attractive human image. Everything is tangled, interconnected and fragmented, with images of pain, mutilation and anger predominating.

Huppauf is interesting on how the military use of aerial photography altered perceptions and (sometimes) removed humans from the pictures, although at other times, it allowed the scale of destruction to be grasped. His essay ends by discussing the technological triumphalism of the Gulf War, and has a pessimistic challenge. Unless we find ways of representing war that match its causal complexities, its scale, its abstract, functional destructiveness, its remoteness from normal human experience and agency, we are condemned to trivialize it and to glamorize it. The sharply opposed conclusions of Huppauf and Moeller suggest that there are difficult issues to be considered. But we must also add another dimension, which is particularly concerned with the documentary film as a purveyor and creator of 'victims'.

A duty of care?

My title comes from an essay by Brian Winston (1988) on what he called 'the victim' in Griersonian documentary. He modified his arguments in certain ways in a later book (Winston, 1995). He suggested that since Grierson's day, documentary film-makers have made thousands of films about people being harmed in various ways, but most of these films have apparently led to no discernible action-in-the-world to improve matters. So, he asks, what good are the films? The satisfaction of the film-makers, and little else? He proposes that many film-makers regard their right to make films as pretty much sovereign – the divine right of documentarists, we might call it. He emphasizes that film and photography subjects have few rights that protect their privacy, and that there are often, sponsoring the film-makers, powerful communications corporations which do well out of all these victims. The essay and later book include a plea for a major rethink by documentarists on the rights of subjects, and the purposes of films. A 'duty of care' means a duty to put the interests of the film's subjects above any desire for dramatic or aesthetic impact, and above any notional public 'right to know' if that right is at odds with the needs for privacy and a sensitive handling of people who have suffered harm. Winston's general argument fits well with Huppauf's unease about the particular difficulties of war films and photographs as effective pacifism. And there are other scholars, with yet other concerns about war, media and the documentary.

The causes of wars as a filmic problem

Academics frequently complain that television news and newspaper reports trivialize the causes and human meanings of wars (for example, Keen, 1996). One can see on any evening's television news that this can be factually true, and this book is concerned particularly with 'essentialist' explanations using ethnic labels of more complex conflicts. Because the media are powerful and persuasive, the problems of distortion, trivialization and oversimplifications are serious. But any discussion of media contributions requires the same degree of specificity and contextualization that anthropologists normally apply to their fieldwork subjects.

If a scholar were giving five one-hour lectures on the causes of the partition of Cyprus in 1974, it would be appropriate to do some intellectual justice to the historical complexity of the issues. A start might be made with the battle of Manzikert in 1176, between Byzantine imperial troops and the armies of the Seljuks, although some scholars would insist that this would be to treat a modern issue as a 'primordial' one, and that we should start the historical explanations much later. Some discussion of these 'timing' views would be essential. But if someone were giving a one-hour lecture on the sufferings of the Cypriot war refugees from 1974 (earlier, for some Turkish Cypriots), that person could cut the causes of the conflict down to five minutes, and five overheads: the role of Greek and Turkish Cypriot nationalists; Greece; Turkey; the UK; the USA, using about three sentences for each. It could still be objected that this had inevitably 'trivialized' the complex causes, but if the remaining 55 minutes dealt even-handedly with an interesting issue, this foreshortening might be 'taken on trust'.

Serious television can take pains to do justice to a war. There have been major historical series in many episodes on the First and Second World Wars, on the Vietnam War, on the Falklands War, on the Cyprus conflict (Norma Percy and Brian Lapping) and on the American Civil War, and in early 1998, on the Israeli–Arab conflict. In spite of being the intellectual prisoner of images, the writers have tried to do something like intellectual justice to the causes, but they have needed plenty of broadcasting time to do it. Much of their story is inevitably 'narrative' rather than complex abstraction, but distinguished modern historians like A. J. P. Taylor and Eric Hobsbawm use analytic narrative, and indeed, it is hard to imagine history without narrative. It would be an interesting exercise for a good war historian to analyse several of these series, to discover what is gained and what is lost when a massively large-scale and complex event is intellectually packaged for the small screen and mass consumption.

I have made this point at some length, simply because the charge of 'trivialization' needs context. Television is a system of programmed time slots, built around editorial assumptions about 'what the viewer wants'. These slots are culturally institutionalized, and act in certain ways as social foci. In fact, in the last 20 years, and possibly responding to the criticisms of the Glasgow Media Group's studies 'Bad News' (1976) and 'More Bad News' (1980), British television news editors have tried to do fewer news stories in somewhat greater depth, and to avoid some of the clichés of earlier reporting. Events are now shown to be slightly more complex, and the possibility of the reporter not having vital information, or not being able to understand an issue, is now an admissible possibility. That is not to say that 'all is well' with news reporting, particularly of warfare. If the war correspondents themselves are worried (and some of them are) there indeed must be something to worry about. Typically, they worry: (1) that there is a trivializing emphasis on shooting, air strikes, missile launches, the seductive glitz of hi-tech weaponry, and what they call 'bang-bangs' in their coverage; (2) that the worst effects of human destruction (extreme agonized suffering, disfigurements) are usually not shown, so that the true costs of war are hidden from the viewer; (3) that the 'media circus' as an input has negative effects of its own; and (4) that war is somehow glamorized by the media.

If those are the problems of news coverage, are documentaries, with their greater freedom from the news time-slot constraints, doing a better job? And, given that there are news slots and current affairs programmes that deal with conflicts in terms of goals, sides and issues, do the more 'ethnographic' films feel the need to devote their time to what the viewer may be informed about from reading, or watching, other programmes? Need a documentary spend its precious time on background causes as if it were the only conceivable source of information for the audience, which can hardly ever be the case?

Granada Television's 'Disappearing World' trilogy, 'War'

Granada Television's 'Disappearing World' series, which normally involves an anthropologist as an expert consultant and facilitator, had three earlier attempts to deal with violent conflict: Brian Moser and

Bernard Arcand's 'The Last of the Cuiva' (1971) charted the violent incursion into the homelands of the Cuiva Indians by land-hungry farmers and ranchers; later, Moser and Lemoine's 'The Meo' (1972) showed how the hill peoples of north-east Laos were drawn into the conflict between Soviet-backed communists and American-backed anti-communists; and the Woodhead–Turton film, 'The Mursi' (1974), was a study of a pastoral people in south-west Ethiopia, under pressure from neighbours, on the point of deciding in their assembly of all adult males whether they should 'go to war' or not. Each of these films was distinguished by attempts to explain both the roots and the meanings of the conflicts, albeit in terse, foreshortened ways. In each case, there were people who were portrayed as being overwhelmed by external aggressions, people with whom we were invited to sympathize, if not identify. I have written about all three films in two previous articles (Loizos, 1980, 1992) and will not repeat the arguments here.

By the time we get to the more recent series of three war-related films, the concern with causes seems to have diminished somewhat. War has become more a taken-for-granted background fact of life, an event assumed by the broadcasters to be part of the viewers' expectations, at least for other peoples in other places. Its human initiating agents are more remote, even though their disruptive influences reach down into local situations. In 'The Last of the Cuiva' some agents were interviewed, as were spokesmen for the anti-communist side in 'The Meo'. But this is not the case in two of the three current Granada films. Is this a retreat from an ethical 'responsibility to explain'? Or is it more of a concentration on the experiential side of the conflicts? Is this an element in a significant widespread media documentary shift, or merely idiosyncratic to the 'Disappearing World' series? Is it an accident that much of contemporary social science, in the 20 years since the first three films were made, has in some sectors disengaged with causal questions and opened up more to interpretative ones, and that the very factors (e.g. political economy) which would have been accepted as causal then, would be treated more sceptically, now, by some disciplines at least, though not by all?

In 'The Longest War' (1993), we are told a number of times that the Karen people in Burma have been fighting for between 40 and 50 years. Individuals are interviewed; they tell stories in which 'the Burmese' have stolen from them, have killed members of their family, including unarmed civilians, have made people carry out forced labour, have placed them in camps. 'The Burmese' are never seen in the film, but are a menacing absent presence. The film is decidedly sympathetic to the people it calls 'the Karens'. Their small numbers *vis-à-vis* 'the

Burmese' are stressed. Their wish for self-government is reported as uncontroversial, even natural. We are told that their struggle is no longer, in a simple sense, an 'ethnic conflict' because some non-Karen Burmese democratic dissidents have come over to the Karen side, and live and fight with them. This positioning invites our sympathies for an oppressed minority. This treatment says nothing about the difficulties of deciding the grounds for 'being Karen' or 'being Burmese', or about internal divisions among Karens. It says nothing about the many difficulties which accompany autonomist or separatist movements (see, for example, Roberts, 1994).

In 'Orphans of Passage' (1993), a film about the Central Sudanese Uduk people as refugees in Ethiopia, there are references made to attacks by 'the Arabs', and to the entry of the SPLA (the Southern Peoples' Liberation Army) into Uduk lives. The conflict in the Sudan is not given more than a passing reference. The Uduk, like the Meo, are shown as innocent people caught up in a situation which apparently means little to them.

In one sense the film-makers are simply playing back to the audiences the terms used by their informants. It is the language of diplomacy to say 'The Rangoon regime' or 'the Burmese Army' rather than 'the Burmese', or 'The Khartoum regime' or 'the Northern Sudanese Army'. Informants tend to use simplifying categories, and films need to take pains to overcome the simplifying implications. Films dedicated to presenting the point of view of local people may easily become constrained, if not to tunnel vision, at least to micro-vision. They need not be, but they often are.

However much liberal academics or academic liberals hate the thought, some wars are reasonably characterized as wars of ethnic secession, or domination. This does not imply that all members of an ethnic group wholeheartedly support one side. Ethnic war usually divides an ethnic group, even while claiming to unite it, but that does not mean it ceases to have the mobilization of ethnicity as a core component. Is it so irresponsible for a film to say as much? That surely depends on the film as a whole. Yet some critics now write as if, but for a few ill-chosen phrases by broadcasters, reporters, editorialists and academics, the intensity of ethnic conflict in the world would be significantly diminished. This is a form of linguistic determinism, a neo-idealism promoted, among others, by Jacques Derrida. The philosopher Iris Murdoch has questioned this kind of determinism, in my view, convincingly (Murdoch, 1992: Chapter 7). To call Milosevic 'The Serb leader' may hurt the feelings of those Serbs who detest Milosevic, and have courageously opposed his policies. But it is hard to see how it has made them weaker, or him stronger, and in a useful, common-sense way it is accurate. It would, of course, be even more accurate if it carried a modifier 'the Serb *nationalist* leader'.

In the Karen film, one could ideally have wished for a sharper understanding of the roots of the conflict, but it would inevitably have taken scarce narrative time to go into serious detail, and this would have 'displaced' other material. And it would have been easy to lose the audience in inaccessible particularities. A film exploring 'Karen identity' would have been another film altogether. The Karens, who number several millions, are depicted as being determined to resist Rangoon, whereas the Uduk, who number some 33,000, seem, in the film's commentary presentation, not to have taken sides in the Sudan civil war, and to have reacted to the war largely by flight. It is not that resistance is more interesting than flight, but flight at first glance needs little explanation – it is an all-too-human response, and persistent effective resistance needs rather more explanation.

The third of this linked set of films about war is 'We are All Neighbours' (1993), a film about how a political conflict with strong ethnic/religious overtones overruns a village in Bosnia which had both Muslim and Catholic residents. It was made in a media context of incessant news and current affairs coverage of the destruction of Yugoslavia, so there had been no lack of television, radio and written comment and interpretation. From the first moments of the film we hear the sound of artillery shelling Sarajevo. This continues throughout the film, and the village is, initially, 15 miles from the Bosnian front-line. The war is not about to start, it is already on, and the film is about people living under the very great threat of the war overtaking them in their own homes. They have lost their jobs, lost their certainties. We see the film largely through the eyes of a Muslim couple, Nusreta, the wife, and Nirija, the husband. He spends days in uniform at the Bosnian front, and days at home chopping wood. The film starts with strong statements from Nusreta about how the Muslims, Catholics and Serbs must live together in Bosnia, how they have always done so and the future must be like the past. But she admits early on to great anxiety that the situation will change, as it finally does, when HVO (Croatian and Bosnian-Croat army) forces drive all the Muslims from the village, killing some and burning the Muslims' homes.

To conclude this section, the three films, in varying degrees, and with different justifications, say the bare minimum about the roots of the three wars, and say a little less than earlier 'Disappearing World' films did when dealing with violent conflict. For two of these wars (Karens, Uduk) most of the audiences could safely be assumed to have had little advance knowledge of the historical background, while for the third there was a safe assumption that there would be a much higher level of background information, but probably a good deal of residual confusion. Given that they are free-standing 52-minute films, and not in an epic series, and that their focus is on the experiences and attitudes of their protagonists, I can accept the foreshortening as the price to be paid for what is offered as the central focus.

Enduring war: the Karens

What, then, do these three films offer us, if it is not deep insight into the roots of their respective wars? Each film does something different. 'The Longest War' in some ways is most like a typical 'Disappearing World' programme, in that it gives us glimpses of events that have been filmed again and again in the series – a wedding, a funeral, an animal sacrifice, a collective baptism.[3]

But the dominant themes of the film are the sheer length of the Karen struggle, Karen sufferings and their determination to resist, and the apparently robust normality of Karen lives in spite of the military situation. We see young, apparently well-disciplined, confident-looking soldiers in smart uniforms, with modern weapons. They are sometimes in the background, sometimes in the foreground. So, instead of the commonplace picture of war as deeply disruptive of civilian lives, with suffering victims, a sense of robustness is created. We are explicitly told that 'people do not go around permanently bowed down by fear' because, among other things, the imperatives of livelihood, house-building and food production do not allow them the luxury of inactivity. Normality is only 'apparent' because people have to take 'elaborate precautions', such as being ready to hide food in the forest if attacked.

A number of people report the loss of close kin, and the use of mines is shown to be an ambiguous mode of defence because the defensive mines sometimes maim Karens themselves. But the emphasis is on calm resistance, and only a small number of apparently low-key statements stress loss and disruption. Here, I have a problem as a viewer since I do not know Karen codes for expressing emotion. Perhaps the 'low-key', 'quiet' statements constitute a Karen way of expressing the deepest pain. The film gives me little help here, and the issue will arise in later films. If you have been accustomed to the powerful wailing of bereaved or simply distraught women from the Yugoslav war zone, shown frequently on European television, it is all too possible to misinterpret Karen 'understatement'. Certainly, Karens report losses of close relatives which, however spoken of, we can assume to have been painful beyond words. Here, then, is a variant of the point David MacDougall has alerted us to about the 'complicity' between a film-maker's intentions and the cultural styles of the subjects filmed. This could be a 'double negative' – film-makers overstating 'stoicism' and film subjects 'undercommunicating' (in European terms) their grief.

It is not possible to know from the film how much is a result of the particularities of the three weeks the crew were present, and the current military situation. Clearly, if filming had taken place during or after a Burmese attack, things might have looked very different. This is a problem inherent in filming – the way it gets entrapped in what is available for filming – and it contrasts strongly to what can be done by writing. Discussion with the field anthropologist (Sheahan, personal communication) suggests that the film reflected the particularities of one very specific situation, and the character of the particular local military commander. Elsewhere, the film would not have found the relationship between the Karen National Liberation Army and local villagers looking quite so relaxed. In any event, the film reports that villagers are taxed in rice by the KNLA, and are expected to provide a son to fight. They would also have been expected to do unpaid portering.

But it is not unreasonable for the film to present the villagers as getting on with their lives as it does, for two specific reasons. First, we are learning to appreciate that the stereotypes of war and peace we carry in our minds, much influenced by fiction films and photographs, tend to emphasize extreme differences. In so-called 'low-intensity' wars, which are intermittent and chronic rather than acute, there may be long periods of relative normality, and only short periods of active violent encounter. The parties may keep their distance, frustrating rather than disabling each other.

The second reason is to do with shifts in our perceptions of the general resilience of people everywhere. We have been invited in recent years to adopt the view that most people exposed to warfare are almost automatically 'traumatized' – deeply harmed in thoroughly disabling ways. These assumptions grow out of elements in European cultural individualism, on the one hand, in spin-offs from psychoanalytic assumptions, themselves highly congruent with individualistic societies, on the other, both cross-fertilized by the desire of Western charities and UN aid agencies to reduce suffering in poorer countries. There is now a major 'trauma industry' of professionals seeking to assist sufferers through programmes of medicine and psychotherapy which has been active in both former Yugoslavia and Rwanda. The spread of the idea of 'post-traumatic stress syndrome' is related to this industry and its practitioners. However, countering this approach is another one, which

Filming 'The Longest War' for Granada Television's 'Disappearing World' series (photo credit: Granada Television, John Sheppard).

is more interested in applying anthropological insights to the understandings of conflict situations (Save the Children Alliance, 1996).

Key suggestions from this counter-view are that many people cope with disruptive conflicts by addressing themselves to the issues of economic recovery, by giving and receiving social support to fellow sufferers, by using indigenous religious and ritual procedures for coming to terms with the disruptions. This group does not deny the possibility of deeply disabling trauma, but it does propose that it is more rare than is widely assumed, and that large numbers of people affected by war get on with their lives effectively without help from psychiatric professionals.

Thus, for the Karen film to stress the robustness of the Karen response to a very long war is neither eccentric nor fanciful. It implicitly accords with a shift to be found in areas of social theory, reacting against the view from political economy of the mass of people as victims of historical structures and forces, and finding in them more conscious resistance to what intrudes.

Suffering war: the Uduk

At first sight, the Uduk film is about victims, for the film presents the Uduk as if they really are victims, however unfashionable it may be to do so. Winston (1988) has argued that there is a long documentary tradition of 'films about victims', and I return to his arguments below. But the Uduk are not passive victims, since they actively and rationally flee when attacked, and regroup as best they can, when an opportunity arises. The best we could do to 'save' the Uduk for a 'resistance' emphasis, if that were an important thing to do, would be to say that in spite of grave losses and exhausting disruption, they were still capable of song, of dance, of laughter, and social reproduction. In 1992 they were down, but not out.[4]

This film presents a challenge to European audiences by virtue of the style with which some of the people recount horrific experiences: one Uduk woman, seemingly smiling sadly, wistfully, spoke of the death of her children, a matter which apparently confused some television critics. Whereas the Bosnian film had offered people who showed emotions in ways already familiar to North Europeans, the Uduk often tended, by Bosnian standards, to undercommunicate grief. (For a subtle discussion of the Uduk, their notions of 'fear', and some further context on their political involvements and the making of the film, see James, 1997.)

But the Uduk film has a very different construction and logic from the other two films. The Uduk, a people numbering more than 33,000, have had a history of fleeing into the bush from slave raiders in the nineteenth and early twentieth century. The second phase of the Sudan civil war caused them to flee again, and to move from place to place in the Sudan and Ethiopia. Flight has been crucial to their survival. The early interviews are concerned with people who have survived, but who have lost contact with their children, and feel great fear for them, or children who know that their parents have been killed, and must now face life without them. These interviews, which open the film, are full of exceptionally sad and moving material.

The film moves from this opening sequence into a somewhat 'lighter' passage of recollection, and gender tensions, with older women, friends of the anthropologist Wendy James, laughing to hear her play back tape recordings of their younger, happier days. The fact of their laughter, that they can laugh when reminded of their youth, seems an important aspect of how we should understand them. Those of us who brought to the film an expectation that refugees would have to be presented and represented as unremittingly sad are brought to more informed appreciations. There is also some Rouchian playback of 8-millimetre film shot when Wendy James first worked among the Uduk in the 1960s. In those days the Uduk wore no clothes. Now they have clothes, but they do not have their homes, due in large part to the political and economic ambitions of those same rulers. The apparent vulnerability of the unclothed, unprotected bodies in that 'innocent' tribal past contrast pathetically with the dependent but protected status they now enjoy under the eyes of UNHCR. Their bodies have been counted, clothed, registered, fed.

On behalf of the film crew, and the television audience, Wendy James asks a group of men playing a gambling game why are they sitting around doing nothing, 'here' in Ethiopia? This helps the viewer with a situation – refugee men playing a game – which they might otherwise easily have misunderstood. The men give a series of individual answers which express degrees of disorientation, feelings that they are a long way from their homelands, that they cannot cultivate at this time, and that there is nothing constructive to do. 'We've been thrown off course by these ideas.' 'Our livers are afraid.' 'We don't know how to get back home.' They are, we infer, being given relief food. So, the purposefulness of the Karen, securing their food supplies, putting the roof on a house, chopping down trees for fortifications is not available to the Uduk in their transit camp, where, the anthropologist reports (personal communication), there really was nothing to do.

A later theme is the disruption of normal male–female relations, because men are 'scarce' and can easily have sexual relations with several different women. Adultery is an issue – some of the Uduk are Christians and there are attempts to prevent adultery. Some women, who are separated from their husbands, are termed free women, and the complex relationship between relief food and sexual partnerships is expressed in a song:

> The face of the free woman flashes lightning
> The face of the free woman sparkles
> No, don't deceive me so
> You haven't named me on your ration card.

This song is sung at a dance, and it is at dances, particularly in the evening, that sexual troubles and fights arise. There is also the theme of spirit-attack, and divination to control bad spirits. It is suggested that these things are in the ascendant because of the tensions of dislocation and flight. Some children are reunited with their mothers, but against my expectations of tearful and vocal expressiveness, this is done in a muted way. A man is found making baskets, and we learn that when people were fleeing, they carried old people or children in such baskets on their heads. In fact, this picks up a very early statement made by a woman whose child died: 'we carried it in a basket …'.

Two key sequences remain: in the first, the girl who was rescued by the Anuak is asked how life was with them. She replies, 'What is there to say? I played with the Anuak children. We ate fish. What is there to say?' and her long silences were intended by the film-makers to evoke the speechlessness of her traumatized condition when she first reached UNHCR from her bush wanderings. Next, we have some end titles, as this girl pours tea, at Wendy James's invitation. Then, we hear from another mother who is separated from some children. She declares that if her children know where she is, they will come, because this is the way the *Kwanim 'Pa* (the Uduk) join up together. She has tears in her eyes. 'It was like this before,' she adds.

The film is composed of many threads, rather than a single strong narrative, or real-time observation of unfolding events. Flight, separation, death, disruption of gender relations, dangerous spirits, and dispersed people coming together again. As many powerful documentary films prefer to do, it raises questions by implication rather than by explicit commentary formulation: the viewer should ask, what have people suffered in going through all this? What hopes and fears do they have? What unspoken criticisms do they make of themselves and of each other?

And we may think outside the film's explicit framework, of yet other questions, which are, perhaps, implicit, and if we do not ask them ourselves because as anthropologists we have learned to ask less obviously simplifying questions, we can certainly imagine the 'ordinary viewer' wanting them answered. Do these mothers of many children mourn the loss of children in the same way that a woman with fewer children might do? Has the task of survival for the Uduk been such a difficult one that they manage their feelings of loss and longing in less painful ways, or are all humans, cultural appearances notwithstanding, empathetically tuned to very similar emotional wavelengths? Several Uduk mothers speak of the fear in their livers for missing children. The film, at least, wishes us to hear that as one of the 'last words' on the subject. Suffering has not 'hardened' the woman whose thoughts end the film. She ran for her life, but she cannot forget the children who did not run with her. Does it matter in the slightest that she speaks of fear being in her liver, where an English mother might speak of her heart?

It is not, I think, eccentric to raise these questions – they have been raised in a different way by David Turton in an essay on the Ethiopian Mursi pastoralists and their adaptations to a difficult terrain (Turton, 1977). He concluded that the Mursi could not afford to care for the seriously infirm and the severely handicapped. It would not have been compatible with the way they have had to live. For the Uduk, rapid flight has historically been an essential adaptive response, and it leaves as one cost orphans and separations.

Surviving war: Bosnians

The film 'We are All Neighbours' (director: Debbie Christie; anthropologist: Dr Tone Bringa) is different again from the previous two. It is very unusual because it shows 'before our eyes', but in the safety of our homes and classrooms, the unravelling of an ethnically mixed community as it is drawn deeper and deeper into the conflict over Bosnia. It is not a reconstruction, but gives the feeling of following events unfolding in 'real time'.

The villagers are not shown as 'caught up' in the war, as if they were nothing to do with the events that finally overwhelm them. They are, in a small way, agents too. They have hopes and goals, identities and loyalties. But these are shown to shift as the war gets closer. Old trusts and friendships are dissolved, and the only safety by the end seems to be among one's own ethnic kind. They had hoped that the conflict would not worsen, would not enter into their local space. But they could not contain the war, a few kilometres from the village. It came to them and rent the social fabric, staining it with blood and ashes.

Early in the film an old Muslim woman called Ramzia visits a Catholic neighbour Adna and they declare that they will continue to drink coffee together – the implication is in spite of everything. 'What can we do but drink coffee?' One thanks the other for having fed her child when he came and found his mother out. Later in the film, the Muslim woman calls her Catholic neighbour out for coffee, and the Catholic woman does not come. But, significantly, nor can the Muslim woman find the courage to visit her. It is now too dangerous for friends and neighbours of 40 years' standing to have coffee together. The civil war has sent its molten lava to divide this village as well.

Should the film-makers have attempted to put the notion of 'ethnic conflict' into quotes, and introduced us to the complex history of wider, older encompassing conflicts? Should we have heard about the political fortunes of Yugoslavia under Tito's leadership? Of the political–ethnic conflicts of the German Occupation and the resistance period? I think little would have been gained and much lost. I have already indicated that within the 52-minute time slot this would have left too little space for the local drama that will unfold. The film's narrative movement is very much in the film's present, starting in January 1993, and in editing terms at least moving forward on a day-by-day, problem-by-problem basis, over a period of three months, at most.

How even-handed is this film? This depends on how we should understand the term even-handed, or any of its synonyms, such as impartial or detached. A formal, traditional BBC current affairs approach would give the two sides to a dispute 'equal time' to put their views, and might avoid taking sides. It would face near-insoluble difficulties over selecting from a mass of material what most fairly represents one side's view, and it would always have difficulties over who has the last word. It risks being superficial if the two parties are very different in power, or there are suppressed historical features of their relationships which do not get covered by the 'two parties in debate' format. This mode of formal impartiality is still widely used in studio confrontations between political leaders.

The problems with documentaries are not so easily resolved by formal 'equal time, equal voice' treatments. A documentarist, or an anthropologist might choose different criteria to engage with a conflict. These might involve a determination to be truthful in reporting, to omit no significant facts, to take account of relevant historical relationships, and to apply the same standards of judgement to both parties. But the even-handedness would not abstain from *judgement*.[5] There would be no avoidance of a conclusion that A rather than B was the primary or initial aggressor, or that B rather than A was the victim or loser.

In some ways the film has a formal 'current affairs' even-handedness. It does not point fingers or call people by adjectives such as 'aggressive'. It is very sparing of adjectives and judgements all the way through. But its editors faced a problem of narrative construction: they knew (although the audience did not) that at the start of the film we are looking at a mixed village, but that by the end of the film Croatian militiamen will have occupied the village and driven out the Muslims. The local Muslims resisted, and lost. The Muslims have not driven out the Croats in this village, but we hear from Croat refugees that elsewhere they have done so, and it is to the credit of the film that it did not edit this out. So, although we may feel the greatest sympathy for Nusreta, Nurija, Ramzia, and other Muslim villagers we have come to know, we do not have the moral luxury of seeing Bosnian Muslims as passive or pacifists. In the early stages of the Bosnian war, the Bosnian Muslim forces were *fighting* to protect Bosnia as a multi-ethnic republic.

In line with the formal even-handedness throughout the film, many sentiments are balanced, in the sense that they are shown to be felt by both communities. Both Muslims and Croats complain of a kind of madness taking people over, and changing them unexpectedly. Both sides are shown to be increasingly fearful and mistrustful of those they thought they knew. Both sides say 'How could they do this?' Both sides are shown to suffer victimization. But there are issues in the construction which operate at an oblique angle to the formal, balanced items just mentioned, and can be understood in the second, substantive sense of even-handedness. The key Muslim family has a dominant position in the film's construction. This is clearly a deliberate element in casting and characterization, and also reflects Tone Bringa's original fieldwork – Nusreta and Nurija get more air-time, more space to express their fears, than anyone else. Their concern for the safety of their son is involving. Their commitment to defend their home likewise. They typify the Muslims as losers in this village, and, by implication, in the Bosnian conflict more generally. We are invited to identify with them.

Some of the film's construction would not meet the 'equal time' formalist criteria. First, the Catholic Slavka's husband is hardly a developed character. He is not named, nor given any depth – he is altogether a background person. He does not 'balance' Nurija at all. Second, when we approach Kiseljak, a town under Croat military occupation, the editing associates Slavka, selling produce in the market, with the Croatian soldiers, an association that was based on kinship information known to the anthropologist. Third, we enter the mosque twice, and see general shots of many Muslims, first women, and then men, at prayer; but we enter the Catholic Church only once, and then the shots are more confined, less rhetorically attractive. It is over the Catholic Church sequence that we are told how religion is becoming nationalistic, whereas over the mosque sections, we hear only of Muslim fears. I make these points formally, for the record. I am not suggesting that the film 'ought to' have had two fully balanced couples throughout, or 'ought to' have been to the church twice, and used commentary about Croat fears over the church sequences. One side suffered more in this village, and, indeed, the Muslims were the victims of aggression in Bosnia before they took up arms. In that sense, the film's commitment to tell the story of neighbours being turned into enemies is valid.

In correspondence with Tone Bringa, she confirmed that there were instances when Croat neighbours warned Muslims of danger, and these might have made the audience see the Croat side as less comprehensively aggressive. The technical editing problem was that there was no filmed material about these events. In such a case it would, arguably, have been worth making the point in commentary alone – it would only have taken 15 seconds. But the film was edited against pressing deadlines, and a critic's hindsight, with ample time to reflect, is always 20/20.

The 'duty of care', again

This was the way Winston suggests film-makers should think about their film subjects, particularly if they are chosen because they have suffered harm. His concerns are privacy, the negative consequences of being filmed, and in what sense the films help the subjects or the issues they represent. He stressed that the communications corporations are often powerful, and the subjects often poor and marginal. It is also true that it is usually too late to set the record straight once the programme has been broadcast. One problem, which Winston must have considered when he was writing, is that the future is unpredictable, so that a decision taken in good faith about participating in a film might be regretted later on. It is, of course, the duty of the film-maker to think ahead on behalf of the subjects.

So what about the duty of care? How do our three war films measure up to Winston's revised criteria? The Karen film could be viewed (among other things) as advocacy for the Karen Liberation Movement (which by mid-1998 seems to have moved closer to losing the war, and to splitting into two political camps). It is certainly a celebration of the resilience of those who appeared in it at the time. We need not be concerned that the State Peace and Development Council, which confined Aung San Suu Kyi to house arrest and refused to step down when her party won national elections, needs protection from media victimization. God may have allegedly been on the side of the Big Battalions, but on this occasion Granada Television was on the side of the small ones. This film was, in a right-to-reply current affairs sense, 'one-sided'. But why exactly should this worry us? Winston is happy for documentarists to become advocates, and leaves it to the audiences to assess the films. To have 'cared for', even to this limited extent, the previously uncared-for and diplomatically unrecognized Karens will, for the moment, have to do (Falla, 1990). Most viewers would have known nothing about the Karens but for the film. Their 'knowing' is unlikely to help the Karens (a point for Winston), but it is highly probable that many Karens would prefer their stories to have been told, rather than not, even had they been assured that the film would change nothing (a point Winston hardly considers). And that meets one of Winston's criteria – about film subjects being active participants in shaping a film. SLORC will have to find their own film-makers, and television documentary slots.[6]

What about the Uduk? It is hard to see how they can be seen as harmed or victimized by the film. It is clear from correspondence with one of the film's authors that care was taken to report nothing that might have harmed them politically, caught, as they have been, between the Khartoum government and the SPLA. The film team were involved in stopping an escalation of violence between Uduk and Nuer during the filming and the anthropologist has acted as an adviser to UNHCR to assist in relief to the Uduk (James, 1997). Will any audience sympathy for their plight translate into action? On a mass scale, no, but for a few individuals, it is not impossible. The film might well motivate some idealistic doctors, nurses or child protection workers to concerned action. It could equally have convinced a depressed person that the world is getting worse, if he or she did not remember the moments of laughter, and the resilient hope expressed by the last mother we hear from.

And what of the Bosnians? Many articulate victims of modern ethnic wars, particularly if they have been forced out of their homes, want to 'tell the world' what has happened to them. That was certainly my experience listening to and filming refugees in Cyprus. The state-controlled Yugoslav and former Yugoslav media have been heavily implicated in the destruction of that state, by their systematic misreporting of the realities. Croat Nationalist objections to the Granada film would have to be understood in that precipitating context (Thompson, 1994).

The Granada films suggest that we need to understand more about how modern wars disturb, distress and displace people. Some of the victims are, at the film's moment in time, totally disoriented, others more actively resist their adversaries. I would argue that their makers have shown a duty of care, and have gone beyond the Griersonian appetite for 'victims' which so disturbs Winston. There is a social spectrum of apparent 'victims', from the utterly powerless and exploited all the way to active, expressive, persuasive, determined, anti-victims, whom we can neither pity nor patronize, and for whom we may muster some admiration.

How, if at all, do the films impinge on the issues raised implicitly by Susan Moeller, on one side, and by Winston and Huppauf on the other? Clearly, they could argue that an understanding of the complex causes of even these much smaller-scale wars is not advanced, nor are wars apparently prevented by such films. I have partly conceded, but also modified both points. But do we have to accept the more negative implications as well, that somehow, by a humanist focus on suffering or resistant individuals and small groups, we are profoundly misled as to the costs and scale of the conflicts? That wars are trivialized and glamorized? I do not think so, for two basic reasons: the growing sophistication of audiences, and their ability to read, think and act 'after the image'. Indeed, audiences should not be imagined by scholars as a 'mass', for audience research shows they are segmented. For a viewer with a channel-change button in hand, to stay watching any one of these three films would have been a commitment, an active engagement with an uncomfortable experience. The audiences for film and photography are increasingly sophisticated about the limiting contexts of what they are offered, and they can do simple arithmetic, too. Surely, they can 'multiply up' empathetically, and imaginatively, from the images they see and the voices they hear, to the fuller contexts. They can read on for themselves, and find out about the issues which the film only dramatized in miniature. They can learn about the arms trade, the Cold War interventions in the Horn of Africa, the roots of Karen nationalism (Falla, 1990; Smith, 1991), the pre-war social fabric of a Bosnian village (Bringa, 1995) and the history of nationalist wars in the region more generally (Glenny, 1995), or in Europe (Howard, 1983). Why should academics treat photographs and films as if they were ever the sole decisive influences on popular thinking, when a little reflection reminds us that in a complex world they are almost never the sole source of knowledge? We should value the better ones for what they do well, and for the ways they provoke us to sympathy, to thought and, sometimes, to appropriate action.

Notes

1. 'The Mursi' (1974); 'The Meo' (1972); 'The Last of the Cuiva' (1971); 'Black Harvest' (1992); 'Dead Birds' (1963); 'The Pepsi Cola War' (1993); 'Sophia's People' (1985); 'Out of Place' (1993); 'Amir' (1985); 'The Opium Warlords' (1974); 'Our Wall' (1993);

2. The workshop was convened by John Ryle and David Keen, at the Institute of Social and Cultural Anthropology, Oxford, in an ongoing ESRC-supported seminar series on North East Africa, organized by Wendy James and Douglas Johnson.

3. One theme of the film is the complex influence of the Baptist evangelicals, a movement which first reached the Karens via American missionaries, but which now has a strong indigenous hold. We are told that the early leaders of Karen nationalism were mostly Christians, and in the film we hear a Baptist preacher assert that God is on the side of the Karens. This harnessing of Christianity to an ethnic resistance movement is one of the film's surprises.

4. Inevitably, the film leaves some issues of some Uduk involvements deliberately unclear, under the rubric of 'a duty of care'.

5. I am indebted to Dr Tone Bringa for criticisms that helped me to clarify the 'even-handedness' issue.

6. Advocacy carries risks to the filmed subjects. The Karen who speak their minds in this film might be at risk in a nightmare scenario if the film were used by their opponents to identify and incriminate them.

References

Allen, T., Hudson, K. and Seaton, J. (1996) *War, Ethnicity and the Media*, London: South Bank University (reprinted from *Contemporary Politics*, Vol. 2, Nos 1 & 2).

Benthall, J. (1993) *Disasters, Relief and the Media*, London: I.B.Tauris.

Bringa, T. (1995) *Being Muslim the Bosnian Way*, Princeton, NJ: Princeton University Press.

Falla, J. (1990) *True Love and Bartholomew Rebels on the Burmese Border*, Cambridge: Cambridge University Press.

Glenny, M. (1995) 'Who are the Macedonians?', *New York Review of Books*, Vol. XLII, No. 18, 16 November, pp. 24–7.

Howard, M. (1983) *The Causes of Wars*, London: Maurice Temple Smith.

Huppauf, B. (1995) 'Modernism and the Photographic Representation of War and Destruction', in L. Devereaux and R. Hillman (eds), *Fields of Vision: Essays in Film Studies, Visual Anthropology and Photography*, Berkeley: University of California Press, pp. 94–126.

James, W. (1997) 'The Names of Fear: Memory, History, and the Ethnography of Feeling among Uduk Refugees', *Journal of the Royal Anthropological Institute*, n.s., Vol. 3, No. 1, pp. 115–31.

Keen, D. (1996) 'War: What is It Good For?' in T. Allen, K. Hudson and J. Seaton (eds), *War, Ethnicity and the Media*, London: South Bank University.

Loizos, P. (1980) 'Granada Television's Disappearing World Series: An Appraisal', *American Anthropologist*, Vol. LXXXII, No. 3, pp. 573–94.

— (1992) 'Admissible Evidence? Ethnographic Films about Death and their Relevance for Anthropological Theory', in P. I. Crawford and D. Turton (eds), *Film as Ethnography*, Manchester: Manchester University Press, pp. 50–65.

McDermott, A. (ed.) (1994) *Ethnic Conflict and International Peacekeeping*, Oslo: Special Publications of the Norwegian Institute of International Affairs (NUPI).

Moeller, S. (1989) *Shooting War: Photography and the American Experience of Combat*, New York: Basic Books.

Murdoch, Iris (1992), *Metaphysics as a Guide to Morals*, London: Chatto & Windus.

Roberts, A. (1994) 'Introduction' in A. McDermott (ed.), *Ethnic Conflict and International Peacekeeping*, Oslo: Special Publications of the Norwegian Institute of International Affairs.

Ruby, J. (1991) 'Speaking for, Speaking about, Speaking with, or Speaking alongside – an Anthropological and Documentary Dilemma', *Visual Anthropology Review*, Fall, Vol. VII, No. 2, pp. 50–63.

Save the Children Alliance (1996) 'Promoting Psychosocial Well-being among Children Affected by Armed Conflict and Displacement: Principles and Approaches' (Working Paper No. 1), London: Save the Children Fund.

Smith, M. (1991) *Burma: Insurgency and the Politics of Ethnicity*, London: Zed Books.

Thompson, M. (1994) *Forging War: The Media in Serbia, Croatia and Bosnia-Hercegovina*, London: Article 19.

Turton, D. (1977) 'Response to Drought: The Mursi of Southwest Ethiopia', in J. P. Garlick and R. W. J. Kay (eds), *Human Ecology in the Tropics*, London: Taylor & Francis.

Winston, B. (1988) 'The Tradition of the Victim in Griersonian Documentary', in L. Gross et al. (eds), *Image Ethics: The Moral Rights of Subjects in Photographs, Film, and Television*, New York and London: Oxford University Press.

— (1995) *Claiming the Real: The Documentary Film Revisited*, London: British Film Institute.

. . . .

PART TWO

Case Studies

This gymnasium turned collective centre houses more than 400 displaced persons. They are part of the estimated 120,000 who had to flee western Bosnia during the Croat recapture of Krajina in 1996 (photo credit: UNHCR, A. Hollman).

Following the Tanzanian government's decision to close the camps for Rwandan refugees by the end of 1996, about 100,000 were on the move by 19 December, forming a column that stretched some 43 kms towards the Rwandan border (photo credit: UNHCR, R. Chalasani).

CHAPTER 6

. . . .

Manipulation and Limits: Media Coverage of the Gulf War, 1990–91

Fred Halliday

There is nothing like a war to generate controversy, the apoplexy of the established or the conspiracy theories of the subaltern, about the role of the media in covering international affairs. Every modern war has involved disputes on the media coverage of that war, disputes that, explicitly or implicitly, abut on to broader concerns about the role of the media, and of war, in a democratic society. The political assumption of full disclosure of information, and the media's concern with rapid, near immediate, communication of news, conflict both with the pre-occupation of states with security on military matters and with the broader, political, impact that news may have on public opinion. This is not simply a matter that pits civil society, in the form of the public, against government officials: for those serving in armed forces, or those related to, or sympathetic in general terms to, these forces, reportage and disclosure raise obvious conflicts of interest. Wars are, therefore, tests of a range of assumptions about the place of the media in a democratic society, as they are of broader understandings of how far it is media coverage as such, above all in a TV age, that shapes public attitudes.

The 1990–91 conflict over Kuwait was no exception. On the one hand, all the states involved sought to use the media, their own and those of their opponents, to promote their cause, positively and negatively. Journalists of the international media found themselves in the familiar, divided, context of those seeking to provide coverage of such events: while government officials sought to control them through 'news management', and domestic audiences were divided, the professional instincts of the critical and independent pushed them to produce un-censored coverage. Not surprisingly the media coverage of the war produced widespread criticism both after but also during the conflict.

At the time, those who criticized the Western war effort in their countries of origin were attacked as undermining the national effort (Casey, 1991; Keegan, 1991). On the other hand, some journalists who reported from Saudi Arabia later wrote that they had been the victims of unwarranted censorship – 'Operation Desert Muzzle' as John Macarthur termed it (Fialka, 1992; Thomson, 1992; Macarthur, 1993).

Outside the media themselves the public debate about the war was suffused with charges of official and media manipulation. 'The mainstream media complicity with US government policies in the Gulf war has intensified the crisis of democracy in the United States,' wrote one critic (Kellner, 1992). Another critic linked media coverage of this war to broader themes:

> Informational events such as the Gulf war are endemic to postmodern public life. Since they are by definition always open to interpretation, they may be made to serve a variety of political ends. They are an important vector of power. What matters is to control the production and meaning of information in a given context. (Paul Patton, in Baudrillard, 1995: 12–13)

A range of issues, some political, some ethical, some pertaining to the techniques of media presentation itself, especially television, were therefore raised by this war. Necessarily, however, judgements on the media coverage of the war correlate closely with views on the legitimacy of the war itself, those regarding the war as legitimate tending to endorse news coverage, those opposed to it regarding coverage as suspect.[1]

The passage of time, and the availability of more information, provide a vantage point from which to identify, and assess, some of these questions. What follows aims, basing itself on the British and US records, to look at three aspects of the media coverage of the war: first, at the broad character of the media coverage; second, at the forms of news management; third, at underlying political and ethical issues involved. These may help to set not only the coverage of the Gulf War in some broader context, but also to use the analysis of this particular case to address concerns about the role of the media in contemporary society. We seem at the moment to be faced with two rival ideologies: one that sees the media as a part of the democratic process, the information explosion serving to challenge states and established interests; the other which ascribes to the media a determining, manipulative and anti-democratic role within states and internationally. The former runs the risks of complacency, towards those with power in the state or media ownership, the latter often implies a conspiracy theory based on unwarranted generalizations about 'the media' as a whole, and the linkage of news coverage to corporate or state interests. The latter position is associated too easily with assertions as to the degree to which public opinion, if not our very thought processes, are controlled by television in particular. Between indulgence of power and neo-Frankfurtian 'manipulation' some more careful, less generic, picture may emerge. If it does it may also allow for some more discriminating assessment of political, and ethical, issues raised by such wars.

Media coverage

The Gulf conflict was a media event in itself, dominating the TV screens and the press for months, and providing, in its final few weeks, a topic for intense coverage. There were 1,600 correspondents from all over the world in Saudi Arabia. Certain features of the media treatment can be easily noted: TV coverage, aided by selective film from both sides in the conflict, dominated the perception of the public – accounting in the British case for 76% of information, as against 10% from the radio and 7% from the press (Morrison, 1992; Taylor, 1992). There was a high resort in the UK and USA at least to 'rolling news', that is to additional news programmes, discussion items late at night, permanent radio coverage. Also distinctive was the direct coverage from the enemy camp, something not seen before. In the period of the air war, and again in the final phase of the Iraqi occupation of Kuwait, CNN was able to carry live reporting of the progress of the war itself, lending an immediacy, and a pressure for political judgement, unprecedented in international conflict. A British government that banned interviews with Sinn Fein spokesman Gerry Adams saw no need to do the same to Saddam Hussein. Yet this coverage was, even from the technical point of view, highly restricted. There was almost no coverage of fighting, carnage, loss of life itself: this remained off screen (Fialka, 1992; Morrison, 1992). Only 3% of British TV news coverage involved actual fighting. The Iraqi occupation of Kuwait and the US bombing of Iraqi forces were invisible at the time. The US armed forces released film of missile attacks on Iraqi buildings, not of its destruction of Iraqi tanks or machine-gunning of fleeing troops.

Coverage was also shaped by the way in which the conflict fell into very distinct, contrasted, phases. The first was the long period from the moment of the Iraqi invasion, on 2 August 1990, through to the launching of the air offensive against Iraq on 17 January 1991. This was the period of diplomatic reaction to the Iraqi intervention, negotiations over a possible Iraqi withdrawal, and preparations for war itself. The second phase was the air war, from 17 January through to 25 February.

The third phase was the ground war, the one hundred hours, leading to the withdrawal of the Iraqis from Kuwait and the subsequent ceasefire on 28 February. Each phase imposed its own limits: the long five-month run from August to January was one in which, in combat terms, and therefore in terms of news actuality, nothing happened. The Iraqis were in Kuwait and there were occupation and resistance stories. The Western forces gradually built up in Saudi Arabia and the region generally. Diplomatic positions were adopted by Baghdad, Washington and many in between, and duly reported. However, from August to January, the real 'story' was none of these, but rather the on–off speculation about whether Iraq would pull out of Kuwait, and whether, if it did not, the West would attack.

The point of this long wait was not that some great story was being kept from the press, but rather that it was a period of profound uncertainty on all sides: nobody knew either what was going to happen, or indeed what was happening at any one time. In the end we do know the outcome: Iraq did not withdraw, the Western forces attacked. But, at least until early January, when negotiations broke down at Geneva, no one could have foreseen this with certainty. All the media could do was reflect a variety of opinion – on the likelihood or otherwise – of the war occurring, and on the rights and wrongs of going to war to expel Saddam from Kuwait. Perhaps for this reason some effort went into what were taken to be suppressed stories – about whether the USA had enticed Saddam into Kuwait, or was secretly plotting to prevent Saddam from leaving. The US enticement story rested on supposed intimations to this effect given to Saddam by the US ambassador to Iraq, April Glaspie. The claim that Saddam was being prevented from leaving confused this claim, which was false, with the fact that Saddam said he would leave *on certain conditions* which neither the USA nor the Arab state was willing to accept. Even in the combat period itself, from 17 January onwards, speculation was as important as hard reporting: there was no footage, from either side, of the impact of the US bombing on the Iraqi front-line, which took place off-stage, but only of attacks on Baghdad itself. It was only the ground war that offered opportunities for war reporting, for a story, in the traditional sense, of the ebb and flow of battle, and the experience of soldiers under combat. But this was almost too short for extended coverage and, given the one-sided nature of the conflict itself, did not present major opportunities for testing the media, either as reporters, or in their relationship to the states involved.

News management

Every party to the media coverage of a particular war does what generals do – they fight the new conflict by reference to those that have gone before. News management, that is control by states of coverage of wars, has been an element of media work in such conflicts for more than a century: the Gulf War was the occasion to put certain well-tried practices into operation, but also to correct for what were seen as errors of previous cases. In the British case, the mechanisms of such a policy had been well honed by the Second World War, and supplemented by the Cold War and subsequent colonial conflicts (*Index on Censorship*, 1991). Censorship played a role, as did denial of physical access to combat sites, but so too did a set of shared guidelines on broadcasting in war news. For example, there were three Second World War principles: (1) to get bad news out quickly; (2) to broadcast the same news in different languages; and (3) to avoid rhetoric – 'No Ranting'. This had been made easier by the broader recruitment of journalists to sympathy with the national cause, and a culture of cosy association between military and press (Halliday, 1987; Norton-Taylor in *Index on Censorship*, 1991). Only once, when the Eden government accused the BBC of betrayal during the Suez crisis of 1956, had this gone badly wrong.

Yet in the case of the Gulf War the lessons of the last major conflict, the Falklands War, were also present for government officials: while British officials felt that they had done a relatively 'good' job in managing the news, made all the easier by the fact that journalists were stuck on ships and relied on the armed forces for all information and communication with home, there had been at least two instances of failure to achieve the right result. One involved the revelation by a Ministry of Defence briefing official that a significant number of Argentine bombs had failed to explode when hitting British ships, because they had been wrongly commissioned. The other related to speculation on British television of where the British forces might next strike, a discussion which, allegedly, led to the death of a parachute commander, Colonel Jones, in the following days. For American officials, the 'positive' exemplars were the recent campaigns in Grenada and Panama, where the media had been largely shut out, the negative example was that of Vietnam (Macarthur, 1993: Chapter 4). All were aware that, ultimately, the impact of the media would depend on whether or not public opinion was behind the military campaign or not, but that, conversely, the media could play a role in affecting that outcome. For the journalists the lessons were, in part, different: on the US side there were those who resented the controls of Panama and Grenada, and wished to emulate the independent reporting of Vietnam; but there were also those who believed, for a combination of political and commercial reasons, in going along with the policy of the military news managers.

With these experiences, and with the particularly favourable conditions for controlling the media provided by Saudi Arabia, a desert in which the average correspondent would soon get lost if unaccompanied, US and UK officials set up a tight system of control for news management well before the actual outbreak of hostilities. No journalists were allowed access to Saudi Arabia in the first place without official permission, and once there, were under the control of the Joint Information Bureau, run by US, UK and Saudi officials. Journalists were placed in Media Resource Teams, chaperoned by Public Affairs officers, or by minders, who organized their movement, vetted their film and read their copy. From the official Western point of view there were certain obvious problems to be addressed beyond the security of military operations themselves. In the first place, in both the USA and the UK, public opinion was divided about the legitimacy of using force to oust Iraq from Kuwait. While, as the months after the original Iraqi invasion passed, support for military action grew, there was always a concern that this could erode. In the period of fighting itself the prime concern was to sustain political support for the decision to use force, and for the kinds of force used. Doubts about this support played an important part in leading President Bush to stop on 28 February and not to press on to oust the Iraqi regime. While some of this 'positive' coverage related to the mobilization of political support for the military action, considerable efforts were also put, in this as in other wars, into the projection of images of the troops that would mobilize support at home and reassure service families. Stories that would have demoralized, about tactical blunders, mechanical breakdowns, or 'friendly fire' deaths, were suppressed. Only later did it emerge, for example, that 23% of all US casualties were a result of fire from their own side.

Second, news management from the Western side had to take account of the fact that for the first time in warfare simultaneous broadcasting, including of TV images, was taking place from the capital of the enemy. This did not reveal much, beyond skies lit up by tracer bullets and explosions, but the availability of pictures from Iraq, coupled with the availability of Iraqi officials for interview, imposed an important limit. It is doubtful if coverage from Baghdad did the Iraqis much good overall, but prior to the outbreak of hostilities US officials had urged American reporters in the city to leave (Cockburn, 1992; Macarthur, 1993: 184–5).

There was, third, the matter of what were termed 'host nation sensitivities', that is the concerns of the Arab states, and most of all of Saudi Arabia, to prevent hostile or, for them, provocative coverage of their own societies. This related most obviously to women – a group of Saudi women staged a demonstration in late 1990 to protest about the ban on their driving cars – but it also related to the fact that, again for the first time in history, Western troops stationed in a friendly country were prohibited from access to alcohol. This became available only once the troops had crossed into Iraq, where no such bans operate. Saudi Arabia was central to both the military and news efforts in the war, yet reporting from it remained curiously off limits throughout the whole crisis: there were no spontaneous interviews with Saudi men, let alone with Saudi women. It was the host country that somehow disappeared.

When it came to the actual period of fighting, the air war that began on 17 January and the one hundred hours of land war at the end of February, censorship guidelines operated. In general they covered obvious issues of military security, and were not such as fundamentally to obscure either political or military developments. Thus the British Ministry of Defence guidelines issued to reporters list those kinds of operational information, and speculation, not to be published. Dispute over this censorship centred less on the guidelines themselves, than on charges of over-restrictive interpretation. There was, however, a considerable degree of concealment of military matters, along the lines already indicated.

Revision of the image projected at the time has been necessary in four major ways. First, the claims made for the Patriot anti-missile, shots of which were shown allegedly shooting down incoming Scud missiles over Saudi Arabia or Israel, were exaggerated; of the 86 Scuds fired in the war, only ten were destroyed by Patriots (*The Economist*, 1992). Equally claims made about the destruction of Scuds on the ground in Iraq were wholly false – some mobile launchers were hit, but no actual Scuds (Macarthur, 1993). This media misrepresentation compounded a serious underestimation by Western intelligence of the number of Scuds in Iraq's hands. On the other hand, the arguments made as to the importance of the new missile technology in the overall war effort were also misplaced: 90% or more of the equipment used was a generation old, going back to the time of the Vietnam War. This also reflected a shift in the relationship between military and civilian technology over the previous decade or so. During the 1950s and 1960s the military sector had been the most advanced technologically, endowing the civilian through spin-offs with new devices. The reverse now operated – the leading area of technology was now the civilian, the most advanced equipment being not that for military use but that available in any high-street computer salesroom. A third issue on which subsequent revision is necessary is that of Iraqi casualties: figures of up to 200,000 were given at the time, and implicitly accepted by both Iraqi and Western sources, if for different, political, reasons. Later evaluations give much lower figures, of between 5,000 and 30,000, reflecting the low level of civilian, collateral, casualties, and the fact that, to a degree probably not appreciated at the time, large numbers of Iraqi troops deserted during the weeks of the air war (Cockburn, P., 1992; Heidenrich, 1993; Macarthur, 1993: 252–3, 255–7). Finally, there is the issue of what later became known as 'Gulf War Syndrome', the illnesses to which many tens of thousands of Western forces who fought in the Gulf later became subjected. Many explanations for this suggest themselves: reckless inoculation of troops, Iraqi chemical attacks, contamination from the destruction of Iraqi arms dumps, radiation from the use by US forces of depleted uranium ammunition (Mesler, 1996). Whatever the cause, or causes, and none of the possible explanations is necessarily exclusive, the result was a massive cover-up by military authorities for years after the war, until, in 1996, repeated evidence and pressure forced a revision of policy.

A different form of distortion, again one common to all modern war, was that of disinformation, or the provision of information known at the time to be false. On their side, the Iraqis were not slow to put out their own side of the case, beginning with the claim, made immediately after the invasion of 2 August, that their forces had been 'invited' into Kuwait by a friendly, popular, uprising. When the fighting itself began the Iraqis had a number of further disinformation stories: they claimed that Israeli planes were taking part in the air attacks on Iraq; they alleged that 5,000 Egyptian prostitutes had been flown into Saudi Arabia to service the troops; film was shown of large numbers of alleged US POWs being paraded in front of Iraqi crowds; other Iraqi reports talked of mutinies by Arab forces stationed in Saudi Arabia (Passmore, 1991).

On the Western side, some standard disinformation ploys also operated (Kellner, 1992: 132–9). The strength of the Iraqi army was played up, apparently deliberately, as was the degree of damage caused by an oil slick off the Kuwaiti coast – an ecological threat blamed on Iraq but which was, to some degree at least, itself caused by Western bombing of oil storage tankers (Kellner, 1992: 226). One story, repeated at various points in the conflict, was that Saddam Hussein had sent his family to Mauritania, or, in other reports, the Gambia: this story had all the hallmarks of a wartime plant. On other occasions Saddam and his associates were said to be avoiding attacks in a cowardly manner by 'hiding in hotels', locations where Western journalists were present and which would not, presumably, be attacked. Deliberate disinformation on military matters was also evident in the way in which, prior to the launching of the ground war, TV crews were allowed to film preparations for seaborne landings along the Kuwaiti coast. Such landings were not to be part of the land assault on Kuwait, but suggestions that they were formed part of an attempt to deceive the Iraqis about where the main brunt of the final attack was to come from (Fialka, 1992: 7). Film of US planes loading napalm prior to the ground war may also have had an intimidating intent. The most controversial disinformation reported came, however, not during the war itself but in the earlier period, and involved the story, related by Nayirah al-Sabah, the daughter of a Kuwaiti diplomat masquerading as an ordinary civilian, to a US Congressional committee, about the Iraqis taking babies from incubators in the al-Addan hospital. This was a piece of deliberate disinformation, later exposed and used by critics of the war to show how deceptive press coverage was. Given that Saddam had gassed tens of thousands of his own people only two years before, it did not present a misleading moral picture of the regime involved: nevertheless it was itself a lie.

Alternative perspectives: 'breaking out' and media manipulation

Discussion of how the media actually covered the war, and of the state–media relation, involves not only questions of the record, but also consideration of what alternative coverage might have been. It also requires examination of the ethical issues present, if not always acknowledged, in discussion of this coverage. In broad terms the course of the discussion of the moral issues involved is predictable enough: those opposed to the war consider media coverage to have been biased, and their critiques use examples of distortion in the media coverage to make broader, political, points about the war itself (Kellner, 1992; Campbell, 1993); those who regarded the war as, broadly, justified tend to argue that the coverage was, within the necessary constraints of any war coverage and of the censorship which is associated with war, legitimate. This is not the place to adjudicate between the different views of the war itself: it is, however, impossible to exclude the influence which this casts on any discussion of the media coverage. My own view, for what it is worth, is that the war was in general justified but that some of the media treatment, as well as some actions in the war itself, were not so (Halliday, 1996: Chapter 3). What will be examined here are some more specific issues pertaining to the way the war was covered.

(i) 'Breaking out'   During the conflict, and after, a number of reporters did protest about the way in which the media were reporting, and in particular the manner in which state officials, in Saudi Arabia, restricted what journalists could do. These critics argued that journalists should have done more to 'break out', in journalistic terms by covering aspects of the story that were being hidden, in physical terms by getting away from their government handlers and getting independently to the front-line. That journalists working in Saudi Arabia were subjected to severe controls is indisputable. As Robert Fisk of the *Independent* wrote: 'So thorough has been the preparation for this war, so dependent have journalists become upon information dispensed by the Western military authorities in Saudi Arabia, so enamoured of their technology, that Press and television reports have found themselves trapped' (Fisk, 1991). This has been the brunt of the critical argument made by others (Fialka, 1992; Thomson, 1992; Macarthur, 1993). However, the issue of 'breaking out' may be more complex than that. On the one hand, while journalists were controlled, and stories unwelcome to the state officials blocked or delayed, there is little evidence, from the time of the fighting or sub-sequently, that there were major stories that a more independent-minded journalist could have found out. The things we now know that were covered up at the time – for example, on the inaccuracy of the Patriot missiles or the causes of Gulf War Syndrome – were known to very few even in the military.

The argument as to a 'story' that censorship prevented from being reported was, in general, never put to the test, because with such a short period of ground combat the relations between state and press were not put to the test. Had the ground war dragged on for weeks or months, let alone going on for as long as the US involvement in Viet-nam, then the scope for such disputes would have been all the greater. In the words of one senior *Guardian* writer:

> reporters often pose the wrong questions. Their concept of the truth is that it is something the interested parties always want to hide: if nothing dramatic or discreditable is coming out, it is only because it has been successfully concealed. But the long period of preparation by the ground forces in Saudi Arabia was by its nature rather boring, and the air war after the first few days was repetitive. Some reporters still imagined that behind the wall of minders was something very important that was being kept from them ... Yet the reality of war, even one with as little heavy fighting as

the Gulf conflict, is its amorphous, dislocated, uncertain nature. The allied censors may have compounded this a little but they did not create it. (Woollacott, 1992)

This criticism, that the news was being manipulated, itself falls into a trap, that of accepting that the most important task is to be first or exclusive with the 'story'. From a journalistic point of view, this may be so; from the perspective of informing the public and allowing for democratic debate, it is not. The place where 'breaking out' would have been more possible, and desirable, was not in news at all, but in current affairs, that is in the programmes and discussion of issues pertaining to the war that accompanied news programmes. The failure to 'break out' in current affairs had nothing to do with state controls, or restrictions on the ground in Saudi Arabia, but with the lack of initiative, and timidity, of editors back in the broadcasting countries, and with acceptance, common to critics and conformers alike, of the priority of 'news'. Thus a range of issues pertaining to the historical background to the war, or the range of ethical issues involved, which could, and arguably should, have been discussed at the time, were not (Kellner, 1992: 92–103). For example, throughout the whole period of the crisis there was virtually no discussion of the character of the political regime in Iraq, in particular of the ideology and history of the ruling Arab Ba'th Socialist Party. Analysis of Ba'th thinking could have revealed much about Saddam's thinking on the war, not least with regard to the role of war as a purgative experience for society, or the significance of the military leader.

The restriction of the current affairs agenda served not only to simplify the historical record, but also to present ethical and legal issues in a one-sided manner. One striking example was in discussion of Iraq's ecological crimes: that Iraq did commit serious ecological crimes is beyond doubt, most noticeably by blowing up over 600 Kuwaiti oil fields, with consequent damage to land, atmosphere and subterranean areas. However, as the story of the oil slick provoked by Western bombing of storage tankers reveals, not all ecological damage was committed by the Iraqis. Moreover, as was later revealed, the US armed forces used highly dangerous radioactive depleted uranium shells, the consequences of which for soldiers and, subsequently, civilians are extremely serious (Mesler, 1996).

The implication of media coverage, that Iraq was the first country to carry out such crimes in war, was also quite unwarranted: one has only to think of the First and Second World Wars, or of the US use of 11 million gallons of the defoliant Agent Orange in Vietnam, destroying

4.5 million acres of countryside, to see that those excoriating Saddam for his ecological crimes were presenting a partial historical record.

Another moral issue of which much was made was the treatment of prisoners of war: the Iraqi regime had already established, in its 22 years in power, a sinister record of human rights abuses, including mass murder of its own citizens and the repeated violations of international conventions when it came to the tens of thousands of Iranian POWs it held after the 1980–88 war (Middle East Watch, 1990). Its treatment of the population in the occupied Kuwaiti territories, be these Kuwaitis or third-party nationals, was in many respects criminal (Makiya, 1993). Iraq also, most obviously, held large numbers of Western civilians hostage for weeks after the 2 August occupation of Kuwait. There was, therefore, precedent, as well as wartime interest, in portraying the Iraqis as maltreating Western prisoners of war, particularly pilots, captured during the 1991 conflict itself. Moreover, this is indeed what occurred: when captured British pilots were shown on Iraqi TV making confessions, it appeared that they had been badly beaten up, and this later turned out to be the case. But the manner in which the POW issue was presented was none the less distorted, and for wartime purposes: the message put across was that Iraqi treatment of POWs was singularly evil, with the further suggestion that the Arabs, perhaps like the Japanese, behaved in an especially barbarous manner towards white prisoners.

Coverage of the POW issue involved a false, irresponsibly selective, picture for two reasons: first, while the Iraqi regime did maltreat its Western prisoners, it treated them better than its own subjects or the Kuwaitis who disappeared when the invasion happened; second, by implicitly phrasing the issue in racial terms the media served to exonerate Western armies for their treatment of prisoners of war in other contexts. One need only think of the US murder and mutilation of the corpses of Vietnamese prisoners in the Vietnam War, or of the systematic starving to death of German prisoners after the Second World War (Herr, 1979; Bacque, 1989). The legitimacy of the expulsion of Saddam from Kuwait rested on a number of strong arguments, but not on the innocence of Western armies with regard to POWs. There was a moral, and legal, case to·be made for forcing Iraq to leave Kuwait by force. It did not require gross simplification of the moral, and historical, issues involved (Campbell, 1993).

(ii) Wartime censorship That some controls operate in wartime is inevitable. It is facile to say, as some journalistic critics did, that since the war was being fought for freedom, the press and media coverage should

be entirely free. Certainly this was not the view of the majority of public opinion in either the UK or the USA (Fialka, 1992: 62; Morrison, 1992: 25). The more difficult question is how far, in a democratic society, such control is justified, especially when it affects not only the security of military operations but also political debate on the legitimacy of the war, or certain aspects of the war, itself. Ideally, these two realms should remain distinct, censorship applying only to the former area. But the line is not so clear: war involves political and moral issues as much as fighting itself, and states pursue the goal of sustaining domestic support, and the support of their armed forces, in such conflicts. The result is that news management, in both its negative and positive forms, comes to cover a wider range of political questions. The presumption has to be that, in a democratic society, the line is drawn as near the core of security issues as possible: debate on the conduct of the war, its aims, the prolongation of conflict are all legitimate, even as states, and supporters of the conflict, seek to minimize them.

In the Gulf War news management operated, and for those either opposed to any such controls, or who took this issue to de-legitimate the war as a whole, this constituted a reason for denouncing the policies pursued (Kellner, 1992). It is harder, however, to make a strong case that news management went beyond the bounds of the legitimate. The overall issue of whether to go to war at all, the *jus ad bellum* argument, was widely and exhaustively debated in the long run-up to 17 January, in both the British Parliament and the US Congress, and in the respective electronic media and press. Those opposed to action, whether they were British MPs or American generals, had the opportunity to voice their objections, and to have them broadcast and reported. Indeed, although, legally and technically, the conflict was a war from 2 August onwards, no significant controls on political debate operated at all. Nor was there shortage of speculation as to what might happen once full war broke out: while some thought a speedy outcome was possible, many a sage observer, civilian and military, predicted a long-drawn-out involvement, a 'quagmire', in which Western casualties would be very high. Others feared insurrection in the Arab and non-Arab Muslim worlds.

As for controls of information in the war itself, that is from 17 January 1991, such controls were certainly there: we have seen above issues on which retrospective information leads to a revision of what was thought at the time. How far such control served unduly to manipulate public opinion, or constrain the democratic process is harder to say. There were clear cases of manipulation, of which the Kuwaiti government story of the killing of babies in the al-Addan hospital in Kuwait was one case, but it is harder to make a case for the fact that an overall, illegitimate, distortion of the democratic process occurred. On the other hand, there were those who argued that coverage, and comment, was in some instances too critical. For example, the coverage of the killings in the al-Amariya shelter on February were seen as unduly pro-Iraqi, yet defended on the grounds that they had occurred and should be so covered (Jenkins, 1991; Simpson and d'Ancona in *Index on Censorship*, 1991). In Britain interviewers who queried the legitimacy of the war, or the military arguments, were subjected to chauvinist and populist abuse (Casey, 1991; Keegan, 1991). Similar diatribes were heard in the USA: one Vietnam veteran turned *Washington Post* commentator denounced his fellow reporters as 'dinner party commandos, slouching inquisitors, collegiate spitball artists ... a whining, self-righteous, upper middle class mob' (Fialka, 1992: 62). In retrospect the arguments made at the time pale: those so criticized were perfectly justified in expressing their views. No one, to my knowledge, has been charged with revealing anything of military value at any time in the whole crisis.

(iii) Jus in nuntio   Media coverage of the war abutted inevitably on to a much broader question: that of the legitimacy of the war itself. Those who endorsed the war wanted the coverage to be in broad terms supportive, and, when it was not, criticized it as such. Alternatively, critics sought to use the biased character of the media coverage as a means of challenging the legitimacy of the war as a whole. Discussion of the legitimacy of war has, traditionally, revolved around two issues: the right to go to war in the first place, *jus ad bellum*, and the right to use certain kinds of violence in war, *jus in bello*. While conceptually distinct, the temptation has always been to use the second, and in particular violations of the legitimate use of violence, to question the legitimacy of the act of war itself. In argument, the distinction is not respected: those who justify the act of war justify all that is done in it, those who deny war's justification focus on the crimes committed in it. Thus arguments against national liberation movements seek to delegitimate them as 'terrorists', while supporters of the overall campaign of the Second World War are unable to admit that crimes were committed at, say, Dresden and Hiroshima.

To these two categories of legitimacy in violence is not, it seems, being added a third, namely the ethics of reporting and media coverage, what may be termed *jus in nuntio* (my coinage, after the Latin for 'message', *nuntium*). Here the linkages, and confusions, of the *ad bellum/in bello* are compounded by a third arena of legitimation and delegitimation. Those who opposed the war focus on censorship, ethnic stereotyping, masculinist and bellicist imagery, and the general air of jingoism and chauvinism, to be seen in much of the printed press and, to some degree, in the electronic media as well (Kellner, 1992). Such arguments draw on a number of traditional critical sources – pacifism, feminism, cosmopolitanism – but the attractions of this approach have undoubtedly been enhanced by interest in discourse theory and post-modernist concerns generally. In this latter context, the critique of the war rests on the fact that, for the Western public and indeed much of the military deployed, the war was not lived as direct combat, but as something seen on television screens, a 'simulacrum' or 'hyperreality' characteristic of the postmodern age (Baudrillard, 1995). It is not difficult to make a case as to the distortions, and inherent prejudices, in much media coverage: once that is done, the transition to arguing that, because the reporting or message is ideological, the war as a whole is illegitimate, is not difficult to make. Equally, the postmodernist can see the 'hyperreality' of the Gulf War as a denial of the moral claims of the other, in this case the Iraqis, and as masking a one-sided slaughter of a 'third world' people.

Postmodernism has, in general, been subjected to repeated, in my view telling, critique, not least in regard to the Gulf War and Baud-rillard's famous remark that it had 'never happened'. Baudrillard's argument was that the war had not happened because it was experienced by the Western world not as a real-life conflict, but as 'virtual reality', an event in which moral certainty, linked to overwhelming power, suppressed political and moral alternatives (Norris, 1992; Baudrillard, 1995). There are, however, difficulties with this approach even in this specific context. The first is simply one of comparison: whatever the distortions involved in the Western media coverage of the war, be these in terms of misrepresentation of facts or projections of stereotypes, they paled before those of the Iraqi media, who regularly indulged in lies and racisms against all that they opposed (Al-Khalil, 1989). This does not legitimate Western distortions, but it may affect judgements as to the relative merits of different sides in the war. Second, while distortion there certainly was, the question remains as to whether it was of such an extent that it invalidated the legitimacy of the war itself: as with the use of *in bello* violations, so with those of *in nuntio*, there has at some point to be a rate of conversion, a tariff, that enables identification of a violation of principle to be used to challenge the overall claim that it is justified to go to war. There is no automatic conversion here: one lie, one stereotype, does not invalidate a war. In the case of the Gulf War it would be hard to argue that the distortion and propaganda (official or unofficial) was such as to support a case against the war itself.

The extensive critical literature on media bias in the war is about the media themselves, no more. As for the broader postmodern critique, of this and other contemporary political events, it shifts from a justified recognition of the role of discourse, narrative and, in the contemporary world, media images in the conduct of war to a different and less justifiable denial of the possibility of legitimate actions in war. Too easily such an apparently open epistemological critique slides into a relativism and an epistemological confusion that dodges the political choices involved. The work of David Campbell (1993) is a particularly interesting instance of this approach. Campbell recognizes and meets the challenge of arguing about what actually happened and provides a cogent, if not necessarily persuasive, alternative account of how the Gulf crisis should have been confronted. At the same time, he is driven, by the logic of his argument, into questionable conclusions: on the one hand (1993: 13–14) he goes from the recognition that war is an object of widespread media attention into asserting that war itself has become a performance; on the other (1993: 82–3) his, in itself valid, questioning of the concept of sovereignty slides into an implicit endorsement of Iraq's occupation of Kuwait. Faced with Saddam's, or for that matter General Mladic's, tanks one might be forgiven for caution in the face of calls for 'deterritorialization'. A similar problem besets some of the writing of Edward Said on Western media representation of the Middle East (Said, 1981). Identifying myths about Islam, Arabs or Iranians does not entail either that some of the political forces so stereotyped cannot legitimately be opposed, nor that the 'Western' media are as a whole an unreliable source of information on a Third World region. The critique of imperialist ideology needs to be carefully distinguished from collusion with retrograde indigenous movements (Halliday, 1996: Chapter 7).

(iv) Democracy misled: manipulation and conspiracy theory While it is difficult to assess the overall impact of this official news management on the public perception of the war, there can be little doubt that it had some impact, at least in keeping some information from the enemy side, and in reinforcing support for the war. But the extent of this management of the media should not be exaggerated. In the first place, the broad character and course of the conflict was visible to anyone with access to electronic media or the press: there were no great mysteries which subsequent revelations have established. Second, a considerable part of the control of information was one which, given public attitudes, the public themselves would have endorsed. There was, for example, very little violence shown on TV throughout this conflict: more was, indeed, shown from Lithuania, then in the last

throes of Soviet rule, than from the Gulf. But this may as much as anything have reflected a general public reluctance to see carnage on TV. By analogy with car crashes or plane accidents, there is a desire to know what has happened, but not to see graphic footage of the bodies. Second, and more important, where the news did have an impact, this was in ways quite independent of the intentions of state news managers, in either a 'positive' or 'negative', that is censorship, sense. At least as far as the UK was concerned, the greatest media damage to Saddam Hussein's image in the West came from something he himself did. Thus scenes shown in the aftermath of the invasion of Kuwait of the Iraqi President meeting with Western hostages and affecting to talk to a very frightened English boy being held with his parents did Saddam most damage. This was a story of evident monstrosity, but it had required no state intervention to produce it. Another example, with considerable political impact, was the coverage of the Iraqi withdrawal from Kuwait, with reports, confirmed in still photographs, of large numbers of Iraqi troops having been killed in their stalled convoy. This provoked considerable concern at the time, and was a factor in the decision not to prosecute the war further. Finally there was the dramatic instance of the footage showing Iraqi Kurds trying to flee into Turkey at the end of March 1991 following the defeat of the uprising against Saddam Hussein. It may not be that it was this footage that persuaded the British Prime Minister John Major to support the sending of troops into northern Iraq, under Operation Provide Comfort, but it does seem that public concern was such that the Western states were led to act. The implication of each of these three instances is that it was not so much politicians or states managing the news as the reverse: here, it would appear the news managed politics, by inflecting public opinion and so enabling or encouraging politicians to pursue a particular course of action. In the case of Vietnam this had, of course, served to erode public support for the US government position, yet Vietnam shared with the Gulf the virtue of showing how media images can have an autonomous, potentially democratic, impact.

Conclusion

If the first casualty of war is truth, it is closely followed by the possibility of a measured assessment of the role of reporting, and of the media, in that war. The three main reasons for this have already been identified: (1) the desire of states to control information for security and political purposes; (2) the subordination of assessment of media coverage to other, often unstated, views of the legitimacy of the war itself; and (3) the pervasive view, fuelled by conspiracy theories of Left and Right, that public attitudes and the democratic process as a whole are easily subverted by manipulation of fact and image.

The Gulf War of 1990–91 lends support to each of these charges and will no doubt be added to the long list of conflicts in which such distortion has occurred. Yet the conclusion of this chapter sits uncomfortably with these debates: one can accept that the war to oust Saddam Hussein from Kuwait was legitimate, but, as has been argued here, one can also show that in many instances, and in a broader approach, the press and media handling of the war was unduly narrow and indulgent. In fulfilling a responsibility to provide news, and to avoid undermining a country's war effort, other responsibilities, including those to educate the public in the broader issues involved, were neglected.

At the same time the Gulf conflict also allows other interpretations, and distinctions that a simple conspiratorial agenda may underplay. There were, first of all, presentations of military activity which in retrospect we know to be false. This falsity does relate to the issue of 'manipulation', that is to the inflection of public attitudes at a time of crisis in favour of the state concerned. How important, or decisive, such inflection was is, however, harder to assess: on its own it does not resolve the issue of distortion of democracy, nor does it, obviously, affect assessment of the final military outcome. The relationship of journalists to the state was also an area of dispute, during and after the war, but, again, no easy judgement is possible: collusion took place as much through spontaneous, self-generated, voluntary support as it did through direct control. It was to be found as much, if not more so, among editors and commentators in the home countries and editing offices as it was on the ground. In other words, direct state control, and particularly at the point of combat, was only a small part of the overall collaboration of media with the state.

Finally, emphasis on the role of the media, however justified in detail, may downplay, or suppress, discussion of other, broader, factors in the shaping of public opinion. That opinion, be it in the USA or Britain, was, and to some extent remained, divided over the legitimacy of using force to oust Saddam Hussein from Kuwait. This was a legitimate disagreement, revolving around issues of sovereignty, frontiers, the legitimacy of force, and the relation between material interest (in this case oil), the risks to human life, and the upholding of legal and moral principles. The majority which emerged in favour of the use of force owed something to the role of the media, and to the ability of politicians to bring public, and their respective legislatures, behind them. At the same time, debate also reflected judgements which public opinion made on the basis of the facts and images presented to them, some of these directly by the Iraqi state itself. It is impossible to test the counter-factual as to whether, with a different media coverage, public opinion would have supported a different policy. One can argue persuasively that a more informative and responsible coverage was possible during the Gulf crisis. One is, however, entitled to doubt whether the opinion that did emerge in the latter part of 1990 and early 1991 was funda-mentally affected by the messages that were conveyed to it.

Note

1. The original version of this chapter was published in *Citizenship Studies*, Vol. 1, No. 2, 1997.

References

Al-Khalil, S. (1989) *Republic of Fear*, London: Radius/Hutchinson.

Bacque, J. (1989) *Other Losses: An Investigation into the Mass Deaths of German Prisoners at the Hands of the French and Americans after World War II*, Toronto: Stoddart Publishing Company.

Baudrillard, J. (1995) *The Gulf War did not Happen*, Bloomington, IN: Indiana University Press.

Campbell, D. (1993) *Politics without Principle. Sovereignty, Ethics, and the Narratives of the Gulf War*, London: Lynne Reinner.

Casey, J. (1991) 'A Pox on the Pilgers', *Evening Standard*, 1 March.

Cockburn, A. (1992) 'When the US Press Fled Baghdad', *The Nation*, 27 January.

Cockburn, P. (1992) 'Lower Death Toll Helped Saddam', *Independent*, 5 February.

Economist, The (1992) 'Armchair generalship', 2 May.

Fialka, J. (1992) *Hotel Warriors. Covering the Gulf War*, Washington, DC: The Woodrow Wilson Center Press.

Fisk, R. (1991) 'Free to Report What We're Told', *Independent*, 6 February.

Halliday, F. (1987) 'Counterinsurgency and News Management: The Case of Oman', in Jean Seaton and Ben Pimlott (eds), *The Media in British Politics*, Aldershot: Gower.

— (1996) *Islam and the Myth of Confrontation*, London: I.B.Tauris.

Heidenrich, J. (1993) 'The Gulf War: How Many Iraqis Died?', *Foreign Policy*, Vol. 90, Spring, pp. 108–25.

Herr, M. (1979) *Dispatches*, London: Picador.

Index on Censorship (1991) 'Warspeak: The Gulf and the News Media', April/May, Special Issue.

Jenkins, S. (1991) 'When the Truth Takes a Direct Hit', *The Times*, 18 February.

Keegan, J. (1991) 'A Plague on the BBC', *The Spectator*, 2 March.

Kellner, D. (1992) *The Persian Gulf Media War*, Boulder, CO: Westview Press.

Macarthur, J. (1993) *Second Front. Censorship and Propaganda in the Gulf War*, London: University of California Press.

Makiya, K. (1993) *Cruelty & Silence*, London: Jonathan Cape.

Mesler, B. (1996) 'The Pentagon's Radioactive Bullet', *The Nation*, 21 October.

Middle East Watch (1990) *Human Rights in Iraq*, London: Human Rights Watch Books.

Morrison, D. (1992) *Television and the Gulf War*, London: John Libbey.

Norris, C. (1992) *Uncritical Theory. Post-modernism, Intellectuals and the Gulf War*, London: Lawrence & Wishart.

Passmore, J. (1991) 'Prostituting the News, Iraqi Style', *Evening Standard*, 12 February.

Said, E. (1981) *Covering Islam. How the Media and the Experts Determine How We See the Rest of the World*, New York: Pantheon Books.

Taylor, P. (1992) *War and the Media. Propaganda and Persuasion in the Gulf War*, Manchester: Manchester University Press.

Thomson, A. (1992) *Smokescreen*, Tunbridge Wells: Laburnham and Spellmount.

Woollacott, M. (1992) 'Warriors in a Minefield', *Guardian*, 1 October.

. . . .

CHAPTER 7

Ethnicity and Reports of the 1992–95 Bosnian Conflict

Marcus Banks and Monica Wolfe Murray

The language of ethnicity

From the 1940s, and increasingly from the 1970s, the terms 'ethnicity' and 'ethnic' have been used by sociologists, anthropologists and others in their academic writings. In particular, from the early 1970s anthropologists began to substitute the term 'ethnic group' for 'tribe' (attributable, in part, to the influence of Barth, 1969). While there are differences in the ways in which terms from this growing ethnicity discourse were used, 'ethnic group' in particular continued to carry with it certain essentialized assumptions about the boundedness of such groups and the homogeneity of their contents. Following on from the earlier discourse on 'tribe', assumptions were made regarding the congruity of name, language, territory, customs and culture, in reinforcing a sense of identity and thus defining a human population as a 'group'. Following Barth (1969), attention was paid to the construction and maintenance of boundaries surrounding and containing 'ethnic groups', but generally these issues were not considered to be especially problematic. Frequently there was a happy conjunction of the anthropologists' or sociologists' assessment of the constituent factors in the group's ethnic identity and the views of members of the group itself. Often, the only point of difference lay in the common assertion on the part of members of the group that their corporate identity was ancient or primordial, a claim often underwritten by some presumption of shared ancestry or blood, and the observer's assessment that this was either untrue or unprovable and that the group's motivation in manifesting a shared identity was rooted in more immediate political or economic advantage.

In recent years anthropologists and sociologists have begun to develop a less essentialized discourse on ethnicity, one which continues to be sceptical of primordialist claims on the part of members of the group, but which seeks to contextualize such claims within a deeper historical perspective and to explore fully the ruptures of colonialism and decolonization where relevant (Comaroff and Comaroff, 1992). In so doing, assumptions regarding the stability or homogeneity of an 'ethnic group's' contents are challenged, to the point where terms such as 'ethnic group' and 'ethnicity' themselves are becoming increasingly limited in their applicability or abandoned altogether.

In contrast to the 'ethnicity discourse' which has been strong in anthropology for at least the past quarter-century, there is a marked absence of an equivalent 'race discourse' in post-war anthropology (although not in sociology). At the end of the nineteenth century anthropology played a part (the extent, nature and motivation of which are subject to debate) in establishing the discourse of so-called scientific racism (Stocking, 1968; Banton, 1987). Once the harmful and destructive nature of this discourse had become apparent, and social anthropology had established itself as a discipline concerned with cultural difference, the word 'race', and the implicit biological associations of the term, largely dropped out of social anthropological discourse, occurring only very occasionally as some kind of synonym for people or population.

However, for reasons that have yet to be explored in detail, a popular, non-academic discourse of ethnicity and 'culture' has developed in recent years, one which appears to draw in part on generally older and for the most part essentialist understandings in anthropology and sociology, as well as being a development of a much older popular discourse on 'race' (which of course was also informed by earlier anthropological understandings). In our opinion, it is this popular discourse, rather than recent academic discourse on these issues, that informs much journalistic writing on, for example, the role of 'ethnicity' in conflicts such as the Bosnian one. It is for this reason we have attempted above to map out some of the contours of earlier academic discourse on these issues. For the same reason, a preliminary assessment of the popular discourse must also be attempted before we go on to discuss reports of the Bosnian conflict in more detail.

The popular discourse generally conflates the terms 'race' and 'ethnicity', although sometimes a distinction is made on the basis of phenotypical difference between people. That is, where the phenotypical difference between individuals or groups is perceived to be high, then the term 'race' is deemed to be appropriate (e.g. between persons of presumed Afro-Caribbean descent and persons of presumed Anglo-Saxon descent in the UK); where the phenotypical difference is presumed to be low, then the terms 'ethnic' or 'ethnicity' (and, increasingly, 'culture') are deemed to be appropriate (e.g. between persons of presumed Irish descent and persons of presumed 'pure' British descent in the UK). Unfortunately, this is not a mere terminological matter, nor is the situation as clear-cut as the discussion of phenotypes would appear to indicate.

First, the popular discourse of ethnicity – very much unlike the current academic discourse – not only presumes an essentialism and fixity of identity and behaviour, it also shares with the older 'race' discourse upon which it builds, a sense of inevitability and a kind of biological rootedness, where description of difference all too easily slips into an explanation of difference, and where, therefore, the antagonistic expression of difference (as in 'ethnic conflict') is seen to be both inalterable and inevitable. Second, there is an unstated nexus of concepts in the popular discourse which turns on the concept of nationalism and national identity. For example, most of the geographical and nation-state labels used above ('Afro-Caribbean', 'British' and 'Irish') are used metonymically and metaphorically in popular discourse (as they can be in academic discourse) to refer to broader 'race' categories – paradigmatically, 'black' and 'white'. 'British' metonymically stands for 'white' in formulations such as 'British National Party' (just as 'national' metonymically stands for 'white' in 'National Front').

In the Bosnian context, as elsewhere in post-socialist East Central Europe, such geo-national labels have a particular salience when allied with presumed ethnic labels, as a result of the Soviet nationalities policy which was applied in the former Soviet Union and elsewhere in the region. Popular, and specifically journalistic, discourse on 'ethnicity' in the region recognizes this salience, but frequently misunderstands it, introducing a false conflation of specifically Socialist period designations of national identity with an already confused set of understandings surrounding the conflated 'race'/ethnicity category.

In Britain, the popular discourse of ethnicity seems increasingly associated with violence and disorder. In 1994 the *Guardian* newspaper carried a report of an electronic database of contemporary English created by Collins, the dictionary publisher, and Birmingham University. With reference to the database and the way language use is changing, John Sinclair, Professor of Modern English at Birmingham, was reported as saying: 'If you say someone has ethnic tendencies you are taken to mean that he is a murderer' (*Guardian*, 14 July 1994). The article makes it clear that this linkage has arisen in the context of the Bosnian conflict.

With reference to other parts of the world it is also clear that such a linkage is being made. Another newspaper article from 1989 employs the terms 'ethnic', 'communal', 'ancient communities', 'nationalist', and 'multi-racial' all in the context of unrest and bloodshed in the then Soviet Union (*Observer*, 3 September 1989). While the tone of such journalistic accounts generally tends towards a primordialist under-standing of ethnicity (that is, seeing its presence as inevitable and expressive of deep-rooted and unalterable sentiments), there is also a strand of a rationalist or instrumentalist explanation. In these accounts, the expression of ethnicity, while inevitable, none the less has some aim or purpose that can be understood by the presumably white readers of the journal who are presumed to have no ethnicity themselves. 'Ethnic' then becomes a marker of otherness and, when coupled with expres-sions of antagonism or violence, can serve to mark a border between those who have no ethnicity and who engage in conflict for presumably rational and justifiable reasons, and those who have ethnicity and engage in conflict because of irreconcilable ethnic difference.

On occasion, anthropologists have sought to counter such views. For example, in the early 1990s the anthropologist Alex de Waal, co-director of a human rights organization focusing on Africa, outlined his view of the Rwandan civil war (de Waal, 1994a, 1994b). In both pieces he decried the tendency of journalists to describe 'the current mass killing in Rwanda as the expression of age-old tribal animosities' (1994a: 1) and blamed the (German and Belgian) colonial administrations for mis-takenly transforming an occupational stratification between Hutu, Tutsi and Twa 'groups' into a distinction between separate 'tribes' or 'ethnic groups'. This reified a notion of 'racial' difference between the groups, that in the context of the war was inevitably seen by journalists to lead to conflict, bloodshed and even genocide. De Waal cites the anthropo-logist David Turton, writing about local warfare between groups in North East Africa, particularly the Mursi of Ethiopia: 'If groups such as the Mursi are treated ... as "given in nature", then the conflict which is seen to define their boundaries is also given in nature' (Turton, 1994: 20, cited in de Waal, 1994b: 3).

De Waal's comments on the Rwandan situation were interpreted by one anthropologist as 'stabbing [anthropological] colleagues in the back and implicating them ... in this genocide' (Pottier, 1994: 28). Although in fact de Waal had stated elsewhere that '[a]nthropologists and his-torians unite in deriding the descriptions of the Hutu and Tutsi as "tribes", and even as distinct "ethnic groups"' (de Waal, 1994b: 3), he partially agreed with his critic. Past anthropologists were indeed to blame for giving academic respectability to what is elsewhere known as scientific racism, and their professional descendants must share some of their sins; at the very least, argued de Waal, 'we should popularize our refutations of our ancestors' errors' (de Waal, 1994c: 28).

In a similar attempt to counter popular misconceptions, in 1993 a group of British anthropologists organized a network under the name 'The Forum Against Ethnic Violence', prompted in part by the conflict in Bosnia. In their initial statement the group argued that 'it is the responsibility of anthropologists to expose the seductive simplicities which invoke primordial loyalties to ethnic origins' and called for a 'greater public awareness of how dangerous will be the consequences of an illusory concept of ethnic or racial purity'. One member of the group, Pat Caplan, later wrote a review of a booklet on Bosnia, put together by journalists and academics to accompany a series of programmes broadcast by Channel 4 in 1993 (Caplan, 1994). In the review, Caplan repeats again the claim made by many that 'explanations' of the Bosnian conflict in the mass media tend to rest on primordialist understandings of ethnicity (Caplan, 1994: 38).

While there are exceptions (and Caplan notes that they tend to be found in the *Guardian* newspaper), this is probably a fair assessment. However, we should note that news reporting, by its very nature, tends to focus on change (good or bad, peaceful or violent, actual or anticipated). Away from the features pages and the magazine programmes, a journalist would presumably see little that was newsworthy in describing peaceful and unexceptional relations between two neighbouring 'ethnic' groups, no matter how 'age-old' their tribal or ethnic loyalties. For this reason, there tends also to be an instrumentalist strand to journalistic accounts. The As and the Bs may draw up the battle-lines between them along an 'age-old' fault-line of ethnic difference, but they are fighting for something – for territory, for jobs, even for survival.

Below, we present a more closely considered example of the popular and academic discourse on ethnicity, that surrounding a single, chilling term – 'ethnic cleansing'. In examining the journalistic discourse of ethnicity we do not wish to trivialize the pain and suffering involved in the Bosnian conflicts or in the Rwandan conflict touched on briefly above. Our aim is to highlight some of the ways in which the popular and particularly journalistic accounts of ethnicity seem to structure public knowledge and understanding, in the hope that clearer understanding may lead to easier solutions in the future.

'Ethnic cleansing'

We have seen above how the term 'ethnic', and more rarely 'ethnicity', have entered the vocabulary of everyday British English speech. One of the newspaper articles cited above made a specific link between ethnicity and violence, grounding the link to the conflict in Bosnia. The article, which reported on trends in contemporary English usage, claimed that 'the word "ethnic" is being redefined thanks to Bosnia, which means it can no longer be used for groups differentiated by race alone' (*Guardian*, 14 July 1994). Setting aside the confusion, noted above, between the terms 'race' and 'ethnic' in both popular and official discourse, the article confirms our opinion that in journalistic use at least, the term 'ethnic' was used most frequently in British English in the first half of the 1990s with regard to the Bosnian conflict. It tended to appear in phrases such as 'ethnic populations', 'ethnic characteristics', 'ethnic fights', 'ethnic segregation', and 'ethnic hatred'. But the phrase that took greatest hold and that was repeated again and again was the phrase 'ethnic cleansing'.

It is difficult to write about the Bosnian conflict, not least because at the time of writing the repercussions of the 1992–95 war still continue. From the start, there were so many shifts in the fighting, and so many twists and turns in policy (local and international) that the task of deciding which were the focal points, and which were the decisive events must be left to future historians. Similarly, the task of outlining the situation as it stands currently would need far more knowledge of the region and its history, of political science and strategic studies than we can provide. Nevertheless, it seems unlikely that any future account of the conflict could avoid reference to the policy and practice of 'ethnic cleansing'. We therefore offer some brief notes and comments on the term as it was used by the British press, in the hope of providing materials and leads for future writers.

Early on in the conflict the term 'ethnic cleansing' appeared in the British press. Among the historical connotations of the term is the Nazi-planned extermination of the Jews during the Second World War, known as *endlosung* (literally, 'final solution'). Linguistically closer is the Slav term *etnicheskoye chishcheniye* (literally, 'ethnic cleansing') which was used by the Soviet authorities to describe the Azeri efforts to drive the Armenian population away from their territory in the Nagorno-Karabakh crisis of the late 1980s. More recently, the term was used in a variety of contexts but generally served to describe the violent actions of Serb forces in their pursuit of creating 'ethnically pure' pockets of land in those areas of Bosnia-Herzegovina they claimed as Serbian. This occurred, of course, after the break-up of Tito's Federal Republic of Yugoslavia, when both Serbia and Croatia laid claims on Bosnian areas inhabited by Serbs and Croats respectively. The term does not seem to have been used in reporting of the war between Serbia and Croatia (1991–92), but surfaced in the summer of 1992 in the context of the Bosnian conflict (*Guardian*, 1 June 1992; *Independent*, 25 May 1992, *The Times*, 5 June 1992).

Although the term seems to have entered the British press vocabulary only in mid-1992, it began to lose its quotation marks a year or so later (especially when Bosnian Serb authorities were being quoted), though for the most part they were retained. It was used by the press throughout 1992 and into 1993, but by 1994 was becoming rarer (probably not so much because the actions it described were becoming rarer, but because journalistic attention had shifted to other matters).

Some journalists were opposed to the use of the phrase from the start – 'journalists should take more care before they repeat this Nazi epithet so blithely on radio or television' (*Independent*, 15 August 1992). The reference to the Nazis made here links to two historical strands from the Second World War: first, the German Nazi policy of rendering parts of the territory of the Third Reich *Judenrein* (clean or pure of Jews); second, the Croatian *Ustashe* (fascist) policy of expelling Serbs (and others) that was described as 'cleansing' (*ciscenje*) during the brief existence of the independent Croatian state under Nazi tutelage. Some journalists at least explicitly noted these antecedents (*Independent*, 27 June 1992 and 15 August 1992), and parallels were made with the Holocaust: 'Are the people of Sarajevo, like the Jews of the Warsaw ghetto, to be starved and shelled into submission while armed troops go from house to house in their chilling "ethnic cleansing" operation?' (*The Times*, 29 June 1992).

The term was widely used by the press during 1992 and was usually defined as a forcible expulsion of population (e.g. *Independent*, 22 August 1992, 28 August 1992, 29 July 1992), although some journalists attempted to examine the meaning of the words a little more closely. The 'cleansing' part was relatively easy: 'The reality behind the Serbian government's clinical phrase is that villages, suburbs or streets inhabited by ethnically "unclean" and unwelcome minorities are deliberately targeted for rocket and shellfire' (*Independent*, 27 June 1992); 'houses are empty, cleansed of their inhabitants' (*Guardian*, 21 August 1992). In fact, many people were not so much shelled out as simply ordered out, and indeed had to pay towards the cost of their own 'cleansing' by paying compulsory 'evacuation taxes' and bus fares.

Somewhat more troublesome was the 'ethnic' component. Most journalists tended to refer either to 'populations' or to a group name (Serb, Croat, Muslim) without further comment, so that 'ethnic cleansing' was a policy of 'kicking out minority populations' (*Independent*, 29 July 1992), or the 'mass expulsion of non-Serbs' (*Independent*, 12 August 1992). But some were a little more reflective: 'The callous and cynical

gratuitousness of the idea that millions of people should uproot themselves at the behest of politicians and regroup themselves under the
meaningless labels of Serbs, Croats and Muslims appalled us all' (*New
Statesman and Society*, 11 December 1992). This idea of the 'meaning-
lessness' of the labels harks back to the discussion at the start of this
chapter of the Rwandan 'ethnic groups'; the *Guardian*, for example,
declared that '[d]espite the horrible expression "ethnic cleansing" there
are no ethnic divisions among the Slavs of Yugoslavia' (12 August 1992)
and went on to claim that the inhabitants of the former state were the
same people, divided along religious and cultural lines.

The 'religious' issue is a complex one. The presence of an indigenous
Islamic minority within Europe had long been of interest to observers,
including some early ethnographers (see, for example, Evans, 1877;
Lodge, 1941: Chapter 7; for a far more recent and anthropologically
sensitive account, see Bringa, 1995). Although a religious division between the Orthodox Serbs and Catholic Croats had occasionally been
noted during the Serbian–Croatian war of the early 1990s, for largely
Protestant Britain this was a rather flimsy and minor distinction, despite
the parallels with Ireland. By contrast, the otherness of Islam, particularly in the aftermath of the Iranian Revolution, the Gulf War, and
the *Satanic Verses* controversy, created a strange and paradoxical focal
point. On the one hand, the Bosnian Muslims were Muslims – if of an
apparently rather secular sort – and therefore would normally be placed
in a 'feared other' category. On the other hand, they were also clearly
the underdogs, the victims of 'ethnic cleansing', not its perpetrators
(despite an early claim to the contrary by Franjo Tudjman, the Croatian
President – *Independent*, 29 July 1992).

Ernest Gellner, writing some years before the Bosnian conflict, out-
lines the 'transition from faith to culture' experienced by the Bosnian
Muslims under Tito. That is, a confessional identity was transformed
under Soviet-style nationality policy not merely into an ethnic identity
but into a legally and constitutionally recognized 'national' identity. As
Gellner goes on to note: '[They] secured at long last the right to describe
themselves as Muslim, when filling in the "nationality" slot on the
census. This did not mean that they were still believing and practising
Muslims ... identifying as one nationality with other Muslims ... They
were Serbo-Croat speakers of Slav ancestry and Muslim cultural background ... [and] thereby Bosnian, Slav ex-Muslims who feel as one
ethnic group' (Gellner, 1983: 71–2). Gellner is clear that this 'Muslim'
identity was an oppositional one, one that was understood and experienced as meaning not-Serb or not-Croat as much as a thing in itself.

The claim of the *Guardian* that there are no 'ethnic groups' in the former Yugoslavia, merely cultural divisions, is perhaps partially correct as far as ethnicity is concerned, but ignores the whole issue of nationality politics in the former Yugoslavia and elsewhere in the former Soviet Union and East Central Europe. '[M]erely cultural divisions' seems to indicate the familiar conflation of popular understandings of race and ethnicity. The *Guardian* writer seems to feel that religion and 'culture' are both transient ephemeral things, not worthy of being deemed 'ethnic'. Ethnicity then is clearly about rootedness, permanence and clear-cut categories (although even at the time 'culture' was becoming popular as a synonym for 'ethnicity' in certain contexts – see Banks, 1996: 17–48; and Dresch, 1995).

This perspective on the solidity of ethnicity is apparent in much of the press reporting of 'ethnic cleansing' in Bosnia. It was reported, for example, that the policy was enforced 'to create ethnically pure regions' (*Independent*, 29 July 1992), as though this were a straightforward task, however distasteful. As the normalcy of the idea of unambiguous ethnic difference resulting in unambiguous groups became established, so too the term itself became normalized. Journalists ceased to define it and used it as a label without comment, like the name of a disease or an item in a catalogue of disaster. *New Statesman and Society* informed its readers that '[our] commitment must be to the civilian population of Bosnia suffering daily bombardment, ethnic cleansing, starvation, hypothermia and God knows what else' (23 October 1992).

Some journalists elevated 'ethnic cleansing' to the top of the list of privations by identifying it as a central goal of the Bosnian Serb war effort – it was the '*subject matter*, not a side-effect of the war' (Vulliamy, 1994: 96, emphasis in original). Others disagreed that it was necessarily the original aim, but implied that an inexorable logic made it so as the war progressed. Misha Glenny, for example, a journalist with extensive experience of East Central Europe and who produced a book on the war, comments: 'Initially, "cleansing" is a military tactic which is mistaken for the central war aim because it is executed in such a horrifying fashion. Of course, as the war continues ... the idea of including a minority population in the conquered territory becomes less acceptable as the doctrine of "national purity" strengthens' (Glenny, 1992: 187). Glenny's use of the ironic 'of course' and his placing of 'national purity' in inverted commas indicate that he is sceptical of any naturalism implied in this process. His comment also reveals again the mixed strands of primordialist and instrumentalist approaches in journalistic discourse on ethnicity.

Even if the ethnicity of 'Serbs', 'Croats' and 'Muslims' was assumed to be perduring, obvious and a natural focus for group division, it was also thought to be expressed for a purpose, for some reason. The reason given in the accounts was almost always territorial gain, but the journalists seemed to be assuming an underlying logic of nationalism. As other authors have commented (Anderson, 1983; Gellner, 1983; Eriksen, 1993: Chapter 6; Banks, 1996: Chapter 5) successful nationalisms must always lay claim to territory, and strive for a congruence of the political, the national and the territorial. This assumption is reflected by most journalists writing about the Bosnian conflict, revealed by the fact that the terms 'ethnic cleansing' and 'national[ity]' frequently occur together in their writing, perhaps aided by the terminology of the former Yugoslavian state which, like the Soviet Union, employed the notion of 'national' (*nacija*) populations. However, there is a category error at work, by which journalists seem to assume that the bureaucratic category of 'national' populations in countries such as the former Yugoslavia is equivalent to the historically evolved nationalist conscious-ness which led to the nationalist consolidation of the European nation states in the eighteenth and nineteenth centuries. 'Nationality' in countries such as the Soviet Union and the former Yugoslavia was an imposed administrative category (rather than necessarily the product of any 'nationalist' feeling) and always had to be seen in the context of any overarching responsibilities the members of such populations might have had as citizens within the wider state.

The term 'ethnic cleansing' was employed by all parties in the Bosnian conflict, and reported as such by the media. It progressed from being a shocking new term requiring a definition, to being an accepted fact. Journalistic explanation of the Bosnian conflict was largely in terms of shifts and changes of local and international policy, with an occasionally expressed historical 'explanation' that the roots of the conflict lie in the Second World War. The first reports of ethnic cleansing were from the Banja region in north-western Bosnia, the area that had suffered ap-parently similar atrocities in the Second World War. The aggressors at that time were the Croats, and their victims were Serbs, Jews, Gypsies and Muslims. On the whole, however, the term tended to provide its own explanation by resting on largely primordialist understandings of ethnicity. As an item in journalistic discourse, the term also began to spread away from its initial use in the Bosnian context, to be applied to other, apparently similar conflicts: 'Talk of ethnic cleansing is growing louder as another Balkan feud unfolds [in southern Albania], this time pitting Muslims against Orthodox Christians' (*Guardian*, 8 June 1994).

Conclusion

We are not in a position to 'explain' the Bosnian conflict, nor even to offer any firm clues as to why 'ethnic' became a key term in the reporting of that conflict. We would note, however, that a number of strands came together in the 1990s that made it a handy term, in which description could stand for explanation. Those strands include policy decisions in the former Socialist states of East Central Europe (informed in part by academics) to administer culturally heterogeneous populations, a terminological confusion surrounding the relevant terms in Slavic languages (such as the Russian *natsional'nost'*, or Serbo-Croat *nacionalnost*), a rise in the use of the term 'ethnic' more generally in British and American English, and a general conflation of 'race', 'ethnic', and 'blood' in the popular imagination which can, in part, be traced back to the scientific racism of Victorian anthropology.

What we can say is that in non-academic, mainly journalistic, discourse, ethnicity – defined as a fixed, inalterable and inevitable identity – became increasingly interpreted as a destructive social force. Having looked at the use by the media of a particularly salient term – 'ethnic cleansing' – in the context of the Bosnian War, we will now briefly cast our eye over the evolution of the same term in the aftermath of the war, while the country struggled with a difficult peace.

The Dayton Peace Agreement for Bosnia was signed, under great political pressure, in December 1995, after 44 months of war. By this time, statistics showed, well over two million people had been displaced within Bosnia or were refugees beyond its borders (UN figures, cited in Peace Net, n.d.) and more than 50% of its Muslim inhabitants had been expelled from their homes. It is hardly surprising, under these circumstances, that the return of refugees would pose a great challenge to the frail peace in Bosnia, not surprising at all that by mid-1997, almost two years later, the issue was still far from resolved. The Accord has come under almost constant attack from politicians, journalists and academics alike, its shortcomings deplored, its confusing sections highlighted and endlessly reinterpreted.

The Dayton Accord was 'guarding ethnic cleansing rather than ensuring refugee return' according to a television news report ('Channel 4 News', 4 August 1997), voicing the most common charge. The report went on to note that ethnic distinction, which had so far been used as a justification, explanation, motive, motto and motor of warfare, had now permeated the same peace accords that sought to put an end to it and show the way forward to a multi-ethnic, pluralistic and democratic society. In the more specialized context of our research, the report shows that 'ethnic cleansing' is still in the headlines, continuing its destructive journey, this time with the indirect effect of blocking the frail peace imposed by great political pressure. Our research shows that the term 'ethnic' (with its more or less grisly derivatives), previously used by the press as a key to understanding the Bosnian conflict, was becoming used to explain the failure of the peace process.

In an analysis of the printed press between 1995 and 1997, it is evident that while Bosnia was less and less frequently the lead story, the term 'ethnic cleansing' still clung to the journalist's pen every time he or she reported from that part of the world. Journalists – and consequently readers too – seem to be more comfortable using, and reading, the term. Its semantic boundaries were challenged regularly, and its grammatical usage became increasingly liberal. From *Time* magazine alone since 1995, we find ethnic cleansing described as a process, campaign, practice, incident, agent, state policy, or simply, as an independent phenomenon (not accompanied by any explanatory noun) (*Time*, 11 March 1996, 23 September 1996, 3 February 1997, 19 May 1997, 21 July 1997). Moreover, in 1997 ethnic cleansing became a recognized legal offence when the war tribunal in The Hague delivered its first verdict against an accused Bosnian Serb war criminal. Ethnic cleansing was for the first time defined beyond newspaper pages and into legal tomes as 'a widespread and systematic attack on the civilian population' (*Observer*, 11 May 1997).

Daring grammatical usage ranged from the definite article – 'they engineered the ethnic cleansing of ...' (*Time*, 3 February 1997) – to the plural – 'witnesses at the ethnic *cleansings* of several towns ...; he had knowledge of these ethnic *cleansings*' (*Time*, 3 February 1997) – and from the past participle used as an adjective – 'camp survivors and *"cleansed"* Muslims' (*Observer*, 11 May 1997) – to the agent suffix 'er' – ' ... were among the worst of Bosnia's ethnic *cleansers*' (*Time*, 21 July 1997), 'Croat *cleansers*' (*Time*, 11 March 1996).

Popular understandings of the term continued to fuse the concepts of race and ethnicity into a simplistic, essentialist, all-encompassing discourse: '"Momo" ... seems an unlikely exemplar of ethnic hatred. Born just outside Sarajevo, into a well-off farming family, "he wasn't at all a racist" as a youth, recalls Kemo Mulic ...' (*Time*, 23 September 1996). Similarly, the links with the Holocaust and the Nazis' 'final solution' continued to be raised in journalistic accounts: 'this hurricane of violence was a racial pogrom initiated by the Serbs and by them alone, in pursuit of an ethnically "pure" Greater Serbia' (*Time*, 11 May 1997).

'Ethnic cleansing' also hit the Internet, discussed in the USENET newsgroups, and the subject of many World Wide Web sites. An online text and photographic exhibition, 'Faces of Sorrow: Agony in the Former Yugoslavia' from Photo Perspectives, New York, offered a comprehensive definition:

> Ethnic cleansing is warfare against civilians identified as targets solely because of their nationality or religion. Civilians are harassed and intimidated, their property confiscated, and their jobs eliminated. They are driven from their villages and forced to cross battle lines. The chief technique of ethnic cleansing is terror, and the means chosen include mass murder, torture, pillage, abuse in detention, rape, castration and other forms of violence. (Photo Perspectives, 1996)

The Internet has been used by all sides in the conflict: a user of the 'Serbian Unity Congress' Web site, for example, supplied statistics as unquestionable proof of the completed 'cleansing' of the Serbian population of Bosnia: 'Mostar 1991 – 20,000; Mostar today [February 1996] – 1,000 … In total around 300,000 Bosnian-Serbs have been displaced by "ethnic cleansing"' (Serbian Unity Congress, 1996). The Internet is particularly well suited to the dissemination of news reports, official (and unofficial) statistics, and opinion pieces by exiled and diaspora members of groups involved in 'ethnic' conflicts. The medium nevertheless perpetuates the essentialized and static understandings of ethnicity discussed earlier in this chapter.

In conclusion, then, we have seen how political agendas, violence and warfare have created and perpetuated dangerous stereotypes based on the notion of ethnicity – ethnic identity, ethnic differentiation, ethnic hatred. Before Dayton, these fuelled the war; after Dayton, they have been obstructing the peace. The war seems to have polarized all political life in Bosnia along ethnic lines – the main political parties base their appeal and electoral success on ethnic ideologies, while independent, multi-ethnic opposition parties were pushed in the background of political life if they survived at all (US Government, 1995). In this context, the peace accords, unable to break away from the pattern, seem to have consolidated ethnicity as the organizing principle of Bosnia's political structures. 'Ethnic incompatibility' suggests itself as the next in the line of hostile stereotypes – used to explain inaction and failure on the road to peace.

References

Anderson, Benedict (1983) *Imagined Communities: Reflections on the Origins and Spread of Nationalism,* London: Verso.

Banks, Marcus (1996) *Ethnicity: Anthropological Constructions*, London: Routledge.

Banton, Michael (1987) *Racial Theories*, Cambridge: Cambridge University Press.

Barth, Frederik (1969) 'Introduction', in Frederik Barth (ed.), *Ethnic Groups and Boundaries: The Social Organisation of Culture Difference*, Bergen/London: Universitets Forlaget/George Allen and Unwin.

Bringa, Tone (1995) *Being Muslim the Bosnian Way: Identity and Community in a Central Bosnian Village*, Princeton, NJ: Princeton University Press.

Caplan, Pat (1994) 'Review of: Bloody Bosnia: A European Tragedy (Channel 4 Television and the *Guardian* publication)', *Anthropology in Action*, Vol. 1, No. 1, pp. 38–9.

Comaroff, John and Comaroff, Jean (1992) 'Of Totemism and Ethnicity', in John Comaroff and Jean Comaroff (eds), *Ethnography and the Historical Imagination*, Boulder, CO: Westview Press.

de Waal, Alex (1994a) 'Genocide in Rwanda (Editorial)', *Anthropology Today*, Vol. 10, No. 3, pp. 1–2.

— (1994b) 'The Genocidal State: Hutu Extremism and the Origins of the "Final Solution" in Rwanda', *Times Literary Supplement*, 1 July 1994, pp. 3–4.

— (1994c) 'Letter: Genocide in Rwanda', *Anthropology Today*, Vol. 10, No. 4, pp. 28–9.

Dresch, Paul (1995) 'Race, Culture and – What?: Pluralist Certainties in the United States', in Wendy James (ed.), *The Pursuit of Certainty*, London: Routledge.

Eriksen, Thomas Hylland (1993) *Ethnicity and Nationalism: Anthropological Perspectives*, London: Pluto Press.

Evans, Arthur J. (1877) *Through Bosnia and Herzegovina on Foot, During the Insurrection, August and September 1875, and a Glimpse at the Croats, Slavonians, and the Ancient Republic of Ragusa*, London: Longmans, Green, and Co.

Gellner, Ernest (1983) *Nations and Nationalism*, Oxford: Blackwell.

Glenny, Misha (1992) *The Fall of Yugoslavia: The Third Balkan War*, London: Harmondsworth.

Lodge, Olive (1941[?]) *Peasant Life in Jugoslavia*, London: Seeley, Service and Co.

Peace Net (n.d.) 'Refugees and Beneficiaries of UN Humanitarian Aid in the Former Yugoslavia'. *WWW document*, Peace Net, Institute for Global Communications, Palo Alto, CA [http://www.peacenet.org/balkans/refugees.html].

Photo Perspectives (1996) 'Faces of Sorrow', *WWW document*, Photo Perspectives, New York [http://www.i3tele.com/photoperspectives/facesof sorrow/html/exhibition.html].

Pottier, Johan (1994) 'Letter: Genocide in Rwanda', *Anthropology Today*, Vol. 10, No. 4, p. 28.

Serbian Unity Congress (1996) 'Mess in the Bosnia and Herzegovina: Ethnic Cleansing against Bosnian Serbs in Bosnia and Herzegovina Contrasted with the Census of 1991', *WWW document*, Serbian Unity Congress, Napa, CA [http://suc.suc.org/~kosta/tar/bosna/b-INDEX.html].

Stocking, George W. (1968) *Race, Culture, and Evolution: Essays in the History of Anthropology*, New York: The Free Press.

Turton, David (1994) 'Mursi Political Identity and Warfare: the Survival of an Idea', in Katsuyoshi Fukui and John Markakis (eds), *Ethnicity and Conflict in the Horn of Africa*, London/Athens, OH: James Currey/Ohio University Press.

US Government (1995) *Office of Transitions Initiatives Report*, April, Washington, DC.

Vulliamy, Ed (1994) *Seasons in Hell: Understanding Bosnia's War*, London: Simon and Schuster.

CHAPTER 8

Culture, Media and the Politics of Disintegration and Ethnic Division in Former Yugoslavia

Spyros A. Sofos

Nationhood exists as a system of cultural signification. The discourse of nationhood and that of ethnicity, or, the imagining of communities, as Benedict Anderson has so aptly put it, comprises 'processes, categories and knowledges through which communities are defined as such: that is how they are rendered specific and differentiated'.[1] Historically, mass communication has played a crucial role in these processes of imagination of national communities. It has enabled the formation and maintenance of public spheres roughly coextensive to modern nations and been central in the homogenization and creation of national cultures and identities. The role of mass communication in these processes of imagination has been complex. It ranged from constituting frames of shared interpretation, public debate and collective action, to standardizing cultural resources and publicizing definitions of the situation which reified and naturalized national communities. However, the contribution of mass communication to the *construction* or *imagination* of national communities has also another, negative, aspect – that of *destruction* and *oblivion* of alternative frames of interpretation, debate and action and of alternative versions of community.

Yugoslavia, thought to have been a relatively successful example of forging such links, enabling coexistence and constructing a civic community, has turned out to be a rather more painful example of the volatility of the notion of community and of the malleability of nationhood. Its undoing has been inextricably linked to the fragmentation of the sphere of public debate and the processes of mass communication that could sustain it.

The establishment of the People's Federal Republic of Yugoslavia after the Second World War was an ambitious but precarious political project. Even before the end of the war, the leadership of the Communist Party of Yugoslavia (CPY) had realized that the success of a post-war Yugoslavia depended upon its ability to deal with the politics of ethnicity which had been unleashed in the inter-war period and exacerbated during the occupation of the country by the Axis powers, and to invent a collective imaginary – a version of Yugoslavism that would be sustained by a social contract that would achieve the economic development of a destroyed and differentially developed country and sustain economic and social progress and a vision for the future.

Post-war Yugoslavia was premised on the principle of federalism within the context of a supra-national Yugoslav socialist order. Although political power resided with the CPY, the republics were endowed with their own republican administrative – and later, political – and cultural institutions and were allowed to promote the distinct identities of the nations they were supposed to be 'homelands' of within the limits, however, of the official policy of *bratstvo i jedinstvo* (brotherhood and unity). In this sense, post-war Yugoslavism was developed not as antagonistic, but rather as complementary to the other identities of former Yugoslavia, as a form of civic-socialist identity. During the first two decades of post-war Yugoslavia, however, the regime attempted to stress similarities and to suppress divisive factors among the South Slav ethnic groups. Efforts to reinforce Yugoslav unity were officially sponsored: such as the official sanctioning of the 1954 Novi Sad declaration of Croat, Montenegrin and Serb linguists, regarding the 'oneness' of the Serbo-Croat language, the promotion of official versions of 'Marxist' Yugoslav history and the support of attempts to establish a Yugoslav 'cultural space', especially in the sphere of high culture.

However, these attempts were largely confined to the relatively small milieu of the urban intelligentsia and the 'Yugoslav cultural space' did not lead to the formation of an all-Yugoslav public sphere. What is more, the inability of Yugoslavia to resolve the problem of an increasingly unequal differential development between the republics[2] and to cushion the economy from the effects of the international economic crisis of the early 1970s threatened to undermine the post-war social contract and clearly marked the beginning of the end of the Yugoslav project.

As early as the late 1960s, a mixture of discontent with the economic situation and awakening nationalism gave rise to a chain of political protest.[3] Despite the crackdown on the protest movements, the regime sanctioned many of their demands, changing radically the centre/republic balance of power within the federation. The 1974 constitution endowed republics with extensive economic and political powers and virtual sovereignty, upgraded autonomous provinces to almost equal status to the republics and left limited powers to the federal authorities. The post-1974 Yugoslavia was premised on the recognition of the so-called 'constitutive nations' of the federation as holders of supreme power; whereas the federation retained nominal sovereignty, the republics were increasingly perceived as quasi-nation states and republican and, by extension, ethnic and national identities were *reified* and *naturalized* at the expense of other social and political identities which remained suppressed, or at least excluded from the universe of political debate.

The post-1974 period also saw the progressive 'confederalization' of most federation-wide organizations, in a way shadowing the confederalization of the country. This process did not leave the media unaffected. As political, economic and cultural powers resided with the republics and provinces, commercial, cultural institutions and the mass media became primarily or entirely 'republican' as far as their control and framework of reference were concerned. Virtually each republic and province, despite the pluri-cultural and multi-ethnic composition of Yugoslavia's constituent units, progressively provided a framework for the promotion of the national identity and attainment of sovereignty of a specific ethnic group, facilitating in this way the fragmentation of the already precarious Yugoslav public sphere.

The 'public sphere' of socialist Yugoslavia was, even before the 1974 constitution, segmented along republic borders. Despite its name, Yugoslav Radio-Television was not a really 'Yugoslav' (federation-wide) institution. It had progressively become an effectively coordinating network of republic broadcasting organizations – each of the republics and autonomous provinces had its own broadcasting system and its own press with at least one daily newspaper as its official or semi-official publication.

Yugoslavia's artificial and arbitrary internal, administrative borders were progressively 'upgraded' to national or 'civilizational' fault-lines[4] and increasingly to communications barriers. However, it was in the 1980s, after the death of the Yugoslav leader, Josip Broz Tito, one of the last factors of cohesion within Yugoslavia, that the weakening of the already loose ties among federal units and their institutions reached its climax and the official discourse and system started to break down. The political vacuum created by Tito's death and the struggle for power and legitimation that ensued at the federal and republic levels, set in motion the process of disintegration of the Federation as a result of the intensification of the 'ethnicization' or 'nationalization' of its constituent units and their institutions. By the late 1980s the federal authorities were well in the process of becoming mere caretakers of a transitory political structure, while the republics were being transformed into nation states.[5] Slovene and Croat communists – the Party of Democratic Renewal, and the Party of Social Reform as they had been renamed – paid the price of their reluctance to confront Milosevic's constitutional coups by losing, in the first multi-party elections in their republics, to more uncompromising nationalists untarnished by participation in the federal government. In the same year, the Serbian Socialist Party (SPS, formed by the Serbian Communist Party and the Socialist Alliance) won 40% of the votes and 77.6% of the parliamentary seats, while its leader, Slobodan Milosevic, received two-thirds of the votes in the second round of the presidential election. What is more, his Montenegrin allies, the League of Communists of Montenegro, won an impressive 66.4% of the legislature seats and its leader, Momir Bulatovic, became president of the republic. In Macedonia, despite a majority electoral system during the elections of 1989, a hung parliament led to the formation of a coalition government of communists, Macedonian and Albanian nationalists, and the election of the reform communist Kiro Gligorov as president. In Bosnia-Herzegovina, the legalization of multi-party competition led to the formation of ethnic parties – Muslim (Party of Democratic Action – SDA and the more secular Muslim Bosniak Organization – MBO), Serbian (Serbian Democratic Party – SDS), and Croat (the Bosnian branch of the Zagreb-based party of Franjo Tudjman, Croatian Democratic Community – HDZ) which defeated the communists and federalists in the 1990 elections. The three ethnic parties formed a shortlived coalition government, before the outbreak of the war in March 1992.

Republics increasingly behaved as sovereign states by concluding international agreements, seeking credit in the international markets and by opening diplomatic representations abroad; at the same time, they became more introspective. What is certain is that interaction at the economic and cultural level among members of the Federation decreased rapidly. By the late 1980s intra-republic communications and commercial transactions had grown disproportionally to inter-republic ones. In addition, the educational system increasingly became fragmented and by the mid-1980s it could be argued that there were effectively eight distinct curricula for primary education in different republics and provinces of Yugoslavia. In this process, the mass media played a very significant role by actively supporting, publicizing and amplifying nationalist definitions of the situation and by demarcating national and ethnic boundaries in the social imaginaries of the post-Yugoslav order.[6]

As the political climate changed and the political elites of former Yugoslavia realized the political capital that an alliance with the nationalist movements could generate, control over the media became the apple of discord between those who chose nationalism as their preferred political idiom and those who, for reasons varying from an adherence to Yugoslavia and its civic connotations to retaining political control, elected to follow the increasingly unpopular route of resistance to nationalism. From the early 1980s, Serbian nationalist intellectuals like Dobrica Cosic were acquiring unusual prominence in the public sphere of Serbia and among Serbs living in other republics and in the diaspora, and the authorities, despite occasional criticisms against them for their tolerance of 'petit-bourgeois nationalism' seemed to be unwilling to suppress the nationalist voices. Similarly, however, nationalist voices were increasingly heard and treated as legitimate in other parts of Yugoslavia. In February 1987, the Slovenian cultural review *Nova Revija* (*New Review*) published a controversial issue focusing on aspects of Slovenian nationhood, distinctiveness and need for sovereignty, while other newspapers and magazines throughout Yugoslavia increasingly accepted the legitimacy and desirability of reports which emphasized ethnic difference and, more importantly, antagonism, although not necessary in an anti-Yugoslav context.[7] As republic leaderships slowly moved towards permitting multi-party elections in the late 1980s, the assertion of national identity, often articulated to nationalist discourses, became more common and a legitimate feature of public debate and media coverage.

I will focus here on two significant areas in which mass communication has been central in the maintenance and spread of nationalism in former Yugoslavia: the performance of *public rituals* and the formation of *moral panics*.

Public rituals

The centrality of the concept of *ritual* in social anthropological research has associated rituals with non-urban and non-industrial societies. Rituals have been seen as belonging to the realm of the sacred and therefore as alien to more 'secular' societies. Recently, however, there have been attempts to introduce the concept of ritual into the study of industrialized and secular societies in general and to the area of mass communications in particular. Philip Elliott's treatment of press performance as 'political ritual' constituted one of the first attempts to operationalize the concept in mass communications research. According to Elliott, ritual should be seen as 'Rule-governed activity of a symbolic character involving mystical notions which draw the attention of participants to objects of thought or feeling which the leadership of the society or group hold to be of special significance'.[8] He went on by stressing the role rituals play in the forging of the unity of a collectivity by inviting subordinate social groups to participate emotionally in the reaffirmation of a collective identity. I will here stress the elements of this definition that I consider to be of importance in attempting to examine the relationship between mass communications, public rituals and nationalism:

1. The affirmation or imagination of community among participants.
2. The element of 'negotiation' in ritual performance: rituals are not simply offering ready-made definitions of collective or national identity; they often draw on customary, familiar, traditional cultural elements in order to invite subordinate social groups to participate.
3. The element of 'emotional' (i.e. non-rational) participation. In particular, Elliott argued that '[ritual] tries to add spiritual, and emotional communion to any sense of political unity ...'.[9]

The rituals examined here are of national regeneration which took place throughout the republics of former Yugoslavia, but especially in Serbia during the late 1980s. These include two sets of officially sanctioned 'national' rituals organized by the Serbian Orthodox Church: mass baptisms of Serbs and Montenegrins in Kosovo Polje, and the 'procession' of the alleged remnants of Prince Lazar through Serb-populated villages and monasteries, from Croatia, through Bosnia-Herzegovina to Kosovo Polje (1988–89) where they were eventually reinterred after a public funeral ceremony.

Both rituals were represented by Serbian media as confirmation of the will of the Serb nation to restore and reclaim its 'dignity' and 'rights' which, according to Serbian nationalists, had been undermined by successive conquerors of the area and former Yugoslavia. The mass baptisms of Serbs in Kosovo, as well as the return of Prince Lazar's relics to Kosovo, in fact constituted meaning-creating or, more precisely, nation-instituting rituals. The former were effectively *pilgrimages* whereas the latter had an effect somewhat similar to those that Turner associates to *pilgrimage*.[10] Unlike pilgrimages, however, in this case it was not travelling to, or coexistence at, a given sacred or administrative centre that constituted the main meaning-creating experience; it was the route of the procession that demarcated the 'territories of the Serbian nation' and brought together Serbs from Serbia proper and those areas within different republics and provinces of former Yugoslavia. An important aspect of both types of ritual is their emphasis to 'cultural regeneration'. However, the centrality of Prince Lazar's remnants (bones) in the latter ritual affirms the cultural/spiritual as well as physical/biological endurance of the national community as, in the Christian-Orthodox tradition, relics of saintly figures (and Prince Lazar has been considered to be such a figure) have a spiritual value.

Although these events constitute rituals in their own right, it could be argued that their televising by Serbian Radio-Television (RTS) altered their character and significance. In both cases, sacred rituals were transformed into televised performances. Televising affected the mode of participation in these rituals; in fact, it produced new rituals of a different order. In the original ritual physical presence is a necessary precondition for participation and the meaning-creating experiences this participation entails are restricted to those who are present in the specific locus where the ritual is performed. However, the televised version rendered physical presence unnecessary and provided a common, shared (among the viewers), imagined 'locus' and time in which the existence of the national community could be reaffirmed. More importantly, these rituals, in their televised form, transcended their 'local' character and played a significant part in the maintenance of a nationalist geography, reaffirming the bonds between Serbia proper and geographically remote territories inhabited by Serbs (Herzegovina or the Krajina), or 'spiritually' Serbian territories inhabited by non-Serbs (Kosovo). In addition, the link between areas that can be considered as *liminally* Serbian, to Serbia proper, was generalized. These televised public rituals brought home to the Serbian viewers a sense of societal insecurity premised on the perceived danger faced by the Serbian nation. It is to the nationalist definitions of the Serbian nation as a *community under threat* that I will now turn by examining the role of moral panics in the forging of a particular version of national identity among Serbs.

Mass media, moral panics and populist definitions of community

The Serbian media were central in the process of defining the Serbian nation as a community under threat in a variety of ways. Throughout the 1980s, but especially since late 1987, Serbian state- and Church-controlled media published and broadcast materials which stressed 'the victimization of Serbs in Yugoslavia' and 'the danger faced by the Serbian nation if the Federation continued to ignore its plight'. By focusing on, and promoting, specific interpretations of the systematic wartime persecution of Croatian and Bosnian Serbs by the Croatian *Ustashe* (and of other similar historical experiences) as 'genocide', state-controlled media transposed these historically specific instances of persecution to the present and attempted to (re)construct nationalist versions of history marked by the continuous subjection to 'genocide' and 'suffering' of the Serbian nation by numerous enemies. The year 1987 marked the beginning of an intensive process of identification of enemies of Serbia and the threats they represented. The press featured articles in which Albanians, Croats, Slovenes, Muslims, the Vatican and the USA were identified, individually or in various combinations, as mortal enemies of the Serbian nation. Serbian Radio-Television soon followed suit. This process of selection, stereotyping and demonization of 'enemies' and the societal reaction it entailed could be analysed as a *moral panic*. Stanley Cohen defines *moral panic* as a process whereby

> [a] condition, episode, person or group of persons emerges to become defined as a threat to societal values and interests; its nature is presented in a stylized and stereotypical fashion by the mass media; the moral barricades are manned by editors, bishops, politicians and other right-thinking people; socially accredited experts pronounce their diagnoses and solutions; ways of coping are evolved or (more often) resorted to ... Sometimes the panic passes over and is forgotten, except in folklore and collective memory; at other times it has more serious and long-lasting repercussions and might produce such changes as those in legal or social policy or even in the way society conceives itself.[11]

Although Cohen's definition refers to the study of societal reaction to (mainly youth) deviance, it seems to me that the concept of moral panic can be fruitfully used in the study of mobilization of nationalist movements in general and of the Serbian nationalist movement in the mid- and late 1980s in particular. Here, I shall focus on the emergence and eventual predominance of the issue of the 'Albanization' of Kosovo in the public debate during this period.

Serbs consider Kosovo to have been the spiritual cradle of Serbian Christendom, the centre of the medieval Serbian Empire which was eventually destroyed by the Ottoman conquest of the Balkans. The modern Serbian nation-building project was premised on the promotion of a collective memory associated with the sanctity of Kosovo, and the significance of the Serbian sacrifice there. A collective memory of the battle survived in local oral tradition and folk songs, while the Serbian Orthodox Church invested the defeat and death of Prince Lazar with a mystical dimension. Such is the power of the history and mythology of Kosovo that the head of the Association of Serb Writers, Matija Beckovic, stated that Kosovo would be Serbian even if not a single Serb lived there, while in 1986, members of the Serbian Academy of Sciences, in their *Memorandum*, presented the situation in Kosovo as equivalent to a national defeat. Although in modern-day Kosovo the Albanian population outnumbers the Serbs and Montenegrins nine to one, the province still occupies a central position among the markers and symbols of Serbian identity.

The campaign against the 'Albanization' of the province started in 1987, shortly after the leader of the Serbian League of Communists, Slobodan Milosevic, while visiting Kosovo, pledged to protect the members of the Serbian and Montenegrin minority of the province from 'persecution by the Albanian majority'. Realizing the power of nationalism, he put himself in the centre of the emerging nationalist movement by adopting a nationalist rhetoric, allying himself with the Serbian Orthodox Church, and mobilizing aspects of folk and popular culture.[12] In addition, he used a variety of elements of popular concern, such as the ever-widening perception that Yugoslavia was undermining 'Serbian rights' or the emotional ties of Serbs with Kosovo. In this climate of antagonism between Serbs and Albanians, the nationalist movement and the Serbian mass media initiated a process of scapegoating Kosovo Albanians. Although anti-Albanian prejudice was not an invention of the time (narratives of antagonism between Serbs and Albanians and suspicion have been deeply embedded in Serb folk and popular culture and memory), never before had the Serbian nationalist movement enjoyed virtually unimpeded access to the mass media of the Republic of Serbia with the approval of the leadership of the Republic.

Politika, a major Belgrade newspaper group, which published the semi-official, republic-controlled and influential dailies *Politika* and *Politika Ekspres*, set the example by publishing news, reports of rumours and historical accounts of the 'suffering' and 'glory' of the Serbian nation. Soon, however, its example was followed by the government-controlled Serbian Radio-Television (RTS), the weekly *Duga* and the daily *Vecernje Novosti*. These media increasingly relied on ultra-nationalist definitions and interpretations of the situation regarding the Kosovo issue and events in the province. In addition, in this context, 'rumours' acquired significant news value and were often treated as 'facts' that needed no further investigation. Thus, Albanians were often described as primitive, backward, illiterate,[13] and were implicated in thefts, robberies, murders and rapes that took place, or were rumoured to have taken place, in Kosovo. Allegations of Albanian criminality became a permanent or recurrent theme of news reports from the province and triggered a series of responses by political, religious and cultural leaders as well as the public.

However, what is significant in Serbian media representations of the Albanians and in the societal response to them is the convergence of hitherto unorganized prejudice, stereotypes, allegations, rumours and testimonies, and their articulation into an aggressive populist discourse. This discourse posited the relationship between Kosovo Albanians and the Serbian nation in terms of an irreconcilable opposition. In the context of the moral panic about the 'Albanization' of Kosovo, therefore, alleged Albanian criminality was not important *per se*; it was seen as merely a part of a broader Albanian 'conspiracy' to drive Serbs and Montenegrins out of Kosovo and to erase any signs or memories of their presence there, as proof of the total opposition between Serbs and Albanians.

One of the most decisive moments in the development of this moral panic came when cases and rumours of rape of Serbian women by Albanians were taken up and exploited by the media. Although the theme of rape was by no means new – as early as 1981 Serbian clergy accused Albanian Kosovars of having raped Serbian nuns[14] – in the mid-1980s allegations of rape of Serbian women by Albanian males increased considerably.[15] The traditional reluctance of the local Serbian and Montenegrin population to acknowledge publicly cases of rape gave way during the mid-1980s to a series of allegations of rape or sexual assault of Serbian or Montenegrin women perpetrated by Albanians. The local committees of Serbs and Montenegrins, nationalist circles in Serbia, the Serbian Orthodox Church and the media drew upon these allegations and rumours of the increasing incidence of rape and produced definitions of the situation in which these rapes were considered to be premeditated attacks against the Kosovo Serbs and, by extension, the Serbian nation.

In this context, the printed and, a little later, broadcasting media interpreted the situation in Kosovo as *genocide* against the Serbian people. A central narrative of Serbian nationalism, that of the nation under threat, was therefore supported by the redefinition of rape as a weapon used in the ethnic conflict between Albanians and Serbs. Of course, rape is a well-documented weapon of war, and one which the Serbs themselves have allegedly used. However, its use may have been legitimized by the elaboration of Serbian martyrdom. From then on, in media and political discourse, rape victims were redefined as *Serbs* at the expense of their individual and collective identities as *women*; they were often referred to or visually represented as *Serbian mothers* or *wives* – their prescribed roles of actual or potential reproducers of the nation, as instrumental to the preservation of the patriline – while the alleged perpetrators were primarily recognized as *Albanians*. As a result, public interest was directed not towards the individual cases of rape but towards the 'rape of the nation by Albanians'.[16] Thus, in the context of the political antagonism in Kosovo, in the popular imagination, women became symbols and property of the national community, markers of national identity, and their violation was transformed into an act of ethnic violence. On the other hand, the Albanians assumed the role of the rapists of these women, hence of the Serbian culture and national identity.

The identification of Albanians as the main enemy of the Serbian nation was further used to reinforce the nationalist definition of the Serbian nation as a *community under threat* by linking other 'enemies' to the former. A quite common strategy of the government-controlled media was to establish a linkage between other 'enemies' and Albanian separatism. In October 1990, for example, the Belgrade daily *Politika* carried reports of 'Croatian specials speaking Albanian' in an attempt to link the special forces of the Croatian Republic, which was on its way to secession from the Yugoslav Federation, with Albanian separatism.

Media performance and populist politics

Through their contribution to the performance of public rituals and in the creation of a series of moral panics, Serbian state-controlled and pro-government media, aided by the media of the Serbian Orthodox Church and of nationalist groups and organizations, reinforced nationalist definitions of the situation and definitions of community. In fact, they posited the national community in opposition to enemies, or informed the imagination of the Serbian nation as a community under threat. This particular modality of imagination of the national community is premised on processes of simplification of the political field into two opposing camps, or the positing of an irreconcilable antagonistic relationship between the 'people', or the 'nation', and its 'other'. In fact, the positing of this binary political and social division not only simplifies the political field, but also entails the maintenance of some sense of homogeneity within the ranks of the community in question, as it unifies it on the basis of establishing a relation of equivalence among its constituent elements. In the case of Serbian nationalism, the mass media identified the nation's 'enemy' in several ways (Albanians, Croats, Slovenes, Muslims, the Vatican and the USA). However, in the context of this antagonistic relationship, these others, or enemies, and the threats they are thought to represent, have been treated as equivalent facets of one enemy/threat.[17]

The disintegration of Yugoslavia has been linked with the emergence of populist discourses in the political spheres of the former Yugoslav republics: national identities have been asserted through the positing of oppositional or antagonistic relationships between the nation and its 'other', and the complexity of the 'political' has been reduced to bipolar antagonisms. Although we should not succumb to the temptation to attribute the emergence of Yugoslavia's populist nationalisms to the mass media, we cannot ignore the contribution of the latter in the performance of public rituals and the creation of moral panics which reinforced closed definitions of community and provided fertile ground for the development of the sharp divisions that are still tearing the former Yugoslavia apart.

Notes

1. Donald, J. and Rattansi, A. (1992) 'Introduction', in J. Donald and A. Rattansi (eds), *'Race', Culture & Difference*, London: Sage, p. 4.

2. Plestina, D. (1991) 'From "Democratic Centralism" to Decentralised Democracy? Trials and Tribulations of Yugoslavia's Development', in J. B. Allcock et al. (eds), *Yugoslavia in Transition: Choices and Constraints*, Providence, RI: Berg, pp. 133–4.

3. The 1968 Kosovo riots, the Belgrade Summer of the same year, the Croatian Spring of 1971, the Bosnian-Muslim campaign to redesignate Bosnia a 'Muslim Republic' in the late 1970s and the Albanian–Macedonian dispute over the 'national status' of Macedonian Muslims are some of the key protest movements of the period.

4. Bacic-Hayden, M. and Hayden, R. M. (1992) 'Orientalist Variations, on the Theme "Balkans": Symbolic Geography in Recent Yugoslav Cultural Politics', *Slavic Review*, Vol. 51, pp. 3–6.

5. Sofos, S. A. (1996) 'Culture, Politics and Identity in Former Yugoslavia', in B. Jenkins and S. A. Sofos (eds), *Nation and Identity in Contemporary Europe*, London: Routledge, pp. 256–75.

6. For a more detailed analysis of the nationalization of the public sphere of former Yugoslavia, see Sofos, S. A. (1997) 'From "Yugoslav" to National Cultures: Ethnic Conflict and the Nationalization of the Public Spheres of Former Yugoslavia', *Res Publica*, Vol. XXXIX, No. 2 (April), pp. 259–70.

7. It is important to stress at this point that although the late 1980s witnessed the progressive ascendance of anti-Yugoslav discourse in the republican media, other discourses stressing ethnic antagonism and incompatibility, but not articulated in the anti-Yugoslav universe of discourse of the period, should not be overlooked. For example, Macedonian media often reflected anti-Albanian feelings among Slav Macedonians by sensationalizing incidents of ethnic tension and conflict between Slav and Albanian Macedonians. For developments in the press in the 1980s, see Ramet, S. P. (1992) *Balkan Babel: The Disintegration of Yugoslavia from the Death of Tito to Ethnic War*, Boulder, CO: Westview Press, pp. 63–90.

8. Elliott, P. (1980) 'Press Performance as Political Ritual', in H. Christian (ed.), *The Sociology of Journalism* (Sociological Review Monograph, 29), Keele: Keele University Press, p. 147.

9. Ibid., p. 146.

10. Turner, V. (1974) *Dramas, Fields and Metaphors: Symbolic Action in Human Society*, Ithaca, NY: Cornell University Press; also Anderson, B. (1983) *Imagined Communities: Reflections on the Origin and Spread of Nationalism*, London: Verso, p. 56.

11. Cohen, S. (1987) *Folk Devils and Moral Panics: The Creation of the Mods and Rockers*, Basingstoke: Macmillan, p. 9.

12. The regime encouraged revived Serbian Orthodox rituals such as those examined in the previous pages. Other instances of mobilization of popular culture were the revival of a Chetnik sub-culture, as uniforms, insignia, flags and other aspects of the dress code of the Chetniks became popular among the youth of the fringe of the nationalist movement: the Radical Party of *Vojslav Seselj* (*Radikalna Stranka*), and the ultra-nationalist circle of Belgrade politician and warlord *Zeljko Raznjatovic* (*Arkan*). Finally, the revival of Serbian folk culture, including the emergence of the popular *turbofolk* (neo-folk) or the 'rediscovery' by parts of the Serbian intelligentsia of the school of contemporary naïve painting formed around Martin Jonas and other leading painters, were also linked to the nationalist movement.

13. Radoncic, F. (1990) 'Teku dani kosmara', *Danas*, 13 March 1990, p. 21.

14. Ramet, S. (1995) 'The Serbian Church and the Serbian Nation', in S. Ramet and L. S. Adamovic (eds), *Beyond Yugoslavia: Politics, Economics and Culture in a Shattered Community*, Boulder, CO: Westview Press, p. 111.

15. Milic, A. (1993) 'Women and Nationalism in the Former Yugoslavia', in N. Funk and M. Mueller (eds), *Gender, Politics and Post-Communism*, New York: Routledge, pp. 114–15.

16. Ibid, pp. 115–16. See also Salecl, R. (1994) *The Spoils of Freedom: Psychoanalysis and Feminism after the Fall of Socialism*, London: Routledge; Sofos, S. A. (1996) 'Interethnic Violence and Gendered Constructions of Ethnicity: Abortion, Rape and Nationalism in Former Yugoslavia', *Social Identities*, Vol. 2, No. 1, pp. 73–91.

17. For a more detailed discussion of 'equivalence' and the 'binarism', see Laclau, E. and Mouffe, C. (1985) *Hegemony and Socialist Strategy*, London: Verso; Sofos, S. A. (1994) 'Popular Identity and Political Culture in Post-dictatorship Greece: Towards a Cultural Approach to Populism', in N. Demertzis (ed.), *Greek Political Culture Today*, Athens: Odysseas and Bowman, G. (1994) 'Xenophobia, Phantasy and the Nation: The Logic of Ethnic Violence in Former Yugoslavia', in V. Goddard, J. Llobera and C. Shore (eds), *Anthropology of Europe: Identity and Boundaries in Conflict*, London: Berg.

. . . .

CHAPTER 9

Nationalism, Ethnic Antagonism and Mass Communications in Greece

Roza Tsagarousianou

On 10 December 1992, hundreds of thousands of Greek television viewers and radio listeners in Greece and Cyprus 'witnessed' a massive demonstration of 1,300,000 people against EC recognition of Greece's new northern neighbour 'Macedonia'. On the same day, members of Εθνικη Σταυροφορια (National Crusade), a small extreme nationalist group, entered a magistrate's court in Athens and attacked three Greek citizens who were being prosecuted for claiming they were ethnic 'Macedonians'. This event received only marginal coverage as both broadcast and print media either ignored it or presented it as an incident of minor importance. This was partly because that day's mass demonstration, combined with the Greek government's efforts to safeguard the 'national interests' (i.e. the non-recognition of the former Yugoslav Republic of Macedonia) at the Edinburgh EC summit was considered to be by far the most significant news item of the day, but also because of the increasing 'nationalization' of the universe of public debate in Greece. The markedly distinct media attitudes towards each of these two events were representative of a more general process of permeation of Greek public life – including the mass media – by nationalist discourse since the late 1980s.

My aim in this chapter is to examine, first, the relation between mass communication and nationalist discourse and, second, the ways in which the prevalence of nationalist discourse in the communication process has affected political and cultural life in Greece after the recent political and social changes in East-Central Europe. Taking the proposition that the 'nation' is a discursive formation, the product of imaginative vision (Anderson, 1983: 7), the outcome of the 'invention' of national traditions and symbols of national existence and continuity (Hobsbawm and Ranger, 1983) as a point of departure, and drawing upon the initial findings of research on media discourses in Greece, I shall look at some of the ways in which mass communications contribute to the unfolding of, and sustain, these processes of imagination and invention.[1]

One of the main concerns of this chaper will be the examination of *scientific nationalism*, that is, of the strategies of construction of the 'nation' and its 'others' as an object of 'scientific knowledge', and the processes of dissemination of the definitions the former entail. A second aspect of the construction of the nation and its enemies which I am particularly concerned with is the role of the mass media in the enactment of public rituals, that is, the transformation, through mass communication, of public events, such as public rallies, demonstrations, or court proceedings, into rituals contributing to the exclusion and criminalization of dissent regarding the 'national issues', and to the forging of 'unity' among the members of the 'national community'. Finally, I shall attempt to assess the impact of the unfolding of these discursive strategies in common-sense representations of the nation as a homogeneous 'moral' and 'authentic' community, and of others as its enemies, and to consider the ramifications of these processes as far as the openness of the universe of public debate in Greece is concerned.

Although this chapter is concerned with the 'nationalization' of mass communications in Greece, a note of caution is in order at this point: this process of 'nationalization' of communications or, more generally, of the universe of public discourse, is not an exclusively Greek, or Balkan phenomenon.[2] Indeed, as Schlesinger pointed out in his analysis of the BBC coverage of developments in Northern Ireland in the 1970s (1978: 205–43), it could be argued that the abandonment of the normative principle of 'media impartiality' in extraordinary conflict situations for an – at least partial – adoption of 'national' considerations, is not confined to the Balkans, but is also characteristic of 'Western' European and other 'non-oriental' societies.

Nationalism in Greece: some background notes

Nationalism in Greek society is by no means a new phenomenon. For the purpose of this chapter, it suffices to point out that nationalist rhetoric has been inextricably intermixed with different modalities of Greek national identity since the latter half of the eighteenth century. Nationalism and ethnocentrism have been prominent elements of Greek culture since the emergence of the intellectual movement of the 'neohellenic enlightenment' which helped shape the modern Greek state and society. Ethnocentrism was used as the raw material for several nationalist outbreaks throughout the nineteenth and twentieth centuries as well as for several military adventures in the Balkans and the Near East (see Campbell and Sherrard, 1968: 83–155). What is more, the ethnocentric elements of Greek culture provided the cornerstone of the post-war ideology of εθνικοφροσύνη (national-mindedness), that is the post-war use of the 'nation' as the main principle upon which the regime based its legitimation, and of the establishment of authoritarian state apparatuses. Indeed, this element of ethnocentrism has been re-produced and reinforced in numerous social contexts. Through the cultivation of 'patriotism' in the school, the day-to-day contact with the state bureaucracy, the church, or military service, generations of Greeks have been inculcated with the unproblematic continuity and sacredness of the Greek nation.[3] By the same token, social, political, ethnic and religious minorities inside Greece, and other societies outside it, were defined as the 'other', this 'other' being perceived at different times as linked to 'oriental backwardness', the 'communist threat', the 'Slavic or Islamic danger', 'Western imperialism' or a combination of these elements.

The political situation after the Greek Civil War (1945–49) was legitimized through the constitutional assertion of what we could call 'national rights' at the expense of human rights. Political dissent was often classified as 'anti-national' behaviour (αντεθνική συμπεριφορά), and the limits of acceptable political action were set and regulated by the politically dominant Greek army and its nationalist/anti-communist allies within the country and abroad (see Haralambis, 1985: 47–104 and 222–42). Ethnic and religious minorities were either isolated and op-pressed, or their very existence was not acknowledged as they were considered to be a 'fifth column' within a state which had striven to achieve and convince itself of its ethnic homogeneity for most of the twentieth century.[4]

The fall of the dictatorship did lead to significant changes in the political system, notably the restoration of democracy and the end to the ban on the communist Left. However, despite hopes of the deepen-ing of political democracy in Greece, ethnocentrism and nationalism have constituted serious obstacles to the process of democratization as they played a major role in the maintenance of constitutional national-ism, and of the mechanisms of exclusion this entails. What is more, the emphasis on the Greeks' ancient ancestry or the heritage of classical antiquity, or on the need for national unity and the obligation of supporting it – as these were mobilized in 1990, for example, when Athens was a candidate for hosting the 1996 'Golden Olympic Games' – usually in order to divert attention from social, economic and political problems, has posed restrictions to the realization of democratic politics.

The Greek mass media played a significant role in the processes of reproduction and reinforcement of ethnocentric and nationalist discourse. They sustain an 'official' representation of Greece as being a nation under threat from its neighbouring states, and a sense of societal insecurity among Greeks.[5] These representations have been crucial in the formation and maintenance of public attitudes regarding both ethno-religious minorities within Greece, and ethnic and religious groups in neighbouring countries. In addition, they have been central in the closure of the universe of political discourse and in the construction of a frame whose boundaries Greek government policy regarding Greece's neighbours cannot easily transcend.[6]

Media structure and performance in Greece: some brief remarks

In the remainder of this chapter I shall discuss issues which are raised by a preliminary analysis of material from the Greek print and broadcast media. Before doing so, however, some brief remarks regarding the material reviewed and, more generally, mass communication in Greece, are in order.

Starting from the Greek daily press, it should be pointed out that, on the basis of the material reviewed so far, there appear to be two distinct trends in the coverage of ethnic and nationalist conflict in the Balkans. The first, which is the prevalent one, is characteristic of most newspapers, both 'popular' and 'quality'. It generally consists of the 'demonization' of minorities and refugees, and of neighbouring states and ethnic or religious groups. The second trend, which is much more marginalized, consists of what could be called 'opinion articles', usually written by intellectuals and human rights activists who are critical of nationalist and racist tendencies manifested in Greek society and politics, including the mass media. These 'dissident' opinion articles appear mostly in 'quality' papers, often in issues featuring sensational first-page articles of the first category.

Whereas one might argue that the existence of two sets of attitudes, and modes of representation of ethnic-religious minorities and groups, is a sign of the pluralistic character of the Greek press, it should be emphasized that opinion articles (that is, articles considered to be expressing 'subjective' opinions open to contestation and counter-arguments) generally play a less important role than 'reportage'. Whereas reportage is considered to be about 'real news' – and thus is thought to be characterized by objectivity – opinion articles are less significant, as they are not dealing with 'news' but with 'opinions' of intellectuals detached from everyday life. This effective marginalization of opinion articles is also reflected in their relatively marginal position in the newspaper layout as they are never featured on the first or last page where 'the news' can be found. In this way – and at the expense of alternative accounts of the situation – official, nationalist, definitions of the situation are represented as 'news', and therefore are more likely to form the raw material of which hegemonic perceptions of reality are constructed. In addition, as it has been argued elsewhere, economic pressures lead editorial policy-makers to opt for sensational accounts of the situation, mainly drawing upon fears, prejudice, fantasies and memories incorporated in the realm of popular culture.

The case of television is quite similar to that of the daily press as far the tendencies towards sensationalization are concerned. It has indeed been argued that, during the liberalization of the broadcast media market, the fact that new private television channel licences and frequencies were primarily reserved for press publishers has contributed to the existence of similarities between the print and broadcast media in terms of editorial priorities and work ethic. As media professionals working in the press moved to television, it could be suggested (although research to support this has yet to be undertaken) that much of the work ethic and editorial objectives of the print media (especially of 'political' newspapers) were transferred to the television industry. In addition, due to the limited regulation of the broadcasting industry, television became an unregulated field of competition between entrepreneurs in the pursuit of a share of the increasing advertising market in Greece. Sensationalization again has been considered to be one of the preferred strategies to this end. It is therefore in this context of limited regulation, increasing competition and a 'tabloid ethic' that the material from the Greek broadcast media will be considered.

Mass communication and scientific nationalism

As mentioned earlier, one of the strategies of construction of the 'nation' and its 'other' is the treatment of the 'nation' as an object of scientific knowledge, or what I have called 'scientific nationalism'. Areas affected by the emergence of nationalist discourse, which at the same time have sustained and reproduced it, are those of history, and of other social and human sciences such as linguistics and anthropology. These 'scientific' discourses are extremely important as they are vehicles for narrating the nation and its 'other' while maintaining a sense of objective knowledge. This is not a phenomenon which appears exclusively in Greek society. Indeed, as it has been argued, the 'politicization of history' (and one might add, of allied disciplines) constitutes a response to 'the ideological dislocations caused by the ending of the Cold War' (Füredi, 1992: 1–16). However, it could be argued that in the case of Greece, as in the case of most of its Balkan neighbours, this politicization occupies a prominent position in the processes of forming and sustaining nationalist discourse and national identity.

Ethno-religious conflict assumes, therefore, the form of antagonism over history; as competing communities seek to project themselves into the past in an attempt to achieve their retrospective foundation, competing claims to that past are formulated and publicized. As it has been argued elsewhere, it is in this context of ethno-religious conflict that the phenomenon of 'scientific nationalism', that is, the 'nationalization' of scientific discourse (mainly of the social and human sciences), emerges (Sofos and Tsagarousianou, 1993: 55–6). In the case of Greece, the phenomenon of 'scientific nationalism' has been characterized mainly by the increasing activity and importance of nationalist cultural and political networks which has manifested itself through three distinct phenomena:

1. The establishment of a number of publishing houses (such as Ellopia and Risos) whose 'mission' is to increase 'national self-awareness' through the dissemination of information to the average reader (and not the academic).
2. The reprinting of older 'nationalist' studies on Balkan history, folk-lore and ethnolinguistics.
3. The emergence or re-emergence of writers and researchers focusing on the so-called 'national issues', ranging from international relations to social anthropology. Also there is the activation of prominent personalities within nationalist cultural networks, including well-known nationalist politicians and intellectuals who, since the early 1990s, have been enjoying considerable publicity and access to the mass media, thus being able to reach a wide readership/audience, extending far beyond academia.

It should thus be emphasized that 'scientific nationalism' is not confined to the production of 'scientific' texts for academic use. Rather, it encompasses the production and diffusion of 'scientific' discourses which promote particular versions of the nation and its 'other' through both 'specialist' and 'popular' media. It is characteristic that in April 1992 the five most popular non-fiction books in Greek bookshops were all about the geopolitical and ethnological situation in the Balkans.[7] Even outside the 'Top 5' books, one cannot avoid noticing the publication of numerous new books and articles claiming to constitute authoritative contributions to the 'scientific' support of Greece's 'national issues'. Several of these publications concentrated on the issue of the alleged 'artificial' character of the Macedonian state and nation, and attempted to prove this in a variety of ways. Most often, historical evidence was used to prove that the contemporary inhabitants of the former Yugoslav Republic of Macedonia are by no means related to ancient Macedonians and therefore have no right to use the name 'Macedonia' and its derivatives, or to 'claim' part of the Macedonian heritage. One of the most common arguments – indicative of the underlying logic of the debate – used to this effect is encapsulated in the following extract which was recycled in several articles that appeared in the daily, weekly and fortnightly press in 1991 and 1992: 'Skopje did not belong to [ancient] Macedonia, it was the capital of the "tribe of the Dardanes" who, according to Roman sources, were the main enemy of the Macedonians' (Vasileiou, 1991: 35; and 1992).

It is quite obvious that arguments of this sort are premised on a reified notion of history, in accordance with which the hybridity of national, ethnic and religious cultures or the discontinuities and gaps characterizing history are suppressed to the benefit of a static and naturalized view of 'national' history. Similar remarks can be made about linguistic approaches to the 'Macedonian problem', which, however, are divided into two main tendencies, one seeking to prove that Slav-Macedonians are ethnic Bulgarians (Andriotis, 1991), and a second, that their language, or idiom as it is called in Greece, does not constitute the basis for any ethnic or national identity:

> [Those who claim that there is a Macedonian language] did not examine how it [the slavic language or idiom spoken in areas of Northern Greece] was created and did not acknowledge that it contains many hundreds of Greek words, even from Homer's era; it has Bulgarian, Turkish and Latin [words], but this does not constitute [proof of the existence of] ethnicity. (Martis, 1991: 41)

Although these arguments often reach the point of absurdity, as this extract indicates, they occupy a very important position in the debate. The popularity of these specialists, and the publicity attracted by their work, interviews and lectures, make scientific nationalism a very significant factor in the reproduction of nationalist discourse.

In addition to the appearance of these studies, the Ministry of Education has published a school book for 'the national issues [sic]'[8] which has been used in secondary education since 1993–94, and has already published and distributed to schools in Greece and diaspora communities a 59-page information booklet titled *Macedonia, History and Politics* in order to 'offer authoritative information to students, teachers and parents, about the Macedonian [issue]'. According to the Education Minister during 1991–93, G. Souflias, the information contained in the book has been 'adapted to the needs of school usage'. It appears that this adaptation includes the selective and misleading use of statistics in order to prove the continuity and predominance of the presence of Hellenism in Macedonia, especially at the beginning of the twentieth century. By eliminating the Slav-Macedonians from history and by denying the existence of the small Slav-Macedonian minority of Northern Greece, scientific nationalism paves the way for the political demands of prominent ultra-nationalists in Greece, as well as in neighbouring Serbia and Bulgaria, for the creation of 'sanitary zones' for the settlement of anticipated refugees from the warring republics and provinces of former Yugoslavia, and even for the absorption of Macedonia by Serbia (see Lazaridis, 1991a: 45–6 and 1991b: 44–5; Dountas, 1992).

The trend of scientific nationalism has been characterized by the development of a booming industry of national identity studies. Most of these studies are based on an uncritical approach to historical and anthropological research, and are geared towards pinpointing linguistic, historical, or anthropological evidence of the continuity of the Greek nation, or towards proving the Greekness of minority groups within Greece, such as the Vlachs or Pomaks. Although the 'Macedonian issue' has probably been the most prominent topic, it has not been the only one to which the efforts of historical, anthropological and linguistic researchers were directed. The issue of the ethnic, linguistic and demographic characteristics of Tsamouria, an area of north-western Greece, often mentioned as a part of 'Greater Albania' by Albanian nationalist politicians, governmental officials and intellectuals, or of western Thrace where Greece's Muslim minority is concentrated, are also present in the relevant literature (see Papadopoulos, 1992; Magriotis, n.d.).

Most arguments introduced by nationalist historians or political commentators are characterized by the naturalization of contemporary political alliances, and the organization of selective remembering of historical alliances and relationships among the Balkan states. This is illustrated by the widespread claims that Serbians and Greeks are 'natural' allies and friends, or that Albanians are 'natural' enemies of Greece, or finally that the 'Serbs, Bulgarians and Greeks are the three historical [sic] nations of the Southern Balkans', reducing the rest to virtual non-existence.[9] This homogenization of national communities, the naturalization of historical contigency, and the ensuing typification of nations support stereotypical 'common-sense' assumptions regarding the current situation in the Balkans and constitute aspects of a strategy with alarming repercussions. Scientific nationalism has contributed to the essentialization and reification of history, and to the introduction and reinforcement of racist distinctions by setting arbitrary and closed criteria for the recognition of ethnicities and nations. The implication of this closure in the universe of public discourse is the denial of the existence, or the symbolic elimination of the others, be they an ethnic or religious minority, or a whole national community.

Media performance, public rituals and moral panics

Another aspect of contemporary Greek nationalism, closely related to mass communication, is the construction of the nation and its enemies through the enactment of public rituals such as nationalist rallies and demonstrations, and their media coverage, or the creation of moral panics through particular ways of representation of minorities and refugees in Greece. The enactment of public rituals, or the creation of moral panics based on media representations of ethnic/religious differences have played a quite significant role in the assertion of a sense of national unity and in the suppression or, in the case of the latter, exclusion and criminalization of dissent regarding the 'national issues'. Here I shall focus on the media coverage of two mass rallies which could be treated as representative cases of public rituals, and on media representations of the 'other'. They have particular reference to the Albanian nationals in Greece, to Islam in the Balkans and to the former Yugoslav Republic of Macedonia.

Media coverage of mass rallies could be treated as public rituals, that is, activities of a symbolic character which draw on customary and familiar elements of the hegemonic culture and are intended to add spiritual and emotional communion to a sense of political unity (see Elliott, 1980: 141–7). In this context, I shall focus on the media coverage of two demonstrations and mass rallies which took place in Thessaloniki (14 February 1992) and Athens (10 December 1992) in order to demonstrate the national/popular unity against the international recognition of the former Yugoslav Republic of Macedonia. According to moderate estimations, the rallies were attended by over 1,000,000 and 1,300,000 persons respectively and received extensive media coverage. Although these rallies were not formally organized by the state, it should be pointed out that they were facilitated by a significant degree of state cooperation. Civil service offices, organizations of the public sector, state-owned or -controlled enterprises, secondary schools and higher education institutions allowed their employees to take time off and participate in the rallies. In fact, employers in the public and, to a lesser extent, the private sector consented to virtually closing down offices and workplaces during these rallies. In addition, public transport was free for those wishing to attend, while schools closed in order to allow their students to participate in the rallies. In both rallies, 'national' symbols from classical, hellenistic or more recent Greek history were prominently featured on flags and banners, while the speakers stressed the national/popular unity demonstrated by the turnout at the rally, and the 'plebiscitary' character of the latter. In the case of the Athens rally, its plebiscitary character was more explicit as the participants were invited to pass a 'popular' resolution to be presented to the EC Edinburgh summit meeting which was to discuss the possibility of recognition of the former Yugoslav Republic of Macedonia.

The rallies received extensive coverage by the mass media as most state and private television and radio stations transmitted the events live, in addition to their inclusion in the regular news slots of the day. What is more, the rallies were broadcast live in the Republic of Cyprus, as one of the Greek television and radio stations, ANT1, persistently reminded its audience, throughout its joint broadcast with RIK (the Republic of Cyprus Public Service Broadcasting Corporation). The television coverage of the rallies complemented the rallies themselves as it transformed the participants/audience into protagonists/enunciators. Instead of focusing on the speakers, the cameras focused on the audience, wandering over the masses of people, zooming in on banners and flags featuring national and religious symbols, or on groups of eager participants. More precisely, particular emphasis was placed on the transmission of visual evidence of the unity and 'unanimity' of the 'people', the centrality of national and religious symbols in the space occupied by the masses of participants and, consequently, the size and importance of the event. Generally, the rallies were represented as a celebration of national/ popular solidarity, as a rediscovery of the national community.

Another area in which the role of mass communication has been significant is that of the construction of the nation and its enemies through the creation of moral panics premised upon particular ways of representation of minorities and refugees in Greece. Media representations of ethnic/religious difference have been central to the construction of a particular notion of national identity, premised on the suppression or exclusion and criminalization of other ethnic and religious groups. Here I will examine briefly three sets of strategies of media representation of the 'other': first, the representation of Albanian nationals in Greece; second, the perceived threat of Islam in the Balkans; and third, the former Yugoslav Republic of Macedonia.

After the collapse of the state socialist regime of Albania and the relaxation of border controls between that country and Greece, Albanian nationals – members of the Greek minority as well as ethnic Albanians – crossed the Albanian–Greek border to Greece in search of employment. The initial reaction among the public and opinion leaders was positive and the mass media concentrated on the humanitarian aspects of these migrants. However, this initial reaction was soon to change radically as a result of the mobilization of public fears regarding the increase in crime rates and its convergence with the anti-immigration rhetorics of nationalist circles. In this process, the mass media played a significant role as they publicized 'definitions of the situation' which were central to these processes. After a short 'period of grace', the media focused on the issue of 'Albanian criminality'. As early as 1991, in search of sensational news items, print and broadcast media carried news stories about the alleged spread of an organized 'Albanian mafia' in Greece. These stories were given credibility by the routine attribution of any unsolved crime to this 'Albanian mafia'. In the period between December 1991 and May 1993, apart from the regular news reports in which 'Albanians' were alleged to have been involved in crimes, there were several special 'investigations' of the so-called 'Albanian mafia' – however, without any credible evidence emerging. Some of the headlines of these investigations in the Greek press are indicative of the attitude of the media towards Albanians in Greece: 'Greece is appalled and scared. Send the monsters away' (*Apogevmatini*, December 1991); 'Albanians: a bomb in our hands' (*Apogevmatini*, September 1992); 'Freedom to robbers and criminals: Albanians are legalized in Greece' (*Eleftheros Typos*, May 1993); 'Albanians landing to Crete' (*Eleftheros Typos*, May 1993); 'Thousands of Albanian illegal immigrants in Macedonia. An atmosphere of terror and fear among the local population' (*Ethnos*, May 1993).

The media orchestration of this moral panic is even clearer if one takes into account the shift that has been taking place since 1991 regarding media definitions of the identity of Albanian citizens involved in illegal activities. More precisely, an analysis of the coverage of crimes allegedly perpetrated by Albanian citizens by three popular tabloids (*Apogevmatini*, *Eleftheros Typos* and *Ethnos*) and the evening bulletins of the two major TV private channels (ANT1 and MEGA) during May 1993, indicated that when the alleged perpetrator of an illegal act was Greek-Albanian, he/she was invariably identified as 'Albanian'. This practice was quite deliberate as the distinction between Albanian Greeks and other Albanians was retained and revived on other occasions. It could be argued that the word 'Albanian' was used by the mass media interchangeably with the term 'criminal'. In this way Albanians are stereotypically defined, not only as ethnically different, but also as socially undesirable and dangerous.

A similar panic has also been present since 1991 in news items and interviews regarding the formation of an 'Islamic arch' or 'transversal'[10] to the north and east of Greece. These were obviously intended to 'remind' the people of the imminent geopolitical isolation of Greece from the rest of Europe. In addition, hints at the alleged 'Islamization' of the republic of Bosnia-Herzegovina (or of its leadership) have been quite frequent during the TV coverage of the war in Bosnia. It is characteristic that during May 1994, in the evening news bulletins of ET1 (Channel 1 of the Greek Public Broadcasting Corporation) and ANT1 (one of the two major commercial stations), the Bosnian government was associated with Saudi Arabia, as most news bulletins featured reports referring to Bosnian Muslims, including the republic's president Alija Izetbegovic, leaving Sarajevo for the annual *hadj* to Mecca, emphasizing that all their expenses were paid by Saudi Arabia. In the same period, ANT1 also presented the refusal of the religious leader of the Bosnian Muslims to meet with the Serb Patriarch in Sarajevo as an act of intransigence. This frequent evocation of the alleged Islamic threat to Greek security and culture adds a religious element to a set of relations primarily characterized by ethnic and geopolitical antagonism.

In the majority of the material reviewed, not only is Islam represented as antagonistic to Christianity; it also carries the connotation of the 'barbaric Orient' as opposed to Western values and civilization, but more significantly, it connotes Turkey, and its geopolitical penetration into the Southern Balkans, and thus into Europe. Through this process, the European credentials of Christian Greece are asserted and reinforced, and Greek identity becomes inextricably linked to its antagonistic relationship to Turkey and its allegedly Islamic, hence non-European, Balkan neighbours. In addition, Greeks are reminded that they are a 'nation in danger', fighting for survival against numerous international foes.

Finally, as far as media representations of the former Yugoslav Republic of Macedonia are concerned, two complementary strategies can be discerned. The first banishes the Macedonian republic and its people from the realms of history and politics. It is characteristic that the mass media have been reproducing the official discourse regarding the new state, referring to the former Yugoslav Republic of Macedonia as a 'statelet' ($\kappa\rho\alpha\tau\iota\delta\iota o$) – a word applied to a small, inferior political entity, not enjoying full rights of sovereignty and self-determination. Other terms are also highly indicative: 'Skopje', pseudo-state, and 'Skopjean entity', are all derogatory names that do not allude to any sort of recognition of a political entity. As far as the inhabitants of the Republic are concerned, they are called 'pseudo-Macedonians', while more populist media (especially, but not exclusively, newspapers) have occasionally referred to them as 'barefoot' ($\xi\iota\pi\acute{o}\lambda\eta\tau o\iota$) – a term connoting poverty and lack of culture – and 'gipsy-skopjeans'. In addition to this, the dispute between Greece and the former Yugoslav Republic of Macedonia has often been personalized as Macedonia has frequently been referred to as 'Gligorov's state' and its policies as 'Gligorov's policies'. In this way the new state is represented as the product of the personal ambitions of its current leader, and the socio-political dynamics which led to its formation are concealed. Thus, the Republic of Macedonia and the Macedonian nation do not exist; rather, they are artificial entities, the product of personal ambition and conspiracy.

A second set of representational strategies posits the 'enemy' as existent and threatening. Here, the 'enemy' is represented as a homogeneous, internally undifferentiated entity poised to deprive Greece of its territory, identity and history. In the case of the former Yugoslav Republic of Macedonia, the symbolic unification of the 'Skopjeans' behind the label of 'evil nationalists' is achieved by the simplification of the political map of the country. The Greek mass media also ignore the political divisions of Macedonian politics. A characteristic example is the presentation by the Greek media of maps produced by nationalist political parties and organizations in the Republic of Macedonia (including the largest party, VMRO) and the Slav-Macedonian diaspora in order to demonstrate the expansive intentions of the 'Skopjeans' or of 'Skopje' as a whole. The presentation of this visual 'proof' of threat (according to these maps, the largest part of Northern Greece, inhabited by an overwhelming majority of ethnic Greek populations, is represented as part of the Macedonian national territory), combined with the use of the vague terms 'Skopjeans' or 'Skopje', which have been consistently used instead of the more specific 'Slav-Macedonian nationalists', or instead of the names of the particular Slav-Macedonian political parties and diaspora organizations responsible for these maps, has prevented the formulation of alternative and more complex explanations of the political situation in the Republic of Macedonia. The consequence of this strategy of dissimulation has been the representation of the citizens, the political forces, the government and the Slav-Macedonian diaspora organizations as an undifferentiated entity, as its constituent elements are treated as 'equivalent' in terms of their expansionist policy and chauvinism.[11] As a result, the political field has been simplified into two antagonistic forces, Greek and Macedonian, moral and immoral, good and evil. This division in turn facilitates the closure of the universe of political discourse in Greece; through the displacement of more complex representations of the Macedonians, nationalist discourse achieves the elimination of diversity in Greek politics and society. Thus, whoever transcends the boundaries of the universe of political discourse is represented as part of the 'enemy', and is therefore excluded from the national – and therefore the political – community.

Nationalism, mass communication and citizenship

On the basis of the media and cultural representations I outlined above, the 'other' is perceived as the aggregate of internal and external opposition, in the form of an imaginary 'enemy'. Internal dissidents and political adversaries are therefore transformed into national enemies as the achieved simplification of the 'political' does not allow room for diversity and difference within the framework of national politics. Instead of recognizing the centrality of self-expression, nationalist discourse is set against the formation and maintenance of public spaces (including the mass media) for representation and identity negotiation, independent from state institutions or the party system. Indeed, restricted access to the Greek mass media and the systematic publicizing of official definitions of the situation and of nationalist discourse have achieved the closure of the universe of political discourse in general.

Greek nationalist discourse incorporates apparently contradictory strategies which, however, deny with consistency the existence of the 'enemy'. Through the demonization of the 'other' and the restriction of the possibilities of recognizing internal complexity and plurality, the Greek mass media have contributed to the construction of national identity in such a way that it is decoupled from freedom and plurality. In the light of these developments, I would argue that the Greek mass media have been reinforcing the binary divisions between 'good' and 'bad' that prevail in popular consciousness and in the nationalist imaginary promoted and sustained by certain institutional actors in Greece, and playing a significant rôle in the maintenance and strengthening of obstacles to the formation of a pluralistic social and political map, as the imperative of national unity that they have been promoting consistently dissimulates structured inequalities, displaces representations of 'difference' and privileges ethnicity at the expence of citizenship.

It should be noted, however, that the mass media should not be seen as the primary agents promoting a nationalist and xenophobic hysteria in Greek society. Rather, they are one component of a complex public sphere comprising a constellation of social actors and discourses which continuously negotiate and redefine their identities and relationships at both the domestic and international level. This is illustrated, for example, by the slow but clear transformation of media discourse on the former Yugoslav Republic of Macedonia in late 1996 and 1997, at a time when the domestic and regional/international situation was also changing considerably as the balance of power tilted towards the more moderate political forces in Greece which attempted first a *rapprochement* and then active cooperation with the Republic of Macedonia and civic organizations operating in it. In line with the new relationship, media discourse on Macedonia has become more diverse and now reflects a broad range of political opinions with reference to Greece's neighbour and the relationships between the two countries.

Still, media discourse, reflecting the near-unanimous positions of the major political parties and organizations in Greece, remains rigid and closed on a sensitive aspect of Greek–Macedonian relations – that related to Macedonian allegations that a Macedonian minority lives in Northern Greece and is denied its minority rights. This allegation, regardless of its validity, remains outside public discussion and prompts blanket condemnations of Macedonian expansionism. Despite the *'détente'* marking the Greek–Macedonian relations, which has had an impact on how Macedonia and the Macedonians are represented in the Greek media, other 'national dangers and enemies' (some of which have been dealt with in this chapter) are evoked and constructed in both political debate and media discourse, depending on the particular power relations in Greek society.

Finally, and perhaps more importantly, it should be noted that although media discourse on the Balkans and the Near East continues to draw upon the resources of ethnocentrism and nationalism, its content and intensity vary considerably depending on the particular ways in which nationalist 'themes' are articulated to the hegemonic political discourse.

Notes

1. It should be emphasized that the proposed link between nationalism and communication should be distinguished from the functionalist communicative approach introduced by Deutsch (1966), primarily concerned with the role of communication in nation-building. In this chapter, I intend to examine the processes of definition of the nation through 'exclusion' and boundary-setting, and not through processes of nation-building in general.

2. The existing research and information on the 'nationalization' of mass communication in former Yugoslavia (e.g. Radojkovic, 1994; Thompson, 1994; Turkovic, 1994) has led to arguments of this sort.

3. For a good general analysis of the historical and cultural aspects of Greek society, see Campbell and Sherrard (1968).

4. This is by no means exclusive to the Greek nation state, as most Balkan and Near East nation states have emerged from the disintegrating multi-ethnic Ottoman empire. The twentieth century was marked by attempts to 'rectify' the 'incongruence' between the ethnic map of the area and the imperative of establishing nation states based on the principle of ethnic homogeneity and monoculturalism.

5. For a discussion and definition of the term 'societal insecurity', see O. Wæver et al. (1993).

6. This was, for example, the case of the Greek conservative government of 1990–93 whose leading faction seemed willing to reach a compromise in the dispute between Greece and the former Yugoslav Republic of Macedonia but was unable to do so as, in addition to the existence of a dissenting minority within the ruling party's own ranks, and of an opposition stressing the primacy of safeguarding the country's 'national interests', the majority of the mass media offered unprecedented publicity to nationalist political personalities and intellectuals. The mass media in this way contributed to the reinforcement of nationalist discourse in public debate, and to the restriction of policy options for the government. The same seems to be true in the case of the current, socialist government, especially as the Socialists had themselves voluntarily entrapped into nationalist politics.

7. 'Hit List: Greece', *Guardian*, 10 April 1992, p. 29.

8. All books used in primary and secondary education are commissioned and published by the Ministry of Education and the Organization for the Publication of School Books.

9. These claims are made in detail in Lazaridis (1991a, 1991b), although they have been repeatedly recycled in the daily press and radio and, to a lesser extent, on television.

10. This very popular term in Greece is used in order to emphasize the existence or formation of a chain of Islamic states and regions in the Southern Balkans (Turkey, regions containing Turkish/Muslim minorities in Western Thrace and Southern Bulgaria, Kosovo, Bosnia, Albania). Although Macedonia is not an Islamic state, it is consistently depicted in the Greek mass media as part of this Islamic arch, mainly on the basis of the good relationship the Republic of Macedonia enjoys with Turkey.

11. For a discussion of the notion of equivalence, see Laclau and Mouffe (1985: 127–34).

References

Anderson, B. (1983) *Imagined Communities*, London: Verso.

Andriotis, N. (1960) *Το Ομόσπονδο Κράτοσ των Σκοπίων και η Γλωσσα του*, Thessaloniki: Institute for Balkan Studies; reprinted in 1991. Also in English as (1957) *The Federative Republic of Skopje and its Language*, Athens.

Campbell, J. and Sherrard, P. (1968) *Modern Greece*, London: Ernest Benn.

Deutsch, K. W. (1966) *Nationalism and Social Communication: An Inquiry into the Foundations of Nationality*, Cambridge, MA: MIT Press.

Dountas, Michalis (1992) 'Interview', *Anti*, 30 October.

Elliott, P. (1980) 'Press Performance as Political Ritual', in H. Christian (ed.), *The Sociology of Journalism* (Sociological Review Monograph No. 29), Keele.

Füredi, F. (1992) *Mythical Past, Elusive Future*, London: Pluto.

Haralambis, D. (1985) *Ετρατός και Πολιτική Εξουσία* (Army and Political Power), Athens: Themelio.

Hobsbawm, E. J. and Ranger, T. (1983) *The Invention of Tradition*, Cambridge: Cambridge University Press.

Laclau, E. and Mouffe, C. (1985) *Hegemony and Socialist Strategy*, London: Verso.

Lazaridis, C. (1991a) 'Ελλάδα–Σερβία, Ευμμαχία' (Greece–Serbia, Alliance), *Anti*, 20 September.

— (1991b) 'Ελληνική Πολιτική στα Βαλκάνια: Κριτική στην Κριτική' (Greek Policy in the Balkans: A Counter-criticism), *Anti*, 4 October.

Lyotard, J.-F. (1984) *The Postmodern Condition: A Report on Knowledge*, Manchester: Manchester University Press.

Magriotis, I. (n.d) *Πομάκοι ή Ροδοπαίοι: Οι 'Ελληνες Μουσουλμάτσοι* (Pomaks or Rodopeans: The Greek Muslims), Athens: Rissos.

Martis, N. (1991) 'Η Υποπτη Μεθοδευση Κατασκευης του Ανεζαρτητου Κρατους της Μακεδονιας' (The Suspicious Attempt of Construction of the Independent State of Macedonia), *Anti*, 4 October.

Papadopoulos, A. (1992) *Απειρος Χωρα* (Infinite Country), Athens.

Radojkovic, M. (1994) 'Mass Media Between State Monopoly and Individual Freedom: Media Restructuring and Restriction in Former Yugoslavia', *European Journal of Communication*, Vol. 9, pp. 137–48.

Schlesinger, P. (1978) *Putting 'Reality' Together: BBC News*, London: Constable.

Sofos, S. and Tsagarousianu, R. (1993) 'Greek Nationalism Revisited', in José Amodia (ed.) *The Resurgence of Nationalism in Europe*, Bradford: University of Bradford Press, pp. 51–55.

Thompson, M. (1994) *Forging War: the Media in Serbia, Croatia and Bosnia-Hercegovina*, London: Article 19.

Turkovic, H. (1994) 'Control of National Attitudinal Homogeneity – War Prime News Programme in Croatia', paper presented at the 1994 European Film and Television Studies Conference, London (19–22 July).

Vasileiou, K. (1991) 'Η Μάχη για την Ελληνική Μακεδονία' (The Battle for Greek Macedonia), *Anti*, Vol. 476.

— (1992) 'Special Section', *To Vima*, 9 February.

Wæver, O. et al. (1993) *Identity, Migration and the New Security Agenda in Europe*, London: Pinter.

. . . .

CHAPTER 10

Deconstructing Media Mythologies of Ethnic War in Liberia

Philippa Atkinson

'Tribal rivalries envenom bitter civil war'; 'Orgy of ethnic militia warfare ...'[1]

This kind of quote typifies much media coverage of the civil war in Liberia, which, as in other cases, has focused on ethnicity as a convenient and encompassing label with which to describe and explain the conflict. While the seven-year war in Liberia and its ethnic aspects have been highly complex and so difficult either for outsiders to grasp or to convey to their audiences, the superficiality of media representations is both misleading and potentially dangerous. Media concentration on primordial ethnic identity as a cause of war, with its apparent manifestations in savagery and even cannibalism, helps to obscure critical political and economic factors driving the violence. It contributes to increasingly popular misconceptions of African wars as being fought for primitive causes beyond the understanding or influence of the West. The imagery of 'new barbarism', a term coined in response to Robert Kaplan's infamous article 'The Coming Anarchy', in which he describes the supposed irrationality of the wars in West Africa and elsewhere, reflects this lack of deeper structural analysis (Kaplan, 1994). This new discourse works, perhaps deliberately, to obscure the role in such wars of national political struggles and their relationships with the post-Cold War global capitalist system (Duffield, 1996). Ethnic misrepresentation of African wars is part of a more general failure of analysis which feeds into the policy formulation of the Western powers that dominate the international community, and helps produce the policy disasters which have characterized much of the international response to so-called complex emergencies in the 1990s. While journalists cannot be attributed with all the blame for these policy failures, the dangers of superficial or misleading analysis from all sides is clear.

In this chapter, an attempt will be made to explore, albeit very briefly, something of what is in fact meant and understood in Liberia by the term 'ethnicity'. The various aspects of ethnicity manifested in the civil war will then be critically examined. Ethnicity has been important in the war in terms of its use and manipulation by powerful groups for political ends. Liberians themselves have always formed alliances in various ways at national and local levels with different patrons or politicians, and sometimes perceive and articulate their strategies in ethnic terms. There is, however, nothing preordained, primordial or primitive in their choices or justifications. Categories of alliance shift and develop according to different circumstances, and are used dynamically, to serve political and economic purposes, rather than as ends in themselves. Through this discussion on the realities of ethnicity in Liberia and its role in the conflict, the inherent complexities will be highlighted, and it will become clearer in what senses the media reporting on the war has failed to capture important aspects of the conflict. The impact of this failure, in terms of its contribution to the inadequacy of Western responses to the civil war, will also be briefly examined. The chapter draws on the small literature on Liberian history and the conflict, and from testimonies from numerous Liberians interviewed in the course of various field trips to the country and region in 1991, 1992, 1996 and 1997. Rather than attempting a detailed examination of ethnicity in Liberia, or of the conflict, this chapter is an effort to demonstrate through an analysis of some of the empirical data available, the complexities of local uses of ethnic categories and their political roles, and some of the factors driving the violence of the war.[2]

Ethnic identities and nationalism

Historical aspects of Liberian identity Ethnic identities in Liberia, as elsewhere, are highly complex and fluid, defined by time- and place-specific social conceptions rather than by biological or actual racial factors. The basic cleavage in Liberian society historically has been between descendants of the freed slaves from the USA who founded the nation of Liberia in 1847, known as Americo-Liberians, and the indigenous or 'native' people, commonly classified as 16 different tribes, many of which are interrelated, linguistically and culturally, and are referred to in this chapter as African Liberians. This division has endured until modern times, and has shaped much of the political development of the country.

The so-called tribes are in fact themselves made up of confederations of chiefdomships and villages, and have been defined differently according to different classifications and at different times (Henries, 1966: 104; Grimes, 1996). Many of the peoples of the Liberian hinterland were organized, before their incorporation, as so-called stateless societies, without any explicit centralized political authority, a system that does not lend itself to rigid tribal boundaries. Alliances between groups across topological boundaries were common, and trade and cultural links spanned the region. The secret Poro and Sande societies, mechanisms of social and religious control, also had cross-tribal and regional significance. Migration has been a major and continuing factor in the social and political organization of this area since at least the seventeenth century, from when the arrival of some of the older tribes identifiable today can be traced. Ethnic identities have always been highly negotiable, and were used as a method to consolidate authority at the local level, with marriage the key institution in forging alliances between competing kinship groups (Murphy and Bledsoe, 1987: 127–9).

The Americo-Liberians are also a mix of different original ethnic groups, consisting of descendants of the men and women on the original shipments from America between the 1820s and 1840s, who settled on different points of the coast, forming first a confederation of settlements and later a nation. Recaptured slaves arrived throughout the nineteenth century, and later shipments were brought from the West Indies in the 1880s and the 1920s and 1930s, the latter groups inspired by Marcus Garvey's Back to Africa movement. The early Liberian settlers were themselves mainly of West and Central African origin, but they brought to Liberia many qualities from America and Europe, especially a pioneering and evangelical spirit, and formed a distinct cultural group from the beginning. The Americo-Liberians founded their nation state in a civilizing mission similar in tone to the missionary aspects of European colonists, and the Liberian state has from its conception been built on imported Western-based values of democracy and Christianity. The native cultures were viewed as fundamentally misguided, and the role of the settlers was to educate, civilize and modernize them. Natives were allowed to join the Liberian project, and vote in elections, but only if they converted to one of the brands of Protestantism on offer.

The Americo-Liberians incorporated the country beyond the coast into the new nation, dominating more and more of the native areas upcountry by a combination of force and conflict. Although there was some affiliation, particularly of coastal groups, and in spite of the major variations within the two groups, the basic division between African and

Americo-Liberians has endured to modern times. This divide has served to define political and class roles in Liberian society, with the Americo-Liberians dominating the state from the start, and controlling most aspects of national public life until the last two decades. The perceived superiority of the settlers over the natives, and their proclaimed civilizing mission, served to justify this domination and contributed to the formation, by the late nineteenth century, of an elite with similar exploitative characteristics as the white rulers of the European colonies. The expansion of direct economic and military control of the hinterland, and the increasingly corrupt practices used by the elite to maintain their position, heightened the divisions between Americos and African Liberians, and the resentment of the latter.

Although the basic ethnic differentiation has endured, and the Americos have retained their elite status, the processes of modernization helped to blur the divisions between the groups, and gradually allowed educated or wealthy African Liberians to join the national elite. Other factors besides pure ethnic origin have always played a role in making up identity in Liberia, including the characteristic of 'civilized', denoting the qualities supposed to be required for natives to participate in national 'modern' life, including the religion of the settlers and their social and political institutions (Brown, 1982a). Ethnic identities in Liberia have been complicated further by the tradition of fostering, where African Liberian children from the hinterland have been brought up and educated by settlers or other modern, urban inhabitants, thus weakening their particular tribal identity. Some natives have been able to join the ranks of the elite through these channels. The involvement in national life by the various powerful native or non-Americo elements, including chiefs and traders, have also played a part in defining national in-stitutions, contributing to the 'creolization' of the Liberian culture, as in Sierra Leone (Richards, 1996).

Ethnicity and nation-building The extension of Liberian state struc-tures into the hinterland this century, and the development of economic enclaves in various locations based around rubber and iron ore pro-duction, have played an important role in breaking down the Americo–African Liberian divide. This state-building has been characterized as an aspect of the expansion by the Americo-Liberian elite of their power over the human and economic resources of the hinterland, and it had many exploitative aspects, including the collection of taxation by the military (Liebenov, 1987; Sawyer, 1992). Land appropriation and labour contributions from chiefdoms helped to strengthen the financial basis for control by the Americo-Liberian ruling class, and also created new

wealth upcountry. Individual tribal identities, which had perhaps consolidated during the initial Liberian expansion, were further formalized
by the delimitation of administrative districts upcountry (Osaghae, 1996:
9). Tribal structures of authority were coopted by the Monrovia-based
elite in patron–client relationships, with some levels of chief being made
salaried government posts (Brown, 1989: 373). Competition among
upcountry elites thus gradually took on a national dimension, with
resources and status conferred by the national government playing a
role in local-level disputes over power.

Local systems of allocation of political power, involving the creation
and sustaining of patron–client relationships by leaders and aspirants,
have always made ethnic definitions very loose and fluid, and subject to
redefinition for political purposes (Murphy and Bledsoe, 1987). One
case study from central Liberia describes a series of inter-marriages
which eventually created an important Kpelle kinship group, comprising
Kpelle, Gola and Loma families, themselves all large and relatively well-
defined tribal groupings (Murphy and Bledsoe, 1987: 130–8). The control
of the administrative power that had been allocated by the central
government played a crucial role in the competition for succession
within this group, with those who were able to exploit these new forms
of patronage being successful in consolidating power at this level. This
process has also been observed in other parts of the country (Brown,
1989). The ability of one contender within the kinship group to register
the land of the Kpelle through a government-sponsored survey both
cemented his power as the most important chief within the kinship,
with ultimate control over land allocation, and defined the boundaries
of the group in relation to others. His ability to survey the Kpelle land
benefited from his alliances with the elite in Monrovia, forged during
time spent as a ward in the family of a former President (Murphy and
Bledsoe, 1987: 136).

The processes set in motion by the Americo-Liberian elite thus had
the inevitable effect of opening up the country to the entire population,
with modernization resulting in both the gradual erosion of the
Americo-Liberian hegemony and in the creation of a real national
identity. Opportunities for education and progress were created, and
although the Americos benefited disproportionately due to their greater
access to such opportunities, no groups were excluded. Modernization
from the era of President Tubman (1944–70) was specifically designed
to contribute to the erosion of tribal identities and to the building of a
national one, with one of the two national slogans for three decades
being unification. The building or extension of national state institutions, including the civil service, health and education, combined with

the impact of the changes brought by the growing export economy and infrastructural developments to help create a national Liberian identity and fast-modernizing Liberian economy and society. The language of Liberian English developed over this period as the means of communication for the new country.

However, although clear boundaries between the two basic groups diminished with the consolidation of a modern nation state, the division still exists, and many America-Liberians still belong to the richer class, although now more by virtue of their international networks than through national-level power. Tribal identities have also endured, especially in areas beyond the road network and economic enclaves. Traditional practices, including the powerful Poro and other secret societies, continue in many parts of the country and play some political role at the national level. The majority of Liberians still speak a tribal language as their mother tongue and identify themselves as both from a tribe and as Liberian. Thus more localized ethnic identities, and the cleavage between Americos and African Liberians, has retained some relevance into the present.

Ethnicity and war

Background to the conflict   The immediate background to the civil war can be traced to the military coup in 1980 in which African Liberians took control of the state for the first time from the Americo-Liberians. Tubman was succeeded on his death by his former Vice-President Tolbert, who continued to drive the process of Americo-controlled modernization, but in a climate of economic decline and uncertainty, and increasingly radical opposition. Opposition had been building up throughout the Tubman era, and was allowed in the 1970s to be expressed more openly. Many intellectuals phrased their objections to Americo domination in class rather than purely ethnic terms, and were able to form alliances with the growing working class against the exploitation of the old elite. The coup was carried out by NCOs (non-commissioned officers), but the pressure for change from the radical opposition was a crucial factor in its success. Although the coup was aimed at a transfer of power from the minority Americos, the ethnic dimension was itself an aspect of the issue of political power and its distribution.

The rate of growth of the Liberian economy had slowed considerably in the 1970s due to world economic conditions, and opportunities for progress were perceived to be diminishing as unemployment increased and government services were cut back. Distribution of income and wealth remained highly skewed, with the continued domination of economic power by the Americo elite. Resentment about the shrinking of opportunities was channelled into political opposition to the Tolbert government, which, although more progressive than its predecessor, was seen as corrupt and nepotistic. The lower ranks of the army, resentful of the domination of higher positions by the same elite system, seized the opportunity created by the growing radical opposition to stage a coup. The coup was portrayed by the radicals as a revolution, similar to those in Ghana and elsewhere, led by the people against a corrupt system, and the widespread sentiment against the corrupt old guard was expressed in the public acceptance of the execution of members of Tolbert's cabinet.

Following the coup, the presidency was taken by Samuel Doe, as the oldest of the NCOs involved, and a so-called Krahn from Grand Gedah in the east of the country. He was the first African Liberian to hold the position. Other important political positions were divided between the NCOs who had been directly involved, many of whom were from the north and north-east of the country, of Mano, Gio and Krahn origin. The last Americo-Liberian administration had recruited from these and other groups in Monrovia in a bid to reduce youth unemployment and unrest. Ministerial posts were initially offered to some of the group of educated radicals who had been actively opposing the Americo-Liberian hegemony throughout the 1970s. Most, however, soon left Doe's administration, unable to deal with the growing corruption and mismanagement, or unable to survive in the increasingly competitive environment. Doe then recruited from the more malleable African Liberian members of the True Whig Party, who represented the acceptable face of the old regime (Osaghae, 1996: 61–5).

As competition in the political sphere intensified during the 1980s, Doe consolidated his own hold on power through the traditional methods of creating patron–client ties with his allies, and excluding his competitors and critics. While these alliances are commonly understood as having promoted Doe's fellow Krahns or Grand Gedahans to powerful positions, in practice, Doe was pragmatic, allying with anyone judged useful, and relying closely on his own immediate kin group rather than any wider group of 'Krahn' people. By the mid-1980s, some sectors of the Americo-Liberian community had been reincorporated in strategic alliances with Doe's regime. Their economic power made it necessary for the new government to offer them concessions in return for their support, and tax exemptions and compensation for businesses that had been damaged during the coup were arranged. Some became senior officials in Doe's government, continuing their pre-coup practices of corruption, and contributing to the increasingly illegal political economy. Other Americos in exile were active in supporting opposition to Doe's government, and some encouraged the later rise of Charles Taylor, a mixed Americo who, originally one of the radicals, had fallen out with Doe and left the government early on under charges of embezzlement.

Competition among the original coupists had led to the early removal by Doe of his major rival, a Gio man from Nimba county who had taken the vice-presidency in 1980. As with Taylor, this man, Thomas Quiwonkpa, spent time in exile gathering support to depose Doe's government. A coup attempt was made following Doe's faked victory at the 1985 election, to which the latter retaliated by targeting Quiwonkpa's followers and kinsmen. The ethnic complexion was heightened by the fact that the man generally thought to have won the election, Jackson Doe, was also a Gio. Gios and a related group from the same area, Manos, were targeted in a series of brutal reprisals. The government army was ordered to burn villages in Nimba county, and disappearances were reported in Monrovia (Berkeley, 1986). The severity of the attacks and their overtly tribal nature contributed greatly to later ethnically based violence. These actions were the first use of mass ethnically targeted violence, and formed part of Doe's wider strategy designed to intimidate both his enemies and supporters.

By the late 1980s, Liberia was degenerating into a state of insecurity. The nature of accumulation by the political elite had changed from a long-term and relatively rational process, albeit exploitative, to one in which a 'get rich quick' mentality prevailed, as the hold on power by the new elite became increasingly tenuous. Although there had always been corruption, many elements of a modern state had previously functioned under Americo-Liberian rule, and had worked to regulate law, order and development. Under Doe, repression of political opposition became increasingly violent, with disappearances and extra-judicial executions of some of those attempting to challenge Doe's hold on power. The opposition to the regime was made up of powerful players from a cross-section of Liberian society and Liberians in exile, and although Americos, Manos and Gios were involved, there was no overt ethnic dimension.

The first war During the first part of the war, from its launch on 24 December 1989 as an incursion led by Charles Taylor until the first ceasefire agreement was signed in November 1990, ethnicity appeared as a major factor in the conflict. The fighting between the government army, the AFL (Armed Forces of Liberia), and Taylor's rebels, the NPFL

(National Patriotic Front of Liberia), involved civilians from the start, and perceived supporters of each side, some identified by their ethnic group, were targeted by the other. In effect, certain groups were treated by fighters as an integral part of the war, and were therefore regarded as legitimate targets. Early AFL actions in the northern Mano and Gio areas, through which the NPFL entered the country, prompted mass flight, and the refugees reported the widespread burning of villages and violence directed against themselves, including mass executions (Human Rights Watch, 1990). Reprisals against these groups were also carried out in Monrovia by Doe's mainly Krahn presidential guard and other supporters, and within the AFL itself. These attacks fuelled the resentment and fear of the AFL and its Krahn members among the northerners.

Taylor is widely believed to have chosen Nimba county specifically to launch his attack on the government, in order to exploit the anti-government sentiment created by the earlier violence (Osaghae, 1996: 93). The original NPFL consisted of only about 150 trained guerrilla soldiers, including former AFL members, some of whom had left Liberia following the failed 1985 coup, and mercenaries from Burkina Faso and elsewhere. These were augmented by new recruits as they advanced. The brutal tactics used by the AFL to try to crush the rebellion encouraged Manos and Gios to join the NPFL, partly in self-defence, and partly for revenge. Although the AFL contained all Liberia's ethnic groups, the elite forces had become Krahn-dominated, and it was these units which were sent to repulse the NPFL advance, using the same 'scorched earth' tactics employed in 1985. Many AFL soldiers of other ethnic groups deserted early on, some joining the rebels, and in May 1990 Mano and Gio soldiers were disarmed, imprisoned or killed (Osaghae, 1996: 95).

Although the rebel incursions were initially welcomed by the Liberian population, which was keen to see the end of the Doe regime, the methods used by the rebels quickly alienated them from the majority. Certain groups were targeted by rebels, either as part of the overall strategy of overthrowing the government, or as an effect of the violence rebels had themselves been subjected to. Many NPFL recruits were child soldiers and teenagers, taken from villages that had been attacked, and reportedly favoured by Taylor because of their vulnerability and malleability (Human Rights Watch, 1990). Groups targeted by NPFL fighters were the Krahn people, defined imprecisely by appearance or dialect; the Mandingo, seen as associated with Doe's corrupt government and as having aided the AFL during the initial attacks in the north; so-called 'fat bellies', again those associated with the corruption of the government, but encompassing professionals and anyone deemed successful; and, later, members of ECOWAS (Economic Community of West Africa) countries.

There were many battles between the AFL and NPFL, as the rebels progressed towards the capital, and stories of massacres and violence perpetrated by them against civilians increased. The AFL was also responsible for further attacks against civilians, with Mano and Gio people being targeted, as in the Lutheran Church massacre in June 1990, in which 600 displaced people from Nimba, many of them women, children and the elderly, were killed. AFL soldiers also targeted wealthy groups in Monrovia, with Americo-Liberians being singled out for theft and assassination. NPFL attacks usually took the form of executions. The reasons given to the civilians were based on the above categories of people targeted. Those fleeing the war would be accosted on the roads, and forced to pay or give up valuables, and then be sentenced based on ethnic group or profession. Those unconnected with the targeted groups would normally be allowed to go if they could pay their way, although many people were killed randomly on the roads by 'gun-happy' rebels. In villages, rebels often singled out and killed civic and religious leaders in order to establish their own authority. Fear was used deliberately as a potent weapon. Killing also took place in displaced camps, particularly Fendall campus outside Monrovia, where some rebels had self-imposed quotas of people to kill each day.

The inclusion in the violence of this period of Mandingos, government officials, and ECOWAS nationals, as well as random civilians, demonstrates clearly that the violence was not primarily ethnic in cause or intent. Ethnicity was used by the government army and by the rebel groups as a category through which to direct their wider strategies. The previous linking by Doe of political allegiance with ethnic identity fed into a cycle of revenge and counter-attack, which motivated the attacks on Krahn people by the rebels, and on Manos and Gios by the AFL. These groups were presented to each other as enemies by their leaders and by those who had themselves suffered the violence. The other groups were seen by NPFL fighters as part of a more general enemy, those responsible for corruption and mismanagement, and those supporting the status quo.

The extent of the violence of this discrete period suggests that a vicious cycle was created, where the frustrations of a generation and more of government repression and corruption were vented in an orgy of violence. Anyone associated with the state and its institutions was a potential target for summary execution by the rebels. Following Doe's model, extreme violence was used by rebel groups against civilians as a way of instilling fear of, and therefore loyalty to, the new rulers. Civilians were viewed as targets within the fighting, as they constituted the necessary legitimizers or support groups for the competing leaders. The related power and impunity that was created through the fighting fuelled the violence further as individual soldiers and rebels became increasingly out of control. This period was ended by the serious famine in Monrovia in late 1990 and the imposition of some semblance of order in November by ECOMOG (ECOWAS Monitoring Group), the US government and Liberian leaders.

The second war The second war in Liberia started during 1992. Although the ceasefire had held since November 1990, the political stalemate between the interim government in Monrovia and Taylor's administration based upcountry in Gbarnga had prevented any permanent resolution. Taylor held over 90% of Liberia's territory as Greater Liberia, in which he established parallel economic and political institutions in order to consolidate power and in an attempt to build a constituency among civilians. Taylor reopened much of the extractive industry based upcountry, and invested in the media and in arms. Levels of open violence decreased markedly, but it continued as an underlying threat for civilians, particularly where economic issues were at stake. Both the major international players – Nigeria, as the main force within ECOMOG, and the USA – remained opposed to Taylor, the latter due to his links with Libya and the atrocities committed during the war, and the former due to the close connection between then President Babangida and the late President Doe.

A new armed group was formed in 1991 by powerful AFL refugees in Sierra Leone and former Mandingo politicians and businessmen based out of Guinea. The United Liberation Movement or ULIMO launched attacks on Greater Liberia from Sierra Leone, and gained ground in the western counties throughout 1992. ULIMO had previously fought with the Sierra Leone army against the rebel uprising there, and had close links with US military and ECOMOG stationed in Sierra Leone. In October 1992, the NPFL launched a major attack on Monrovia, which was resisted by ECOMOG forces with the help of the reconstituted AFL. There commenced a short period of what might be called real war, with the direct involvement of an international force (in effect, mainly Nigerian) against Charles Taylor and the NPFL.

Until July the following year, when an agreement was signed by the warring parties at Cotonou, Benin, ECOMOG fought in a coalition against Taylor, with ULIMO and the AFL attacking on the ground and the Nigerian airforce and warships concentrating on damaging important economic infrastructure in Taylor's territory. Some international attention was given to the partisan nature of ECOMOG's actions, and a small UN military contingent, UNOMIL (United Nations Military Observers), was sent in as a monitoring force with observer status. Sporadic media coverage helped to expose the dubious role of ECOMOG, but informed reporting was not sustained (Atkinson, 1996). Between Cotonou and the signing of a new accord in September 1995 at Abuja, Nigeria, fighting continued along the same lines: ECOMOG and Nigeria continued to lend support and supply arms to factions opposed to Taylor, but limited direct military engagement with the NPFL. ULIMO, the LPC (Liberian Peace Council), a proxy faction for the AFL set up after Cotonou, and another breakaway NPFL group, the CDC–NPFL, all took territory from the NPFL, and, as a coalition, occupied Taylor's headquarters at Gbarnga for a few months in 1994.

The factions opposing Taylor were led predominantly by former associates of Doe's government. The Mandingo element of ULIMO split from their former allies in early 1994 forming ULIMO–K (Kromah, after its leader). This break was triggered by a failure to agree on the allocation of seats in the transitional government, which, according to the Cotonou agreement, were distributed among the factions. Since the split the ULIMO groups have fought each other over valuable diamond territories in western Liberia, sometimes involving ECOMOG soldiers, also competing over the trade. The LPC managed to hold large parts of the south-east during 1994 and 1995, including the strategic ports, hardwood forests and gold deposits. While defending this land from the NPFL, the LPC exploited the local economy, allying itself with ECOMOG to ship goods and import arms along the coast. Taylor and the NPFL also continued to survive through the exploitation of local resources, taxing harvests and trade, stealing at gun-point, and illegally extracting and exporting the country's natural resources (Atkinson, 1997). The allocation of government seats in Monrovia to factional appointees following Cotonou allowed for the integration of the upcountry war economy developed by Taylor in Greater Liberia, with the corruption endemic in the interim administrations (Atkinson, 1997).

All the factions used highly illegal methods to control territory and extract resources, often involving serious human rights abuses against local civilian populations. These include: the prevention of civilians from leaving dangerous front-line areas, the use of civilians as forced labour; rape, torture and other physical attacks; and widespread extortion and stealing. As in the first war, civilians have also been subjected to summary execution, and there have been small- and large-scale massacres. Testimonies from a variety of sources suggest that these tactics have been used by all factions, and for similar ends, although intensity and types of violence used have varied. The systematic use of forced labour has been reported particularly by LPC fighters in the south-east and by ULIMO–J in the west. ULIMO–K appears to be implicated in more incidents involving cannibalism and the desecration of religious or cultural symbols in their attacks on villages. Direct violence was reported less in NPFL areas after the first war and more sustainable economic systems have been allowed. NPFL control has been more implicit, as Taylor focused on building local political constituencies, making use of the media to spread his influence, and encouraging the resumption of local taxable economic activities. However, NPFL fighters have continued to commit atrocities, particularly in the treatment of those accused of collaboration with other factions, and in the forcible extraction of economic resources from civilians.

Taylor regained some lost territory during the April 1996 war, which was his final attempt to take Monrovia by force. This time he was allied to ULIMO–K, with the support of ECOMOG following his *rapprochement* with the Nigerians, which had been consolidated in the Abuja I accord in September 1995. Taylor teamed up with ULIMO–K to try to weaken the other, mainly Krahn factions (ULIMO–J, the AFL and LPC), by attacking them within Monrovia itself. Although the attempt failed in Monrovia, as fighters on both sides went on looting sprees and attacked civilians, Taylor was able to take back much of the south-east from the LPC, their fighters having been drawn into Monrovia to support the AFL and ULIMO–J. This territorial gain greatly strengthened Taylor's strategic position in relation to the other factions, and contributed to his willing participation in the electoral process. In spite of his loss of face in Monrovia, the balance of power shifted in Taylor's favour at the same time as international interests converged in a new commitment to seek a real solution to the conflict. A new agreement signed in September 1996, Abuja II, included targeted sanctions on those failing to comply. An ostensibly successful disarmament process culminated in July 1997 in the holding of free and fair elections, won by Taylor in a landslide victory, with up to 75% majorities across much of the country.

Ethnicity and the functions of violence

Ethnicity has ostensibly played an important role in the Liberian war, both as a causal factor and in the techniques used by those fighting. However, its role must be understood in the context of the competition between and among various groups, with ethnicity being only one of many factors compelling people to instigate violence against others. The perceptions of those perpetrating the violence are important, but while hostility may be expressed in terms of ethnicity, this may be symbolic of other causes. The identification of enemies by ethnic group had been unknown in Liberia since earlier in the century when land or trade-route disputes continued sporadically between some neighbouring groups. In these localized conflicts, however, ethnicity was a symbol of geographic or political boundaries between groups, while during the civil war it became a symbol of civilian support for those contesting power at the national level. The association of politicians or warlords with particular ethnic groups was not universal, and only arose as one mechanism used by those seeking a constituency. While during the first war ethnic identification gained currency as a means of targeting violence, it was again only one of many factors driving the deeper political conflict.

The Liberian war is often portrayed as having involved little real fighting between the factions, but rather predation on civilians was pursued for individual ends. Violence directed against civilians was used as an integral part of attempts by factions to accumulate and demonstrate power and control. The various factions and alliances that have developed during the war have always been struggling to take and hold territory, partly for direct and often personal economic gain, but also, importantly, as part of their wider strategy of establishing themselves in control of specific areas, with the ultimate goal being the presidency of the nation. Even Mandingo leader Alhaji Kromah, acknowledged by most Liberians to have little hope of gaining a national constituency because of his minority ethnicity, has always considered himself to be a serious contender for the presidency, or the national political arena, while LPC leader George Boley, identified as a Krahn south-easterner, likewise competes at the national level. The political struggles at the national level influence and dominate those played out at local levels, and the violence perpetrated at all levels is a function of this national struggle for power.

The nature of violence used during the war evolved according to the tactics of leaders and fighters. While the initial struggle to oust Doe released an outpouring of violence that was expressed through ethnic targeting, as the war developed violence became more directly functional, in terms of being used at local levels for economic survival and empowerment by individual fighters and commandos, while their leaders attempted to accumulate territory and wealth to support their own higher ambitions. Other factions adopted the strategy used by Taylor of attempting to control all economic flows in their own areas, and the coping mechanisms of more and more people thus became linked to this violent system. Mechanisms for economic exploitation included direct theft, and the increasing use of forced labour, for digging alluvial gold, and in the diamond mines, harvesting and carrying food and cash crops. The splintering of factions and emergence of later groups demonstrated both that it was increasingly difficult to survive, causing people to try increasingly desperate strategies, but also that opportunities were being continuously created within the culture of impunity that could be seized by any aspiring rebels or politicians, thus adding to the problem. Following the Cotonou agreement that integrated the upcountry military and territorial struggles with the national political arena based in Monrovia, the culture of impunity was widened and strengthened.

Violence also became more unpredictable as the war developed, as the identification of victims was based on fewer constant factors than before. Historical local conflicts, over land rights for example, economic exploitation, and perceived loyalty to opposing groups, sometimes seen in terms of ethnicity, all played a role in local-level violence perpetrated by individual fighters. Much of the violence took place at the frontlines, mainly within Central Liberia, although encompassing parts of all counties. Atrocities were often directed against those civilians who were perceived as having been harbourers of the previous occupying faction, and who were thus understood to be legitimate targets. Violence was used as a method to instil fear and thus ensure the loyalty or submission of civilian populations. The strategies of the factions, and techniques used by fighters, changed according to circumstances. On arrival in some areas, some factions would announce themselves as saviours of the village, and demonstrate their power only through firing weapons, or even through displays of magic. Many civilians accounted for later violence as being due to the failure of factions to provide supplies for the fighters, who were forced into increasingly violent strategies in order to provide for themselves and the clients who inevitably come to depend on them. Thus while specific national political and economic processes were driving the overall course of the war, diverse and unpredictable factors were involved in determining the nature of more localized violence.

One widely reported massacre highlights the complexity of the motivation involved, including its ethnic aspect. Both ULIMO groups targeted villagers in their territorial attacks on each other, often killing individuals on the basis of their perceived collaboration with the enemy ULIMO. Sinje, a small, predominantly Vai, village in the south-west, was seen by the local ULIMO–K fighters as having close links with a notorious ULIMO–J commando. Although the Vai people are traditionally mainly Muslim, and thus share more cultural ties with the Mandingo people than others, ULIMO–K targeted the village and massacred at least 24 people in one attack alone. The ostensible reason for the attack was the large delivery of relief aid, including food, that the village had just received. Although this was undoubtedly an important factor in provoking the attack, it was in fact judged by survivors to have been the secondary motive, the primary being the punishment of the Vai people for their perceived support of ULIMO–J (Justice and Peace Commission, 1996).

The Mandingo case further demonstrates the complexity of the motivations involved in provoking violence. Mandingos have been involved in the conflict both at national political levels, and in terms of localized, targeted 'ethnic' violence, and some conflict between Mandingos and other groups continues in parts of the country. While the Mandingo diaspora has throughout its history retained its separate identity, in Liberia Mandingos have become integrated to the extent that in some northern and western areas they hold hereditary chiefdoms, including land rights. Their Muslim religion is shared by approximately 20% of Liberia's population. They have, however, always been seen by Liberians as 'foreign', with some referring to them as Guineans, and have been resented in a way similar to Jewish people elsewhere, in terms of their success in business, and their cultural differences. Although they have gained political representation and power through their economic clout, they have been excluded from secret societies, and this has led to tension at times, especially in central Liberia in the mid-1980s. The immediate reason for the targeting of Mandingos during 1990 has been given differently by various sources, suggesting that although it might have been sparked by some initial action by particular Mandingo people in a specific case in the early months of the war, the impulses behind the violence must be attributed to broader social issues of envy and exclusion.

While the basic logic of the conflict can be found in the competition over political and economic resources, violence also has its own logic and built-in reasons for escalation. The need for survival at local levels, combined with the desire for revenge of those themselves subjected to violence, fed into a vicious circle of violence that could sometimes be manifested in ethnic targeting. Psychologists have suggested that mass violence can be instigated merely through the creation by leaders of a strong ideology around which populations can be motivated. In Nazi Germany or Hutu-dominated Rwanda, the threat to the majority group by a powerful minority was used to rouse civilians to commit violence against the perceived enemy. The threat is sold to civilians as relating to their own security, but the objective of the violence is to strengthen the power of those in control. In Liberia during the 1980s and in the first war, ethnicity served this same purpose – as one of the many tools used by leaders to build support. Leaders have relied on the subjective interpretations of ethnicity by the groups involved, but have themselves specifically cultivated animosities between groups by helping to instigate the initial violence.

The very recent emergence of these ethnic animosities in Liberia can be seen clearly in the case of the conflict between Krahns and Manos and Gios. The former category was not even identified as an ethnic group by anthropologists before Doe's time. Lexicostatistical research carried out in the 1970s showed major semantic differences between the western and eastern areas, and mutual unintelligibility be-tween some of the various dialects (Ingemann et al., 1974). The Krahn identity has become cohesive only through its use by Doe as a means to garner support and ensure loyalty among close followers. The fact that the challenge to Doe during the 1980s came from a Gio man is purely coincidental. If another opponent of the regime had mounted the 1985 coup, it is likely that a different ethnic group would have been targeted for reprisal. The marginal role being played by ethnicity by the end of the war is demonstrated in the figures for the geographical background of fighters (collected during the disarmament period), which showed that fighters in all factions came from all areas of the country (UNDHA, 1997).

Taylor himself initially exploited the ethnic animosity encouraged by Doe, which served his purpose as a means of garnering support for the incursion. The strategy in fact backfired in that the extent of violence that was triggered seriously damaged his international reputa-tion. After the first war, Taylor concentrated on building a national political constituency for his bid for power, based on popular support from civilian populations in NPFL areas. Although he continued to pursue a military strategy for territorial domination and to secure the economic means necessary to achieve it, Taylor always recognized the importance of civilian support, and his win in the election testifies to his success in this area. His ability to build alliances at macro levels with political players across ethnic or other boundaries, as well as with national and international business interests, and to gain the support of civilian populations, again of all ethnic categories, through allowing more sustainable economic and social structures than other factions, as well as through the use of media as propaganda, finally enabled him to prevail over his competitors in the struggle for national power.

Ethnicity, war and the media

Media representations of ethnicity It may be argued that the various international, national and local-level dimensions of the civil war, as discussed above, are in fact far too complicated for journalists either to understand themselves, or to convey to their readers. The complexity of the war, including its ethnic aspects, has been amply demonstrated by the brief foregoing discussion, and journalists cannot be expected to become specialists in anthropology or political science. The purpose of media coverage of distant conflict is not, moreover, to provide detailed analyses of the causes and issues involved, but rather is merely to brief Western audiences on the development of the war as it happens, and perhaps to attempt a superficial analysis of some of the international political implications. The evolving structures of the modern media as fast-moving, profit-driven image industries also work to hinder the development of informed and responsible reporting, particularly of distant wars (Benthall, 1993). However, the importance of the media in terms of their role in shaping perceptions, and thus policies, does assign to them a moral responsibility to represent the realities of such wars in a careful manner, and to avoid adding to stereotyped misrepresentations. When the media make assertions based on primordial ethnic interpretations, and assume a particular position on the causes of the war, then it does become necessary to critique their analysis, and to show in what ways they have promoted misunderstandings.

The media surveyed for this section include most Western press and TV coverage, and African media sources, which have almost universally portrayed the war in a superficial and misleading way, with the few exceptions merely proving the rule. Much media coverage of the war in Liberia has, since 1990, projected essentialist ethnic interpretations of the violence. Many articles about the war in the British press and on the international news wires have, up to the present, included a mention of the ethnic divisions both between the Americo-Liberians and indigenous Liberians, and between the Krahn and other tribal groups. Many, especially from the period of the first war, reflect the tone of a recent BBC book on warfare, which stated that 'African tribalism caused a bloody civil war in Liberia in 1989' (quoted in Allen, see above pp. 32–3). Little of the political issues at stake in Liberia is conveyed by such assertions, and the impression given that the conflict is based in ethnic strife is misleading. Few mentions have been made of the politicized nature of the ethnic aspects of the conflict, with the suggestion made instead, despite no evidence whatsoever, that the tribal issues are deep-seated and intractable.

Journalists have also concentrated heavily on the so-called barbarism displayed by fighters in the war. Photos accompanying articles have often pictured child-fighters with their guns, although these constitute only 10% of the fighters (UNDHA, 1997), and headlines have focused on savagery and cannibalism. 'He killed my brother and ate his heart', appeared as a headline in the *Observer* during the April war in Monrovia, even though the story referred to an event that had taken place in the countryside months if not years earlier (*Observer*, 10 April 1996). *The Economist* headlines include 'Savagery' (9 September 1995), 'Horror Story' (21 November 1992), and 'Shambles' (24 September 1994), with articles referring to 'Liberia's gruesome civil war' (6 April 1991; 31 July 1993), and even the 'Hobbesian chaos that grips Liberia' (1 June 1991). While something of the reality of the violence may be captured through the use of this kind of emotive language, the overall impression given is highly superficial and dangerous in its implication that this war is different, and worse in some way, from wars in Europe or elsewhere.

The conclusions drawn about the war in many press articles suggest that the violence is ethnically motivated, barbaric, mindless and impossible to understand. These perspectives became the accepted analysis of the war, and the image of policy-makers despairing of finding or imposing a solution is the natural consequence of this outlook. This view was encapsulated in an *Economist* article of 1995 which stated 'there was never any convincing reason for the fighting in the first place' (9 September 1995), and went on to disparage the chances of success of the latest attempts at resolution. Most commentaries have failed to recognize the nature of the tactics used by the factions, which necessarily involve violence against civilians, interpreting it instead as gratuitous and thus particularly nasty – for example: 'It is an African *Clockwork Orange* in which militias don't even pretend to stand for anything other than looting villagers of all they own' (*International Herald Tribune*, 22 January 1996).

As the war continued, this attitude gained in prevalence, with much of the coverage of the fighting in April 1996 portraying a similar lack of analysis and understanding. *Time* magazine discussed the 'murderous chaos' and 'swirling new ring of hell' in the country, while making no attempt to provide some history of the conflict (*Time*, 22 April 1996). Most articles focused on the evacuation of relief workers and other expatriates. The history of the war was given in a brief sentence, or was not mentioned at all, as if only the current violence was of interest to readers, and an understanding of the background was unimportant. Journalists moved from a focus on ethnic factors to concentrate on the supposed pointlessness of the war, as if once the clearly ethnic dimension was diminished, no other explanation could be found. A *New York Times* article named 'A War without Purpose in a Country without Identity' (22 January 1995) reflected this trend. The implication was that violence was being perpetrated for no good reason, as if the political and economic motivations behind the conflict, and control of the distribution of the great natural wealth of Liberia, were somehow not worthy causes of war.

There has been some media attention to the development in African wars of mercenary armies, comprising mainly ex-South African troops, which have been employed by governments in Sierra Leone and Angola (*Sunday Times*, 19 October 1997; *The Economist*, 13 July 1996; *Observer*, 19 January 1997). The close links of these military operations to resource extraction, mainly diamonds, has aroused some interest. However, coverage of these issues has been limited, and the implications of such developments have not been explored. Scattered articles appeared in the French press, particularly on the subject of the war economy in Liberia, and the role within it of French timber interests (*La Tribune de L'Economie*, 2 September 1992; *Marchés Tropicaux et Mediteranéens*, 28 July 1995; *Croissance*, February 1996). In this case, the media attention may have had some small positive impact. French NGOs later drew on the information in these articles and produced more detailed analyses of the operations of the war economy, which may have in some way contributed to the subsequent US and EU interest and action (Jean and Rufin, 1996; US State Department, 1996). However, again coverage has been limited and not sustained.

The danger of the superficiality of media coverage and its focus on 'new barbarism' imagery lies in the perpetuation of racist myths about Africa, and in the obscuring of international roles in sustaining conflicts there. Liberia has often been referred to in the international press, along with Somalia, as one of the basket-cases of the continent, and beyond help or even hope. The civil war has been used continuously by media analysts as an example to support theories of the disintegration of the state in Africa, the re-emergence of primitive tribalism, and the general perceived inability of Africans to live together in order and peace. Liberia is mentioned in almost every article that, in the first half of the 1990s, lamented the desperate state of the African continent, and the imagery of its war lends itself to the heart of darkness school of inflammatory African commentary.

This school of thought is typified by Kaplan's 'The Coming Anarchy' (1994), but is well represented throughout the media, including in publications such as the *Guardian* or *The Economist*, which are normally renowned for their independent and sound judgement. Under headlines such as 'Darkest Africa' (13 February 1993), and 'Tribalism Revisited' (21 December 1991), *The Economist* asserts that 'many of the insurgencies ... are simply violent expressions of tribalism', while the *Guardian*, in a piece entitled 'Africa, the Lost Continent', claimed that 'the unravelling of ancient customs and complex civilisations threatens vast areas of the continent with a future in which Conrad's *Heart of Darkness* will be read as a straightforward description' (8 April 1994). A widely reported book by a black American visiting Africa for the first time encapsulates the view of many. Speaking about Rwanda, Keith Richburg states: 'I realised that fully evolved human beings in the twentieth century don't do things like that. These must be cavemen' (reported in the *Sunday Times*, 1 June 1997; *Evening Standard*, 15 April 1997).

The role of narrative The foregoing analysis of the development of the war demonstrated the importance of detail in understanding why the conflict followed particular trajectories and why the violence has taken particular forms. Although complex, such an analysis is crucial so that policy-makers are properly informed of the realities of the conflict and can base their decisions on facts rather than perceptions or assumptions. Clean, sober narrative of this type has, however, become unfashionable in the media world where fast-moving and powerful images are seen as necessary to capture the attention of bored readers or viewers. The focus by the media on the postmodern imagery of small-boy Rambos fighting in the jungle has displaced any deeper analysis of the causes of war, filling in the gaps with empty and stereotyped representations of barbaric Africa. As argued by Paul Richards in relation to Sierra Leone, one of the consequences of the 'new barbarist' paradigm is to obscure the role of those countries involved in the modern war economies of West Africa, and to mask their responsibility for the social damage that results (Richards, 1996). Similarly, in Liberia, the international response was limited by a lack of understanding of the realities of the conflict.

The images presented of African conflicts as primitive and backward reinforce existing prejudices and limit further examination of their causes and impact. Conclusions are drawn, based on this imperfect analysis, that the West can play no positive role to help Africans with their local and historical conflicts, with disengagement seen as the only sensible strategy, and that perhaps humanitarian aid can be offered through the non-committal channel of NGOs. Even in the early 1990s mood of optimism for the potential of international interventions in civil conflict, Liberia was portrayed as too difficult, messy and local a conflict for the West to be able to intervene successfully. As the war continued, it became a supporting case for those arguing for more general Western disengagement (*The Economist*, 1 July 1995). The use of relief aid as a palliative by the international community to avoid political engagement has been discussed by commentators in relation to other contemporary conflicts (Borton et al., 1994). While relief allocations to Liberia have exceeded an average of US$100 million every year, with the majority donated by the US government, direct political intervention in Liberia by the international community was for many years limited and ineffectual.

The USA delegated direct intervention to the ECOWAS, and the UN response consisted of the often questionable interventions by the Special Representatives of the Secretary-General (first sent only after Taylor's 1992 offensive), and resolutions supporting the operations of ECOMOG. Although these interventions suffered from a lack of commitment, they did however have an impact on the development of the conflict. International support for the ECOMOG actions against the NPFL from 1991 to 1995 arguably contributed to the development of new factions, with the US government providing military aid and intelligence, and UN resolutions (788, 896) providing the legal framework. French and Ivoirian support for the NPFL was also a key factor in the war, while many countries were involved in illegal economic trade with all factions. The lack of direct criticism of the role played by international interventions in the war, with most discussion focused on internal, supposedly incomprehensible factors, highlights the failure of analysis by the media. The failure of 13 peace agreements, all backed by regional forces and the international community, has always been portrayed by the media as resulting from continuing squabbling between factions, with little mention of the role of the UN and diplomats in the various failures. There has also been little discussion of the duty of the international community, particularly once it has decided to intervene, to do so in an effective and responsible manner.

The lack of understanding of how national political struggles have been played out, with their local, regional and international dimensions, has thus been a primary factor in the lack of effective action by the international community until six years into the war. The war was seen to be ethnic conflict, with the horrific violence understood as an expression of deep primitive instincts and loyalties. The hidden implication, that Liberians are at some backward phase of their political development, forms part of the more general analysis of the African situation. If conflicts are seen as caused by factors unique to Liberian or African history and culture, with their causes so deeply embedded, then it becomes difficult to see how the West could intervene effectively.

The lack of analysis thus provides a public justification for the lack of engagement, while at the same time obscuring the activities in the international sphere that do in fact have a direct impact on the development of the war. But neither the conclusion that intervention should be limited, nor the covert actions that do take place, are based on any real critique of the war and potential for effective action.

Analyses of the causes of conflict and crisis in Africa rarely make more than a passing reference to the political roles of Western countries or to the importance of Africa's economic resources in the world economy, except perhaps to mention the support for too long by superpowers of greedy dictators. In Liberia too this was a factor, but as the war progressed, the role of its illegal export economy in the conflict, involving leading members of the international economy, became a far more significant influence, contributing to the power of existing warlords and increasing the incentives of competing to aspiring fighters, warlords and politicians. Media and other sources have almost consistently failed to analyse the economic aspects of African wars, which arguably form the crux of many conflicts, providing as they do both the motivation and the means for expressing or resolving competition through violent conflict. The links between the economic strategies of those competing for national power and international businesses operating in the semi-legal or illegal global economy is where analysis of contemporary wars should be focused, and where targeted interventions may have most impact.

Effective action to resolve the Liberian conflict was successful only following serious attention by the international community to the issue of the illegal economy and its role in perpetuating the war. Analysis of the extent of illegal economic activity was publicized by the US government in mid-1996, and the sanctions that were introduced in the Abuja II accord included the threat of freezing bank accounts and holding a war crimes tribunal. Although this coincided with changes in the balance of power nationally, it certainly had an impact on the calculations of faction leaders, arguably contributing to their willingness to participate in elections. The impact of the exposure by US officials of the extent of the war economy and the threats which were introduced, which arguably influenced the decision-making processes of the faction leaders, demonstrates the potential of informed analysis based on clear narrative.

As a mechanism to intervene more effectively in African conflicts, attempts to introduce or enforce controls on the operations of international companies that do business in war zones could actually have a positive impact, through reducing incentives to use violence to resolve conflict. But without analysis from the media and other sources of information it is difficult for policy-makers to develop such strategies. Detailed information is needed to build analyses of the mechanisms of such trade, and thus to help devise ways to restrict it. Superficial imagery focusing on the supposed primitive violence of ethnic war can only fuel misunderstanding. It seems sad that in the age of information, useful knowledge is still scarce, particularly in this field where its application could be so helpful. Greater commitment by media organizations to responsible and high-quality investigative journalism and foreign coverage could go some way to providing it.

Chronology of major events

1847 Establishment of Liberian nation by Americo-Liberians; American-style constitution adopted.

1931 League of Nations Enquiry into allegations against prominent Americo-Liberians of involvement in forced labour.

1944 Election of reformist President Tubman; initiation of twin policies of Unification and Open Door to foreign investment.

1971 Vice-President Tolbert succeeds Tubman on his death; continuation of reforms, including increased toleration of opposition political activity.

1980 Military coup ends Americo-Liberian hegemony; Krahn African Liberian Samuel Doe takes presidency.

1985 Doe fakes victory in elections; failed coup by former rival, Thomas Quiwonkpa, results in reprisals against his Gio ethnic group.

24 December 1989 Launching of insurgency by Taylor's NPFL (National Patriotic Front of Liberia); sparking of ethnic violence as the increasingly Krahn-only national army, the AFL (Armed Forces of Liberia), fights Gio and Mano followers of Taylor.

January–June 1990 Advance of NPFL towards Monrovia; large-scale human rights abuses perpetrated by both sides.

August 1990 Arrival of ECOWAS (Economic Community of West African States) Monitoring Group, ECOMOG; advance of NPFL halted.

November 1990 Ceasefire established at Bamako conference; interim government set up, but not recognized by Taylor, who establishes his own government upcountry.

1991–92 ULIMO (United Liberation Movement for Democracy) is set up by former members of Doe's government; advances made in NPFL territory in western counties.

October 1992 Operation Octopus launched; Taylor fails again to take Monrovia; sparks major combined action against NPFL.

July 1993 Agreement signed at Cotonou, Benin; initiates system of factional representation in national interim governments.

September 1993 LPC (Liberian Peace Council) formed as proxy faction for AFL; make advances in NPFL territory in southeast.

March 1994 Split between Krahn and Mandingo elements of ULIMO to form ULIMO–K (Mandingo) and ULIMO–J (Krahn), following disagreement over allocations of positions in interim government.

September 1994 Coalition forces, including ECOMOG, AFL and ULIMO, briefly take NPFL capital in central Liberia.

September 1995 Abuja I agreement signed in Nigeria, signalling *rapprochement* between Taylor and the Nigerians; Taylor arrives in Monrovia.

April 1996 NPFL, allied to ULIMO–K, launch attack on Monrovia; sparks fighting for six weeks against combined Krahn factions, ULIMO–J, LPC and AFL; NPFL retake most of the south-east from the LPC.

June 1996 Public awareness of war economy increased following testimony before US House of Representatives International Relations Committee.

September 1996 Abuja II agreement signed; targeted sanctions, including the threat of war crimes tribunal, greatly increases pressure on factions to comply.

December 1996–February 1997 Disarmament and demobilization; ostensibly successful with over 20,000 fighters disarmed, although only 8,000 weapons collected.

July 1997 Holding of democratic elections with international supervision; Taylor elected President as his National Patriotic Party takes 75% of the vote.

Notes

1. *The Economist*, 27 April 1991; Reuters, 11 February 1997.
2. For a detailed discussion of historical development and ethnicity in Liberia, see Liebenov, 1987; Sawyer, 1992; Osaghae, 1996.

References

Allen, T. and Eade, J. (1997) 'Anthropological Approaches to Ethnicity and Conflict in Europe and Beyond', *International Journal on Minority and Group Rights*, Vol. 4, pp. 217–46.

Atkinson, P. (1996) 'The Liberian Civil War: Images and Reality', *Contemporary Politics*, Vol. 2, No. 1, Spring, pp. 79–88.

— (1997) *The War Economy of Liberia: A Political Analysis*, London: Relief and Rehabilitation Network, Overseas Development Institute, May.

Benthall, J. (1993) *Disasters, Relief and the Media*, London: I.B.Tauris.

Berkeley, B. (1986) *Liberia: A Promise Betrayed*, New York: Lawyers Committee for Human Rights.

Borton, J. et al. (1994) Study 3 of *The International Response to Conflict and Genocide: Lessons from the Rwanda Experience*, London: Overseas Development Institute, March.

Brown, D. (1982a) 'On the Category "Civilised" in Liberia and Elsewhere', *Journal of Modern African Studies*, Vol. 20, No. 2, pp. 287–303.

— (1982b) 'Politics as Ritual: Rules as Resources in the Politics of the Liberian Hinterland', *African Affairs*, Vol. 81, No. 325, pp. 479–97.

— (1984) 'Warfare, Oracles and Iron: A Case Study of Production among the Pre-colonial Klowe in the Light of Some Recent Marxist Analyses', *Africa*, Vol. 54, No. 2, pp. 29–47.

— (1989) 'Bureaucracy as an Issue in Third World Management: an African Case Study', *Public Administration and Development*, Vol. 9, pp. 369–80.

Captier, C. (1996) *Liberia in the Throes of Civil War*, MA dissertation, War Studies Department, Kings College London.

Duffield, M. (1996) 'The Symphony of the Damned: Racial Discourse, Complex Political Emergencies and Humanitarian Aid', *Disasters*, Vol. 20, No. 3, September, pp. 173–93.

Ellis, S. (1995) 'Liberia 1989–1994: A Study of Ethnic and Spiritual Violence', *African Affairs*, Vol. 94, pp. 165–97.

— (1997) 'Liberia's Warlord Insurgency', mimeo.

Grimes, B. F. (ed.) (1996) 'Ethnologue: Languages of Liberia', part of *Ethnologue: Languages of the World*, 13th edn, London: Institute of Linguistics.

Henries, D. A. B. (1966) *The Liberian Nation: A Short History*, New York: Macmillan.

Human Rights Watch, Africa (1990) *Liberia: A Human Rights Disaster: Violations of the Laws of War by All Parties to the Conflict*, New York: Human Rights Watch.

Ingemann, F., Duitsman, J. and Doe, W. (1974) 'A Survey of the Krahn Dialects in Liberia', paper presented at the Tenth Congress of the West African Linguistic Society, 25 March.

Jean, F. and Rufin, J. (eds) (1996) *Economie des Guerres Civiles*, Paris: Hachette/ Pluriel.

Justice and Peace Commission (1996) *Report on the Sinje Massacre*, Monrovia, Liberia: Justice and Peace Commission.

Kaplan, R. (1994) 'The Coming Anarchy', *Atlantic Monthly*, February, pp. 44–76.

Liebenov, G. (1987) *Liberia: The Quest for Democracy*, Bloomington, IN: University of Indiana Press.

Murphy, W. P. and Bledsoe, C. H. (1987) 'Kinship and Territory in the History of a Kpelle Chiefdom (Liberia)', in I. Kopytoff (ed.), *The African Frontier: The Reproduction of Traditional African Societies*, Bloomington, IN: University of Indiana Press, pp. 123–47.

Osaghae, E. (1996) *Ethnicity, Class and the Struggle for State Power in Liberia*, Codesria Monograph Series, Dakar, Senegal: Codesria.

Richards, P. (1996) *Fighting for the Rain Forest: War, Youth and Resources in Sierra Leone*, London: The International Africa Institute in association with James Currey and Heinemann.

Sawyer, A. (1992) *The Emergence of Autocracy in Liberia: Tragedy and Challenge*, San Francisco, CA: Institute of Contemporary Studies.

UNDHA (1997) *Analysis of Disarmament Exercise*, New York: United Nations Department of Humanitarian Affairs.

US State Department (1996) Testimony of William Twaddell, Assistant Secretary of State for African Affairs, Hearing on Liberia before the House International Relations Committee, June.

. . . .

CHAPTER 11

'The War in the North': Ethnicity in Ugandan Press Explanations of Conflict, 1996–97

Mark Leopold

In recent years, Uganda has been presented as a model of economic, social and political reconstruction.[1] President Yoweri K. Museveni's National Resistance Movement (NRM) government has, since its inception in 1986, made great strides in integrating the country, bringing groups of people previously opposed to his rule into the system. At grassroots level, this has been achieved to a great extent through the role of elected Resistance Councils (RCs), now called Local Councils (LCs), which have enabled the decentralization of many governmental functions, particularly those most important to the everyday lives of ordinary people – land, property and marriage disputes, for example, and much of the criminal justice system.[2] At national level, care is taken that the different 'ethnic groups' of Uganda (still generally called 'tribes' by Ugandans) are represented in executive, legislative and judicial positions. Nevertheless, in Europe and North America, the predominant popular image of Uganda is still that of inexplicable, limitless ethnic violence; its synecdochal image the figure of Idi Amin.

In this chapter, however, I am concerned with an area of continuing conflict, frequently called by Ugandans 'the war in the north'.[3] While this is by no means the only zone of violence in the country, it has been the most bloody and persistent conflict over the past decade, the biggest failure of the NRM's policy of reconciliation and reconstruction. My focus is on Ugandan explanations of the roots of this conflict, particularly as expressed in the contemporary Ugandan press, and on the role of concepts of ethnicity in these explanations, which in many ways resonate with the negative popular image of the country in the West. I relate this discourse to a master trope which has dominated Ugandan politics since independence, one of 'north versus south', in which these terms are understood as standing for an ethnic, 'tribal' distinction. This model has many of its roots in the particularities of the Ugandan experience of colonial rule (more properly of imperial rule, since Uganda was never a British colony but a Protectorate, governed through a system of indirect rule and with no significant settler population).

Press and politics in contemporary Uganda

One reason for focusing on the Ugandan press is that the print media in Uganda are among the freest and most critical, not only in Africa but (in some ways at least) in the world.[4] Even the government-owned English-language paper, *New Vision*, carries material that is not only critical of government policy, but sometimes personally critical of President Museveni or members of his family. Although editors and journalists from more oppositional papers are occasionally arrested or harassed in other ways, the level of press freedom is generally very high and Uganda has some fine journalists. Of course, the English print media provide only one set of representations on offer to Ugandan society.[5] However, my ethnographic experience, both during four months or so spent in the capital, Kampala, and considerably longer in north-western Uganda, leads me to believe that, in respect of the issues considered in this chapter at least, these newspapers reflect and exhibit widespread attitudes. They could certainly be considered the attitudes of an elite, but they have a hegemonic position within a discourse on power and ethnicity that has dominated Ugandan politics, and which is of course reproduced, as well as reflected, by the press.

There is no space in this chapter for anything like a complete analysis of the complex course of post-independence Uganda, and good accounts of the background to, and the establishment of, the NRM regime already exist, particularly in the collections edited by Holger Bernt Hansen and Michael Twaddle (1988, 1991). Recent years have seen, alongside the country's extraordinary economic revival, a gradual extension of representative liberal-democratic institutions, with the election of a Constitutional Assembly in 1994 followed by both parliamentary and presidential elections in early 1996. Praised though they were by most outside observers, these polls clearly demonstrated a major and long-standing fissure in Ugandan society, between the mainly Bantu language-speaking people living south of the River Nile as it flows between Lakes Victoria and Albert, and the Nilotic (and Sudanic) language-speakers north of the river. The northern Acholi and Langi people are associated by southerners with Milton Obote's two regimes, while the north-westerners are seen as having supported Idi Amin. Among northerners,

Museveni's government is regarded as dominated by southerners, despite the presence of northerners and north-westerners in senior positions. The elections of the mid-1990s reflected this split: the north and north-west voting largely for anti-Museveni candidates, the more populous south for the NRM.

The same split was exhibited in continuing armed conflict in the north. Rebel groups operating in the northern districts of Gulu and Kitgum, and the north-western ones of Arua and Moyo, had fought the National Resistance Army (NRA) and its successor, the Ugandan People's Defence Force (UPDF), since the NRM's seizure of power in 1986. In the late 1980s, the predominant rebel group was the Holy Spirit Movement (HSM) led by 'Alice Lakwena', an Acholi prophetess, and rooted in Acholi religious and cultural tradition (Allen, 1991; Behrend, 1991, 1995). By the mid-1990s, the HSM had been succeeded by the Lord's Resistance Army (LRA), under an uncle of Alice Lakwena's known as Joseph Kony (Asowa-Okwe, 1997). In the north-west, the main rebel group was the West Nile Bank Front (WNBF – named after the colonial-era district of West Nile, presently Arua, Nebbi, and Moyo districts). The WNBF was led by Juma Oris, a former cabinet minister under Idi Amin. It had continued to fight after a previous group, the Uganda National Rescue Front (UNRF), led by another of Amin's one-time ministers, Moses Ali, had come to a peace agreement with the NRM. Moses Ali has subsequently held the posts of Second Deputy Prime Minister and Minister of Wildlife and Tourism in Museveni's cabinet.

The 'war in the north' had a further dimension, an international one. The LRA and WNBF were armed and funded by the government of Sudan. Their main bases were on Sudanese territory, and they were used by the Khartoum regime alongside government troops in military operations against the southern Sudanese rebels, the Sudan People's Liberation Army (SPLA – see EIU, 1995). In 1996, the WNBF's main operational base moved to Zaire and they received assistance from Mobuto's regime, eventually even replacing government soldiers in part of north-eastern Zaire, as Mobuto's losing battle against Laurent Kabila's Allied Democratic Forces for the Liberation of Congo–Zaire (ADFL) moved into its penultimate phase (Leopold, 1997). The Ugandan government, meanwhile, was widely seen as supporting the Zairean and Sudanese rebels, the SPLA and ADFL.

By mid-1996, two further factors led to an increased coverage of the northern war in the Ugandan press. The first was a considerable upsurge in the fighting, which led to the near isolation of the north-west, as LRA attacks cut off the road leading to the Nile crossing that links the former West Nile district to the rest of the country. The LRA attacked the civilian population of Gulu and Kitgum, mutilating and killing those who transgressed an ever-growing series of commandments – such as a ban on riding bicycles, keeping pigs, or possessing white animals, and other apparently religious-based instructions. The government responded by appointing the President's brother, a charismatic and controversial soldier and businessman known by his *nom de guerre* Salim Saleh, to command the military effort in the north. A more proactive strategy followed, including mass arrests and screening of local people, and the removal of the civilian population from the worst-affected areas in Gulu and Kitgum into 'protected villages' (Asowa-Okwe, 1997).

The second element behind the upsurge in press interest in the war and the 'northern question' as a whole was the inception in August 1996 of a major inquiry into the causes of, and possible solutions to, the war in the north. This represented the first attempt by the newly established Ugandan Parliament to hold the executive branch of government, Museveni and his cabinet, to account for its actions in such a sensitive area of national security and foreign policy. After a 'long, heated debate on the northern insurgency',[6] the matter was referred to the Sessional Committee of Parliament on Defence and National Security, which established the inquiry. Most of its hearings were held in public and many received near-verbatim coverage in the newspapers. Sessions were held in the north itself and witnesses included local leaders and other public figures from the north, as well as government and opposition politicians, and senior military officers. A wide range of views was expressed and reported over the six months the Committee was sitting.

Press coverage of the northern situation came under severe criticism from the government over this period. The tri-weekly *Monitor* reported in October that Salim Saleh had accused it of 'irresponsible and sensationalist reporting', and had called for the introduction of laws against the publication of such stories. Saleh was reported as warning an audience of journalists, 'if you act irresponsibly, you may oblige me to encroach on some of your freedoms'.[7] A fortnight later, the President himself, addressing a press conference, 'spent over an hour reading an assortment of laws concerning breach of national security and their attendant penalties. He warned that action would be taken if the papers did not take his warning.'[8] In December, the editor of the weekly *Uganda Express* was arrested and held for two days, and Museveni returned to the attack on the *Monitor*, summoning its editor for a dressing-down. The President's Adviser on Media and Public Relations, John Nagenda, told the *Crusader* that 'government would punish newspaper editors and journalists who have been "misreporting" the war in the north ... "Nobody is saying we enjoy crushing little bones of these journalists, but if everything else fails the law has to take its course," he said."[9]

Government criticism tended to concentrate on news stories that were regarded as 'inaccurate' or inopportune, but the press continued to publish critical news and opinion, as well as commenting on attempts to muzzle it. The bulk of the English-language media, including the daily papers,[10] are however generally supportive of the President and the NRM government, reserving criticism for specific policies, albeit on occasion highly sensitive ones.

Ethnicity and conflict in the Ugandan press: the Acholi factor

In this section, I concentrate on explanations for the northern conflict proffered in the Ugandan media over the period between the inception of the Parliamentary Inquiry into the war in August 1996 and the presentation of its report to Parliament in February 1997 (the next section will examine coverage of the Inquiry itself). Partly due to the Inquiry, over this period the media paid greater attention than usual to the root causes of the conflict, rather than simply reporting its developments. Conflicting views of these causes were expressed in interviews, letters to the editor, 'op-ed' pieces by academics and other opinion-formers, and signed or unsigned editorial pieces, as well as in the presentation of news stories. Almost inevitably, much of the argument was conducted in 'ethnic' terms or their standard Ugandan geographical euphemisms, 'north', 'south', 'north-west', and so forth. The war is generally presented as an 'Acholi' war, with its north-western component ignored or minimized. (Where it is not, as we shall see, it is also frequently discussed in ethnic terms.) Different notions of ethnicity are deployed (on all sides of the conflict) over a range from historical constructivism to pure primordialism. Even its international dimension is given an ethnic explanation: the northern tribes are seen as coming originally from Sudan and being historically involved in southern Sudanese politics.

The primordialist position was clearly expressed in a letter from a southern Ugandan correspondent published in the *Monitor*, defending General Saleh's views on the need for media censorship over the war in the north:

The fact is clearly visible that Acholi are killing Acholi whatever journalists and politicians want us to believe. The trend is part of Acholi history when you consider the Labong-Gipir saga, where an infant accidentally swallows your wife's bead and you insist and ensure that the babe gets dissected and the said bead washed from the gory entrails. In a nutshell, most Acholi that other Ugandans have met ... have little respect for human life.[11]

The reference here is to a well-known Nilotic foundation myth, in which two brothers quarrel over the swallowed bead and split apart from each other, forming the eastern (Acholi) and western (Alur) branches of the Ugandan Luo-speaking (Nilotic) peoples (Crazzolara, 1950). The warlike nature of the Acholi is thus explained as 'in their nature' from the very foundation of their society. In November, a 'Special Report' in the *Sunday Vision* explained the war in terms of the Acholi traditional belief in spirits (*Jogi*, sing. *Jok*), under the headline 'Acholi remote control – How the jogi belief fuelled the Kony war'.[12] In December, the *Crusader* published a debate (the terms were not used, but it was essentially between primordialist and constructivist explanations for the warlike behaviour of 'the Acholi'), in which the primordialists were represented by a southerner calling himself *'Byaka'*. Under the headline 'Northerners are natural murderers', he wrote:

> This society needs purification. The likes of Aliro and Onyango [journalists seen as pro-Acholi] should be brought before the law for inciting and encouraging the murderers.
>
> Those Acholi are murderers and they should be isolated from a true human society. The only life they have lived is plundering and shedding blood. Anything short of that, they will not accept. They hate anybody who tries to stop them from killing. That is why they hate Museveni.[13]

Byaka received some support from an apparently repentant Acholi, Charles Oyet p'Ojok:

> One can rightly say that the Acholi are the most barbarous tribe in Uganda. This is because they have been involved in all the atrocities inflicted on the people of Uganda ...
>
> The Acholi must learn to accept defeat and to forgive like other tribes in Uganda for peace to return to their land.[14]

An NRM activist, Kajahago Ka-Karusoke, put a mixed primordialist/ constructivist position. His headline was 'British cursed Acholi to false pride', under which he wrote:

> Many African countries are made up of many tribes, which were amalgamated by the colonial system as a higher stage of capitalism from Europe. But the period of colonisation in Africa could not crush tribal cocoons at once. These tribal cocoons are very much alive in the intestines of post-colonial independent states. They cause social pain in the political abdomens

of the newly independent states. That is why there is no peace in some African states …

… the British tried to convince the Acholi that they were taller, more broad shouldered, tougher, traditional warriors … So the Acholi became psychologically damaged by the British colonialists … The colonial authority also wanted rough and tough elements to implement their immediate colonial orders, and the Acholi were found to be the most suitable of all the tribal cocoons amalgamated by the colonial mechanism. Because the military is the chief component of state power, the Acholi found themselves in a politically significant position in the colonial set-up. They therefore inherited the political muscle and a mentality that became an obsession. (Ibid.)

A thoroughgoing constructivist line was put by the *Monitor*'s editor, Charles Onyango-Obbo, in a series of articles in his own paper, as well as in his column in the regional weekly based in Kenya, the *East African*: 'Throughout the colonial period, the British recruited people mainly from the North, mostly the Acholi, into the army. They propagated the myth that this was because the Northerners were naturally good warriors.'[15]

The Acholi, according to Onyango-Obbo, are a misunderstood people:

It often passes unnoticed, taking into account the problems the Northerners (the Acholi in particular) have had and the colonially implanted disadvantages they still suffer, that no other Ugandan nationality has been able to educate as many of their own as have the Acholi …

… when the 'Northern' armies and governments were eventually defeated by Yoweri Museveni's National Resistance Army in 1986, it was a triple crisis for the North in general and the Acholi in particular. First they lost raw power. Second, with the loss of power they lost access to the resources which they were investing in what was essentially an affirmative action project to 'catch up' with the rest of Uganda. Third, a crisis of self-worth set in since part of the Acholi identity was their view of themselves as great invincible warriors …

Thus, at the psychological level, the Kony war tapped into the need for the Acholi not so much to win back national power, but to restore pride and a sense of self-worth in themselves.[16]

Unsurprisingly, many Acholi commentators themselves tended to represent the problem as lying, not in Acholi ethnicity, but in the ethnic attitudes of southerners. As Amone p'Olak, a Makerere graduate student, put it:

the insurgency in the North is not about any past glory, but about social and economic justice. It is about remaining or not remaining on the map of

Uganda ... Ever since World War I, the Acholi have neither any cause for pride, nor any respect or honour. In fact, today it is not only criminal to talk for the Acholi but also to be an Acholi ... Today the Acholi do not only fear the rebels or the UPDF soldiers, but also fear being Acholi ... [The various Acholi-based rebel groups since 1986] are simply symptoms of a deeply psychologically traumatised society that is relentlessly searching for an identity in a country that does not care whether they exist on the map of Uganda or not.[17]

A similar point was made by Acholi elder, Lawrence Ocen, in an interview headed 'Govt should stop calling Northerners dogs':

The Kony problem is a result of President Museveni's system of government ... The one party system is bad ... Northerners are looked at as dogs. We heard it here on radio during the CA [Constitutional Assembly, the elected body which debated Uganda's new constitution, preceding the election of the Parliament]. We sent people like Celia Ogwal [a leading member of Milton Obote's UPC party] to the CA and every day we heard on radio how they were being called dogs. When they stood up to say anything they were called dogs and laughed at, they were ridiculed. Do you think we were happy? Do you think we are happy when they laugh at our representatives because they are not Movement supporters? ... How different are Northerners from Easterners, Westerners or Baganda? Who is a Northerner, anyway? Are Northerners all the same?[18]

Writing in the *Monitor*, Gad Fix Ruakoah put the issue starkly:

In a nut-shell, the Acholi people see themselves as victims of a long time hidden agenda to demilitarise and disintegrate the North. To them, this war in the North (Acholi) is the last hammer on their coffin's nail. They think that once it is done, the disintegration (pacification) of the North will be completed.

The truth therefore is that the people of Acholi are only fighting for survival, and if the government and the people of Uganda can change their attitudes towards them, restore their traditional culture and have dialogue with the rebels' leaders, that war will come to an end.[19]

The Islamic fundamentalist magazine, the *Shariat*, an extremely anti-government journal whose editors are regularly jailed (in 1995, the magazine's Editor in Chief died, somewhat mysteriously, in police custody) took the same line, quoting a group of anonymous Acholi as accusing the NRM of: 'Carrying out genocide against their tribe under the disguise of fighting Kony rebels in the North ... This government is working round the clock to isolate Acholi from the rest of Uganda and wipe them out.'[20] The controversial *Monitor* columnist Ogen Kevin Aliro, writing from Akron, Ohio, also spoke of government genocide against the Acholi, which he presented as deliberate reprisal for the massacres carried out in the Baganda heartland, the Luwero Triangle, during Obote's second regime:

> I read something in the *Monitor* about Prime Minister Kintu Musoke saying that 'Acholi had to pay for the blood in Luwero' ... The NRM has now been in power for almost 11 years and during each of those years, thousands of Acholi have been killed ... the very survival of Acholi as a people, a nationality, is now threatened ... about two generations of Acholi have almost been wiped out ... Even those young Acholi who find themselves disadvantaged at the time their age-mates from elsewhere are entering the job market ... Those, and other disparities, will further marginalise the Acholi, condemning them to the fringes of Uganda's economy forever.[21]

Replying later to some criticism of the previous article, he accused President Museveni of exploiting anti-Acholi feeling in the south to win the election. One critic

> raised the possibility of Acholi's [sic] being polarised from the rest of the country who would see them as armed 'murderers' or 'killers'. The truth is that the Acholi (and Northerners in general) are already stereotyped this way ... the Museveni campaign resurrected Southerners' anti-Acholi (Northern) sentiments to secure the Ganda vote ... the President reinforced the message by repetitive Luganda references to 'abatemu' (the killers) who Paul Ssemogerere [opposition presidential candidate] was trying to bring back into power ... Even the lousiest political junky knows what that was all about. The Museveni campaign was openly telling the Baganda 'don't vote for Ssemogerere because he has won over the North – the home of "killers"'. To the ordinary Muganda 'abatemu' brought back the horrors of Luwero, it could only mean one thing – 'Abacholi'.[22]

Of course, not all explanations for the war were couched in ethnic terms: it was not always portrayed as Baganda versus the Acholi or southerners versus northerners. The official government line (as expressed, for example, in the Minister of Defence's official 1996–97 policy statement to the Parliamentary Committee on Defence and Internal Affairs) was that:

> Kony and his LRA, and indeed the WNBF of Juma Oris in West Nile, do not enjoy popular support in the areas where they operate or anywhere else in Uganda. It is true that they have some collaborators who benefit from the loot ... But these are few in number. There are also some among the elite from the area who have a very strong sense of nostalgia for the past. They see Kony as their greatest hope to restore their lost glory. They support him.[23]

The LRA itself (in the person of its Nairobi spokesman Dominic

Wanyama, interviewed shortly afterwards in the government paper the *Sunday Vision*) avoided ethnicizing its criticism of the NRM, speaking only of 'the support we get from the people in Acholi and Uganda at large', and defining the LRA's aims in terms of 'root[ing] out Museveni's dictatorial and undemocratic government', which he criticized in terms designed to appeal to an international audience:

> The NRM first of all is not a multi-party government and we are opposed to that. Secondly, the principles under which it is governing our people are not acceptable globally, and given the fact they are power hungry zealots who shan't talk to anyone or take advice from anywhere we have no option other than to take up arms.

But both government and rebels recognize the potency of ethnic arguments and the power of the media – for a while, the LRA even operated a website (from a Columbia University, New York address) (*New Vision*, 29 January 1997). If official statements usually avoided playing the ethnic card, the same was certainly not always true of interviews with government and military spokespeople, nor of would-be representatives of the people of the north. The press coverage of the Parliamentary inquiry into the war provides examples of ethnic arguments from both sides.

The Parliamentary inquiry

The inquiry launched by the Parliamentary Sessional Committee on Defence and National Security began hearing witnesses in September 1996. The first testimony set much of the tone: an 'Acholi singer' named Evelyn Grace Anywar, based in Nairobi, Kenya, accused the government of a 'let the Acholi kill themselves attitude … "What happens in Acholi was not the concern of government," she argued. "The Acholi feel rejected. The Acholi feel hated. The Acholi feel unwanted".'[24] A later witness, a community activist from Gulu named Christine Oryema Lalobo, echoed this critique, at the same time launching an assault on the government for supporting the SPLA. According to the *Monitor*:

> Lalobo's lucid testimony also suggested that government might have intentions to wipe out the Acholi nationality. 'It seems there is a trick to make sure that all the Acholi perish.' The witness also pointed at frequent statements by senior officials in government that the Acholi are responsible for the Luwero deaths as a reflection of government sentiment.[25]

This suggestion was indignantly repudiated by the Minister of State for Defence, the Hon. Amama Mbabazi, who himself appeared in front of the inquiry a few days later. The Hon. Aggrey Awori (MP for a southern constituency) asked him directly: 'Mr Minister, one thing which has come up from time to time, is the question of ethnicity in this whole conflict. Ethnicity comes in both politically and militarily.' The Minister asked, 'What do you mean by ethnic factor?' Awori replied:

> I mean tribalism. People have said that nearly 75 percent of Acholi officers … are idle, mostly non-commissioned officers. People of Gulu and Kitgum feel isolated as if it was a deliberate policy of government to isolate them. I would be grateful, Mr Minister, if you gave the committee information regarding the ethnic factor, more especially in regard to officers of Acholi origin within UPDF.

The Minister answered: 'I don't engage in idle talk.' After a brief exchange between Committee members and the Minister, the latter stated:

> I was really reluctant to engage in this debate because I don't think it is helpful. Generally, the leadership of the Movement government is completely free of tribalism. We engage people in positions of work according to their merit, not according to tribe or religion. If we had that antipathy against the Acholi we would not rely on the LDUs [volunteer Local Defence Units] for the defence in that area or the arrow group in Kitgum, or the home guards. The Head of Intelligence in the Army is an Acholi. How would we have him if we were against the Acholi? Seventy-five percent of the people fighting against the bandits are Acholi.[26]

But the criticisms of government policy continued. One of Obote's former Prime Ministers, Eric Otema Allimadi, asked by a Committee member 'why have the Acholi picked up arms to fight against every government?', said that 'the Acholi took up arms against the NRM as a means of survival'.[27] Makerere University lecturer Dr Morris Ogenga-Latigo charged that in 1980 Museveni 'castigated the Acholi for thinking that they were militarily invincible and swore that he would one day deal with them'. Other government figures, he alleged, admitted to having:

> peddled the war largely as a struggle against northerners and got many recruits … They even toyed with the idea of completely destroying the northerners or fencing them off … During the Luwero war, true to earlier targeting, the NRM propaganda machinery was trained on the Acholi. Thus all non-Bantu soldiers became 'Acholi' and all the Luwero killings were committed by these people. (Ibid.)

A feature article in the *Monitor*, headed 'Kony's bloody trail: Acholi are both victim and culprit', noted in October:

The Northern insurgency has taken on a new dimension ... the prominence of allegations that the NRM leadership has nurtured a paranoid hatred of the Acholi as a tribe and has set in motion a grand design to annihilate them ... Claims about government's secret evil plan to annihilate the Acholi are alarmist and only lay the groundwork for future vicious circles of violence.[28]

When the inquiry moved to conduct hearings in Gulu and Kitgum themselves, many more such allegations flew. A former Constitutional Assembly delegate from Kitgum said that:

> the northern rebellion was sparked off due to the continued suppression of the Acholi from colonial days ... He said that this has been compounded by the abuse of the Acholi as being primitive and backward by the present government, yet the Acholi have just been neglected and denied education and development facilities.[29]

Along similar lines, a Church of Uganda (Anglican) Bishop (who, according to the *New Vision*, 'spoke so movingly with a lot of references from the Holy Bible') told the Committee: 'the war has taken long because in the beginning government looked at it as an Acholi war ... This kind of perception has caused untold suffering to the Acholi in the last ten years.'[30]

Major General Salim Saleh, meanwhile, conceded some truth to the allegations of 'tribalism' in the army, telling the inquiry that 'I have learned of clogging in the army. I have written to the Army Commander about reports of tribalism in the army. The system in the army is so clogged that there is no movement.'[31]

In a detailed joint written submission to the Committee, a group of Acholi MPs[32] reiterated the northern case that a colonially constructed ethnic identity had led to unjustified mistrust of northerners/Acholi, compounded by systematic underdevelopment of the area and prejudiced government propaganda. The first 'underlying cause' of the war listed in their submission states:

> For some reason, the colonial administration found it necessary to recruit the bulk of its army from the north, particularly from Acholiland ... It is not surprising then that by the time of independence northern tribes had dominated the armed forces ... and they were looked at as a potential danger by the post-independence leaders.

'Immediate causes' also included 'discriminatory language against northerners from January 1986 in all public places (especially in the south) and on national radio [which] scared many northerners'.[33]

Another aspect of the debate was the issue raised by the official government line that Kony had no widespread support among the Acholi people. A former follower of Alice Lakwena's HSM, currently a 'Mobilizer' for the NRM in Gulu, told the Committee, 'One reason why the war has lingered on is because 99 percent of the Acholi are rebels themselves', while a former officer in Obote's army claimed that '90 percent of the Acholi were strong supporters of the rebellion'.[34] Given the UPDF's own roots as a rebel army based on the principle that guerrilla struggle depends on a close relationship with the local populace, it was difficult for some soldiers to agree with their Minister of State that support for the LRA was weak in Gulu and Kitgum districts. Colonel Pecos Kutesa told the Sessional Committee: 'I find it difficult to believe that Kony can survive up there without the support of the people ... Why did Obote fail to get us (NRA) in Luwero? It is because people supported and hid us. Fighting a war is like farming; you always look for fertile land. Fish cannot swim without water.'[35]

Towards the end of the Committee's proceedings, however, attention shifted from the underlying causes of the war, towards the measures necessary to end it. Debate polarized between government supporters, who advocated a mainly military strategy, and oppositionists who called for direct talks with Kony. When the report of the Committee was presented to Parliament in February 1997, the Committee was split, with a majority supporting a military strategy while a minority took the line that the government should seek peace talks. In the parliamentary debate that ensued, the same arguments were rehearsed, a characteristic intervention being that of a southern, pro-NRM MP and former District Administrator in Gulu, Dr Fabius Byruhanga, who 'rejected talks and said the war had tribalism as its root cause. He accused some Acholi of intolerance and tribal bigotry, which he said many people in Uganda had.'[36] If, in the eyes of some MPs, the inquiry had been an expensive (a reported 182 million Ugandan Shillings, some $182,000) waste of time,[37] it had at least allowed many issues concerning the war, its root causes, and the role in it of antagonisms related to ideas of ethnicity, to be aired in public, and reported in the press.

The war in the north-west

From the press material cited so far, it is clear that a prominent way of understanding the conflict in the north, among Ugandans on all sides, is as a binary opposition between 'north' and 'south', in which the former is represented by 'the Acholi' and the latter by 'the Baganda'. In the next section, I discuss some theoretical issues raised by this discourse. Here, I want to examine one aspect of the northern war that stands outside such an analysis: the conflict in West Nile (i.e. the north-west corner of Uganda, most of which is west of the White Nile). Of course, other contradictions in the binary model exist: for example, Baganda people frequently express resentment at what they consider to be the dominance of the government by people from the south-west of the country, particularly Museveni's own ethnic group, the Banyankole (and, more specifically, the Bahima, cattle-keeping Banyankole). This occasionally surfaces in the press. An 'op-ed' opinion piece in the *Monitor* in October 1996, for example, claimed that 'Tribalism and regionalism is eating this country. The west, where the majority of government leaders come from, is taking the lion's share',[38] while a feature headline in January 1997 claimed, 'Want to get rich? Marry a Westerner'.[39] But, in terms of the press discourse on civil conflict in the country, the ways in which the West Nile war was discussed over the period with which I am concerned reveals the central contradiction in the binary ethnic model.

Explanations in terms of constructed or inherent Acholi propensities to violence clearly do not work in the north-west: there is no significant Acholi population in the area, and indeed many local people have some dislike of the Acholi (see, for example, Allen, 1994). Moreover, 'tribal' explanations in general are difficult to sustain in relation to the conflict in West Nile: as its name implies, the West Nile Bank Front recruited from, and was led by, people from all the ethnic groups into which the people of the area have been divided since being classified by the British. These include the 'Sudanic' language-speaking Madi and Lugbara, the predominantly 'Nilotic' Alur, and the Kakwa, whose language is also generally regarded as Nilotic. An additional West Nile group has been defined, the 'Nubi' or 'Nubians', believed to be descendants of Sudanese troops from many different ethnic origins, brought into the area in the 1880s, and closely associated with Idi Amin's rule. (On the Nubi, see particularly Furley, 1959; Collins, 1962; Mazrui, 1975a, 1975b, 1977; Pain, 1975; Southall, 1975; Soghayroun, 1981; Johnson, 1988, 1989; Rowe, 1988; Woodward, 1988; Hansen, 1991 and Kokole, 1995). Many Nubi people settled in Aringa County, and in recent years 'Aringa' has come to be widely regarded as another 'tribal' identity, one less tainted, perhaps, by association with Amin. The ethnic make-up of the former West Nile district, then, is complex, and for many southerners, the West Nilers are all tarred with the same brush.

The evident inapplicability of the binary ethnic model has had a number of consequences for press coverage of the war in the north-west. In the first place, it is frequently ignored: as is apparent from many of the articles already quoted, the West Nile is often simply omitted when the war is discussed (although death tolls of rebels, rather than civilians, were reported to be higher there than in Gulu and Kitgum, and the area also faced aerial and mortar bombing from Sudan, unlike the central northern region). Second, when the area is mentioned, the inevitable reference is to Idi Amin, the metonymic figure for West Nile violence in particular, even more than for Ugandan violence as a whole. Third, attempts are sometimes made to understand the war in the north-west in ethnic terms, to speak of it in the 'tribal' language used to analyse group conflict elsewhere in Uganda. The fourth strategy is to present the people of the area as deracinated, people without 'real' tribes, a mish-mash of different Sudanese, Zairean and Ugandan peoples with no legitimate authority and hence inclined to violence and terror (the Nubi are the model here). These aspects of contemporary press discourse are by no means novel; they relate to an image of the north-west that has not only persisted since the area came under colonial rule but, as I have argued elsewhere (Leopold, 1996), has many roots in an even earlier period.

Reference to Idi Amin is ubiquitous in press comment on West Nile, and in the utterances of southern politicians on the conflict in the district. The Minister of State for Defence's policy statement to the Ugandan Parliament in August 1996, quoted above, starts its section on West Nile, 'WNBF, which invaded Uganda in March 1996 and consisted of the remnants of the Idi Amin fascist army, was led by Juma Oris'.[40] The death or capture of WNBF officers was frequently announced in the media with a recitation of the rank they had held under Amin:

West Nile Bank Front (WNBF) overall Artillery Brigade Commander, Maj. Alli Sudi, 50 ... was captured by civilians of Oluko, Arua district on Dec 31 ... Alli Sudi is a half-caste born in Yumbe, Aringa County. He was an artillery sergeant in the Ugandan Army in Idi Amin's regime.[41]

Uganda's former ambassador to Ghana [under Amin], Col. Aziz Amua, was killed on Wednesday in a battle where UPDF clashed with rebels in Ariwara inside Zaire.[42]

Five suspected Oris rebels have been killed, two of them beheaded last Saturday by a mob ... One of those beheaded was a former employee of State House in the 1970s. Masikini Adu of Jiako village in Ayivu County, Arua, was head of the dry-cleaners responsible for dictator Idi Amin's clothes.[43]

Regular feature articles in the press underlined the – perhaps unsurprising – continuing southern Ugandan fascination with Amin. They ranged from a novel serialized in the *Monitor* throughout August and September, which depicted a brave group of Baganda freedom-fighters under Amin's regime, through a special 'Focus on Amin' feature in the *New Vision* on 25 January 1997, which ran to three whole pages, to a reprint of a 1977 *Newsweek* article on the then dictator in the *Monitor* on 15 March 1997. Features on the suffering of people in West Nile during the period of widespread conflict had titles like 'Koboko town paying for being home to Amin'.[44] An interview feature on 'the Nubians' was headed 'Help; we are not Amin's men'.[45] Small wonder that a letter to the *New Vision* from the Chairman of the West Nile Women's Association, writing on behalf of 'members of the West Nile / Madi Community in the United Kingdom', which protested strongly against government policy in the area, had among its demands, 'Your government must stop seeing the people of West Nile/Madi as waiting to bring Idi Amin back'.[46]

The image of Amin in the Ugandan press is one of deracination. This is not simply to do with his violence; it is also a question of the complexities of ethnicity in West Nile (see Allen, 1994), which do not fit the model of 'tribal' identity that is established as strongly among the Bantu-speaking people of southern Ugandan as it was in the British colonial regime, which did so much to form it. One feature on Amin began in a symptomatic manner, both asserting and denying Amin's ethnic identity:

> Field Marshal Idi Amin was born in a village near Koboko, in West Nile, bordering Sudan and Congo. He is a Kakwa. But Idi Amin never seemed to know where he was born, or was he pretending? He once claimed he was born ... in Kampala ... On another occasion he hinted that he was born near Bombo.[47]

A darkly humorous piece in the *Crusader* featured an imagined trip around the borders of Uganda, all of which were portrayed, in different ways, as threatening places. The section on West Nile once again exemplifies the image of hybridity and deracination:

> Beyond, you can see the waters of Lake Albert. A lot of caution. Here do not be sure of anybody. Juma Oris and his men have laid claim to this land and say they are intent on expanding it. Do not ask many questions. Some of the people you see crossing the ferry were last in Uganda some 17 years ago. Most have forgotten their language and speak a mixture of Dinka, Bari, Nuel [sic], Madi and Lugbara. Those many small huts you see over there are not villages, but camps where families here have been relocated.
>
> From this point, please pray. We are in the danger zone. We are now taking the eastern direction on the northern border of Uganda. We shall be only lucky to survive an ambush. And if we do, shall we manage to return with all our limbs?[48]

The obverse strategy to the presentation of the north-west as deracinated is that of attempting an ethnic explanation of events there. This surfaced particularly strongly when a new group appeared in Aringa County, Arua, calling itself the Uganda National Rescue Front II (UNRF II). According to a *New Vision* article headed 'Oris men: Tribal split':

> A wrangle based on tribal and religious division has split the rebel West Nile Bank Front. The West Nile UPDF Commander ... told a local security meeting last week that the rebel force is divided with the Aringa under Moses Gala's command ... the Kakwa commanded by a man identified only as Ali and the Alur under Colonel Athocon ...
>
> 'The Kakwa group were told when they fight and win they would bring Amin back and live the life of the 1970s ... the Aringas instead feel government did not resettle them ... As for the other groups they claim Uganda is being ruled by a foreigner so they should fight to rid Uganda of a President who is a foreigner.' [He added] '... so you can see there is nothing concrete the rebels are fighting for'.[49]

In fact, senior military and intelligence officers I spoke to in Arua over the period from October 1996 to March 1997, as well as local people with family members among the rebels, were clear that ethnic differences played little or no part in the formation of the rebel splinter-group, which was attributed to personal differences among the WNBF commanders and Sudanese government dissatisfaction with the relative lack of success of the rebels in West Nile.

Perhaps the most sophisticated analysis of West Nile ethnicity in the Ugandan press over the period in question emerged in the course of a controversy over a submission to the Parliamentary inquiry on the war. The area's most powerful and controversial political leader, the Hon. Brigadier Moses Ali, Second Deputy Premier and Minister of Tourism, told the Committee:

> It would be unfair of me to talk about the causes of this war without going back to history. The root causes are historical. Since the British came here, the way they handled different ethnic groups determines our history now. We in the North have been graded as warriors; we are fit for the army because we are tall people; we are hunters because of our cultural activities. For many years we were locked up in the security forces. Northerners did not participate in other sectors. We were tailored to poverty straight from the time of British rule. We in the North are poorer than people who grow permanent cash crops. There is also a false belief that we are the only ones suitable for the army ... But the belief that a particular tribe excels in the army has been overrun by those [i.e. the southerners] who were thought

weak and are now warriors. They are now the ones holding the gun. It was not true that only Northerners were expert in the army.[50]

The *New Vision*, which has an English editor, William Pike (a supporter of Museveni since the time the NRA itself was a rebel group), put Ali's testimony as a front-page lead under the header 'Northern poverty blamed on Britain'[51] and attacked the Deputy Prime Minister the next day in an editorial entitled 'Wrong, Mr Ali'. The editorial stated:

> Ali is wrong on two fronts. He is insinuating that there was a deliberate policy to gag development in the north, while the other regions prospered – that the colonial authority discriminated against the north – and he is wrong on the economics of the cash crops ... But most of all it is obscurant of Ali to still blame the British in 1996. True though it may be that many distortions in our social, economic and political structures were caused by uninspired policies, it is unrealistic of us to still blame the colonial administration, long after it has departed.[52]

Ali responded a few weeks later, citing colonial records to support his claim of deliberate underdevelopment. He quoted (from Powesland, 1957) the response of central government in 1925 to an attempt by the Director of Agriculture in West Nile to introduce cotton production in the district:

> The policy of this government is at present to refrain from actively stimulating the production of cotton or other economic crops in outlying districts on which it is dependent for the supply of labour for the carrying out of essential services in the central or producing districts.

Ali concluded:

> I am not saying that the British colonial policies are the only variables in understanding the present crisis in the north. There are other components to the problem. But it is necessary to comprehend the impact of British colonial policies on Uganda's development in order to understand the present crisis in the north ... Present Ugandan society as structured is, to a large extent, a creature of British colonial policies. It is that extent, that aspect of Uganda's development that I referred to in my submission. Any society or community is a creature of its past.[53]

In his analysis, Ali links north-west and central-northern Uganda through their common role under British rule: it is no longer a case of Acholi ethnicity, however created, but a shared history of the peoples of the north and north-west. As such, it keeps the binary north/south model, while incorporating the experience of West Nile. Thoroughly constructivist as the argument is, though, it appeals to the discourse of ethnicity through the same notion of colonial stereotyping of various pre-existing northern ethnic groups as 'warriors' that we saw in the case of the Acholi.

Inside the master trope

The proposition that a central ideological dynamic in Ugandan society, and *a fortiori* in Ugandan political discourse, operates by reference to a series of ideas about ethnicity, is by no means a new one. As Michael Twaddle put it at an early stage in Amin's rule: 'In Uganda, political alliances at the centre of the country sometimes follow an ethnic line, sometimes politico-religious allegiances, sometimes a racial difference. More frequently, they cluster along some combination of these allegiances' (Twaddle 1972: 107).

The issue of ethnicity and the north/south divide in relation to Ugandan politics is discussed by many of the contributors to the collections edited by Hansen and Twaddle (1988, 1991), especially in Wrigley (1988) and Gingyera-Pinycwa (1991) (see also Low, 1988; Mazrui, 1988; Obbo, 1988; O'Connor, 1988; Southall, 1988; and Woodward, 1988, 1991. Other volumes of relevance to the issue include Gingyera-Pinycwa, 1978, 1992; and Rupesinghe, 1989, especially the contribution by Gingyera-Pinycwa).

Uganda is by no means unique in the way in which a discourse of ethnicity can come to dominate political debate; we know this happens in countries all over the world. What is, if not unique to Uganda, at least characteristic of it, is the combination of a highly 'tribally' diverse country with a powerful tendency to dichotomize ethnic discourse into a binary model. The complexities of northern and north-western ethnicity are encompassed by 'the Acholi'; the many kingdoms and smaller political units of the pre-colonial Bantu south are swallowed up, at the ideological level, by 'the Baganda'.

The widespread human tendency to think in terms of binary oppositions has been analysed by many social anthropologists, particularly those working in a broadly Durkheimian tradition (from Herz and Mauss to Claude Lévi-Strauss). In recent decades, the most influential theorist in this tradition has probably been Louis Dumont, whose analyses of, first, the 'traditional' Indian caste system and, more recently, the 'modern' ideology of individualism in European and North American societies provide a model of how ideological hierarchies operate through what he calls 'the encompassing of the contrary' (Dumont, 1970: 239). The best example of this is the process in which 'male' is presented as universal, encompassing its opposite, 'female', as symbolized dramatically in the story of Eve being formed from Adam's rib. 'This hierarchical relation', Dumont says, 'is, very generally, that between a whole (or a set) and an element of this whole (or set); the element belongs to the set and is in this sense consubstantial or identical with it; at the same time, the element is distinct from the set or stands in opposition to it' (ibid.: 240).

In the ideological discourse of the Ugandan nation,[54] 'Buganda', the kingdom of the Baganda people, encompasses, first, the southern Ugandan nations conquered by its forces under British tutelage, then the northern lands later annexed to the colonial polity. The use of the name of one constituent group for the whole country, (B)Uganda, symbolizes this dominance. In the language of the Ugandan press, not merely in its analysis of the conflict in the north but in much broader social and cultural debates, Bagandan views and customs are frequently referred to as 'Ugandan', southern ones as if things are the same in the north. As 'Baganda' encompasses the south, and the south dominates the north, so 'Acholi' comes to dominate the north, in the ethnic discourse, leading to the kind of press coverage of group conflict analysed in this chapter.

Conclusion

It has been possible to write this chapter only because of the unusual freedom of the Ugandan press to present opinions that are substantially, even violently, opposed to government policy and to the present structure of Ugandan society. In emphasizing an important, perhaps the most important, contradiction to the NRM's generally successful strategy for social, political and economic development, the conflict in the north, the achievement of a relatively free media should not be forgotten. The fact that this freedom is used in a way that demonstrates the importance in Ugandan life of an ideology of ethnicity is not a criticism of the press: it is, after all, the normal role of a society's collective representations to exhibit its beliefs and thought-processes.

In the present chapter, I have examined Ugandan press coverage of conflict between rebels in the north and north-west of Uganda and the Ugandan government. I have concentrated on explanations for the root causes of this conflict, relating them to a wider discourse on ethnicity in Ugandan society. I have not covered the real, rather than ideological, progress of the war, nor its results in terms of death and injury, or poverty and displacement, among the people living in the conflict zone.[55] To some, this may seem an unduly abstract way to approach the subject. A concentration on discourse can be seen as anti-human in a moral sense, as well as anti-humanist in the epistemological sense. I would argue, however, that the ideology of ethnicity demonstrated in the press discourse which has been examined here has been an important contributory factor in perpetuating into the post-Independence era the social, economic and political structures of ethnic difference established during imperial rule. The effects have been, and continue to be, real enough. Moreover, the long-term process of reconstruction in Uganda depends crucially on the Ugandan people's understandings of their own history. As the press coverage of the issue of ethnicity shows, there is in contemporary Uganda a lively interest in, and debate over, questions of history and the construction of ethnicity. This can only be a good sign for the future of the country and even, perhaps, ultimately the key to healing the wound that separates the north of Uganda from the south.

Notes

1. This is the case both in much of the academic literature (see, for example, Brett, 1993; Langseth et al., 1995; Hansen and Twaddle, 1995) and by such beacons of world opinion as the International Monetary Fund (e.g. Sharer et al., 1995).

2. On the operation of RCs, in addition to the works on reconstruction cited above, see Tidemand, 1994; Kabera and Muyanja, 1994; and Nsibambi, 1991. Unfortunately, all these are case studies from southern Uganda; I know of no in-depth local study of the operation of RCs/LCs in the north or north-west.

3. Research for the present chapter was carried out as part of my DPhil project, entitled 'The Roots of Violence and the Reconstruction of Society in North-West Uganda', and funded under ESRC postgraduate training award No. R00429534198. Fieldwork in Uganda between August 1996 and April 1997 was facilitated by my attachment to Makerere Institute of Social Research, Makerere University, Kampala, and by the Uganda National Council for Science and Technology. I am grateful to my supervisor, Professor Wendy James, to the many Ugandans from both north and south of the country who gave me (among much else) their views on the war, and to JoAnn McGregor for reading and commenting on drafts of this chapter.

4. A BBC correspondent with whom I discussed this issue argued that the Ugandan press was freer than the British media, largely due to restrictions imposed by UK libel laws.

5. I regret that my examples are taken only from the English-language press. There are thriving print media in the main vernacular languages (though not in those of the area in which I undertook most of my fieldwork) and in Kiswahili. English is, however, the language of most school instruction as well as the official language, so most literate people are literate first in English, and

only second in their mother tongue. In towns, at any rate, English is also used widely in everyday conversation. It is the preferred second language and *lingua franca* of most southern Ugandans, while northerners tend to prefer Kiswahili; in a sense, then, the English-language press reflects the hegemonic role of southerners in contemporary Uganda, an issue discussed in more detail below.

6. *New Times*, 28 August 1996–2 September 1996.

7. *Monitor*, 2–4 October 1996.

8. *Crusader*, 19–24 December 1996.

9. Ibid.

10. The government-owned *New Vision*, and *Monitor*, which went daily in November 1996, are the only English-language dailies, and frequently the only newspapers available outside Kampala and the other major southern towns.

11. *Monitor*, 28–30 August 1996.

12. *Sunday Vision*, 17 November 1997.

13. *Crusader*, 7–10 December 1996.

14. Ibid.

15. *East African*, 26 March 1996, reprinted in the Ugandan magazine the *Independent*, July 1996.

16. *Monitor*, 16–18 October 1996.

17. *Crusader*, 22–4 October 1996.

18. *Monitor*, 11 November 1996.

19. *Monitor*, 25–7 September 1996.

20. *Shariat*, 27 August–2 September 1997.

21. *Monitor*, 16–18 September 1996.

22. *Monitor*, 14–16 October 1996.

23. *Sunday Vision*, 1 September 1996.

24. *New Vision*, 13 September 1996.

25. *Monitor*, 18–20 September 1996.

26. *Crusader*, 19–24 September 1996.

27. *New Vision*, 20 September 1996.

28. *Monitor*, 7–11 October 1996.

29. *New Vision*, 31 October 1996.

30. *New Vision*, 28 October 1996.

31. *New Vision*, 25 October 1996.

32. The letter was initially 'signed' by all Acholi MPs, but one, the Head of Army Intelligence Colonel Fred Tolit (an MP, not for a geographical constituency, but for one of the Parliamentary seats reserved for the Army) later dissociated himself from the submission.

33. *New Vision*, 31 October 1997.

34. *Crusader*, 24–9 October 1996.

35. *Monitor*, 22 November 1996.

36. *New Vision*, 28 February 1997.

37. *New Vision*, 10 March 1997.

38. *Monitor*, 18–21 October 1996.

39. *Sunday Monitor*, 5 January 1997.

40. *Sunday Vision*, 1 September 1996.

41. *Monitor*, 7 January 1997.
42. *New Vision*, 14 February 1997.
43. *New Vision*, 22 February 1997.
44. *Monitor*, 18 December 1997.
45. *Crusader*, 22–4 October 1996.
46. *New Vision*, 17 December 1996.
47. *New Vision*, 25 January 1997.
48. *Crusader*, 19–24 September 1996.
49. *New Vision*, 28 August 1997.
50. *Crusader*, 1 October 1996.
51. *New Vision*, 21 September 1996.
52. *New Vision*, 23 September 1996.
53. *New Vision*, 20 November 1996.
54. It is important to emphasize that I am writing here about an *ideological* dominance – as we have already seen, the Baganda today frequently complain of having a subordinate position within the present Ugandan state structures. Dumont (1970) makes the same point regarding the dominance of the Brahmins within the ideological caste system, which has no necessary relation to real political or economic power.
55. I have written elsewhere of the progress and impact of the war in West Nile over the period covered by the present chapter (Leopold, 1997).

References

Allen, T. (1991) 'Understanding Alice: Uganda's Holy Spirit Movement in Context', *Africa*, Vol. 61, No. 3., pp. 371–99.
— (1994) 'Ethnicity and Tribalism on the Sudan–Uganda Border', in K. Fukui and J. Markakis (eds), *Ethnicity and Conflict in the Horn of Africa*, London/ Athens, OH: James Currey/Ohio University Press.
Asowa-Okwe, C. (1997) 'Insurgency and the Challenges of Social Reconstruction in Northern and North-Eastern Uganda, 1986–1996', in B. F. Frederiksen and F. Wilson (eds), *Livelihood, Identity and Instability*, Copenhagen: Centre for Development Research.
Behrend, H. (1991) 'Is Alice Lakwena a Witch? The Holy Spirit Movement and its Fight against Evil in the North', in Hansen and Twaddle (eds).
— (1995) 'The Holy Spirit Movement and the Forces of Nature in the North of Uganda 1985–1987', in Hansen and Twaddle (eds).
Brett, E. A. (1993) *Providing for the Rural Poor; Institutional Decay and Transformation in Uganda*, Kampala: Fountain Publishers. [Orig. edn 1992. Brighton: University of Sussex Institute of Development Studies.]
Collins, R. O. (1962) *The Southern Sudan, 1883–1898: A Struggle for Control*, New Haven, CT and London: Yale University Press.
Crazzolara, J. P. (1950) *The Lwoo* Part 1: *Lwoo Migrations*, Verona: Istituto Missioni Africane.
Dumont, L. (1970) *Homo Hierarchicus*, Chicago and London: University of Chicago Press.

EIU (Economist Intelligence Unit) (1995) 'Quarterly Country Report, Uganda, Rwanda, Burundi' (3rd quarter), London: EIU.

Furley, O. W. (1959) 'The Sudanese Troops in Uganda', *African Affairs*, Vol. 58, No. 233, pp. 311–28.

Gingyera-Pinycwa, A. G. (1978) *Apolo Milton Obote and His Times*, New York/London: Lagos/NOK Publishers.

— (1989) 'Is there a Northern Question?', in Rupesinge (ed.).

— (1991) 'Towards Constitutional Renovation: Some Political Considerations', in Hansen and Twaddle (eds).

— (1992) *Northern Uganda in National Politics*, Kampala: Fountain Publishers.

Hansen, H. B. (1991) 'Pre-colonial Immigrants and Colonial Servants. The Nubians in Uganda Revisited', *African Affairs*, Vol. 90, No. 2, pp. 559–80.

Hansen, H. B. and Twaddle, M. (eds) (1988) *Uganda Now*, London: James Currey; Nairobi: Heinemann Kenya; Kampala: Fountain Publishers; Athens, OH: Ohio University Press.

— (1991) *Changing Uganda*, London: James Currey; Nairobi: Heinemann Kenya; Kampala: Fountain Press; Athens, OH: Ohio University Press.

— (1995) *Religion and Politics in East Africa*, London: James Currey; Nairobi: East African Educational Publishers; Kampala: Fountain Publishers; Athens, OH: Ohio University Press.

Johnson, D. H. (1988) 'Sudanese Military Slavery from the Eighteenth to the Twentieth Century', in L. Archer (ed.), *Slavery and Other Forms of Unfree Labour*, London: Routledge.

— (1989) 'The Structure of a Legacy: Military Slavery in Northeast Africa', *Ethnohistory*, Vol. 36, No. 1, pp. 72–88.

Kabera, J. B. and Muyanja, C. (1994) 'Homecoming in the Luwero Triangle', in T. Allen and H. Morsink (eds), *When Refugees Go Home*, London: UNRISD/James Currey.

Kokole, O. H. (1995) 'Idi Amin, "the Nubi" and Islam in Ugandan Politics, 1971–1979', in Hansen and Twaddle (eds).

Langseth, P., Katorobo, J., Brett, E., and Munene, J. (eds) (1995) *Uganda, Landmarks in Rebuilding a Nation*, Kampala: Fountain Publishers.

Leopold, M. (1996) 'Drawing a Margin: Violence, Knowledge and History on the West Nile', Paper presented to University of Oxford Africa Research Seminar, June 1996.

— (1997) 'Arua=Prison: A Cosmopolitan Locality under Siege in North-Western Uganda', Paper presented to the SCUSA third inter-university colloquium 'The Meanings of the Local', University of Keele, May.

Low, D. A. (1988) 'The Dislocated Polity', in Hansen and Twaddle (eds).

Mazrui, A. A. (1975a) 'The Resurrection of the Warrior Tradition in African Political Culture', *Journal of Modern African Studies*, Vol. 13, No. 1, pp. 67–84.

— (1975b) *Soldiers and Kinsmen in Uganda: The Making of a Military Ethnocracy*, Beverly Hills, CA/London: Sage.

— (1977) 'Religious Strategies in Uganda: from Emin Pasha to Amin Dada', *African Affairs*, Vol. 76, No. 302, pp. 21–38.

— (1988) 'Is Africa Decaying? The View from Uganda', in Hansen and Twaddle (eds).

Nsibambi, A. (1991) 'Resistance Councils and Committees: A Case Study from Makerere', in Hansen and Twaddle (eds).

Obbo, C. (1988) 'What Went Wrong in Uganda?', in Hansen and Twaddle (eds).

O'Connor, A. (1988) 'Uganda: The Spatial Dimension', in Hansen and Twaddle (eds).

Pain, D. (1975) 'The Nubians, their Perceived Stratification System and its Relation to the Asian Issue', in Twaddle (ed.), *Expulsion of a Minority*, London: University of London/Athlone Press.

Powesland, P. G. (1957) *Economic Policy and Labour: A Study in Uganda's Economic History*, Kampala: East African Institute of Social Research.

Rowe, J. A. (1988) 'Islam under Idi Amin: A Case of *deja vu*?', in Hansen and Twaddle (eds).

Rupesinghe, K. (ed.) (1989) *Conflict Resolution in Uganda*, Oslo: International Peace Research Institute; London: James Currey; Athens, OH: Ohio University Press.

Sharer, R. L., De Zoysa, H. R., and McDonald, C. A. (1995) *Uganda: Adjustment with Growth, 1987–94*, IMF Occasional Paper No. 121. Washington, DC: International Monetary Fund.

Soghayroun, I. (1981) *The Sudanese Muslim Factor in Uganda*, Khartoum: Khartoum University Press.

Southall, A. (1975) 'General Amin and the Coup: Great Man or Historical Inevitability?', *Journal of Modern African Studies*, Vol. 13, No. 1, pp. 85–105.

— (1988) 'The Recent Political Economy of Uganda', in Hansen and Twaddle (eds).

Tidemand, P. (1994) 'The Resistance Councils in Uganda: A Study of Rural Politics and Popular Democracy in Africa', PhD dissertation, Roskilde University, Denmark.

Twaddle, M. (1972) 'The Amin Coup', *Journal of Commonwealth Political Studies*, Vol. 10, No. 2, pp. 99–111.

Woodward, P. (1988) 'Uganda and Southern Sudan', in Hansen and Twaddle (eds).

— (1991) 'Uganda and Southern Sudan 1986–89: New Regimes and Peripheral Politics', in Hansen and Twaddle (eds).

Wrigley, C. (1988) 'Four Steps towards Disaster', in Hansen and Twaddle (eds).

· ·

CHAPTER 12

Representing Violence in Matabeleland, Zimbabwe: Press and Internet Debates[1]

Jocelyn Alexander and JoAnn McGregor

In the 1990s, both Zimbabwe's independent press and the internet provided a forum for public debate about the violence that took place in the country's Matabeleland region between 1982 and 1987.[2] The revelations of the 1990s differed markedly from the portrayals of the conflict in the state-controlled media of the 1980s. There were also important differences between the unmediated internet discussions and journalists' renewed coverage of the violence in Zimbabwe's print media. We investigate these distinctions, examining the uneven power of the media to shape perceptions of events on the one hand, and casting doubt on the supposedly liberating and subversive potential of the internet on the other. Before turning to the media, let us first explore the context of Zimbabwe's post-independence conflict.

In 1980, Zimbabwe emerged from a bitter war between two guerrilla armies and the Rhodesian armed forces. Neither of the two guerrilla movements was ethnically or regionally constituted, and both had leaders and members from throughout the country. Nevertheless, over the course of the war, they had developed regional areas of operation and recruitment which broadly, though far from completely, coincided with ethnic and linguistic divisions. Joshua Nkomo's Zapu (the Zimbabwe African People's Union) and its armed wing Zipra (the Zimbabwe People's Revolutionary Army) had their strongest base in the largely Ndebele-speaking Matabeleland region. Robert Mugabe's Zanu (Zimbabwe African National Union) and its armed wing Zanla (the Zimbabwe African Liberation Army) predominated in largely Shona-speaking areas.[3] In the country's first elections, voter loyalties tended to reflect the operational divisions of the war, thus reinforcing the association between Zapu and the predominantly Ndebele-speaking Mata-

Chronology of conflict

1979–80 In December 1979 a ceasefire ends the liberation war fought by Zimbabwe's two guerrilla armies against the Rhodesian regime. Robert Mugabe's Zimbabwe African National Union (Zanu) wins the elections of February 1980. Joshua Nkomo's Zimbabwe African People's Union (Zapu) is invited into a coalition government. Amid considerable insecurity and ongoing violence, steps are taken to form an integrated Zimbabwe National Army, combining Zanu's armed wing, the Zimbabwe African National Liberation Army (Zanla), Zapu's armed wing, the Zimbabwe People's Liberation Army (Zipra), and the Rhodesian armed forces.

1981–82 Violent clashes between former Zanla and Zipra guerrillas in the integrated army and in assembly points result in the desertion of large numbers of Zipra guerrillas, some of whom take up arms again. This leads to a growing problem of armed 'dissidents' in the Matabeleland region, the heartland of support for Zapu, and a heavy-handed military response from the Zanu government. Joshua Nkomo and other senior Zapu leaders are expelled from the government, and Zipra commanders are charged with treason.

1983–84 The notorious Fifth Brigade of the Zimbabwe National Army is deployed in Matabeleland to deal with 'dissidents'. It unleashes unprecedented violence against civilians and Zapu officials accused of supporting 'dissidents'.

1987–88 In December 1987, the Unity agreement is signed between the ruling party, Zanu, and Zapu. The two parties merge under the name 'Zanu'. Joshua Nkomo and other former Zapu leaders are absorbed into the Zanu party and government; Zapu members follow Nkomo into the new Zanu. Dissidents turn themselves in under a Presidential Amnesty and peace returns to Matabeleland.

beleland region, and Zanu and other regions of the country. Mugabe's Zanu won an overall majority but formed a coalition government which included Zapu leaders in key positions. The coalition lasted an uneasy two years. It foundered as the process of creating the integrated Zimbabwe National Army, combining Zipra, Zanla and the Rhodesian forces, broke down. Clashes between Zipra and Zanla guerrillas led many to flee. Some Zipra guerrillas took up arms again, and came to be called 'dissidents'. The existence of army deserters and dissidents brought heavy-handed government repression which came to be directed at civilians, Zapu officials and armed insurgents alike.

During the conflict itself, the state-controlled media reproduced and popularized the Zanu government's views on violence in Matabeleland. The media portrayed the conflict in predominantly political terms, casting the minority party Zapu and its former guerrilla army, Zipra, as the aggressors, and blaming them for instigating a violent insurgency in Matabeleland out of anger over their 1980 electoral loss. Zanu and the government forces, on the other hand, were cast in a legitimate and reactive role: they were defenders of a hard-won independence vulnerable to South African destabilization; they were upholders of law and order in the face of armed dissent from former Zipra guerrillas and a treacherous Zapu. Although such representations rarely explicitly alluded to ethnicity, they were underlain by an implicit ethnic explanation due to the association between the Matabeleland region, Zapu and Zipra. The Zanu government, and the state-controlled media, blurred distinctions between the armed 'dissidents', the civilians among whom they lived and Zapu supporters. All these groups were marked as subversive and dangerous, and all of them were concentrated within the 'Ndebele' region of Matabeleland. The frequent blurring of political, ethnic, regional and insurgent categories in the media played an important role in popular understandings of the violence as 'tribal' in regions outside Matabeleland. Ethnic interpretations emerged within Matabeleland as well, but these were a response to the direct, and almost wholly unreported, experience of state violence, not the representations of the media.

The conflict in Matabeleland ended in 1987 with the merger of the two parties Zanu and Zapu. Subsequently, a revitalized independent press began to challenge the interpretations of the conflict propagated over its course. This process began with isolated reports of evidence of large-scale government killing. It gained force with the release of a detailed, locally compiled human rights report on abuses in Matabeleland. The report first became available on the internet, and was subsequently covered extensively by the independent press. Elite, usually expatriate Zimbabweans gained access to and debated the report on an internet discussion forum known as Zimnet. Initially, these debates were far from subversive: dominant strands of discussion questioned the report's legitimacy, sought to defend the government's version of events, and focused on the conflict's 'tribal' nature. The Zimnet discussions revealed the difficulty of changing perceptions formed through a decade of exposure to government propaganda in a context where the leaders of that government remained in power and could still inspire loyalty and fear. Such views met a more serious challenge on Zimnet only when the government faced an unprecedented political and economic crisis in the late 1990s.

Below, we consider the contemporary media coverage of the violence before turning to more recent coverage in the independent press and on the internet.

The Zimbabwean media after independence

The question of media control is crucial to understanding how conflict and security problems were reported after independence in Zimbabwe. Increasing government control brought changes in the terminology and interpretation of conflict, eventually leading to the exclusion of views other than those of the ruling Zanu party.

At independence, Zimbabwe inherited foreign-controlled print media long subject to extensive controls by the Rhodesian state:[4] the main newspaper chain was controlled by the Rhodesian Printing and Publishing Company, an affiliate of the South African Argus Printing and Publishing Company.[5] The Rhodesian Printing and Publishing Company renamed itself Zimbabwe Newspapers (Zimpapers) before Zimbabwe's first national election in February 1980, but its reporting remained biased. In the words of the Catholic Institute for International Relations, it 'fail[ed] to provide a balanced picture ... The view of the war and the ceasefire continue[d] to be that of the Rhodesian administration and the security forces' (CIIR, 1980: 19–20; also see Commonwealth Observer Group, 1980: 47).

After Zanu's election victory, Zimpapers publicly declared a new role for itself: it would critically support the government with an 'independent and responsible press' (Saunders, 1991: 55). But management and editorial positions continued to be dominated by whites, and animosity between the press and government escalated. Finally, in January 1981, the Mass Media Trust was established by the Ministry of Information with the stated aim of 'decolonizing' and 'democratizing' the print media. The Trust was created as part of the ambitious and idealistic vision of a 'New World Information and Communication Order' embraced by the Organization of African Unity and the Frontline States.[6] Zimpapers' South African shareholders were bought out by the government and the newspaper chain was placed under the Trust's control.[7]

The Mass Media Trust was a much celebrated initiative. It was neither a parastatal nor a private company; as a public trust it was – in theory – politically and economically independent. However, the Ministry of Information's democratizing aims were from the outset fraught with tension due to the ruling party's desire to control information. The Trust's 'independent' Board of Trustees included senior Zanu figures and had few representatives from the minority Zapu party or from other bodies that had a history of critical engagement with the Rhodesian government in the print media, such as the Catholic Commission for Justice and Peace. The replacement of white editors with black Zimbabweans was organized by the Ministry such that its 'choice of new editors was presented to the Trustees – and indeed, to the Zimpapers' Board of Directors – as a *fait accompli*' (Saunders, 1991: 114). Zapu criticized the Trust from its inception, arguing that the Ministry of Information used 'the news media as Zanu propaganda tools rather than as channels for national development, unity, reconciliation and entertainment'.[8]

Zimbabwe's growing 'security problem' served as both trigger and justification for increased government control of the media. Concerns over the potential for a subversive South African influence on the media persisted for a number of reasons: telecommunication links depended on South Africa until 1983, the effects of past white domination of staffing and management proved difficult to reverse, and Radio Truth broadcasts from Johannesburg encouraged people in Matabeleland to rise against the government. In Saunders' words,

> The [Ministry of Information] directed local journalists to combat foreign 'information aggression' by being aggressively partisan in defending the principles of majority rule, socialism and the aims of the country's 'friends' in the international community. It was a demand which government backed up by ... introducing Rhodesian Front-style vetting for foreign journalists working in Zimbabwe. (Saunders, 1991: 116)

The effects of this control were 'seen most clearly in the series of politically motivated editorial hirings and firings ... throughout the decade. They were also evident in the blanket of self-censorship in the same media [and] the building of a partisan management regime' (Ibid.: 116, and see 58, 113). Elias Rusike, a wartime political propagandist for Zanu and for five years Zimpapers' Chief Executive in the 1980s, described the role of the Ministry of Information as follows:

> [Mass Media Trust Chairman] Dr Davison Sadza and myself were ordered by the Ministry of Information to fire different Zimpapers editors ... The way I saw it, I was being a faithful party cadre ... [W]hat really happened was the Board of Zimpapers and the Mass Media Trust's Board of Trustees were both bypassed – with the Ministry of Information giving its orders to editors and journalists through myself and Dr Sadza.[9]

The content of, and terminology used in, press reports on security problems in the 1980s reflected these changes in media ownership and government intervention. From the ceasefire of December 1979 until Zanu's election victory in February 1980, reporting on security problems focused on the process of bringing guerrillas into assembly points. Those who refused, left them illegally, or engaged in acts of violence were sometimes called 'renegade terrorists', 'terrorist' having been the Rhodesian-era term for guerrilla. More commonly, reporters used the terms chosen by the leaders of both Zanu and Zapu, that is 'outlaws', 'unruly elements' or 'bandits' (Alexander, 1998).

Zanu's electoral victory produced changes in vocabulary. The term 'terrorist' disappeared from media reports and, while apolitical terms continued to be used to describe 'banditry' in most of the country, the reporting of violence in Matabeleland took on an increasingly political hue. From the opening of Parliament, Zanu politicians focused on problems in Matabeleland and on the threat posed by Zipra guerrillas (despite evidence that the situation was at least as bad, if not worse, in other parts of the country where guerrillas loyal to Zanu were concentrated). Errant guerrillas in Matabeleland were increasingly referred to not as 'bandits' but as 'dissidents'. 'Dissidents' were different: in Prime Minister Mugabe's words, they were 'organized bands of Zipra followers' who were 'refusing to recognize the sovereignty of the government'.[10] Though Zipra came under an increasingly politicized scrutiny, the press also continued to cover Zapu's views, including Zapu leader Joshua Nkomo's vehement denials of any Zipra plot, details of his efforts to round up recalcitrant Zipra guerrillas, and verbatim accounts of his public speeches in Matabeleland.

In this period, only one minister, Enos Nkala, expressed explicitly tribal interpretations of the problems in Matabeleland. Nkala was the most senior Ndebele-speaking Zanu minister, and was a highly influential figure. The newspapers reported his many provocative public addresses in Matabeleland: on 30 June 1980, for example, the *Chronicle* covered his speech to a crowd of 3,000, in which he said armed dissidents were

> Ndebeles who were calling for a second war of liberation ... We give them a few weeks to surrender their guns and go back to the assembly points. After that we will round them up and those who resist will be shot down. ... If any party cannot control their military wing we will do it for them Those preaching Ndebeleism should stop before we liquidate them. I myself will lead the forces against them because I am an Ndebele and if the PM were to do so he would be misunderstood because he was a Shona.[11]

In a rally the following week, he argued that the ruling party's task was 'to crush Joshua Nkomo and forget about him. If I remain in this government I will crush Joshua Nkomo, self-appointed Ndebele king.'[12] Nkala's provocations at times led directly to violence: after a rally in Entumbane (a suburb of Bulawayo, the provincial capital of Matabeleland), Zanu and Zapu supporters clashed, Zanla and Zipra guerrillas (who had recently been moved into barracks in the suburb) were drawn in, and a two-day battle ensued. In the aftermath, the press gave coverage to both sides' accusations of the other.

The formation of the Mass Media Trust in January 1981 coincided with the demotion of Zapu leader Joshua Nkomo from his position as Minister of Home Affairs. But it was Nkomo's dismissal from the government in February 1982, following the discovery of arms caches said to be intended for use in a Zapu insurrection against the government, which marked the breakdown in political relations between Zanu and Zapu. Explicit accusations of treachery against Zapu, and increased political control over the media followed. Joshua Nkomo was banned from speaking in public outside Parliament. He claims his views were distorted or ignored in the media thereafter: 'Hostile publicity was directed against me in the government-controlled press'; Mugabe compared Zapu to a cobra and declared that the only way to deal with it was to 'destroy its head':

> My replies to the verbal attacks were passed over in silence, ignored by the press, radio and television … In parliament the prime minister pointed the finger at me and proclaimed before the television cameras that the father of Zimbabwe had become the father of the dissidents. (Nkomo, 1985: 229–30)

Nkomo felt a hostile political climate was being created in order to justify violent repression in Matabeleland.

The media coverage of the main period of violence in Matabeleland between 1982 and 1987 presented almost exclusively the government view. This view exaggerated the dissident threat, and held a near total silence on acts of violence against civilians perpetrated by government forces. Press coverage of violence in Matabeleland in this period has been systematically analysed in a human rights report recently released by two Zimbabwean non-governmental organizations, the Catholic Commission for Justice and Peace and the Legal Resources Foundation. Based on a survey of 562 offences reported in 1,500 *Chronicle* articles between June 1982 and March 1988, the report noted:

> The perpetrator is almost invariably given as 'dissidents' or 'bandits', with very few acknowledgements of atrocities by security forces. It is only in instances where individual members of the security forces were prosecuted, which were rare, that the newspaper reported such atrocities. Most refer-

ences to security force atrocities take the form of vociferous denials. When acknowledged, deaths of civilians at the hands of the security forces are at times referred to as being 'deaths in crossfire', implying the unintentional killing of innocents where dissidents were the target ... Of the approximately 3,500 named victims on file from other sources [than the press], there are, in fact, only seven interviews which refer to five people killed and two homesteads destroyed in genuine crossfire. (CCJP/LRF, 1997: 16)

The exaggeration of dissident violence in Matabeleland took various forms. Violent attacks in parts of the country far from where dissidents operated – such as those committed by the Mozambican rebel group, Renamo, along Zimbabwe's eastern border – were attributed to dissidents. The numbers of specific cases of violence reported in the press were far lower than the numbers of incidents reported in Parliament, suggesting the lumping together of different sorts of cases, from genuine dissident acts, to those of criminals, to those of security forces either acting as such, or posing as dissidents (CCJP/LRF, 1997: 16–17, 165–6). The latter – cases of atrocities committed by security forces posing as dissidents – were common.[13] The Catholic Commission report discusses seven specific incidents in detail, including a bus burning, the murders of three chiefs, a shoot-out at a rural shopping centre, and the murders of clinic staff in an ambush on their car. In each case, the *Chronicle* attributed responsibility to dissidents, but eye-witnesses put forward convincing arguments (to independent observers) that the perpetrators were in fact government agents (CCJP/LRF, 1997: 17; also see Lawyers' Committee for Human Rights, 1986).

Dissidents certainly did commit acts of violence, but the emphasis in the press on dissident violence was wholly disproportionate. Government security forces were in fact responsible for the vast majority of deaths, beatings, rapes and other abuses. The Catholic Commission report's extremely diligent compilation of the numbers killed and missing lists 2,052 named victims, and estimates that at least 6,000 died in total. Of these, an estimated 98% died at the hands of government forces, and only 2% at the hands of dissidents (CCJP/LRF, 1997: 156–7). In our own research in the Nkayi and Lupane Districts of Matabeleland, we estimated a similar ratio: at least 1,250 killed by government forces, and at most 45 killed by dissidents.[14] Such findings should not be surprising: the dissidents were a poorly armed group of less than 400 at their peak, and substantially less than that number for most of the 1980s, who survived largely by avoiding confrontation (Alexander, 1998), while the government wielded the full might of not only the Zimbabwe National Army, including the notorious Fifth Brigade, but also of the Central Intelligence Organization, police and various other units.[15]

The killing of unarmed civilians was justified by government officials through their elision of the categories of dissidents, Zapu members and civilians residing in regions where dissidents operated. Their statements, dutifully reported in the press, played an important role in giving the government's armed forces *carte blanche*. They also encouraged rank-and-file Zanu supporters – particularly the zealous Zanu Youth – to attack Zapu members, as they often did, notably during elections. The practice of painting all civilians in Matabeleland as dangerous and hence as legitimate targets intensified in 1983 with the deployment of the Fifth Brigade, the army unit responsible for the vast majority of atrocities against civilians. For example, the *Chronicle* reported Minister Emmerson Mnangagwa as telling a rally that the government had come to burn down 'all the villages infested with dissidents ... The campaign against dissidents can only succeed if the infrastructure that nurtures them is destroyed.' He referred to the dissidents as 'cockroaches' and to the Fifth Brigade as the 'DDT' which would eliminate them, a metaphor which both dehumanized the dissidents and legitimated indiscriminate killing.[16] Responding to critics of Fifth Brigade activity in Matabeleland, Mugabe explained the impossibility of distinguishing a dissident from an ordinary person: 'Where men and women provide food for dissidents, when we get there we eradicate them. We don't differentiate when we fight, because we can't tell who is a dissident and who is not.'[17]

When the Fifth Brigade was commissioned in August 1981, Joshua Nkomo still had a voice in the media: he objected to the Brigade, both due to the secrecy which surrounded its formation, and due to its stated purpose. The Brigade was composed largely of Shona-speaking, ex-Zanla forces, was directly answerable to the Prime Minister, and was trained by the North Koreans for use in maintaining 'internal' security, and more specifically to 'crush dissidents'.[18] Nkomo argued that Zimbabwe already had in place 'efficient forces of law, including the civil police, to handle any internal problems'. He feared that the Fifth Brigade 'is for the possible imposition of a one party state in our country': the Fifth Brigade 'is obviously a separate army, since it has different instructors from those we publicly know'.[19] Critical voices were increasingly silenced thereafter. The first censorship of a Zimbabwean journalist followed a critical report on the creation of the Fifth Brigade in August 1981 in the *Umtali Post*. Mrs Jean Maitland-Stuart, a white, former Rhodesian Printing and Publishing Company journalist, questioned the use of North Korean instructors for the Fifth Brigade. She was subsequently summoned to explain why she had adopted 'the South African line' on Zimbabwe's cooperation with friendly socialist countries. Within a month the Mass Media Trust advised Zimpapers to remove her from her post. As Saunders (1991: 116) notes, the case sounded a warning to those who would be critical of the government on security questions. With the deployment of the Fifth Brigade in Matabeleland in 1983, controls on press reporting increased. Curfew regulations were applied to large parts of the region, and strict controls were placed on the movement of both civilians and journalists.[20] As the Catholic Commission report noted:

> Journalists were banned from leaving Bulawayo without permission, and no unauthorised people were allowed into and out of the curfew areas. There were road blocks established on all roads into these areas. In short, these measures, together with the curfew, ensured that there was a near-total information black-out. (CCJP/LRF, 1997: 50)

Virtually the only way in which information about the activities of government forces in Matabeleland seeped into the press during the conflict itself was through government denials of charges made by human rights groups, church groups or foreign journalists, denials that invariably incorporated either an attack on the messenger or the heaping of calumny on Zapu.[21] For example, at the time of some of the Fifth Brigade's largest civilian massacres in Matabeleland North in February 1983, Minister of Information Nathan Shamuyarira responded to a Catholic Commission press release criticizing the actions of the security forces by denying that the government had 'inflamed the situation' or committed wanton killing: instead, he launched an attack on Zapu.[22] In April of the same year, Mugabe rebutted allegations of security force atrocities by calling his critics 'a band of Jeremiahs [who] included reactionary foreign journalists, non-governmental organisations of dubious status in our midst and sanctimonious prelates'.[23] In 1983 a press tour of carefully selected parts of Matabeleland was organized by the government to counter accusations of human rights violations. Director of Information Justin Nyoka told journalists that the supposed 'full-scale war' was 'no more than a figment of the imagination of foreign correspondents'.[24] While some civilian deaths were acknowledged, they were justified by the now familiar tactic of placing civilians in the same camp as dissidents. The *Chronicle* reported Minister Emmerson Mnangagwa's explanation to a forcibly assembled crowd in Matabeleland: the army had come to Matabeleland like fire, Mnangagwa said, 'and in the process of cleansing the area of the dissident menace had also wiped out their supporters'.[25]

The reporting of the conflict in Matabeleland thus reflected the Zanu government's point of view. It served to create a perception of the conflict as one in which the government was legitimately engaged in fighting the 'dissident menace', a menace that was made all the more dangerous and difficult to combat due to South African attempts to exploit disaffection as part of its destabilization strategy, and due to the political support of Zapu and the popular support of the civilian (i.e. Ndebele) population of Matabeleland for dissidents. Outside Matabeleland, people had little or no knowledge of the extent of state violence, but were regularly fed graphic details of dissident atrocities. By reading the government-controlled press between 1982 and 1987, they would have learned that violence in Matabeleland was perpetrated largely by dissidents loyal to, if not organized by, Zipra and Zapu and supported by Ndebele-speaking civilians in Matabeleland. They would have learned that those killed by the state were either themselves dissidents or were legitimate targets in so far as the people of Matabeleland supported dissidents.

The perceptions of the conflict within Matabeleland were formed very differently. People in Matabeleland, and particularly those in the rural areas, had little access to the media during the conflict due to a series of curfews and controls on travel. To the extent that they did see media reports, they regarded them as unreliable government propaganda. Their perceptions were the product of their direct experience of state violence.[26] The Fifth Brigade was critical in this regard. It targeted civilians: women were killed as the mothers of dissidents, children as future dissidents, others for failing to understand Shona. The Brigade politicized language, justified its attacks on tribalist grounds, and blurred the distinction between being Ndebele and being Zapu. Fifth Brigade commanders and soldiers often publicly explained their violence as revenge for nineteenth-century Ndebele raids on 'the Shona'. Many of the Fifth Brigade's victims felt its attacks were directed at them as a people.[27] The Central Intelligence Organization's systematic targeting of Zapu members, and the violence directed against Zapu during elections, served to harden a political interpretation of violence. State violence as a whole thus produced a deep alienation from the ruling party and central government, and aggravated resentment against 'the Shona'. The perception of tribalism outside Matabeleland was thus mirrored within it.

After Unity: a revitalized independent press

The critical turning-point in newspaper reporting on the conflict followed from the signing of the Unity agreement between Zanu and Zapu in late 1987. The agreement provided for the merger of the two political parties under the (unchanged) name of Zanu. Zapu ceased to exist:

senior Zapu politicians were incorporated into the government as Zanu ministers and Zapu members joined the new Zanu. The agreement brought an almost immediate cessation to the violence and opened the doors to a more critical attitude towards the government and robust discussions of press freedom in the independent media.[28]

The most immediate sign of a new willingness to criticize the government was the coverage given the 'Willowgate' scandal of 1988 by the Bulawayo-based Zimpapers' daily the *Chronicle*. The scandal concerned politicians' and state officials' illegal acquisition and resale of price-controlled vehicles for personal profit. After *Chronicle* editor Geoff Nyarota broke the story, the issue of corruption more broadly sparked a crisis in confidence in the government, marked by university student demonstrations, strikes and, in 1989, the formation of a new opposition party, the Zimbabwe Unity Movement. Intense pressure was put on Nyarota, who was threatened and forcibly 'promoted', but the independent press – particularly the *Financial Gazette* and the monthly magazines *Moto* and *Parade* – kept critical discussion of this and other issues alive. In the end, an official commission of inquiry was established and several key Zanu politicians and ministers were forced from office.

In this climate of more open criticism of the government, the independent press revisited the Matabeleland conflict of the early 1980s, through editorials, letters to the editor and investigative journalism. Coverage was given to the government's failure to release certain Zapu and Zipra prisoners under its general amnesty; wide-ranging discussions of the implications of the Matabeleland violence were published; and the particular problems of individuals in obtaining death certificates for those killed in the 1980s, and attempts by victims of violence to obtain compensation, were explored.[29] From 1991, cases of massacres and 'disappearances' were increasingly reported, often drawing on information collected by the ever-active Catholic Commission. These included a mass grave uncovered at Mpindo by heavy rains, the case of the 'Silobela 9' and other lower-level Zapu officials who had 'disappeared' at the time of the 1985 elections, and the discovery of mine shafts filled with bodies at Antelope and Silobela.[30] In each case, the government was called upon to respond, but senior members of the former Zapu (who were now in Zanu and in government) refused to comment, and Zanu leaders either denied responsibility or maintained that violence had been justified.[31] Police and the Central Intelligence Organization were reported to have threatened those who came forward with information, or who sought to visit places where mass graves had been found.[32] Despite the hostile government response, these reports played an important role within Matabeleland for their public confirmation for the first time of the existence of government atrocities, and their sparking of a public debate about the need for acknowledgement and healing.[33]

The most far-reaching public debate on the 1980s conflict followed the publication of the Catholic Commission for Justice and Peace/ Legal Resources Foundation human rights report, *Breaking the Silence, Building True Peace: A Report on the Disturbances in Matabeleland and the Midlands 1980–1988* (1997). We have drawn on this extraordinary report above. It is by far the most painstaking and detailed exploration of the violence in Matabeleland; its conclusions present a powerful challenge to the portrayal of the conflict propagated in the media during the 1980s.[34] The report showed how the organized violence perpetrated by the various arms of the state and Zanu party hugely outweighed the actions of the small number of dissidents they were ostensibly countering. It explored the conflict's background, examining the relationship between Zapu and Zanu, the problems encountered in creating an integrated army after independence, and the interventions of South African agents. It emphasized the central role of the Fifth Brigade in targeting civilians. The report called on the government to acknowledge human rights abuses in the interest of a lasting peace and proposed a 'reconciliation trust' to provide compensation to affected areas in the form of funds for community projects.

President Mugabe was handed a copy of the report in March 1997. It was not to be publicly circulated until Mugabe had had a chance to respond. A copy was nevertheless leaked to the South African *Weekly Mail and Guardian* in the first week in May. The *Mail and Guardian* (which is readily available in Zimbabwe's main cities) published long excerpts, and made the report available on its website. *Breaking the Silence* subsequently received extensive and positive coverage in the independent press, particularly in the *Zimbabwe Independent*, and the monthly magazines *Parade* and *Horizon*.[35] It was, however, largely ignored by the government-controlled press, and where it was not ignored it was attacked as a divisive tool designed to divert attention from the Zanu government's positive programmes (see Wetherell, 1997: 21–2).

Mugabe was forced to respond, but did so ambiguously. While addressing mourning crowds at the funeral of Zapu leader Stephen Vuma, he criticized the bishops for opening old wounds and threatening the nation's unity, implicitly suggesting that it was the publication of their report rather than the violence about which it was written that would dangerously divide the nation: 'If we dig up history, then we wreck the nation ... and we tear our people apart into factions, into tribes.' He nevertheless seemed to take a small step towards acknowledging government human rights abuses: 'The [historical] register or record will remind us what never to do. If that was wrong, if that went against the sacred tenets of humanity, we must never repeat it.'[36] Though decidedly ambiguous, Mugabe's response marked an important shift from previous blanket denials of security-force abuses. When the country entered a period of political and economic crisis in late 1997, Mugabe and the Zanu government faced an unprecedented challenge to its legitimacy. In this context, two prominent political figures, who had been powerful in Zanu in the early 1980s, made public 'apologies' for the violence unleashed by the state in Matabeleland.

The opening up of the press in the post-Unity period thus made possible the dissemination and discussion of information about the 1980s conflict as never before. But this change was not due to the press alone: the Catholic Commission report played a key role in making informed discussion possible. Without the extensive documentation presented in the report, the pattern of piecemeal revelations and periodic government denials would likely have continued. Nevertheless, the media coverage given to the report was key in making it accessible to a wider audience and forcing a government response, however in-adequate. The internet had played a key role in making that coverage possible, and it is to other internet debates to which we now turn.

Internet debates: Zimnet

The internet has been lauded as a liberating communicative utopia: the revolutionary and subversive potential of its free information flows, decentralized access and global links has been much heralded.[37] But the internet is simply a new tool with diverse users. Those who provide or use its facilities may have conflicting understandings of, and interests in, freedom and security, and the discussion groups which 'meet' on the internet are only as subversive as their members. Access to informa-tion may be 'direct' in the sense of being unmediated by journalists, but access to the equipment and knowledge necessary to use the inter-net is limited, and the political context in which it is used may constrain truly 'free' debate. As James Boyle has argued, even 'if information wants to be free, we aren't always ready to sign the emancipation proclamation ... Information technology can provide methods to lock *itself* up' (Boyle 1997b). The internet has already sparked new debates and conflicts over the long-standing issues of copyright, political access, monopoly control, civil liberties and freedom of speech. The impact of internet information flows is not simply a question of 'more is better', but depends on what messages are being sent, by whom, and how those with access to information react to and use it. The case of Zimnet, an internet forum that largely serves elite, expatriate Zimbabweans, many of whom are studying for university degrees abroad, shows the internet's role in the dissemination of human rights information, but also demonstrates that such information can be received and discussed in a manner that is precisely the opposite of subversive.[38]

When the Catholic Commission report on human rights abuses in Matabeleland was released on the *Weekly Mail and Guardian* website it was eagerly consulted and debated on Zimnet. The Zimnet subscribers, many of whom self-consciously saw themselves as Zimbabwe's future leaders, had had little or no direct experience of the conflict. Their reactions to the report were shaped most strongly by the earlier coverage of Zimbabwe's state-controlled media; they were also shaped by current media reports on a number of vaguely parallel international events. Thus those hailing from the USA made reference to the American debates over reparations for slavery and Clinton's apology for medical experiments undertaken on the black community of Tuskegee; others referred to events in Rwanda and Zaire. Debates on the role of the Catholic Church in Zimbabwe were influenced by broader debates over the 'cult of Rome' in upholding white supremacy and colonialism in the past, and the Church's recent apology for its role in the Second World War.

For some, the report was cause for frank admissions of shock at the extent of state violence. One contributor, for example, commented, 'I have been reading the gruesome reports of the atrocities by the Fifth Brigade in Matabeleland. Like most people, I am appalled by the breadth and scope of the violence, the brutality, the destruction, the displacement and deaths during this period.'[39] But many others were less concerned with the substance of the report than with its authors. The Catholic Church came under sustained attack. Contributors questioned its moral authority and suggested it had a 'hidden agenda' or 'external paymaster', thus consciously or unconsciously echoing the denunciations of the Catholic Commission made by Mugabe during the conflict. One subscriber, whose views were widely supported, wrote:

> I question the veracity of the [Catholic Commission] report, and the motivations of those who financed the development of the report. True research requires that you first research the author. If the Catholics truly knew evil they would first have done a report to make restitution for centuries of atrocities committed against Africans.[40]

Some contributors called for violent retribution: 'Now those who published the report can be taken to court and may be shot in public.'[41]

Minority dissenting voices pointed out that, although some members of the Catholic Church had supported the white settlers, others ('even white ones') 'threw their lot behind the armed struggle'.[42]

Efforts to defend the Zanu government, and the interpretation of the conflict that had been presented in the state-controlled media in the 1980s, were prominent in Zimnet discussions. These efforts took little notice of the substance of the Catholic Commission report, emphasizing instead the importance of loyalty to Zanu. One contributor was particularly zealous in this regard, and his lengthy and provocative contributions often set the tone for subsequent debates. He trumpeted his Zanu membership, declaring, 'I will shout it to everyone.'[43] He argued that the government's actions were legitimate because they brought peace: 'I can confidently say that the genocidal tactic is the one that brought stability in that part of the region.'[44] In exchanges with an outraged Ndebele-speaker, he developed an historical justification for the violence that sounded all too close to that which had been propounded by the Fifth Brigade itself:

> The extermination of the support base, although unfortunate, was one of the alternatives that worked. I sympathize with the victims, but for the victors it was a question of life and death as well ... Was dissidentry necessary? Was it anybody's fault that you [i.e. the Ndebele] lost elections? Was that the only option? Now ... the strategists ... decided to hammer the support base and you cry for a human rights inquiry. Do you want us to also cry for a human rights inquiry for the [nineteenth-century] warriors (thieves) who roamed Mashonaland? ... Our [i.e. the Shonas'] only sin was that we toiled the soil and had better produce. Don't the Matabeles beat their chests with pride for having stolen Mashona produce, women and children[?][45]

He held that Joshua Nkomo and Zapu were the leaders of the dissidents, and added for good measure that the Ndebele had not suffered in the war for independence as the Shona had.

Many other contributors condemned the Catholic Commission report as divisive, and the call for acknowledgement and compensation as misplaced. Historical and ethnic arguments were often taken up. Some assumed a lengthy and antagonistic relationship between 'the Shona' and 'the Ndebele', and expressed their views in a deeply intolerant and emotional tone. As one contributor commented: 'If you tell me anything about the war in early 80s Zimbabwe I will say to hell, you are an interested part[y]. You will definitely say the same if I tell you about the loss I suffered through my ancestors on the hands of the Matabele warrior.'[46] Ethnicity was discussed explicitly. Contributors presented a range of views, but most argued that ethnicity was in some way central to the conflict. One contributor initiated a lengthy debate with the following message:

> I write here to raise at least one question, specifically was that war an ethnic war? The analysis of this question is in my opinion tricky but at the same time very important. It is clear that, by and large, Zanla and Zipra were constituted along ethnic lines. It is also clear that, by and large, the armed combatants in that war were divided along ethnic lines. On the other hand, one should point out however, that soldiers do not start wars, they fight them ... Whereas those who executed the war and a certain propor- tion of the civilians may have seen it through ethnic eyes, others (perhaps the majority) did not. It is this reality, this simple truth which some of us choose to ignore. Instead we embrace and propagate the emotive and dangerous perception that every Shona is anti-Ndebele and every Ndebele anti-Shona. True, ethnicists like racists and sexists will be with us for a long time if only because society propagates them.[47]

Responses varied. Some concurred with the argument that politicians had used ethnicity for their own ends, and that an ethnic consciousness had since become widespread and entrenched. Others stressed the role of specifically the Fifth Brigade and dissidents in creating ethnic pol- arity.[48] For still other contributors, ethnicity was 'natural' but ethnic wars needed to be understood as conflicts over resources.[49] Some stressed the role of the colonial powers and historians in creating 'tribal labels', sparking debate over the nature of the Ndebele state, and the 'constructedness' of ethnicity.[50] These debates at times degenerated into acrimony: 'All you want is for us to say Mugabe be condemned and resign, so that you may Buldoze [sic] your tribe into power,' wrote one angry contributor. An equally angry individual responded:

> All this Ndebele and Nkomo is coming from your tribally intoxicated mind ... Your shallow-mindedness is clearly evidenced by the fact that you simply jump to the conclusion that everyone against the Gukura [Fifth Brigade] atrocities is a Nkomo supporter, [Catholic Commission] supporter or a Ndebele. WAKE UP! This is not the case. Where do you come from? Have you ever lived in a city?[51]

Significant time and energy was spent in debating the nature of ethnicity, sometimes resulting in attacks on fellow contributors on the basis of their assumed ethnic identity despite some postings that insisted on the irrelevance and divisive nature of such debates. Others tried to stimulate a reading and discussion of the substance of the Catholic Commission report. One contributor, seeking to bring the debate back to the report itself, commented:

You asked if this was an ethnic war. I feel at first the 'war' was genuinely against dissidents. But, frustrated with the lack of progress, particularly in tracking down the more notorious bandits, and at the encouragement of politicians (who also wanted to crush Zapu political opposition), the security forces blanketed dissidents, Zapu supporters and Ndebeles into one category and simply unleashed a reign of terror. The dissidents themselves were mainly Zipra soldiers who had fled from the army when Zipra members of the ZNA began to disappear, or ex-Zipras who were unhappy about the treatment that had been handed their leaders by the Shona leadership. To them the Shona were an enemy.[52]

This contributor continued, 'At some point during that war the people of Matabeleland felt persecuted as a people. The next crucial question is who did the persecution. And the answer is, the government.'[53]

Dominant strands in the Zimnet debates sparked by the release of the Catholic Commission report on the internet were initially far less concerned with grappling with the substance of the report than with defending an interpretation of events that shadowed those of the state-controlled press, the Zanu government, and even the Fifth Brigade. Ethnicity was a central topic of debate. Zimnet discussions were defined by the nature of Zimnet members, the majority of whom hailed from outside Matabeleland and came from elite families. The self-confident and provocative defences of state violence in Matabeleland were reinforced by self-censorship: at least one participant in the debate withdrew explicitly, pronouncing the topic too sensitive for a medium such as the internet.[54] Certainly, only a fraction of the total Zimnet membership contributed to this particular debate – it was thus not a fully free exchange. Though the internet facilitated increased access to information, the impact of that information was profoundly shaped by its political context, by the source of the information, and by the attitudes and beliefs of those receiving it. The importance of political context has been underlined subsequently: when Zimbabwe entered a severe political and economic crisis in late 1997, and the Zanu government's legitimacy was challenged as never before, critical views of government violence in Matabeleland began to be voiced more frequently and confidently on Zimnet.

Conclusion

The press played a central role in shaping attitudes towards Zimbabwe's post-independence conflict. The rapid change in ownership of the press after independence, in part to redress South African and white domination, opened the door to government control. The burgeoning insecurity and violence of the immediate post-independence period subsequently legitimated an expansion of state intervention in the media. Government controls ensured strongly biased coverage of the developing conflict in Matabeleland. Dissenting voices were quickly silenced; a distorted view of the conflict took hold in the popular imagination. Outside Matabeleland, it seemed that the vast majority of violence was perpetrated by 'dissidents' bent on the illegitimate project of overthrowing the government, probably with the aid of Zapu leaders, and certainly with the backing of civilians in Matabeleland. The focus of the violence in the predominantly Ndebele-speaking Matabeleland region, and the historical connection of both Zapu and Zipra to the region, made the jump to an ethnic interpretation of the conflict all too easy. The media coverage given to government ministers' often intolerant denunciations of Zapu, dissidents and the people of Matabeleland, created a climate in which the armed forces, as well as local-level backers of Zanu, could justify resorting to extreme violence. Within Matabeleland, civilians also began to interpret the conflict in ethnic terms, due not to media coverage but to the explicit use of ethnic justifications in attacks by government forces, particularly the Fifth Brigade.

In the post-Unity period, a newly self-confident and critical, independent press began to question the official account of the conflict. Reports of government atrocities were certainly important to the people of Matabeleland for publicly confirming the reality of their suffering. However, it took the publication of a locally compiled human rights report to reinvigorate debate on a new scale. Media coverage of this document forced President Mugabe into his first, deeply ambivalent, acknowledgement of some level of government responsibility for the violence. The circulation of the report on the internet was key in its dissemination to Zimbabwe's media as well as more widely. The internet discussions contrasted with the newspaper coverage of the conflict in the sense that they were unmediated by journalists. But the internet was not a straightforwardly democratizing and liberating instrument of free discussion: Zimnet debates demonstrated that discussion was only as free as the political views of the participants allowed, and showed the lasting and profound influence of the interpretations of the violence propagated in Zimbabwe's media during the conflict.

Notes

1. The research on which this chapter draws was undertaken between 1994 and 1997 as part of a collaborative research project carried out by Jocelyn

Alexander and Terence Ranger, funded by the Leverhulme Trust, and JoAnn McGregor, funded by the ESRC, Grant No. R00023 527601.

2. The Matabeleland region was the main arena for conflict in the 1980s, but neighbouring provinces, notably the Midlands, also suffered violence.

3. We use the shorthand terms Zanu and Zapu throughout this chapter in lieu of Zanu (Patriotic Front) and Patriotic Front–Zapu, the full post-independence names of Zimbabwe's nationalist parties.

4. On Rhodesian era press censorship, particularly the barrage of restrictions introduced by the Rhodesian Front after 1965 and the practice of self-censorship, see Frederikse, 1982; Todd, 1972; Watson, 1976; Windrich, 1981. For a recent brief review, see Maxwell (forthcoming).

5. For an extended discussion of the media in Zimbabwe, see Saunders, 1991. This section draws on Saunders' account.

6. On the New World Information and Communication Order, see Harrell-Bond and Carlson, 1996.

7. In 1981 Zimpapers consisted of the *Herald*, the *Chronicle*, the *Sunday Mail*, the *Sunday News* and the *Manica Post*. In 1985, *Kwaedza* and *Umthunya* were added (subsequently merged to *Kwadeza/Umthunywa*). The only other major paper was the privately owned *Financial Gazette*.

8. *Herald*, 8 January 1981. Zapu leader Joshua Nkomo commented cynically, 'I would have thought that radio and television were enough as a propaganda tool.' See *Herald*, 5 January 1981.

9. Interview with Elias Rusike in 'Of Hatchets and Hacks', *Moto*, July 1991, pp. 5–6. At the time of this interview, Rusike had become Chief Executive and Publisher of the independent *Financial Gazette*, and had recently published a book (Rusike, 1990) detailing his experience as Zimpapers' supremo.

10. *Chronicle*, 27 June 1980. See also *Chronicle*, 21 and 23 May 1980; 20 June 1980.

11. *Chronicle*, 30 June 1980.

12. *Chronicle*, 7 July 1980. For a lengthier compilation of Nkala's many provocative statements, see Reginald Thabani Gola, 'Nkala's Record Speaks for Itself', *Parade*, September 1992, pp. 13, 16.

13. In our research, such cases were regularly reported (see Alexander, McGregor and Ranger, forthcoming).

14. We estimated these figures based on extensive interviewing in the two districts. The number of deaths at government hands is almost certainly underestimated (see Alexander and McGregor, forthcoming).

15. The CCJP/LRF (1997: 47) estimated more than 5,000 troops (including the Police Support Unit and other army units) were deployed in Matabeleland North after the arrival of the Fifth Brigade in 1983. *Africa Confidential*, 11 April 1984, estimated 15,000 soldiers were in Matabeleland South in 1984.

16. *Chronicle*, 5 March 1983.

17. *Chronicle*, 18 April 1983. Other Zanu ministers such as Enos Nkala and Sydney Sekeramayi made similar, widely reported comments (see *Chronicle*, 4 and 12 February 1983).

18. *Chronicle*, 22 August 1981.

19. *Chronicle*, 25 August 1981.

20. The curfews had important implications not only for the free flow of information, but also for the health of civilians who found themselves denied drought relief and unable to travel to shops to buy food during an extreme drought.

21. Virtually the only critical voice in the media was that of the independent monthly magazine *Moto* which covered the Matabeleland violence in a series of articles in March 1983. These included: 'The situation in Matabeleland' and 'The bruising of the dissidents'. *Moto* was also the only magazine to give critical coverage of the trial of Zapu and Zipra leaders for treason.

22. *Chronicle*, 30 March 1983.

23. *Chronicle*, 6 April 1983.

24. *Chronicle*, 26 February 1983.

25. *Chronicle*, 5 April 1983.

26. Civilian perceptions and experiences of state violence are discussed at greater length in Alexander and McGregor (forthcoming) and Alexander, McGregor and Ranger (forthcoming).

27. The Fifth Brigade's violence was unique. Other units of the national army and the police did not normally target civilians or explain their mission as one aimed at tribal vengeance (see CCJP/LRF, 1997; Alexander and McGregor, forthcoming; Alexander, McGregor and Ranger, forthcoming).

28. Debates about press freedom were regularly reported in the monthly magazines *Moto*, *Parade*, and *Horizon* after the Unity agreement. They reflected efforts to debate press freedom by new opposition parties, local human rights groups, university lecturers, and even senior members of Zanu such as Eddison Zvobgo, and former members of Zimpapers such as Elias Rusike.

29. For example, see 'The forgotten prisoners', *Moto*, December 1988/January 1989; B. Sodindwa, 'The people and their wounds' and A. Z. Nhamo, 'Shock and disbelief in Matabeleland' both in *Moto*, January 1993; Collet Nkala, 'Matabeleland's missing persons mystery', *Horizon*, November 1991; 'Looking back over the decade', *Parade*, April 1990; Collet Nkala, 'Tsholotsho folk challenge death certificate ruling', *Horizon*, October 1990. *Horizon* magazine also ran a series of articles on South African involvement in the 1980s violence, and on Zipra. The latter was an important effort to right some of the historical distortion of that army's contribution to the liberation struggle.

30. See, for example, Thabane Kunene, 'Gukurahundi murders exposed', *Horizon*, March 1992; 'Silobela abductees declared dead' and 'The mystery continues', *Horizon*, June 1992; 'Tragedy at Tsholotsho', *Horizon*, July 1992; 'Missing men mystery: no records from state' and 'CCJP wants army atrocities published', *Parade*, November 1991; 'Human remains continue to surface in Matabeleland', *Parade*, October 1992; 'Miner who found Silobela bones now fears for his life', *Parade*, April 1993; 'Villagers blame Fifth Brigade atrocities for drought as famine hits Matabeleland', *Parade*, January 1996.

31. That the long-time senior members of Zanu continued to deny responsibility is far less surprising than the quick conversion of the former Zapu's senior leaders to the merits of silence. In 1992, confronted with the discovery

of human remains at Antelope Mine in Kezi District (his home area and political stronghold), former Zapu leader and then Vice President Joshua Nkomo told assembled crowds that he 'could not answer any questions in the absence of his colleague [and co-Vice President], Simon Muzenda'. See 'Human remains continue to surface in Matabeleland', *Parade*, October 1992. Other, less senior, former Zapu leaders were less willing to keep quiet.

32. In the Antelope Mine case, police immediately mounted a guard post at the site, and the Central Intelligence Organization deterred locals from making visits. In the case of the Silobela mine shaft, police threatened the mine owner (a local man), intimidated others, and tampered with evidence. Such threats, coming so soon after the violence of the 1980s, were terrifying for local people. See 'Human remains continue to surface in Matabeleland', *Parade*, October 1992; 'Miner who found Silobela bones now fears for his life', *Parade*, April 1993.

33. For example, see Letters to Editor page of *Horizon*, September 1992. We were often told that the coverage of the Antelope Mine discoveries was important in local eyes for the legitimacy it gave to people's long-denied grievances against the government.

34. The report is based on interviews with victims in two case-study districts in Matabeleland (Nyamandhlovu and Kezi), cross-referenced with and supplemented by a compilation of all other available material, from hospital records, Catholic Commission correspondence and reports, legal cases, press and human rights reports. It is an exemplary case of careful and nuanced reporting, and was praised as such by Amnesty International.

35. See, for example, *Zimbabwe Independent*, 9 to 15 May 1997; *Financial Gazette*, 8 May 1997; 'Zimbabwe's killing fields', *Horizon*, July 1997; 'Are Catholic Bishops developing cold feet over explosive report?', *Parade*, June 1997; 'Mugabe taken to task over human rights', *Parade*, August 1997.

36. *Sunday Mail*, 11 May 1997.

37. A more considered and sceptical recent literature is discussed in the *Times Literary Supplement*, 4 July 1997, including Boyle, 1997a; Brown, 1997; Mulgan, 1997; and Sardar and Ravetz, 1997.

38. This is of course not the case with all internet sites: Camnet, a discussion forum for Cameroonians, is highly subversive, as its members are drawn predominantly from dissenting exiled groups (Francis Nyamnjoh, personal communication). Dissidents in Mexico have also made use of the internet (see Castells, 1997).

39. Zimnet, 3 May 1997.

40. Zimnet, 8 May 1997.

41. Zimnet, 13 May 1997.

42. Zimnet, 3 May 1997.

43. Zimnet, 12 May 1997.

44. Zimnet, 4 March 1997.

45. Zimnet, 5 May 1997.

46. Zimnet, 8 May 1997.

47. Zimnet, 3 May 1997.

48. E.g., see Zimnet, 3 May 1997 and 6 May 1997.
49. Zimnet, 4 May 1997.
50. Zimnet, 5 May 1997 and 7 May 1997.
51. Zimnet, 8 May 1997.
52. Zimnet, 3 May 1997.
53. Zimnet, 3 May 1997.
54. E.g., Zimnet, 8 May 1997.

References

Alexander, J. (1998) 'Dissident Perspectives on Zimbabwe's Post-Independence War', *Africa*, Vol. 68, No. 2, pp. 151–82.

Alexander, J. and McGregor, J. (forthcoming) 'Democracy, Development and Political Conflict: Rural Institutions in Matabeleland North after Independence', in N. Bhebe and T. Ranger (eds), *Historical Perspectives on Democracy and Human Rights* (3 vols), Harare/Oxford: University of Zimbabwe Press/James Currey.

Alexander, J., McGregor, J. and Ranger, T. (forthcoming) *Violence and Memory: Life in the Forests of Northern Matabeleland, 1896–1996*, Oxford: James Currey.

Boyle, J. (1997a) *Shamans, Software and Spleens. Law and the Construction of the Information Society*, Cambridge, MA: Harvard University Press.

— (1997b) 'A Sense of Belonging. Problems of Defining the Limits of Copyright in the Age of the Internet – and of Pop-Music Parody', *Times Literary Supplement*, 4 July.

Brown, D. (1997) *Cybertrends. Chaos, Power and Accountability in the Information Age*, London: Viking.

Castells, M. (1997) *Information Age: Volume Two. The Power of Identity*, Oxford: Blackwell.

CCJP/LRF (Catholic Commission for Justice and Peace/Legal Resources Foundation) (1997) *Breaking the Silence, Building True Peace: A Report on the Disturbances in Matabeleland and the Midlands 1980–1988*, Harare: CCJP/LRF.

CIIR (Catholic Institute for International Relations) (1980) *Halfway to the Elections: Some Notes on the Present Situation in Rhodesia*, Salisbury: CIIR.

Commonwealth Observer Group (1980) *Southern Rhodesia Elections. The Report of the Commonwealth Observer Group*, London: Commonwealth Secretariat.

Frederikse, J. (1982) *None But Ourselves. Masses vs Media in the Making of Independent Zimbabwe*, Harare: Zimbabwe Publishing House.

Harrell-Bond, B. and Carlson, S. (1996) 'Resisting the Dream of a New World Information Order', in T. Allen, K. Hudson and J. Seaton (eds), *War, Ethnicity and the Media*, London: South Bank University, pp. 97–123.

Lawyers' Committee for Human Rights (1986) *Zimbabwe: Wages of War*, New York: LCHR.

Maxwell, D. (forthcoming) 'Southern Rhodesia', in D. James (ed.), *Censorship: An International Encyclopedia*, London: Fitzroy Dearborn Publishers.

Mulgan, G. (1997) *Connexity. How to Live in a Connected World*, London: Chatto & Windus.

Nkomo, J. (1985) *Nkomo. The Story of My Life*, London: Methuen.

Rusike, E. (1990) *The Politics of the Mass Media: A Personal Experience*, Harare: Roblaw Publishers.

Sardar, Z. and Ravetz, J. (eds) (1997) *Cyberfutures. Culture and Politics on the Information Superhighway*, New York: New York University Press/Plymbridge.

Saunders, R. (1991) 'Information in the Interregnum: The Press, State and Civil Society in Struggles for Hegemony, Zimbabwe 1980–1990', Unpublished PhD thesis, Carlton University, Ontario.

Todd, J. (1972) 'Not in Rhodesia's Interest', *Index on Censorship*, Vol. 1, No. 3/4, pp. 85–97.

Watson, E. (1976) *Banned: The Story of the African Daily News, Southern Rhodesia, 1964*, London: Hamish Hamilton.

Wetherell, I. (1997) 'The Matabeleland Report: A Lot to Hide', *Southern African Report*, June 1997.

Windrich, E. (1981) *The Mass Media in the Struggle for Zimbabwe. Censorship and Propaganda under Rhodesian Front Rule*, Gweru, Zimbabwe: Mambo Press.

. . . .

CHAPTER 13

Media Ethnicization and the International Response to War and Genocide in Rwanda

Mel McNulty

This chapter will discuss the response of the international media to the Rwandan crisis, which culminated in the genocide of 1994, and assess whether they contributed to the eventual extension of the civil war to neighbouring Zaire. Misinterpretation of these conflicts as ethnically-driven facilitated Western interventionary responses, the rationale for which may be summarized as 'they are mad, we are sane, we must save them from themselves', and served, whether deliberately or accidentally, to make a bad situation worse. New outbreaks of conflict were interpreted as ethnically-driven ('Laurent Kabila's Tutsi-led rebels', etc.), inviting a further interventionary response. It will be argued that the Western media, by swallowing the deliberate disinformation that the Rwandan war was ethnically-driven, legitimized that view. Thus the media became accomplices in the power politics of external actors with interests in the region.

Media imagery was key in the promotion of a 'humanitarian' reaction to the crisis in the Great Lakes region, by means of which military-strategic interests could be pursued under a cloak of humanitarian concern. The net result of this media-driven agenda was a vicious circle – crisis, images, intervention, further crisis, more images, repeated intervention – that helped exacerbate the Rwandan crisis to the point of genocide, and then exported that crisis to neighbouring Zaire. The local response in late 1996 displayed the extent to which local actors had learned from recent experience; the destruction of the vast camps of refugees and fugitives from justice in eastern Zaire, and massive repatriations to Rwanda in November and December of that year, removed the pretext for a further Western response. The subsequent elimination of the non-returnees – former Rwandan army, militias, Zairean supporters and the civilians among whom they sheltered, numbering anything up to 200,000 – was conducted off-camera, in the full knowledge that where there are no images, there is no story. The fact that Rwanda was able to deny its involvement in the Zairean war, despite the Rwandan Patriotic Army's (RPA) spearheading of the campaign, until that war's successful conclusion – with the seizure of power by the Rwandan-backed AFDL (Alliance of Democratic Forces for the Liberation of Congo) in May 1997 – demonstrates how little purchase the Western media yet had on the true nature of events, seven years after the initial outbreak of war.

The Western media and African crises

The volume of Western coverage of recent African crises is almost always in direct proportion to the scale of direct Western involvement (NGO or military interventions), or to the degree of clamour for such interventions (the 'something must be done' response). No Western troops or high-profile, publicity-hungry NGOs mean no media coverage. Mass murder far from the Western lens is small news (as a comparison of coverage of conflict in Israel and Algeria suggests); mass epidemic (albeit in man-made circumstances), with the potential for Western intervention, is big news. The real exigencies of 'humanitarian' intervention were already apparent at the time of its post-Cold War reinvention, most clearly in the agenda for 1992's high-profile Operation Restore Hope in Somalia. Gérard Prunier, East Africa specialist and sometime adviser to the French Defence Ministry, tells how he met Bruno Delhaye, head of the French President's 'Africa Unit', in December 1992 while French troops were preparing to join the US-led operation. Delhaye explained French involvement:

> You see, it is soon going to be Christmas and it would be unthinkable to have the French public eat its Christmas dinner while seeing on TV all those starving kids. It would be politically disastrous ... But don't worry, as soon as all this stuff blows over and TV cameras are trained in another direction, we will quietly tiptoe out. With luck it shouldn't last more than three to four months and in the meantime we will try our best not to do anything foolish. (Prunier, 1997: 135)

Later, *Médecins sans Frontières* co-founder and Minister for Humanitarian Action Bernard Kouchner was to be seen on French television shouldering a bag of rice with which he splashed ashore on a Somali beach. This manipulation of images has been well documented elsewhere; however, it became a key determinant of the nature of the international response to the Rwandan genocide. France's controversial

Opération Turquoise in 1994 was driven as much by this media imperative as any other. Prunier tells how on that occasion, he saved the Defence Ministry embarrassment by pointing out:

> The first draft of the intervention plan ... was entirely based on the supposition that the French troops would enter the country through Gisenyi [in north-west Rwanda] ... [S]ince the official purpose of the mission was humanitarian, there was precious little to do at that level in Gisenyi and Ruhengeri préfectures. As a local Hutu trader was later to remark to a French journalist, 'We never had many Tutsi here and we killed them all at the beginning without much of a fuss.' The French forces would find absolutely no-one left alive to be paraded in front of TV cameras as a justification for the intervention. (Prunier, 1995: 283–4.)

Coverage of the Rwandan crisis was characterized by war reporting, not conflict reporting. The Western news consumer was fed an occasional series of unlinked reports about seemingly unrelated crises, which generally fitted into the typical African mould of biblical catastrophes. Mechanical ethnicization comforts us in the knowledge that the perpetrators are mad (driven by tribalism, ancient blood lust, etc.); we in contrast are sane, and that something must be done. It is not too far from this new media-driven agenda of humanitarian intervention to the argument that decolonization was a mistake, that Africans are unfit to govern themselves, and to conservative historian Norman Stone's calls for a new imperialism.

News coverage came to set the agenda of international response to the extent that disease (on camera) was equated with, or superseded by, genocide (largely off-camera) in the public imagination. Generally, images of mass movements of 'refugees' in Rwanda suggested that these were the victims, rarely that many of them were the perpetrators of genocide (now fugitives from justice), accompanied by a terrified and intimidated 'human shield' of real refugees. In contrast, there had been no foreign camera crews in Rwanda when the genocide began. All of this may have been accidental, the result of ignorance, indifference, and ready recourse to clichés. But we should also allow for the possibility of a deliberate agenda on the part of those with a vested interest in Western involvement in Central Africa, at government, NGO or indeed media level. One possible theory which may emerge is that the Western media's ethnicization of the conflict justified Western intervention, and was perhaps so used deliberately; subsequent evidence of different sets of motives among press practitioners – reporters, commentators, editors – which distorted public and government perceptions of the war, genocide and their aftermath lends weight to this interpretation. In short, the media left themselves open to charges of neo-colonialism, what anti-colonial playwright and essayist Aimé Césaire called 'collective hypocrisy, skilled at distorting problems all the better to legitimise the odious solutions which are provided' (Césaire, 1955: 7–8).

As a result, the following formula of cause and effect may be offered in response to prevalent interpretations of the media's role in African conflict, and the 'humanitarian intervention' agenda: in response to a crisis, the media portray the conflict as ethnic (i.e. a crisis not of our making, caused not by political or economic circumstances but by ancestral hatreds beyond our ken); a media focus on human suffering rather than its political causes provokes demands for a presumed apolitical response – to freeze the situation if not solve it – which equals forcible 'humanitarian' intervention; intervention by a powerful state into a weak state (and particularly by European states in Africa) cannot be disinterested or free of the suspicion of neo-colonialism; the media, through mechanical ethnicization of conflict in Africa, become the (unwitting) vehicle of a post-Cold War neo-colonial agenda, what has been called the Second Scramble for Africa. The implications of such an agenda will now be discussed, and a possible response offered by way of conclusion.

Ethnicization: the mutual reinforcement of local propaganda and Western stereotypes

The Great Lakes region of eastern Central Africa received little attention in the Western media in the decade before mid-1994. Those not directly interested in the region's politics could perhaps recall nevertheless Uganda's Idi Amin, the caricature grotesque of an African dictator, and the movie-glamorized Israeli commando raid on Entebbe airport during his reign in 1976. Otherwise, the loose collection of states bordering Lakes Victoria, Kivu and Tanganyika were among the continent's most stable and hence least newsworthy: 'Westernized' Kenya, considered 'civilized' and a relic of colonial decency by the wildlife safari jet set; tranquil Tanzania, suffering in silence the poverty, underdevelopment and disillusionment which followed the failure of Nyerere's experiment with African-style socialism; and the heart of darkness itself, mammoth Zaire, vaguely recalled as troublesome in the 1960s and prone to the occasional flare-up, but best known perhaps for 'the rumble in the jungle' (Muhammad Ali's triumphant comeback heavyweight bout against George Foreman in 1974, recently given the Hollywood treatment in *When We were Kings* (1991)), or the 'African authenticity' campaign and grandiose airs of its seemingly comical ruler,

Mobutu Sese Seko. As for tiny, land-locked Rwanda and Burundi, these were, like Andorra or Liechtenstein, best known for their stamps and, by the mid-1980s, for the mountain gorillas befriended by American anthropologist Dian Fossey (played by Sigourney Weaver in *Gorillas in the Mist* (1987)).

Needless to say, few Western news organizations had a permanent correspondent or even a specialist on the region outside of Kenya (Nairobi being East Africa's largest and most 'developed' city). This was not a failing unique to the media. A search of academic literature in the early 1990s for works on Rwanda, Burundi or Mobutu's Zaire (i.e. post-'Congo crisis') would have borne but little fruit in French, and next to none in English (notable exceptions are Newbury, 1988 and Guichaoua, 1992).

Even Gérard Prunier (both academic and sometime participant in events as adviser in 1994 to French Defence Minister François Léotard) was by his own admission a Uganda specialist prior to 1990, and was surprised in that year to be overtaken by events in that country's diminutive and seemingly tranquil neighbour. Published in 1995, his *The Rwanda Crisis: History of a Genocide* was one of just a few voices raised in opposition to the prevailing paradigms of analysis (or non-analysis). The events in Rwanda that culminated in genocide are, he argues,

> a historical product, not a biological fatality or a 'spontaneous' bestial out-burst. Tutsi and Hutu have not been created by God as cats and dogs, predestined from all eternity to disembowel each other ... The Rwandese genocide is the result of a process which can be analysed, studied and explained. (Prunier, 1995: xii)

And yet, references to a 'centuries-old', 'ethnic', 'tribal' conflict between 'races' genetically predisposed to hate each other dominate to an extent unthinkable in other societies where politico-economic factors have brought different social classes or castes into conflict.

Such coverage by many Western journalists (for a detailed analysis, see Sweeney, 1997) in its ignorance and oversimplification, follows directly from its colonial predecessors who rejoiced in the unfathomable mysteries and the exotic thrill of horror provoked by the 'dark continent'. Apolitical invocations by sub-editors and leader-writers of 'the horror, the horror', of Conrad's *Heart of Darkness* (1902) and Coppola's *Apocalypse Now* (1979) have been legion. Representative of the genre and remarkable for its use of cliché was a *Financial Times* editorial, predictably entitled 'Heart of Darkness', which warned: 'Once again the international community watches helplessly as an African state slides into genocidal anarchy ... Two years ago in Rwanda the world was caught unawares by the sheer speed of the slaughter. That is one excuse we cannot give today in neighbouring Burundi' (*Financial Times*, 29 July 1996). Two of France's leading reporters of African affairs, Antoine Glaser and Stephen Smith, guilty themselves of unrelieved Afropessimism in their most recent co-authored work, nevertheless identify the dearth of analysis and the obsession with both the exotic and the apocalyptic that characterizes Western coverage: 'Tribal wars, bloody *coups d'état*, Biblical famines, savage massacres, devastating epidemics ... Africa is another planet' (Glaser and Smith, 1994: 12). Accordingly, Prunier states that he hoped his book would be 'an antidote to the idea that Africa is a place of darkness, where furious savages clobber each other on the head to assuage their dark ancestral bloodlusts', a feeling which, he suggests, 'sneaks even into the recesses of the most "liberal" minds' (Prunier, 1995: xii).

It should have come as no surprise, then, that Western news media, whose coverage of foreign affairs is so frequently limited, sporadic and more ill-informed than actually subjective, should have acquitted themselves poorly in Rwanda. It is doubtful whether the average American or European could offer a cogent analysis of conflicts closer to home in Bosnia, Chechnya, or indeed Northern Ireland, based on news coverage alone. But post-decolonization conflict in Africa – 'black on black violence' as it was labelled in South Africa – conflicts in which, inconveniently, skin colour is not available to distinguish the combatants or classify them either way as good or evil, ring a new set of bells in the media-shaped public imagination. There is a need – perhaps shaped by Serb/Muslim, Catholic/Protestant perceptions of wars elsewhere – for neat descriptors; typically, and tragically, more accurate terminology – sectarian versus pluralist, pro-regime versus anti-regime – has not been considered sufficiently accessible for the simplicity-seeking news consumer.

Add to this an often inherent, automatic, culturally-programmed racism about Africans and African societies which can distort the interpretative lens, as Prunier points out, of the most politically correct, or a prevalent Afro-pessimism which views the whole continent as unfit for self-rule (as voiced more controversially in the recent travelogue by African-American Keith Richburg, 1997), and the agenda for describing the Rwandan war was utterly predictable.

It is not intended here, therefore, to express surprise at ignorance, indifference, racial stereotyping and ethnic labelling in most coverage of events in Rwanda and its region since 1990. Instead, we will consider a chain of cause and effect which was put in place as soon as the

Rwandan war began (in October 1990), the most calamitous effect of which was to legitimize the Rwandan state's own propaganda about the threat it faced in what it portrayed as an ethnic war.

The Rwandan media: facilitator of genocide

The pro-state media within Rwanda – a single-party state based on sectarianism and nepotism which was adapting reluctantly to post-Cold War imperatives for change expected by its Western backers – had an obvious agenda. The role of the Rwandan media – as propaganda organs which gave voice to and mirrored the sectarianism of the state and its capitulation to its extremes – was key in reinforcing sectarianism and promoting a sense of crisis and siege which in turn contributed to the sabotaging of the Arusha peace process, and damned compromise as surrender. This role has already been examined and documented by two excellent accounts, in French and in English (Chrétien, 1995, and Kirschke/Article 19, 1996).

Despite descriptions in some Western coverage of 'genocidal anarchy', recourse to genocide by the former Rwandan regime was possible only due to the state's strength, its tightly controlled administration, and its monopoly of information and use of the media (i.e., radio and propaganda journals, in a non-televisual, predominantly monoglot Rwandophone society with little access to external sources of information) to coordinate systematic massacres throughout the country. The effects of external misinterpretation of the causes and conduct of this war encouraged the proponents of genocide to believe, with reason, that their elimination of a section of the Rwandan population would not be identified by the international media until its principal goals had already been achieved.

A salutary lesson may be drawn from the role of Ferdinand Nahimana. One of the most accomplished Rwandan historians of his generation, Nahimana had completed his doctorate in Paris with the support and supervision of some of Europe's leading Africanists. As the author of a major history of ethnicity in his country (1993), Nahimana would have been keenly aware of both simplistic, Eurocentric, Western interpretations of African history and current affairs, and of the public and official receptiveness in Rwanda for a version of its history which conformed to popular perceptions and prejudices learned from home and school.

Nahimana's academic prominence as rector of the National University of Rwanda was to prove less significant than his skills as the Rwandan genocide's Goebbels, as co-founder of the pro-genocide *Radio-*

Télévision Libre des Milles Collines (RTLM, dubbed, as its role in co-ordinating the genocide became clear, 'Radio-Télévision La Mort'). Nahimana became one of the principal ideologues of the sectarian 'Hutu Power' faction at the heart of the regime, and RTLM, along with extremist publications, became the principal weapon in the anti-RPF (Rwandan Patriotic Front) and anti-compromise propaganda war, used effectively to indoctrinate the population and coordinate the genocidal militias. It is important to emphasize here, as Kirschke rightly concludes, that RTLM 'did not incite genocide so much as organise it ... The genocide would have gone ahead with or without RTLM.' (Kirschke/*Article 19*: 1996: 166, 170).

The theory that pro-regime or pro-extremist radio stations, albeit with a near-monopoly in a tightly controlled society, could whip an otherwise peaceful population into a murderous frenzy draws on a number of stereotypes, not the least insidious of which is that Rwandans (and presumably Africans generally), being 'unsophisticated' and 'undeveloped', are infinitely suggestible. This point is emphasized in recent research on the West's 'humanitarian intervention' agenda: 'The media are not a cause of conflict proper but a terrain of conflict and instruments of enmity and mobilization...' (Pieterse, 1997: 79). It is also a key part of the process of mass self-exoneration which many manifestations of the 'international community' – governments, international organizations, NGOs – have pursued since the near-completion of the genocide (which was stopped, it should be emphasized, by Rwandans). Smith and Glaser, for example, suggested that there is no direct French complicity in genocide – despite massive, long-term military support for the army which oversaw it – because the killings were carried out by machete-wielding peasants incited by Rwandophone radio (Glaser and Smith, 1995: 34–5). Nahimana was evacuated along with other leading pro-genocide figures by the French army in April 1994, and sought refuge in Cameroon, from whence he has since been extradited to face trial at the International Criminal Tribunal for Rwanda at Arusha, Tanzania.

International media: facile repetition of sectarian agenda

International coverage of the Rwandan crisis (used here to mean war, genocide and their aftermath) is most obviously characterized by misinterpretation resulting from oversimplification and the related, racist tendency to label all conflict in Africa as 'tribalism', by means of which a unique set of political circumstances is ethnicized and thus explained away. Rwanda has not been the sole target of this distortion in recent years; Pieterse's article explains how:

Ethnicity, although generally considered a cause of conflict, is not an explanation but rather that which is to be explained. The terminology of ethnicity is part of the conflict and cannot serve as a language of analysis. The core causes of conflict are authoritarian institutions and political cultures and the politics of hard sovereignty, while external influences play a significant role. (Pieterse, 1997: 71)

Ethnicization was singularly inappropriate, and particularly provocative, in Rwanda where, despite attempts by colonists and post-colonial sectarian regimes to prove otherwise, there is only one ethnicity: Rwandan. In a timely interview in November 1996, social geographer Dominique Franche told *Le Monde* that, in contradiction of much of its own coverage:

The Hutus and Tutsis do not form two different ethnic groups. An ethnic group is defined by a unity of language, culture, religion or territory. The Tutsis, Hutus and Twas live together ... They speak the same language and share the same culture and religion. They used to specialize in certain areas of the economy, but not systematically ... The conflict can't be described as ethnic, since there's only one ethnic group in Rwanda, and that's Rwandan. (Interview by Jean-Pierre Langellier, Le *Monde*, 12 November 1996)

Although the societies of the Great Lakes were distinguished by separate castes in pre-colonial days, the current segregation into separate 'ethnicities' is a product of the colonial era, used effectively to divide and rule Rwanda's population. The country's eight million inhabitants pre-1994 are categorized typically as Hutu (84%), Tutsi (15%) and Twa (1%). Rwandan independence in 1962 was achieved on the colonists' terms, via the Belgian-sponsored overthrow and exiling of those favoured (but, by 1959, anti-colonial-minded) Tutsis who previously had administered on the colonists' behalf. The accession to power of the hitherto downtrodden Hutu majority only reinforced sectarian divisions, to the extent that a citizen's ethnic group continued to appear on his or her compulsory identity card. This practice greatly facilitated the work of the genocide's militias, which sought to eliminate Rwanda's remaining Tutsis as an inherently disloyal national minority, along with opposition Hutus and indeed those of any ethnicity who opposed them. However, Prunier points to a (foreign-authored) cultural mythology which, given the dominance of foreign influence in education and information, became reality:

[T]he social and political actors moved by degrees from their real world into the mythological script which had been written for them ... In 1959 [sectarian pogroms marking the start of the Belgian-supported 'social revolution'] the red seal of blood put a final label of historical unavoidability on this mythological construction, which from then on became a new *real* historical framework. (Prunier, 1995: xiii)

The Rwandan conflict was exacerbated by the international media's adoption of the false analysis which was in many ways at the root of the conflict: the original historical distortion became a script that the players acted out.

Pieterse does not presume a press conspiracy in mechanical ethniciza-tion, but 'a media circus of clichés which privileges whatever notions come floating up that are consistent with conventional wisdom, which are then endlessly and uncritically repeated' (Pieterse, 1997: 80). There is no shortage of examples of this style of reporting; much broadcast news coverage in the anglophone and francophone West seemed confined to a narrow lexis which, through repetition, became self-sustaining. Most reporters' sources appear to have been limited to their own organizations' cuttings and audio/video library; interviewees on the ground were almost always fellow Westerners: NGOs, UN troops, or indeed other journalists.

What is surprising is that the international media should have adopted so much of the Habyarimana regime's agenda, so unquestioningly. Much may be attributed to ignorance ('parachute reporting') and a combina-tion of preconceptions, editorial and practical restraints, and plain poor journalism. For example, the frequently repeated idea that the Rwandan genocide was the result of spontaneous and unforeseen violence result-ing from public outrage at the assassination of the country's president when his private plane was shot down on 6 April 1994, was firmly refuted by UN-funded research published in 1996 (Joint Evaluation of Emergency Assistance to Rwanda – hereafter JEEAR – March 1996). In its apportioning of blame for the failure of the international response in Rwanda, the media are highlighted:

> Surveys of the British, French and US media ... show that relatively little change occurred in the media coverage after 6 April compared to the paucity before. There was a blip with the shooting down of the plane and the reporting on the slaughters – generally portrayed as ancient tribal feuds – but with the withdrawal of foreign personnel there was a precipitous drop in coverage. When the genocide was accelerating, the Western press virtu-ally ceased to report on Rwanda. (JEEAR, 1996, Vol. II: 46)

The report also points out:

> The misleading media coverage was echoed in the accounts of events in Rwanda given by both the Security Council and the Secretary-General,

explaining the withdrawal of UNAMIR on 21 April [1994] ... *More generally, the Western media's failure to report adequately on the genocide in Rwanda possibly contributed to international indifference and inaction, and hence the crime itself.* (JEEAR, 1996, Vol. II: 48, emphasis added)

When the UN-commissioned report was published in March 1996, the chairman of its Steering Committee, Neils Dabelstein, summarized the UN response despite warnings from its own force commander in Rwanda: 'Humanitarian aid was substituted for political action' (quoted in Victoria Brittain, 'Chronicle of a genocide foretold', *Guardian*, 13 March 1996). Similarly, one of the report's authors, Norwegian academic Astri Suhrke, asked (at the report's launch in London on 12 March 1996):

The UN failed the test, the early warning signals were simply not heard ... Was it possible to organise the machinery of death without the world knowing, in a country where there were numerous UN organisations including a military force overseeing a peace accord, many NGOs, and where France was very heavily involved with the government's machinery in every sphere, from economic to military? (*Guardian*, 13 March 1996)

The net effect of the failure to report the Rwandan war, the pre-genocide preparations, the conduct of the genocide, the escape of the majority of those responsible, and the complicity of prominent members of the international community (notably France, Egypt and South Africa) in arming and militarily assisting the Habyarimana regime, contributed to an inconsistency and inappropriateness of international response that exacerbated the crisis. The initial distortion, deliberately promoted by the Rwandan regime, provided an effective smokescreen for a meticulously planned and systematically conducted campaign of mass political assassination. Jean-Pierre Chrétien (editor of *Les médias du génocide*) tells how, 'we had to wait until the start of May [1994] for the media, [human rights] associations and then governments to denounce the genocide ... Until then, observers and [the Rwandan government's] partners continued to evoke "interethnic clashes" which, it was suggested, were the legacy of some ancestral barbarism' (Chrétien, 1995: 11).

In retrospect, state-sanctioned preparation for genocide was apparent from shortly after the signing of the Arusha accords in 1993; Chrétien, in common with other concerned chroniclers of the genocide (notably Rakiya Omaar and Alex de Waal of *African Rights*, and journalists Colette Braeckman, Lindsey Hilsum, Chris McGreal and Victoria Brittain), points out that there was nothing inevitable about the outcome of the crisis: 'The spiral of violence since 1991, in words and on the ground, appears retrospectively as the chronicle of a genocide foretold, even if few observers had underlined the depth of the cancer which was eating away at this country' (Chrétien, 1995: 12).

However, as a pattern of events and identifiable actors began to emerge – guerrillas in the mist, if you wish – it became possible to place the genocide in context; and there could be little further excuse for failing to do so. By late 1994, several significant accounts had appeared in print in English or French, and by early 1996 JEEAR offered a useful yardstick by which to judge common perceptions.

Nevertheless, international media coverage of conflict in the Great Lakes region continued to fall into three broad categories: (1) Ignorance – where the reporter, flown in at short notice, has no grasp of the situation and repeats platitudes and errors; (2) A Little Knowledge – where the reporter has read up in the cuttings library and seeks to insert any new information into an existing framework of ethnicity (to the extent of asking Rwandans their ethnic group). Fergal Keane, despite his understandable emotional response to the genocide, fell easily into this trap (see Keane, 1995); and (3) The Hidden Agenda – to be discussed in light of revisionist coverage of more recent events in the region.

Revisionism

Post-genocide revisionism has hinged on two principal arguments: that there was a 'double genocide', and that, as a result, the post-1994 administration in Rwanda is as bad as that which preceded it, that its (the RPF's) war against the Habyarimana regime makes it partly responsible for provoking the 'first' genocide, and that, by extension, it is unfit to judge or to govern. Moreover, its attempts in late 1996 to secure its borders by invading Zaire and breaking up the refugee mini-states there are in fact part of a plan for a campaign of expansionism and ethnic triumphalism which would sweep Central Africa from Kampala, where the 'Tutsi' Museveni (albeit elected) governs, to Kinshasa, where Kagame's presumed puppet Kabila was installed by Rwandan force of arms in May 1997.

The most obvious example of a media-driven agenda which served, and was deliberately exploited, to distort the political reality of events on the ground, was the response to the cholera epidemic in the massive 'refugee' camp at Goma in July 1994, as the genocide within Rwanda was stopped (by the RPF victory). Even the terminology was a distortion. Although described as refugee camps, they were controlled by the former Rwandan army and the genocidal militias, and populated by them, their families, and a human shield of over a million Rwandans who had been forced at gun-point or terrified by propaganda into fleeing with them. The terminology was key: refugees are seen as victims; the news images were powerfully evocative of other (often similarly man-made) humanitarian crises in Ethiopia or Somalia; and the public perception was that the Rwandans in camps in eastern Zaire were fleeing from genocide and not, as was the case for at least 100,000 of them, that they included the perpetrators. The equation of disease – albeit in man-made circumstances – with systematic state-sponsored murder provided the key argument of the revisionist/double genocide lobby. Chrétien points out that: 'The highly-mediatised cholera of July 1994 seemed to erase the bloodbath of the preceding April to June' (Chrétien, 1995: 15).

Accordingly, the *Guardian*'s front-page banner headline of 23 July 1994, 'Rwandan apocalypse', did not describe, as might be supposed, the genocide which had killed up to a million over the previous three months, but the subsequent outbreak of cholera across the Zairean border in the camps of Goma. Plague (and natural disaster, the type of thing that happens in Africa) was to be equated with state-sponsored massacre. Straplines announced, 'Refugee a minute said to be dying', and quoted President Clinton's assessment that: 'The flow of refugees across the borders has now created what could be the world's worst humanitarian crisis in a generation.' This was something the Western reader could understand: a massive disaster, dying children, Western aid needed, make a donation. This was 'Band Aid' reporting; inside, stories told of a 'Vision of hell as cholera stalks camps'. And the leader column, which announced that: 'The hell fires are burning in Goma', alluded only in passing to 'weeks of inaction in the face of genocide' and possible 'suspicions of French motives in erecting their safe haven in south-western Rwanda'. There was no explanation of how or why the 'refugees' came to be in such a sorry plight, and who had forced them into it. JEEAR noted in 1996 that: 'The media's concentration on the visually dramatic story of the refugees was also partly responsible for distorting the distribution of resources into camps and away from survivors. As media interest has ebbed, so have donor commitments' (*Guardian*, 13 March 1996).

Most significantly, in the absence of proof of the predicted RPF counter-genocide, the massive deaths of their compatriots in exile, albeit from disease, were used to undermine and discredit the new RPF-led, post-genocide administration in Kigali. Speaking in the same month of the Rwandan 'genocides', President François Mitterrand was asked at a press conference about his use of the plural. His reply – 'Oh, so you think the genocide finished when the Tutsis took power?' – set the tone for the revisionist agenda that was to follow.

Libération's Stephen Smith was soon to be perceived as the principal advocate of a revisionist lobby, which equates human rights abuses by the new post-genocide Rwandan administration with those of its predecessor. This deliberate re-ethnicization is all the more shocking in one so well-informed. The publication, on 27 February 1996, of a six-page 'Inquiry into Tutsi terror', astonished many observers who had hitherto admired *Libération's* journalists as among the better-informed commentators on Rwanda, particularly with regard to France's role. Smith had earlier been quick to describe *Opération Turquoise* as 'a smoke-screen'. Fundamentally, *Libération* sought to suggest that isolated acts of revenge by RPA troops must be state-sanctioned and systematic, and manipulated statistics to state that 'the RPF has created a new dictatorship in Rwanda'. Starting from lists of 17,000 people unaccounted for (and presumed 'disappeared') in Gitarama, one of Rwanda's ten préfectures, Smith simply multiplied the figure by ten (rounding down to allow for differences in population density) to announce on the paper's front page, 'Relying on lists of victims and witness statements, *Libération* is able to state that the Rwandan Patriotic Front, the former Tutsi rebel movement which has been in power in Kigali since 1994, is responsible for the deaths of more than 100,000 Hutus over 22 months.' Apart from an editorial, the six-page feature was the exclusive work of Smith, and was illustrated with library photographs captioned by a seemingly over-enthusiastic sub-editor: a photo of Zimbabwean UN-AMIR 'blue helmets' at a mass grave became 'Tutsi soldiers spat on the bodies of victims'; unidentifiable babies became 'Hutu orphans whose parents were massacred ... by the RPF army'.

Subsequently, the continued portrayal of conflict as ethnic (or 'tribal') undermined attempts to bring the genocide's planners and perpetrators to justice (either within Rwanda, or to the international tribunal at Arusha). A revisionist lobby soon found a receptive audience for its argument that all deaths were the same, and that state-sponsored genocide – what R. J. Rummell has called 'death by government' – could be equated with death by disease in camps which the genocidists themselves had created, facilitated by the misguided, misdirected and ill-informed concern of the 'international community'. According to this theory of double genocide, what happened in Rwanda was a demonstration of cultural particularism which outsiders could not understand. Belgian Africanist Alain Verhaagen satirizes this viewpoint, which seeks to exonerate by making a virtue of ignorance. By this logic, Rwanda defies explanation because it was 'above all an ethnic war, a civil war.

Everybody killed everybody. Everybody should therefore be punished. But as everybody is guilty, everybody should be pardoned to allow this country to be reborn' (Verhaagen, 1996: 1). Much of this thinking pervades the underfunding and dismissive attitudes surrounding the International Criminal Tribunal for Rwanda (at Arusha, Tanzania), which exists as the poor cousin of The Hague Tribunal for the former Yugoslavia (and came into being only as the latter's offshoot).

However, after the withdrawal of the second United Nations Assistance Mission in Rwanda (UNAMIR II) and the apparent stabilization of the situation (albeit temporarily), Rwanda all but disappeared from Western news reports. Throughout 1995 and most of 1996, there was little reporting of the Rwandan war's direct aftermath: the attempt at reconstruction within Rwanda, the largely unsuccessful attempts to bring the genocide's perpetrators to justice, and the resultant destabilization of Zaire. When in late 1996, just two years after the genocide, the insurrection of the victimized Rwandophone Banyamulenge in eastern Zaire took Mobutu and his demoralized army by surprise, hidden agendas began to emerge in much of the media coverage which, when considered in retrospect, may explain some of the earlier distortion, and much that is ongoing.

Conclusion: new crisis, old clichés

Coverage now fell into two broad categories, supporting a policy of either: (1) non-intervention: the West can do nothing, not our responsibility, not our fault: best to back the strongest group in the region in the interests of stability for fear there would be new clamour for action (the US position); or (2) neo-humanitarian: a traditional interventionary response to freeze the military-political front-line, on the pretext of protecting civilians (the French position). However, on this occasion the former position was to become the only one viable, as the new spinning of the vicious circle prompted pre-emptive regional action: a lightning war and summary justice for the fugitive génocidaires and their hostage human shield before there could be further Western interposition.

As the Great Lakes region reappeared on the West's front pages – pitiful images of refugees – all the old 'heart of darkness' clichés were dusted off. This time, indeed, there was impatience, annoyance, exasperation that these people had not sorted themselves out. 'The world may have to resign itself to the fact that Hutu and Tutsi refuse to live together in peace,' suggested the International Herald Tribune. However, attempts since 1994 by human rights campaigners, essayists and the new, assertive regional powers to expose and embarrass Western governments may have borne fruit in the form of the Western non-intervention response in Zaire in late 1996. Stephen Smith himself pointed out that French policy over Zaire was driven in late 1996 by the need to avoid at all costs 'another indictment (*mise en accusation*) of France' (paper presented to conference 'France, the United States and Africa', Université de Bordeaux, May 1997).

The main charges to be laid against the Western media response to war and genocide in the African Great Lakes region may be summarized according to the following charge-sheet:

1. The most serious error came at the beginning and was at the root of those that followed: the Western media swallowed the ethnic interpretation of conflict promoted by interested parties locally; in those Western countries most concerned (France, and to a lesser extent Belgium), promoters of this historically-resonant sectarian agenda were pushing at an open door. Internally, propaganda was based on fear and ignorance; as elsewhere when sectarianism and genocide became state policy, those stirring the pot were confident that there was a pot to stir. The first link of the vicious circle was soon in place: the Western media described the war as ethnic, hence it must be so; local propaganda was reinforced, and there was no alternative source of information.

2. Portrayal of the war as ethnically-driven facilitated Western intervention; France could skilfully conceal its true role – as a long-term military and economic backer of the Habyarimana regime – through media manipulation. Even as the regime's preparations for genocide became apparent, there was little questioning of France's presumed 'humanitarian' role, or its claims to be protecting its nationals although involved in combat far from the capital where those nationals lived.

3. Failure of UNAMIR (United Nations Assistance Mission in Rwanda) to prevent preparations for genocide in early 1994 was attributed to a failure of observer and early-warning mechanisms. But there had been abundant warning – from human rights organizations, the Rwandan opposition, NGOs and the UN's own commander General Roméo Dallaire – which the organization and the media ignored.

4. France's apparently belated response to the genocide, *Opération Turquoise*, became, in the absence of critical media reporting, a largely successful attempt at raising a smokescreen behind which to conceal the extent of French support for the regime which prepared and perpetrated genocide. Television images of French paras rescuing terrified Rwandans and burying the dead helped restore the country's image for domestic and international consumption; but the exfiltration of France's

former allies – the ex-Rwandan army and the militias they trained – spawned the eastern Zaire camps, cholera in Goma, attacks on genocide survivors and Rwandophone Zaireans, and the subsequent destabilization of Zaire.

5. The second UN intervention (UNAMIR II) post-*Turquoise* demonstrated that such operations could achieve little. However, by late 1994 Rwanda was no longer news and was filed away under 'inexplicable ethnic bloodbaths – Africa'. When war broke out in Zaire as a direct result of (the international response to) the Rwandan crisis, Western reporters were quick to dust off the ethnic labels of 'Hutu' and 'Tutsi' which had previously served them so poorly, and clung to them even as they grew increasingly irrelevant in the broader Zairean context. Notable were repeated references to '[AFDL leader] Laurent Kabila's Tutsi-led rebels' despite the obvious paradox: the Zairean Kabila, from Lubumbashi far south of the Rwandan border, is not a Tutsi.

6. There could be fewer claims this time that there had been no warning of the imminence of conflict in eastern Zaire, although the backfiring of the attempt by Zaire's last president and Africa's longest-ruling dictator, Mobutu Sese Seko, to play the ethnic card – a hitherto failsafe divide-and-rule policy which had kept him in power for 32 years – did reveal the shift in the balance of power across the region. Nevertheless, the mechanical Western response – media ethnicization, call for action, intervention – seemed ready to set the vicious circle in motion once more. However, on this occasion it was the very threat of another media-driven Western intervention that accelerated the swift, seven-month Zairean war. Its rapid conclusion, with the military overthrow of Mobutu while the West – and most surprisingly France – looked on with their hands tied, gave the lie to dominant frames of analysis; ethnicity could not explain away the conflict, and 'humanitarian' intervention was discredited as a Trojan horse for neo-colonial interests. Only belatedly have we seen a media acknowledgement of their failure to come to terms with these changes, or any attempt to address the resultant vacuum of theory and practice.

7. Revisionism – to the point of negationism – greatly exacerbated the post-genocide situation in Rwanda, and a related failure to address the causes of Zairean 'refugee crisis' – by the media and by extension by the international community – precipitated the violent ultra-Realist Rwandan response of late 1996. Media coverage which led to calls for another international intervention (even though extra-regional intervention had been a root cause of the region's conflicts since 1990), was evidence again of episodic reporting.

Nevertheless, despite the watershed that the Zairean war represents, there is still abundant evidence of automatic ethnic labelling and revisionism. As a result, there is an urgent need for alternative analyses to challenge the mechanical and simplistic interpretations of contemporary conflict in Africa which dominate Western media coverage. What alternatives should be pursued in reporting Central Africa? Perhaps it would be a surer course for any journalist to base analysis on a range of local opinion, and to break out of the Eurocentric straitjacket which has so long distorted coverage of African wars.

As everywhere, the regional imperatives in Central Africa are peace, stability, prosperity and security. The destruction of the Zairean camps in December 1996, and the public executions within Rwanda of *génocidaires* in April 1998 demonstrate that these imperatives will take precedence over Western concerns for perceived human rights violations, particularly when such concerns are expressed by institutions – the UN, the Catholic Church, Western governments – which did nothing to prevent and little in response to the 1994 genocide. Indeed, Western selectivity of reporting, condemning and inquiring will increasingly be seen as serving a self-interested, neo-colonial, Western agenda. A new, 'Afrocentric' regional consensus is emerging, which accepts that the West has its uses – and is indispensable for reconstruction – but which can no longer leave it unchallenged in reporting and responding to African crises.

References

Césaire, A. (1955) *Discours sur le colonialisme*, Paris: Présence africaine, pp. 7–8.

Chrétien, J.-P. (ed.) (1995) *Rwanda: Les médias du génocide*, Paris: Karthala.

Glaser, A. and Smith, S. (1995) *L'Afrique sans Africains*, Paris: Fayard.

Guichaoua, A. (ed.) (1992) *Enjeux nationaux et dynamiques régionales dans l'Afrique des Grands Lacs*, Lille: Université des sciences et technologies de Lille.

Joint Evaluation of Emergency Assistance to Rwanda (Steering Committee of the) (1996) *The International Response to Conflict and Genocide: Lessons from the Rwanda Experience* (5 volumes), Copenhagen: JEEAR.

Keane, F. (1995) *Season of Blood: A Rwandan Journey*, Harmondsworth: Penguin/Viking.

Kirschke, L./Article 19 (1996) *Broadcasting Genocide: Censorship, Propaganda and State-Sponsored Violence in Rwanda 1990–1994*, London: Article 19, October.

Nahimana, F. (1993) *Rwanda: L'émergence d'un Etat*, Paris: L'Harmattan.

Newbury, C. (1988) *The Cohesion of Oppression*, New York: Columbia University Press.

Pieterse, Jan Nederveen (1997) 'Sociology of Humanitarian Intervention: Bosnia, Rwanda and Somalia Compared', *International Political Science Review*, Vol. 18, No. 1, pp. 297–359.

Prunier, G. (1995) *The Rwanda Crisis: History of a Genocide*, London: C. Hurst & Co.

— (1997) 'The Experience of European Armies in Operation Restore Hope' in W. Clarke and J. Herbst (eds), *Learning from Somalia: The Lessons of Armed Humanitarian Intervention*, Boulder, CO: Westview Press.

Richburg, K. (1997) *Out of America: A Black Man Confronts Africa*, New York: HarperCollins.

Sweeney, L. (1997) 'Media Coverage of the Genocide in Rwanda 1994–1996: Constructive Reporting or Fuelling Third World Stereotypes?', MSc Development Studies dissertation, London: South Bank University.

Verhaagen, A. (1996) 'Le Rwanda en 20 tableaux', paper presented at Université Paul Valéry de Montpellier, 12 January.

CHAPTER 14

Misrepresenting Ethiopia and the Horn of Africa? Constraints and Dilemmas of Current Reporting

David Styan

This chapter is about some of the contradictions inherent in the generation of media representations both in and of Africa, most of its examples being from Ethiopia. It begins by examining factors shaping international news agency reporting of the Horn of Africa and highlights the role of northern non-governmental organizations (NGOs) in defining news agendas. It goes on to discuss the way in which news is disseminated. The later sections comment on some of the changes and contradictions within both domestic and foreign media reporting of Ethiopia since 1991. It does this by focusing on the government's promotion of ethnic identity as the ostensible basis of a federal political system, and the emergence of privately owned publications.

The context of the discussion is, first, that of long-standing and generally poor Western media reporting of African issues, and second, the specific configuration of media issues generated since the 1991 political and military watershed in the Horn of Africa. In Ethiopia and Eritrea, this brought an end to three decades of war, sparked in large part by rival conceptions of regional identities. In Addis Ababa, the changes brought to power a government claiming legitimacy from the explicit promotion of local linguistic and ethnic identities in an attempt to make real or imagined local identities the ostensible basis of political life. This political and administrative project has been accompanied by ongoing economic liberalization. These economic changes have in turn prompted a proliferation of privately owned newspapers and magazines in Addis Ababa since 1991, with over 70 separate titles being published by 1996. While the chapter focuses on Ethiopia, the end of the war in 1991 evidently brought political changes throughout the region. The new government in neighbouring Eritrea, in contrast to that of Ethiopia, retains state control of all media and all official expression of political identities, be they central or regional. The same is partially true of neighbouring Djibouti, whose 1991–93 civil war was largely ignored by both international and domestic media.[1] Meanwhile, in Somalia, 1991 marked the collapse of a centralized state and a far more radical re-configuration of information flows.[2]

International news agencies: poor resources and pre-determined agendas?

International news agency reporting of Africa in general and the Horn in particular has become increasingly marginalized over the past two decades and is exceedingly poor in terms of both quantity and quality. Most European and North American newspapers have dispensed both with full-time Africa editors and permanent correspondents, relying instead exclusively on news agencies and freelancers, both African and non-African.[3] Thus part-time journalists based in Nairobi may ostensibly 'cover' the Horn. Both the structure and agenda of international news from the Horn of Africa is increasingly determined by the major Western news agencies such as Reuters, Associated Press (AP), Agence France Presse (AFP), Voice of America (VOA) and the BBC. The influence of the BBC stems directy from its own correspondents and indirectly via its Summary of World Broadcasts (SWB). This is a daily BBC publication of translated and edited items of news broadcast locally and – for those countries in the Horn of Africa – monitored in Nairobi.

This is not to say that little news is generated. Information of mediocre quality tends to be abundantly available and is now instantly accessible electronically. The Reuters database, for example, carried around 150 items during the month of January 1996 concerning Ethiopia and Ethiopians (including sporting activities abroad), around one-third of which were its own reports while one-third came from the BBC's SWB.[4] Rival agencies such as AFP and AP carried a slightly lower number of stories. However, very little of this information is sub-sequently reproduced in an edited form in print or broadcast media. African news is a low priority and in general has to fit fairly rigidly defined pre-conceived categories of what is deemed newsworthy by metropolitan-based editors before a decision is made to broadcast or publish such news.

Such decisions appear to fit three categories: (1) stereotypical stories already associated with pre-conceived images of the region (in the Ethiopian case these are, above all, those concerned with famine);

(2) actual or threatened inter-state violence; or (3) stories concerning Westerners (the kidnapping or hijacking of white people being the only thing guaranteed to attract foreign attention). In quantitative terms, the vast majority of stories fall into the middle category. Thus 80% of news generated in the region in 1996 and carried by the agencies was associated either with inter-state tension between Ethiopia, Eritrea and Sudan, or Eritrea's tussle with Yemen over sovereignty of the Red Sea Hanish islands. The domination of the news agenda by such stories begs the broader question of *what and who is news for?* Is news primarily an adjunct of international diplomacy, an avatar of the Horn's pivotal role in the Cold War and a reflection of its location on the perimeter of the Middle East oil reserves? This would be the obvious conclusion from the predominant preoccupations of the news agencies. Or is it that the local official news agencies are state-controlled and thus either, above all, interested in inter-state relations, or simply inept at presenting other stories (on health, sport, environment, etc.) as being newsworthy?

An obvious objection to the foregoing characterization of the media is that it focuses uniquely on Western agencies and the consumption of news from Africa in Western Europe and North America. Other parts of the world and people within the region surely have different, less distorted ways of seeing affairs in the Horn of Africa? Sadly, this is not the case. The vast majority of African countries get their images of other African countries from this same handful of Western-based news agencies. The Pan-African News Agency (PANA) acts as a very partial corrective to this general trend,[5] but newspaper readers in Kenya and Uganda are still most likely to get the bulk of their images of events in Ethiopia from the same news agencies as readers in Europe. Despite the presence of the Organization of African Unity (OAU) in Addis Ababa, few African countries have journalists in Addis, indeed few can afford foreign correspondents. The same goes for most other international publications, although a singular exception to this general pattern is the Arabic London-based daily, *Al-Hayat*, which carries fairly extensive coverage of the Horn from a network of correspondents. This is chiefly because the paper has a large readership among migrant workers and émigrés from the Horn resident in the Gulf. There are also the obvious inter-linkages of regional politics, particularly the interests of Saudi Arabia and Yemen in the Horn, Egypt's concern with Sudan and the Nile Valley as well as the fact that Sudan, Djibouti and Somalia are all Arab League members. Clearly, there is also a danger of English-language analysts forgetting that the former Soviet Union, as well as China and Eastern European socialist states maintain(ed) extensive networks of reporters in Africa. Some of the most durable

images of Haile Selassie's regime were provided by a Polish correspondent (Kapuscinski, 1983).

This dominance of international news agencies is even more pro-
nounced for televisual images and news. Most Africans get what few TV
images they receive of *other* Africa countries via European and American
news agencies. Thus Tanzanians and Zaireans would see events in
Rwanda via images diffused by the BBC, CNN or TF1 (the main French
TV channel) rather than those filmed by their own journalists. While
noting the improvements to Southern African broadcasting due to the
end of apartheid, in general it seems that this external dominance of
TV is likely to be further reinforced by the prevalence of satellite TV.
Satellite broadcasting also requires far more substantial technical feeds,
which many African countries are unable to offer at affordable prices.[6]
This unsatisfactory state of affairs was partially modified in January
1995 by Reuters' experiment with its 'Africa Journal', a TV news programme designed for an African audience commissioned in Nairobi
from the (since deceased) Kenyan journalist Mohamed Amin, using
largely African journalists. This innovation was popular in Anglophone
countries, providing a far wider range of TV images of Africa than were
usually available from foreign sources. Despite its initial success, it ran
into problems of editorial control almost immediately.[7]

These problems reflect the fact that the Horn is a very low priority
for the world's major news agencies. It is an area of residual, marginal
interest. The clearest evidence of this lies in the negligible resources
devoted to news-gathering across vast territories that are so socially
and politically diverse. Africa as a whole is such a low priority that
most agencies have very few permanent staff covering vast geographical
domains. Thus, for the Horn, it is usually journalists operating out of
Nairobi who will be expected to report on all events stretching from
the Comoros in the south to Asmara in the north, taking in a dozen
countries of the Rift Valley, linked by only very rudimentary communications in between.

Convention has it that staff will be from the agency's home base in
Europe or North America, versed in 'house' style where form and
technical competence is more important than the accuracy of content or
knowledge of local conditions. These conditions, plus poor, piece-rate
pay and large countries to cover, linked only by abysmal communications, mean it tends to be young, inexperienced staff at the beginning of
their careers who will attempt such a job, even if those running the
agency offices, usually in Nairobi, are slightly more experienced. Again,
this tendency for non-Africans to report Africa is, if anything, being
reinforced by the changes within the media, particularly the move to 'bi-

media' reporting (i.e. being equally able to report for both TV and radio). This values technical competence and speed over accuracy and content, reinforcing an implicit in-built tendency on the part of editors for white faces with crisp Queen's English accents.

These are the people who collect the news that most Western publications and agencies receive of the Horn of Africa. It is accepted that this is 'normal'. The absurdity of this is best illustrated by a hypothetical analogy. In terms of geography it is as if Africans expected and accepted that the bulk of their images of Europe would be provided by a handful of young, inexperienced recent African-graduate journalists who were poorly paid in Paris or Geneva to report on events in an area which stretched from Belfast to Belgrade, Lisbon to Lithuania, with very little confidence that editors will accept or pay for much of what they produce. Clearly such expectations appear laughable. Yet even with a far, far poorer communications infrastructure, it is through comparable structures that the bulk of 'our' imagery of East Africa is provided. In stressing the absurdity of the situation, I do not imply any criticism of the actual individuals who do such jobs. They often manage to make some sense of the vast region extraordinary well. It simply serves to underline the impossibility of gaining a real understanding of the region via such structures.

Why are local journalists not employed to feed the agencies? To a certain extent they are, but very often the limitations of this comes back to metropolitan-based structures and resources of the main news agencies. These tend to be biased in favour of full-time, in-house-trained staff operating in an environment in which format and speed are of the essence. Local part-timers also tend to be very poorly paid, for a job which can frequently be dangerous. Given that, until recently, state-controlled media was the norm in most African countries, journalists have been actively discouraged from any form of investigative reporting. Second, the very fact that local journalists have greater access to, and understanding of, a country's political situation makes them far more vulnerable.[8] A foreigner falling foul of the authorities runs the risk of expulsion (and occasionally a boost in kudos and career), not persecution and unemployment. This is not to say that foreign journalists do not rely extensively upon local journalists. They have to, as only via local reporters' extensive networks of contacts and insiders' explanations of complexity can they even pretend to understand such a diverse range of countries and peoples.

NGOs and 'news'

An obvious element is missing from the above overview; as general news reporting has become marginalized, one set of external actors have had a growing interest in reporting from regions such as the Horn of Africa. These are the northern-based non-governmental organizations (NGOs) whose increasing presence, and essential need for publicity at home, have inadvertently complemented and thus reinforced the casting of the Horn in terms of development, disaster and 'humanitarian' concerns. As professional media coverage of Africa has declined, so NGOs have stepped in to supply images and representations of Africa in general and the Horn in particular. The relationship between NGOs and the media is necessarily incestuous. NGOs rely upon media coverage of their work to stimulate awareness of their activities. This generates public donations and pressurizes governments to support NGO activities as well as shaping domestic policy towards countries in which they operate (for a brief examination of such issues in the UK, see the section 'The Media, NGOs and Official Cultural Policy' in Styan, 1995). It is insufficient for NGOs simply to be doing something, they need to be *seen* to be doing it on prime-time TV. Nowhere has this mutual interest of foreign journalists and NGOs been more apparent than in the Horn of Africa and Great Lakes region. Given the pressures of operating in East Africa, fostering close relations with locally-based, expatriate NGO staff has obvious attractions for foreign journalists. These range from the sponsoring or subsidizing of journalists to visit their areas of activities, to the provision of points of contact and sources of information, as well as convenient accents and white faces to interview, for hard-pressed freelancers trying to cover a vast territory. NGOs' home offices also tend to be instrumental in lobbying editors in London, Paris, etc. to provide print or broadcast space for stories from the region. This relationship between NGOs and media in generating news about the Horn, notably about disasters, appears to be singularly under-researched, despite the evident importance it played in determining foreign reactions to both the 1984–85 Ethiopian famine, and the 1991–92 political drama in Somalia (African Rights, 1994; Harrison and Palmer, 1986: particularly Chapter 5, 'TV and Revolution in Ethiopia 1973–74').[9]

News dissemination: a lazy game of Chinese whispers?

If these are the structures which actually produce the news, an additional layer of distortions is introduced by how this news, once produced, is disseminated outside of the Horn of Africa. An examination of this raises two questions. First, what is the relationship between domestically produced news and that provided by foreign news agencies? Second, how do people within the Horn receive media images of themselves? The above section focused on the production of news by foreign agencies. Presumably the domestic news sources would operate in a fundamentally different way? Before going on to examine the constraints on domestic news production it is important to note that the notion that there is a clear-cut difference between 'domestic' and 'foreign' news agendas is probably false.

At least until recently in Ethiopia, much of what is reproduced by foreign news agencies in fact originated with the domestic (i.e. the state-owned) news agency and was simply reinterpreted and retransmitted by journalists working for international agencies. A particular feature of the circuits of news from and within the Horn is the existence of the BBC monitoring station in Kenya. Broadcasts are monitored here and republished in the Summary of World Broadcasts. A typical example is an item broadcast on the Ethiopian state radio monitored by the BBC in Nairobi, published the next day in both the BBC's Summary of World Broadcasts and the Ethiopian state-owned newspapers, using the same Ethiopian News Agency (ENA) material broadcast the previous evening. This may be simultaneously mentioned on the BBC's Africa Service radio news, and the Amharic service of the Voice of America (VOA). If Agence France Presse also uses the piece, then it may well be picked up by Radio France International and *Le Monde*. This same single item then invariably gets repeated, rehashed and interpreted abroad in secondary print media and specialist publications on Africa: the *Indian Ocean Newsletter*, *Africa Confidential*, *Marches Tropicaux*, *The Economist* Intelligence Unit, etc.

The outcome of this process is that, at least until the early 1990s, if you talked to diplomats, journalists or NGO staff at any particular time, they would, regardless of whether they were in Paris, Washington or indeed Addis, all have a similar news agenda for the simple reasons that they all fed off the same meagre sources. More particularly, the crucial thing in this circuit of information is that there was too often alarmingly little verification or analysis. News dissemination thus became a rather daft game of Chinese whispers, exacerbating the arbitrary and artificial nature of the construction of what passed for a news agenda. This process is doubly problematic in that it has often been such written sources (i.e. transcripts from the Summary of World Broadcasts, etc.) which subsequently become the basis for contemporary historical analysis of Ethiopia.

The above example illustrates the degree to which there is an interpenetration of domestic and international media. Until 1991, for the Horn, this effect was very much increased because of the predominance of the Summary of World Broadcasts and the fact that Ethiopia was largely closed to foreign journalists. During the civil war, broadcasts by both the government and the rebel fronts served two purposes. First, they informed and mobilized populations within the country. Second, they informed foreigners, most notably diplomats, of events. It is not an exaggeration to suggest that part of the struggle for international awareness and recognition between the liberation fronts and the government in the 1980s was fought via rival broadcasts and their re-dissemination via Summary of World Broadcasts. Since the change of power in 1991, this has been far less so. However, given that evidently political power in Ethiopia is contested, opposition groups continue to broadcast into Ethiopia, while occasionally still reaching a foreign audience via the Summary of World Broadcasts. This has particularly been the case of Oromo fronts and US-based diaspora groups opposed to government, who in recent years have intermittently used shortwave transmitters based in the former Soviet Union to broadcast into Ethiopia. It is nigh impossible to evaluate what audience or impact, if any, such broadcasts have within the country.[10]

Years of state control over domestic media in Ethiopia inevitably prompted reliance upon foreign news media. While prior to 1991 access to foreign newspapers was extremely limited, even six years after the change of government, demand for, and distribution of, foreign-language newspapers and periodicals published abroad remains negligible. However, there has been a long-standing tradition of foreign-controlled radio broadcasting into Ethiopia. Given low literacy and the reliance upon radio as a news medium, this has a significant impact upon how people receive and interpret news. These include not only foreign-language services, such as those in English and French of the BBC and RFI, but also broadcasts in local languages. These include daily Amharic languages from the USA (Voice of America) and German (*Deutsche Welle*) services. The BBC also broadcasts an extensive series of Somali programmes, which have a large audience in Ethiopia as well as neighbouring Somali-speaking countries. Clearly, an exhaustive analysis of the interpenetration of domestic and international media would need to look more closely at the content and domestic impact of these services.[11]

Reporting ethnicity and conflict since 1991: the dilemmas of officially defined ethnicity

Given the constraints and distortions inherent in the reporting of events in the Horn of Africa by outsiders, it is unsurprising that the vast bulk of external media reporting has been unable to provide meaningful or consistent analyses of notions of ethnic identities and their relationship to conflict. All too often the role of ethnicity has been evoked within the clumsy categories of 'tribes' imported inappropriately from elsewhere in the continent. The absurd contradictions that this throws up were well illustrated by Western coverage of the military defeat and change of government in May 1991.[12]

This is not to suggest that there is, or was, ever any simple correlation between war and ethnicity in the Horn, which could have been 'correctly' reported by outsiders. Ethnic, regional and linguistic identities have invariably played exceedingly complex and frequently contradictory roles in the conflicts in northern Ethiopia and elsewhere in the Horn of Africa in recent decades. Invariably, detailed analyses tend to stress that politicized ethnicity is as much a *product* of conflict as a cause of it (Fukui and Markakis, 1994). Such views are reinforced by a deeper historical examination of the forces of repression and rebellion which have been instrumental in forging local and national identities in the region in this century (Gebru Tarke, 1991).

Any attempt to incorporate an ethnic dimension into political or media analysis has to come to terms with three separate considerations. First, that Ethiopia contains a vast number of distinct peoples, languages and dialects; linguists identify over 200 discrete languages, while the current government recognizes around 60 separate 'nationalities'. Second, that these are widely disparate in size and nature; Oromo and Amharic are spoken by tens of millions of people, while some of the peoples on Ethiopia's western borders live in linguistic communities of just a few thousand. Third, that competing political groups have diverse, and often fundamentally conflicting concepts of the relationship between linguistic identity and political mobilization and representation. This final factor is crucial for anyone seeking to report the relationship between politics and local identities in the Horn of Africa.

These conflicting concepts of identity were most clearly illustrated during the 1970s and 1980s in the war in northern Ethiopia and Eritrea. The two principal rebel movements fighting against the Ethiopian government in Eritrea and Tigray each had a different concept of the role of linguistic and ethnic identity in politics. The Eritrean leadership, at least in theory, adhered to the post-colonial concept that national identity and unity superseded all parochial, local identities, indeed stressed national integration via armed struggle and political mobilization. In neighbouring Tigray, the Tigray People's Liberation Front specifically legitimized their struggle on the basis of regional identity, claiming that the Ethiopian army could be overthrown only via co-operation between like-minded political groups representing the diverse peoples of Ethiopia. In practice, during the war this difference, which was variously validated by the then obligatory references to the canonical texts of Marxism-Leninism, made little difference to their mobilization techniques. However, post-1991 it has prompted significantly different approaches to formal structures of political control. Throughout the war, the fronts' adversary, the Ethiopian government and its media, also portrayed local identities cloaked in the threadbare, yet stifling blanket of 'nation-building'. Such an attitude was common to most state-owned media in Africa. Given the class-based rhetoric of the Ethiopian regime, if regional identity was referred to at all, it was usually primarily in cultural or folkloric terms. This is not to say that the government was uninterested in, or insensitive to ethnic differences. In practice (and evidently in people's perceptions), the exigencies of military mobilization made appeal to local identities necessary. In addition, print and broadcast media operated in several languages, as they had done under the imperial regime. Again drawing on Marxist-Leninist interpretations (and the model of the multinational constitution of the USSR), considerable research was done into national differences. While some of these found their way into the short-lived 1987 republican constitution, there remains no convincing analytical literature in English on the role of ethnicity and the state in Ethiopia between 1974 and 1991 (nevertheless, Clapham, 1987 can still be usefully consulted, particularly in the light of current attempts to project an 'ethnic' reading of the Derg). Overall, prior to 1991, inaccessibility and the complex nature of conflict in northern Ethiopia, coupled with the class-based terminology employed by parties to the conflict, meant that outsiders involved in reporting the region tended to neglect ethnicity.

This schematic overview of politics and ethnicity prior to 1991 is recapped simply to stress the degree to which this situation has been completely reversed since then, at least in so far as reporting of Ethiopia is concerned. Whereas ethnicity was almost totally marginalized in both the political discourse of politicians and thus local media and external reporting of the region prior to the end of the war, since 1991 it has become *the* dominant and privileged language of political discourse. This is due to the fact that the new Ethiopian government has tried to explicitly reorganize internal administrative boundaries along 'ethnic' lines. Shortly after taking power, the incoming rulers provisionally divided Ethiopia into 13 new administrative regions. These were defined largely along real or imputed linguistic lines. An amended version of this administrative blueprint was incorporated into the federal constitution, which came into force with the creation of the second republic in August 1995.

At first glance, it might be thought that the new emphasis on ethnic identity would simplify the task of journalists. Would it not allow more accurate reporting of local identities and the country's linguistic and ethnic diversity? Would this not particularly be so if coupled with the establishment of privately owned publications and the government's commitment to greater freedom of expression? The reality has been rather different, and far more complex. In practice, this radically different political configuration has posed a complex set of new problems for both foreign and local journalists.

For Ethiopian journalists in the state sector, this change has been one of style rather than substance. Too often the leaden reporting of the Ethiopian News Agency (ENA, which in addition to reporting in Ethiopian languages fills the English daily, the *Ethiopian Herald* and English-language broadcasts on TV and radio) is characterized by inept adherence to the new government's rhetoric, journalists all too often appearing to have simply swapped one orthodoxy for another. Reporters in the Ethiopian News Agency remain uncritical and journalists do not have the instinct, resources or the editorial backing for investigative reporting. Clearly, a rather different set of criticisms can be levelled at Ethiopian journalists working in the fledgling private sector. These, and related issues concerning the changes in print journalism in Ethiopia since 1991, are touched upon in the section on press ownership below.

For foreign reporters, the fact that politics is conducted in the framework of officially sanctioned ethnic categories throws up a series of new and highly contradictory challenges. Given that the official discourse and categories of political discussion are that of ethnic labels, foreign reporters evidently have to use these terms. Yet in addition they need to be able to explain the new distortions that such terms have introduced into public debate. There are at least four different considerations which need to be borne in mind when discussing such distortions:

1. The fact that the ostensible 'ethnic' composition and the actual boundaries of several regional states are contested. There are numerous cases where this is so, but it is most obvious in the south-west which is very linguistically and ethnically heterogeneous. The original plan for

five separate administrative regions in the south-west was abandoned. The five regions were amalgamated into a single administrative region. Its composition and politics are as contrived as its name: the Southern Nations and Nationalities Peoples' Regional State (SNNPRS). In this case linguistic heterogeneity means that the official vocabulary of ethnicity is of little use in explaining events in the region.

2. The legitimacy of the particular branch of the governing party which rules in a specific region, ostensibly in the interests of the given ethnic group of the region, is invariably contested by people from the same ethnic group in that region. This is most evidently so in the vast Oromo-speaking region (Region 4), where the Oromo Liberation Front (OLF) has conducted sporadic guerrilla warfare against the state army and the ruling Oromo People's Democratic Organization (OPDO, the Oromo-designated affiliate of the Ethiopian Peoples' Revolutionary Democratic Front, EPRDF, which controls the federal government). However, this pattern is repeated to varying degrees in most of the regional states, with the 'official' party being contested most acutely in the two small, largely pastoral, Somali (Region 5) and Afar (Region 2) states.

3. Evidently there are also large numbers of people – particularly in urban areas – who reject the notion of a narrow interpretation of ethnicity as the basis of political representation. This rejection rests on two considerations: (1) rejection on the *principle* that no system of government should be based on parochial identities; and (2) rejection on the practical grounds that Ethiopia's unique mosaic of peoples does not lend itself to such a system of representation. In reality there are also critics who accept the principle of a political system with an element of regional and linguistic devolution, but contest the *form* of the system currently in operation. This consideration is further complicated by the fact that some opponents of the government may, explicitly or implicitly, accept the notion of some variant of ethnic federalism, but are simply agitating for greater representation for what they perceive as their 'own' group.

4. Probably the most problematic consideration facing an outsider attempting to report post-1991 Ethiopian events is that the 'ethnic' vocabulary of politics invariably conceals more than it reveals about the actual political process. This concerns, above all, the allocation of resources and the relationships of patronage and power, cooption and coercion. Frequently, the day-to-day struggles within regional governments, and between the regional and federal administrations have little or nothing to do with the 'ethnic' character of the actors involved. This is most particularly so given the reality of the formal system of political

organization currently in operation. This is a variant on the single-party state. In each of Ethiopia's nine regional states it is a component of the ruling coalition, the EPRDF, which controls the regional assembly and administration. This component, which usually has the same ethnic appellation as the region, thus controls resources and political patronage within the region. Political factionalism – regardless of whether it rests on ideological, personal or material factors – therefore naturally occurs *within* the individual 'ethnically' defined components of the ruling party, rather than between organizationally distinct political groupings or factions.[13] The political process is therefore largely hidden from public view or media attention. Thus the officially sanctioned vocabulary of 'ethnic' representation and politics is of little use in analysing ongoing power struggles within regional administrations or the federal government.

Media ownership and observations on the private press

The changes and challenges to media representations thrown up by the shift in political vocabulary in Ethiopia have been significantly heightened by the simultaneous changes in the ownership of the country's print media. Economic liberalization and a commitment to freedom of expression (which while now embodied in law, is far from being comprehensively implemented)[14] prompted the proliferation of privately owned publications in Addis Ababa from 1991 onwards. Prior to May 1991 all print and broadcast media were state-owned and subject to censorship. The proliferation of new, privately owned newspapers and magazines has considerably modified the circuits of information outlined earlier in this chapter. Thus the existence of thriving, albeit harassed, private publications, has significantly influenced the reporting of the attempt to make real, imagined or manufactured local identities officially the basis of political life within a federal Ethiopia since 1991. Private newspapers have, to varying degrees, thus modified both internal and external perceptions of the explicit introduction of ethnicity into political life. These influences have been felt in two distinct spheres. First, among literate urban Ethiopians, notably in the capital. Literacy is evidently higher in towns than the countryside, where distribution networks are non-existent. Thus an estimated 95% of the already small circulation of private magazines and newspapers is in Addis Ababa (most of the private publications have a print run of 1,000–3,000, although one copy will have multiple readers). The second impact of the private press is upon the foreign, English-language readership, notably the growing numbers of diplomats, aid workers and external analysts interested in the country. By 1997 there were several private English-language publications, alongside the state-run *Ethiopian Herald*, serving this market.[15] Evidently the privately owned print media and their political analysis influence the perceptions of the new 'ethnic politics' by these two distinct groups in very different ways, the impact upon foreigners, who have far more limited sources of information, being rather greater.

The re-emergence of a private press in Ethiopia and its impact upon political life and discourse, particularly upon perceptions of the government's attempts to establish a federal political system based upon ethnic criteria since 1991, warrants more extended analysis than is possible here. The following series of four observations suggest some of the factors that such an analysis should consider. First, as already noted, opposition to the idea of ethnic federalism has been most explicit in the capital, Addis Ababa. Given that virtually all of the new private publications have, to varying degrees, been hostile to the government, it is clear that some publications have been instrumental in debating and disseminating criticism of the government. The private press's hostility to the government accounts for the extent of repression faced by the private press from the government. This has particularly been the case for Amharic-language publications critical of ethnic federalism in general, and the independence of Eritrea in particular.[16] Repression has consisted of repeated arrest, preventative detentions and punitive fines for both editors and journalists, ranking Ethiopia among the countries with the world's highest number of journalists under arrest since 1995 (Kakuna, 1996). Despite such repression, the private sector has continued to flourish. Indeed, the fact that the government has periodically tried, albeit unsuccessfully, to silence editors and journalists suggests it is doing its job. Foreign liberals protesting at the arrest of editors overlook the facts that nowhere were the trappings of liberal democracy gained without struggle. If they are to be durable, civil rights such as freedom of the press have to be fought for, not simply acquired as a ready-made accessory from a foreign donor's prescription list. Notwithstanding extensive use of the legal system to harass private publications, in practice the government has proved ineffective at suppressing comment. The result is that, paradoxically, Ethiopian political discourse thus includes a far wider variety of views in the media, including far more virulent criticism of government and total rejection of the legitimacy of the current political class, than in many liberal democracies.

Second, while it is true the bulk of the private press is hostile to the government, it does not automatically follow that private publications' *raison d'être* is uniquely political. Economics has played a significant part in shaping the evolution of the private media sector. There is clearly a large demand and thus substantial and potentially profitable markets for news and writing, particularly in Amharic and English. The upsurge in the number of private publications in 1991–93 was due in part to the fact that newspaper publishing provided a quick, short-term vehicle for circulating capital and generating profits in an economic environment with few immediate investment opportunities. Similarly, the subsequent, partial shift from daily tabloids to weekly and bi-weekly publications was due to shifts in the market rather than political factors.

Third, the Ethiopian experience demonstrates that it is wrong for Western donors and other foreigners currently promoting nostrums of 'civil society' to assume that a privately owned domestic press will somehow be more liberal and responsible than a state-owned monopoly. In fact in the Ethiopian case a demand-driven private press has excelled in the production of crude stereotypes, inflammatory statements and slander. This has been particularly the case where reporting ethnic identity has been concerned. The confrontational, often demagogic language of some private publications in part explains the government's criticism of, and refusal to enter into dialogue with, privately owned publications.[17] This in turn highlights another misconception among liberal donors: that allowing freedom of the press and encouraging a privately owned press will automatically lead to a more mature, sophisticated government press. In Ethiopia the relationship between state-owned publications and the private sector has, on the whole, to date been a dialogue of the deaf. When there has been commentary and interaction this has too often degenerated into a slanging match of competing stereotypes.

Fourth and finally, it is worth re-emphasizing that it is easy for outsiders to exaggerate the impact of the media changes upon the population as a whole. The flourishing of private newspapers remains a largely urban phenomenon in a country with exceedingly low urbanization (less than 15% of approximately 60 million people living in towns) and literacy rates.[18] Given such limited literacy, the impact of *any* print media, be they private or government-owned, on most rural Ethiopians is extremely limited. In this respect it is significant that while in principle the current media law permits private ownership of radio and television facilities, in practice the government has managed, at least until 1997, to maintain a monopoly over domestic radio and TV broadcasting.[19] The case of radio in particular is anomalous; in the light of the mushrooming of commercial FM stations elsewhere in Africa, Addis Ababa could easily support one or two commercial radio stations.

Particularly given the long tradition and current resurgence of Ethiopia's indigenous music industry, the potential audience (and thus advertising revenues) for such a station would be considerable. Clearly the government has clung to its monopoly on radio because while the private print sector has only a geographically limited impact upon the population, private radio, particularly stations broadcasting news and opinion hostile to the current government, would have an impact on a far larger number of Ethiopians.

Conclusion

This chapter has attempted to consider the ownership and structures of local and international media, through which images of the Horn of Africa and its myriad of ethnic identities are reproduced. The aim has been simply to highlight some of the contradictions within the bodies which determine the production and dissemination of news. While evidently the political and economic watershed of 1991 has modified the situation outlined in the first half of the chapter, in general the quality of information about Ethiopia disseminated outside the country remains piecemeal and poor. Media coverage is clearly insufficient to allow informed analysis of local conflicts, or to evaluate the role of ethnicity in such conflicts. Technical developments, particularly news agencies' demands for live, real-time news, coupled with trends towards multi-media reporting and the increased use of satellite TV, are all likely to exacerbate, rather than improve the distortions highlighted in international news agency coverage of the Horn of Africa. It is far from certain that other technological developments, notably the Internet, will serve to counterbalance this trend.[20]

The changed political and economic climate, and the rapid development of privately owned newspapers in Ethiopia since 1991, has undoubtedly modified the stilted circuits of information flows which characterized reporting of, and from, Ethiopia in the 1980s. However, this does not appear to have facilitated a better understanding of the role of ethnicity in either the formation of political identities or the conflict in the Horn of Africa.[21] This suggests that more thought needs to be given to the question of what difference it makes to media representations of identities if government is actively promoting representations of regional and ethnic groups. Rather than simplifying the problems associated with reporting such identities, it appears that the Ethiopian administration's promotion of a specific set of ethnic labels has created a new set of biases and distortions in both the state and private journalists' presentation of news.

Notes

1. Paradoxically, tiny Djibouti has the region's most technically proficient newspaper, the weekly *La Nation*. Equally paradoxically, political debate in Djibouti tends in fact to be overshadowed by the Paris-based, speculative newsletter, *Indian Ocean Newsletter*, available electronically on www.indigo-net.com/ai.

2. The role of the media in the disintegration of Somalia is beyond the scope of this piece. I note simply that as most Somalis relied almost entirely on the BBC Somali service for broadcast representations of the state of the country, the role of the service perhaps requires a little closer scrutiny.

3. In terms of London-based Africa editors, the *Financial Times* and weekly *Economist* magazine are the notable exceptions.

4. 'Reuters Business Briefing' online news service, this includes all Reuters' stories, the Summary of World Broadcasts and a vast array of print media but not rival agencies. Significantly, the 150 items include only four stories from UK broadsheet newspapers, none of which was on, or from, the Horn, being about Ethiopian athletes in Europe and Ethiopians now living in Israel.

5. PANA is as available via www.africanews.org/pana.

6. See *Issue*, the African Studies Association (USA)'s 'journal of opinion', Vol. XXII No. 1, Spring 1994, on 'the news media and Africa', especially C. Paterson's article 'Who Owns TV Images from Africa?' p. 15.

7. 'Future of "Africa Journal" under Threat', *East African* (weekly, Nairobi), 28 August 1995.

8. Two days before the 1995 'workshop on war, ethnicity and the media' in which these thoughts were originally presented, a local correspondent for the BBC and AFP in Mogadishu, Ali Musa Abdi, was kidnapped by men under the command of Mohammed Farah Aideed.

9. See also J. Ryle in the *Guardian*, 29 September 1995, on a conference on information and disasters held in Oxford on 27 September 1995, which contained a far more nuanced evaluation of news in Ethiopia by Tafari Wossen, currently the editor of the weekly Addis-based news digest, *Seven Days Update*.

10. Such groups also now broadcast directly to diaspora groups. By late 1997, Washington, DC apparently had two local Amharic-language FM stations.

11. In the wake of US President Clinton's visit to Africa in March 1998, the Voice of America announced it would increase its broadcasting in African languages, including Tigrinya, Orominya as well as Amharic.

12. For a selection of muddled reports blending ignorance, incomprehension and Cold War categories, US broadsheet coverage of the events of May 1991 in Ethiopia take some beating. See for example, C. Krauss, 'Ethiopia's New Rulers Try to Shed Ethnic Baggage', *New York Times*, 4 June 1991.

13. It is probably not accidental that the two regions where the model has manifestly failed to produce a semblance of regional authority are the two small, primarily pastoral Afar and Somali regions (numbered 2 and 5).

14. Negarit Gazeta, Press Law (No. 34/1992), October 1992, Addis Ababa.

15. These include the weeklies: *Addis Tribune*, the *Monitor*, the *Reporter* and

the *Entrepreneur*. In addition two publications, *Seven Days Update* and *Press Digest*, provide weekly edited summaries from both government and private press. The latter sell largely to the diplomatic community.

16. Evidently Ethiopia's *internal* experiment with a form of ethnic federalism is a totally distinct political process from the establishment of an independent Eritrea. However, the two are frequently conflated in Ethiopia's domestic political debate.

17. Speaking before the National Assembly in February 1997, Meles Zenawi was bitterly critical of the private press. See Agence France Press, BQA No. 14893, 19 February 1997, p. 42.

18. Literacy is estimated at 35% (World Bank, 1996).

19. While some officials claim that Radio Fana is a 'private' station, like a growing segment of the private economy, it is owned by the ruling party.

20. In 1996–97 the Ethiopian telecommunications agency established a monopoly over Internet provision. The full text of the *Addis Tribune*, a private weekly newspaper, is available at http://AddisTribune.EthiopiaOnline.Net. in English.

21. Evidently this article was written and edited prior to the May 1998 Ethio-Eritrean conflict.

References

African Rights (1994) *Humanitarianism Unbound: Current Dilemmas Facing Multimandate Relief Operations in Political Emergencies*, London: African Rights.

Clapham, C. (1987) *Continuity and Change in Revolutionary Ethiopia*, Cambridge: Cambridge University Press.

Fukui, K. and Markakis J. (1994) *Ethnicity and Conflict in the Horn of Africa*, Oxford: James Currey.

Gebru Tarke (1991) *Ethiopia, Power and Protest: Peasant Revolts in the 20th Century*, Cambridge: Cambridge University Press.

Harrison, P. and Palmer, R. (1986) *News out of Africa: Biafra to Band Aid*, London: Shipman.

Kakuna, K. (October, 1996) *Clampdown in Addis: Ethiopia's Journalists at Risk*, New York: Committee to Protect Journalists, p. 37.

Kapuscinski, R. (1983) *The Emperor*, London: Quartet.

Paterson, C. (1994) 'Who Owns TV Images from Africa?', *Issue, a Journal of Opinion*, African Studies Association (USA), Vol. XXII, No. 1, Spring 1994, p. 15. (Special edition on 'The News Media and Africa'.)

Styan, D. (1995) 'Does Britain Have an African Policy?', *Afrique Politique, 1996*, Paris: Karthala.

World Bank (1996) *Social Indicators of Development*, Washington, DC: World Bank.

Index